# Oracle® Solaris Cluster Essentials

# Oracle® Solaris Cluster Essentials

**Tim Read**

PRENTICE
HALL

Upper Saddle River, NJ • Boston • Indianapolis • San Francisco
New York • Toronto • Montreal • London • Munich • Paris • Madrid
Capetown • Sydney • Tokyo • Singapore • Mexico City

The publisher offers excellent discounts on this book when ordered in quantity for bulk purchases or special sales, which may include electronic versions and/or custom covers and content particular to your business, training goals, marketing focus, and branding interests. For more information, please contact:

U.S. Corporate and Government Sales
(800) 382-3419
corpsales@pearsontechgroup.com

For sales outside the United States, please contact:

International Sales
international@pearsoned.com

Visit us on the Web: informit.com/ph

*Library of Congress Cataloging-in-Publication Data*

Read, Tim, 1963-
  Oracle Solaris Cluster essentials / Tim Read.
       p.  cm.
  Includes bibliographical references and index.
  ISBN 978-0-13-248622-4 (pbk. : alk. paper)
1.  Oracle Solaris Cluster. 2.  Integrated software.  I. Title.
  QA76.76.I57R43 2011
  005.5—dc22

                             2010027191

ISBN-13:  978-0-13-248622-4
ISBN-10:      0-13-248622-9
Text printed in the United States on recycled paper at Courier in Stoughton, Massachusetts.
First printing, September 2010

# Contents

design Solaris Cluster systems suited to providing the levels of availability required by the target applications.

- *System implementers* will derive the most value from the sections that describe how the Solaris Cluster resource group and resource constructs can best be used to encapsulate the target applications.

- *System administrators* will find the book a useful source of background material on how the Solaris Cluster features work. This material as well as the sections on troubleshooting will help them resolve day-to-day issues with the cluster. In addition, the sections on cluster management will provide them with guidance on maintaining a Solaris Cluster system after it has been moved into production.

The book assumes that the reader is familiar with the Oracle Solaris operating system (Oracle Solaris OS).

## How to Use This Book

Readers who just want to know about the high-availability features provided by the Solaris Cluster software, and who are not interested in disaster recovery, will benefit from reading the first four chapters of the book. Chapter 1 focuses on the basic requirements for designing a Solaris Cluster system, and Chapter 2 provides a more in-depth description of the Solaris Cluster features. If you are considering implementing virtualization technologies, Chapter 3 explains how the Solaris Cluster software can coexist with these environments. Finally, Chapter 4 discusses some of the tasks that you perform to manage your Solaris Cluster system.

Readers who want to understand the capabilities of the Solaris Cluster Geographic Edition software, or who are planning a disaster recovery system and are already familiar with the Solaris Cluster software, should start with Chapter 5. In many ways, Chapter 5 mirrors Chapter 1 insofar as it provides a general background to the Solaris Cluster Geographic Edition product. More detailed technical information about the features of the Geographic Edition product is explained in Chapter 6. Finally, Chapter 7 covers some additional tasks that you might need to perform while managing a Solaris Cluster Geographic Edition installation.

If you learn best by playing with a piece of software and then reading the associated background material, then Chapter 8 and Chapter 9 are the places to start. Each chapter has detailed examples that you can follow to create your own Solaris Cluster or Solaris Cluster Geographic Edition installation. Bear in mind that these examples are not necessarily optimal configurations or what might be considered "best practice." Instead, the examples focus on demonstrating feature capabilities to give you a platform on which you can build and experiment.

**Note**

Oracle Corporation acquired Sun Microsystems, Inc., early in 2010, when this book was nearing completion. Although this book mostly uses the new product names, occasional reference is also made to previous names. The following table provides a guide to the old and new product names.

| Sun Product Name | Oracle Product Name |
| --- | --- |
| Solaris | Oracle Solaris |
| Solaris Cluster | Oracle Solaris Cluster |
| Solaris Cluster Geographic Edition | Oracle Solaris Cluster Geographic Edition |
| Solaris Zones or Solaris Containers | Oracle Solaris Zones or Oracle Solaris Containers |
| Logical Domains | Oracle VM Server for SPARC |
| VirtualBox | Oracle VM VirtualBox |
| ZFS | Oracle Solaris ZFS |

# Acknowledgments

First and foremost, I would like to thank Meenakshi Kaul-Basu, Director of Oracle Solaris Cluster engineering, and Burt Clouse, my manager, for allowing me the time to write this book.

I am also indebted to Dr. Ellard Roush for his huge contribution to this book. Without his detailed knowledge of the Solaris Cluster software internals, his tireless reviews of my drafts, and his patient answers to my endless questions, I doubt the book would be half as complete or accurate as it is.

The breadth of features in the Oracle Solaris Cluster software makes it virtually impossible for any one person to have in-depth knowledge of every aspect of the product. Thus, I have relied heavily on many of the Solaris Cluster engineers who have unmatched knowledge of the inner workings of the product. In this respect, I would like to extend my gratitude to Marty Rattner, Honsing Cheng, Leland Chen, Bob Bart, Zoram Thanga, Venkateswarlu Tella, Ashutosh Tripathi, Sambit Nayak, Detlef Ulherr, Prasanna Kunisetty, Madhur Bansal, Bharathi Subramanian, Harish Mallya, and Larry Kriewald for making sure that the book accurately reflects the product's capabilities.

As someone who has been working with Solaris clustering products for almost 15 years, I can easily forget that someone reading this book might not have the same level of experience with the product. Fortunately, I have many colleagues around the world who devoted considerable time and effort to reading and critiquing what I had written, as well as providing me with insight into how they explain and position the product to our customers. Consequently, I am very grateful to

Hartmut Streppel, Mike Ramchand, François Marcoux, Nicolas Houix, Madhan Kumar Balasubramanian, Chris Dekanski, Tomas Persson, Gia-Khanh Nguyen, Thorsten Früauf, Steve McKinty, Maria Nieto, Subarna Ganguly, and Jean Randriam for their feedback. I hope the resulting text does justice to their input.

When writing this book, I often found that I had a technical question that I could not answer. Once more, Sun colleagues from around the world came to my aid by answering the questions I posed by email. For their generous responses to my emails, I would like to thank Juergen Schleich, Jingci Wang, Tirthankar Das, Venkat Chennuru, John Wren Kennedy, Rameshkumar Ramasamy, Pete Dennis, Hisham A. Al-Sheikh, Ray Jang, Thejaswini Singarajipura, Pramod Nandana, Lisa Shepherd, Duncan Hardie, Hemachandran Namachivayam, Terry Smith, Liam Merwick, Prasad Dharmavaram, Neil Garthwaite, Jim Dunham, and Thomas Atkins. In addition, I am grateful to Dave Arrigo at EMC and Bill Martin at Hitachi Data Systems for their help.

One of my biggest hopes for this book is that it provides examples that a reader can use as the basis for setting up a proof of concept of an Oracle Solaris Cluster system. For this to happen, I needed access to a wide range of clusters within Sun's QA department. Without help and support from Roger Autrand and Shyam Bollu, I never would have achieved this goal.

Finally, the process of getting this book published would not have been as smooth as it has been without the expertise and assistance of Jim Siwila and David Lindt, who liaised with Greg Doench at Pearson. Jeff Ramsey and Prakash Damodaran turned my drawings into beautiful graphics. The dedicated technical editorship of Alysson Troffer, development editing of Susan Zahn, and copy editing of Barbara Wood turned my writing into substantially better English.

And, of course, I am grateful to my wife, Hazel, who put up with my monosyllabic reply of "Book" in response to her question "What did you do today?"

# About the Author

**Tim Read** has worked in the UK computer industry since 1985. He joined Sun Microsystems in 1990, in a pre-sales role, as a Systems Engineer. He was responsible for the first Sun Cluster HA 1.0 deployments in the UK. Tim now works as a Software Developer for Oracle's Solaris Availability Engineering group. He has written and coauthored a number of BluePrints and white papers, including "Designing Enterprise Solutions with Sun Cluster 3.0," "Architecting Availability and Disaster Recovery Solutions," "Using Solaris Cluster and Sun Cluster Geographic Edition with Virtualization Technologies," and "Sun Cluster 3.2 Software: Making Oracle Database 10G R2 and 11G RAC Even More Unbreakable." He holds a joint honours degree in physics with astrophysics from the University of Birmingham in the UK. When not working, he enjoys running, tandem riding, and exploring the islands of the Outer Hebrides in the far northwest of Scotland.

# Oracle Solaris Cluster: Overview

The Solaris Cluster 3.2 11/09 software is the twelfth release of the product since Sun Cluster 3.0 was announced in December 2000. Oracle Solaris Cluster is the culmination of 14 years of development work stemming from the Solaris Multicomputer project that was started in Sun Labs in 1995.

This chapter begins by discussing the purpose and value of the Solaris Cluster software. It continues by comparing clustering for high availability (HA) and scalability with high performance computing (HPC) and fault-tolerant systems. It then contrasts HA with the demands of disaster recovery. After describing the benefits of using a third-party clustering framework, such as the Solaris Cluster software, the chapter concludes by explaining how a cluster is created from its constituent parts: servers, storage, and networks.

## The Value of the Solaris Cluster Software

To understand the value of the Solaris Cluster software, you first need to understand the concepts of reliability, availability, and resilience. These concepts are important because of the ramifications they have when applied to the systems on which you run your business applications.

A system is reliable if it does not fail for long periods of time. However, if such a system does fail, it might take a very long time to fix the fault and to get the business applications the system supports running again. In contrast, a system might be very unreliable and fail regularly, yet take very little time to fix. As a result, the services the system supports are unavailable for only a very short time. Therefore, system reliability is related to the likelihood of a failure occurring; system availability is determined by how long the system takes to recover from that failure.

A system is reliable when it does not fail frequently. Reliability is often measured by the "mean time to failure." The resilience of the system is also important, where the "mean time to recover" is often measured. The availability of a system is determined by the percentage of time during which the system is operational. Both the failure rate and the recovery time affect availability. A system that fails frequently but recovers quickly could have the same availability as a system that fails infrequently but takes a long time to recover. Because you want the system to have a high level of availability, both the failure rate and the recovery time need to be addressed.

A system can often be made more reliable through the use of redundant components. A redundant component enables a system to mask the failure of a component by transparently transferring the function or data flows from the failed component to the redundant component. If a system has, or can have, only one of a particular component, then that component is deemed a single point of failure. Although the failure might not be sufficient to cause the system to fail completely, it might render the system or the application useless. For example, the failure of the sole public network connection to a system renders the system inaccessible to external users. Similarly, the failure of the sole data path to data storage will render an application that relies on that data useless because the application will be unable to continue processing. Fortunately, the Oracle Solaris OS has several built-in features that enable redundant components to be combined to remove single points of component failure. These features are mentioned in subsequent sections.

Although computer systems have grown more reliable over the years, mainly because of increased component integration, they can, and do, still fail. The Solaris Cluster software enables you to combine two or more systems to provide a platform on which you can run your business applications. If one of the systems fails, the Solaris Cluster software uses methods to quickly remaster your business applications on one of the remaining systems. This process reduces the service outage by rapidly detecting failures and then recovering promptly. The Solaris Cluster software moves the applications in such a way that any user who was disconnected from the applications can reconnect to them again shortly, without changing his or her connection procedure. In some cases, because of either the communication protocol or the software that the user is using, the user might not even be aware of the failure. Indeed, the user might simply experience a short pause in service.

Although the business application is provided by surviving nodes, you can repair the failed system without incurring more service outages. Combining the Solaris Cluster software with the built-in Solaris redundancy features and redundant components enables you to create an environment that removes virtually all single points of component and service failure. Thus, using the Solaris Cluster software enables your business to increase application availability.

## High Availability, High Performance Computing, and Fault-Tolerant Systems

Although the Solaris Cluster software makes applications highly available and in some cases scalable or parallel (see the section "Resources" in Chapter 2, "Oracle Solaris Cluster: Features and Architecture"), a clear distinction must be made between systems running the Solaris Cluster software and fault-tolerant systems. When a serious hardware or software fault occurs on a Solaris Cluster system, leading to a system panic, all the services managed by the Solaris Cluster software on that server fail over to another node in the cluster. Consequently, users of the service might experience a pause in the service or an outage that requires reconnection. In contrast, fault-tolerant systems use methods such as lockstep computing to shield the operating system and its applications from failures in the underlying hardware.

The advantages of a Solaris Cluster solution over a fault-tolerant solution are threefold:

- A Solaris Cluster solution is considerably less expensive because it is based on general-purpose Solaris servers.
- The wider choice of server platforms enables greater application scalability.
- The Solaris Cluster software can recover from software faults (bugs) that would otherwise be a single point of failure in a fault-tolerant system.

Furthermore, the Solaris Cluster software is not aimed at the HPC market. HPC installations, often called *grids*, can consist of many hundreds or even thousands of servers linked by a high-speed network, usually InfiniBand or 10 Gigabit Ethernet, and a file system optimized for HPC workloads, such as Lustre. The combination of the network, file system, and servers provides a homogeneous environment onto which computation-intensive jobs can be scheduled. Thus, peak performance and throughput, rather than availability, are usually the key metrics for an HPC grid. In such an environment, if a server fails, the jobs running on it are simply resubmitted to the queue to be run on another system. The loss of "state" is tolerated because it can be recalculated. This is clearly not the case with a Solaris Cluster system. If a banking application were to lose all records of a large financial transaction, a simple recalculation would not be possible.

## High Availability Compared with Disaster Recovery

The primary goal of the Solaris Cluster software is to maximize service availability, without requiring manual intervention. When a hardware or software failure is detected, the Solaris Cluster software automatically restarts the service on another logical or physical server. Your application performance requirements combined with the additional infrastructure costs of separating cluster nodes often mean that a single set of cluster nodes is located within two of your data centers, separated by no more than a few kilometers. However, any catastrophic local event might make it impossible for you to provide service from either data center, thus rendering your services unavailable. In such a scenario your services will benefit from having a disaster recovery solution in place.

A disaster recovery solution uses a physically separate copy of your production data to re-instantiate the services. The time it takes to bring the disaster recovery solution online is mainly dependent on the mechanism you use to maintain this second copy of the data, ignoring the time involved in making the decision to switch to the disaster recovery site. Protection strategies can range from tape backup for your least important applications to continuous, online data replication for your most critical applications. Switching to your secondary data copy comes at a price. When the primary site is available again, you might be able to resynchronize the data without having to copy the entire dataset back across the network. Alas, that is not always guaranteed with every replication technology. You also could decide that you want to revert back to the data that was held at the primary site, an option that would not be possible with a highly available system. Thus the decision to switch operational sites is not made lightly or automatically, as would be the case with clusters used purely for the purpose of high availability. Instead, the disaster recovery failover decision should be part of your manually initiated disaster recovery plan.

## Benefits of the Solaris Cluster Framework

Your enterprise runs a wide range of services, not all of which are business- or mission-critical. As such, it is important that you use an appropriate availability solution to support each service's requirements. Your decisions will be based largely on the cost of any outage, both financially and from any consequences from a prolonged outage for your organization's reputation.

Some services are not critical to the organization and can run on single servers without risk to the organization. Critical services need the high availability provided by clusters of servers that utilize a third-party cluster framework such as the Solaris Cluster software.

Although it is feasible to implement your own "home-grown" solution for high availability, the cost of doing so usually makes it financially unattractive. There is not only the cost of initial development but also the costs of ongoing support, maintenance, and testing, particularly with respect to new application releases. Worse still is the approach that uses a long, complex manual procedure. Such a procedure carries significant risk to both your data integrity and service availability when it is not well maintained and tested.

Consequently, the Solaris Cluster software is a very cost-effective way of providing a high-availability framework to a wide range of enterprise applications. The framework automates service restarts when a hardware or software failure occurs. It also provides application-specific fault probes for many popular software products. These software fault probes add significant value to a basic high-availability framework.

A *fault probe* is a custom piece of software that tests the health of a target application. For example, a database fault probe might read various internal database tables to determine if any work is being done. If nothing appears to be happening, the fault probe might then try some database operations such as creating a dummy table, creating a dummy record, deleting the dummy record, and deleting the dummy table. If these operations complete without error, then in all likelihood the database is working correctly. However, if they fail, then there is a strong possibility that the database is experiencing some sort of fault. This fault might be cleared by restarting the database. If that does not resolve the fault, then possibly moving the database to another cluster node will.

Although the Solaris Cluster software responds very quickly to the failure of cluster nodes by restarting the services that were hosted on that node, the software must rely on these fault probes to determine whether a particular service is healthy. When using these probes, you must strike a balance between the length of time that your applications are allowed to remain in an unhealthy state and the consequences of regular and possibly expensive probe operations on your system. Furthermore, the probe timeouts must be chosen to enable your applications to respond to health checks, even when they are under heavy load and responding slowly. Clearly, you want the Solaris Cluster software to restart services that are unhealthy and performing no useful work, but not the services that are slow but otherwise healthy. Fortunately, the Solaris Cluster framework enables the system administrator to choose the probe interval and probe timeout on a per-service basis.

Fault probes are a key feature and benefit of the Solaris Cluster software. Not only are they maintained by Oracle, but they are also tested against each new version of their associated target application to ensure they function correctly.

## Solaris Cluster Architecture

This section covers the basic physical requirements for a Solaris Cluster system. For the most part, this section avoids naming a specific server, storage, host-bus adapter (HBA), or network interface card (NIC) because the supported configurations change regularly as new hardware is announced. Where a section is specific, for example, with respect to the maximum system configuration, note that the configuration is just a snapshot of the current state of affairs and not necessarily a product limitation, unless otherwise stated.

Finally, as the name implies, the Solaris Cluster 3.2 11/09 release runs only on servers using the Oracle Solaris operating system (Oracle Solaris OS). The Solaris Cluster software supports SPARC-based systems using either the Solaris 9 OS or the Solaris 10 OS and supports x64-based systems using the 64-bit version of the Solaris 10 OS. In both cases, you should use the latest supported version.

Starting with the Solaris 10 OS, a cluster node (see the section "Defining a Cluster Node" in Chapter 3, "Combining Virtualization Technologies with Oracle Solaris Cluster Software") and a machine (or system) are not the same. When you use the Solaris 10 OS, a global-cluster node is the Solaris global zone of a physical or virtual machine. The operating system runs on a machine. You cannot use different Oracle Solaris OS releases on the machines within a single cluster. You must use either the Solaris 9 OS or the Solaris 10 OS for all machines. Also, you must run all cluster machines at the same patch level.

> **Note**
>
> A single cluster running the Solaris Cluster software must use a single instruction architecture, either SPARC or x64.

### Server Configurations

You can construct a Solaris Cluster configuration from a mixture of server node types as long as all the servers share the same instruction architecture: either SPARC or x64. You are not required to remove all single points of failure, but you should still aim to eliminate as many of them as is practical. Doing so means that you should have dual paths to both network and storage.

In order to avoid a single point of failure in networking, ideally you would have at least two network connections to each of your public subnets, and these links should connect to separate network switches. You would then place these interfaces into IP network multipathing (IPMP) groups to shield services from failures in individual NICs or switches.

Similarly, you would ideally use two networks for the private cluster networks, as described in "Private Networking." In contrast to the public networks, you must not place the NICs for these networks into IPMP groups. Part of the value of the Solaris Cluster framework is that it creates a highly available and trunked interface for the cluster private interconnect across the interfaces of all the private networks.

With the advent of VLAN tagging technology, a resilient configuration can be achieved with two NICs per node [UsingVLANs].

## Storage Connectivity

Most Solaris Cluster installations use some form of shared storage. For the purposes of this book, *shared storage* is defined as storage that is physically connected to more than one cluster node. Shared storage can be connected in many different ways, including Fibre Channel storage area network (SAN) fabrics, parallel SCSI, serial-attached SCSI (SAS), iSCSI, and network-attached storage (NAS). In some circumstances, the storage technology limits the number of hosts that can be simultaneously connected to a particular device or array.

Although most Solaris Cluster configurations have some form of shared storage, it is possible to construct a Solaris Cluster system that has no shared storage at all. In such configurations the services that are made highly available by the Solaris Cluster software do not use any shared data.

Any shared storage should ideally be protected by built-in hardware RAID capabilities of the storage array, host-based mirroring, or storage replication (see "Data Protection Using Storage-Based Replication"). If Fibre Channel is used, it is best practice to configure multiple paths to your shared storage through redundant SAN switches. The Solaris 10 I/O multipathing feature (formerly called Sun StorEdge Traffic Manager, but also known as MPxIO) is the preferred storage multipathing driver for maintaining data access to the underlying storage system. However, you can instead use one of the supported third-party multipathing products. You must also ensure that LUNs that are used by the cluster are zoned and LUN-masked so that they are accessible from this cluster alone.

The Solaris Cluster software also supports low-end SCSI storage devices, that is, non–Fibre Channel devices. SCSI storage devices can connect to only two cluster nodes. If you use this type of dual-initiator SCSI device, then you must change the `scsi-initiator-id` setting on one of the cluster nodes that connects to the shared storage so that it does not conflict with the setting on the other cluster node or any of the shared disk devices. One option is to change the default from target ID 7 to 6 on the second node. Because the server nodes often have DVD drives that use target ID 6, you might need to make this change separately for each shared SCSI controller rather than at a server-wide level. These changes are made at the `eeprom` or `BIOS` level of the servers.

Within the last decade the iSCSI standard has emerged [iSCSI-RFC]. There are two important participants in this protocol: the storage, or iSCSI target, and the host, or iSCSI initiator. You can use iSCSI targets, such as Oracle's Sun StorageTek 2510 Array or the Sun Storage 7000 Unified Storage System, as shared storage with a Solaris Cluster system. However, current iSCSI implementations might vary considerably in their capabilities and might result in restrictions being placed on their usage with a Solaris Cluster configuration.

If an iSCSI target does not support SCSI-2 reservations or SCSI-3 Persistent Group Reservations, the device can still be used as a quorum device (see the section "Majority Voting" in Chapter 2, "Oracle Solaris Cluster: Features and Architecture"). However, the device must instead use the software quorum feature (see the section "Software Quorum" in Chapter 2). When an iSCSI target uses the software quorum feature, the iSCSI device must be on the same subnet as the cluster.

## Server-to-Storage Connectivity Topologies

The Solaris Cluster software supports four types of storage topology: scalable, clustered pairs, N+1, and pair+M. These storage topologies are equivalent when only two nodes are considered. With the advancement in SAN technologies over the past decade, the scalable storage topology has become the predominant deployment architecture for midrange and high-end cluster configurations of more than two nodes. Low-cost SCSI arrays can only be dual-hosted. Therefore, clusters using these arrays are limited to the dual-host topologies: clustered pairs, N+1, and pair+M.

### Scalable Topology

The scalable topology (see Figure 1.1) is the most popular cluster architecture for configurations that are connected through Fibre Channel SAN fabrics. This topology has all nodes connected to all of the underlying storage. This approach gives you the greatest flexibility to consolidate and balance your services across the computing resources contained within your cluster. However, multiple paths to storage place a heavier burden on the storage array, from the perspective of both correctly handling the fencing protocol (see the section "Storage Device Fencing Subsystem" in Chapter 2, "Oracle Solaris Cluster: Features and Architecture") and its ability to manage the writes that arrive from multiple sources concurrently without starving any one node of service.

Parallel SCSI and SAS storage arrays allow only dual-host connectivity. Thus, they only support the scalable topology using a maximum of two nodes.

Because the shared storage is connected to all of the cluster nodes in a scalable storage topology, you have greater flexibility in choosing the sequence of nodes that

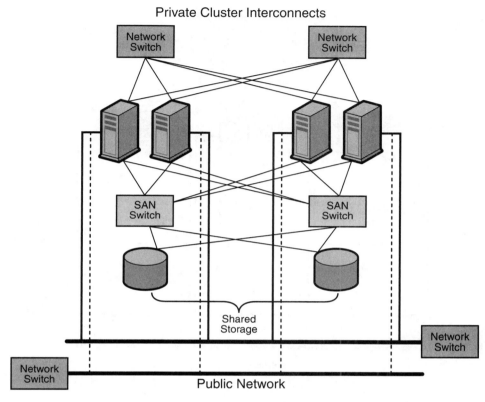

Private Cluster Interconnects

**Figure 1.1** Scalable storage topology

each of your services uses if a failure occurs. The sequence of nodes you pick, in other words, the failover topology, can mirror the storage topologies described in the following sections. For example, one node could provide the backup for several services, giving an N+1 failover topology. Similarly, services could be constrained to nodes grouped in pairs, giving a clustered pair failover topology.

## Clustered Pair Topology

A clustered pair topology (see Figure 1.2) creates a single cluster from pairs of nodes that dual-host storage. Implementing this topology means that unless you use the global file system (see the section "The Cluster File System" in Chapter 2, "Oracle Solaris Cluster: Features and Architecture"), your services will be confined to the nodes to which their storage is connected.

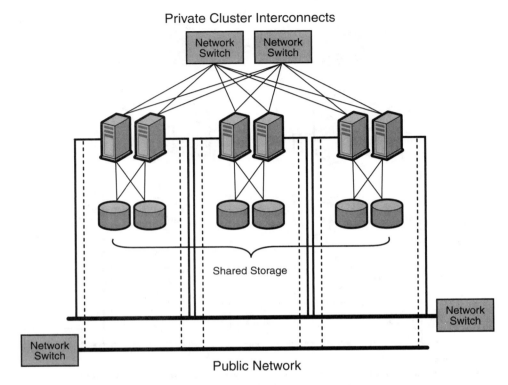

**Figure 1.2** Clustered pair storage topology

### N+1 Topology

Clusters that utilize an N+1 topology (see Figure 1.3) enable a single "backup" node to dual-host storage with up to seven other nodes. If you use this topology with low-cost storage, you will need sufficient expansion slots in the "backup" node to install the host-bus adapters required to connect all the shared storage. This requirement could well constrain the number of nodes you can consolidate into the cluster. However, in a Fibre Channel SAN environment, the number of host-bus adapters required depends only on the performance and redundancy needed, set against the expansion slots required.

If you configure one or more services on each of the N "primary" nodes and leave the backup node idle, the failure of a single server causes failover of its applications to the backup node. Assuming that the CPU power and memory resources of the "backup" node match those of the largest primary node, the migrated applications perform at the same level as before, assuming that no other node also fails over its workload. This approach enables you to meet service-level agreements

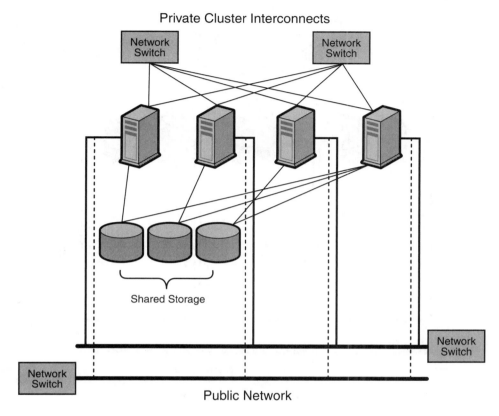

**Figure 1.3** N+1 storage topology

(SLAs) even if a cluster node failure occurs. The alternative is to run additional data services on the backup node and experience some level of service degradation if primary nodes fail over workloads. This approach also assumes that only one node is likely to fail at any one time.

Finally, as with the clustered pair topology, unless the global file service is used, your services will be restricted to just their primary node and the backup node.

## Pair+M Topology

The global features in the Solaris Cluster software make the pair+M storage topology (see Figure 1.4) possible. Using this approach, you can provide storage facilities (see the section "The Cluster File System" in Chapter 2, "Oracle Solaris Cluster: Features and Architecture") to additional M nodes that are also part of

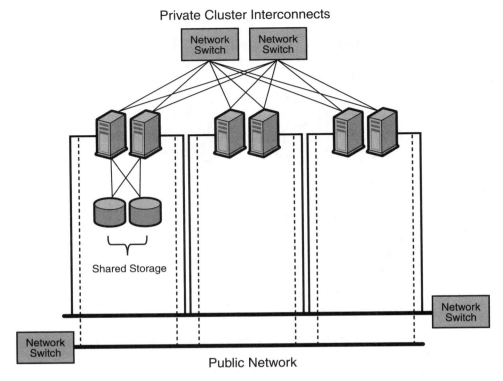

**Figure 1.4** Pair+M storage topology

the cluster with a single clustered pair. This approach is similar to network-attached storage (NAS) for the sole use of the other nodes in the cluster.

This topology minimizes the I/O slot demands on the remaining M nodes but at a cost of making these nodes send all their disk I/O requests to the nodes hosting the storage. M nodes are required to have public and private interconnect networks only.

This approach is ideal if you want to consolidate a combination of back-end databases, application servers, and web servers. Your implementation would use the nodes with local storage as primary hosts for the back-end databases. The M nodes would be used to support the web and application servers. Because the web and application servers typically perform a limited number of writes, remote storage does not significantly impact these servers. The system caches any data these servers read in the local Solaris virtual memory page cache, thus maintaining the overall performance of the servers.

## How to Protect Your Data

Without redundant connectivity from your cluster to your storage subsystems, no amount of host-based mirroring, hardware RAID, or data replication can overcome the loss of access to your data caused by the failure of a single critical path. For many years, the Solaris 10 OS has provided a free storage multipathing feature, formerly called Sun StorEdge Traffic Manager (also known as MPxIO). This feature mainly benefits storage that is connected through a SAN and thus capable of having more than one connection to the same array. MPxIO hides these multiple paths to storage behind a single device name through which I/O requests to disk are load-balanced. Furthermore, any failure in the underlying connectivity is shielded from the application until such point that all links have failed. The multipathing software must update SCSI reservations on the storage when a path failure occurs because these registrations are specific to a host and a storage path.

The Solaris Cluster Open Storage Program (http://www.sun.com/software/cluster/osp) offers certified support for a wide range of third-party storage products, including those from EMC, IBM, Hewlett Packard, and Hitachi Data Systems, to name a few. Some of these vendors have their own multipathing software. However, with the exceptions of EMC PowerPath and Hitachi Dynamic Link Manager (HDLM) software, the Solaris 10 I/O multipathing feature is generally the only option.

After you have addressed storage connectivity, you must then consider data redundancy. The applications that are hosted on your cluster rely on access to their data to enable them to provide a service to your end users. Protecting this data against component failure is therefore vital for high availability. You can protect your data in these ways:

- Using the built-in hardware RAID capabilities of your storage arrays
- Using a host-based volume manager such as Solaris Volume Manager or Veritas Volume Manager, both of which offer host-based mirroring capabilities
- Using the built-in RAID-1 or RAIDZ capability of Oracle Solaris ZFS storage pools, if the Solaris 10 OS is being used
- Using the built-in storage replication facilities of high-end storage arrays, such as EMC Symmetrix Remote Data Facility (SRDF) or Hitachi TrueCopy and Universal Replicator

Although many storage arrays now commonly come with built-in hardware RAID capabilities, they often don't provide quick and easy ways to divide the virtual LUNs that you create into usable chunks. Consequently, many users still prefer to use a volume manager with such arrays. You might choose to use a volume manager to give your system administrator finer-grained control over the storage that has been allocated by the storage administrators. Of course, when you are using low-end "just a bunch of disks" (JBOD) arrays, a volume manager is your only option.

## Disksets, Disk Groups, and Zpools

When you implement a failover service on your cluster, you can move the service, along with its associated data, from one cluster node to another cluster node within the constraints that are imposed by the storage topologies described in the section "Server-to-Storage Connectivity Topologies." If you use Solaris Volume Manager, this collection of LUNs is known as a *metaset* or a *diskset*. If you use Veritas Volume Manager, it is known as a *disk group*.

Both volume managers store configuration details about the software RAID devices (sometimes referred to as *metadevices*) that they maintain in private regions on the disks. By default, Solaris Volume Manager uses disk slice 7 to hold what is called its *state replica database*, and Veritas Volume Manager uses disk slice 4. The data that you store in a diskset or disk group is only ever imported on and accessed directly through one cluster node at any one time. However, as described in the section "The Cluster File System" in Chapter 2, "Oracle Solaris Cluster: Features and Architecture," this single path to storage does not prevent the diskset or disk group from providing the storage for global file systems.

When control of the diskset or disk group is moved from one node to another node, the diskset or disk group is released, or exported, from the initial node and taken, or imported, by the receiving node. When a target machine imports a diskset or disk group, the target machine reads the private regions of the disks in the set to determine the nature and extent of the metadevices that constitute the diskset or disk group. As described in the section "Solaris Volume Manager's State Replica Majority," it is critical that a majority of these private regions be accessible. Otherwise, the data might be imported read-only to preserve data integrity. The following example shows how to create a diskset for non-parallel services.

### Example 1.1  Creating a Single-Owner (Nonshared) Diskset

First, create three copies of the root replica on the two cluster nodes (`phys-earth1`, `phys-earth2`).

This step is done only once before the first disksets or root metadevices are created.

```
phys-earth1# metadb -afc 3 c0t0d0s7
phys-earth2# metadb -afc 3 c0t0d0s7
```

Next, create the diskset (`myset`) with just the cluster nodes as hosts.

```
phys-earth1# metaset -s myset -a -h phys-earth1 phys-earth2.
```
Disks are added at this point.

Both Solaris Volume Manager and Veritas Volume Manager have cluster-aware versions of their basic capabilities, known as *Solaris Volume Manager for Sun Cluster* and *Veritas Volume Manager cluster feature*, respectively. These volume managers are specifically for use by parallel applications such as Oracle Real Application Clusters (Oracle RAC), which manage data concurrency themselves. Unlike the standard disksets or disk groups, these cluster versions import a diskset or disk group on all cluster nodes at once. One node is designated as the master node and coordinates all changes to the set.

Solaris Volume Manager for Sun Cluster multi-owner disksets can also be used to provide host-based mirroring for shared QFS file systems (see the section "SAM-QFS Software" in Chapter 2, "Oracle Solaris Cluster: Features and Architecture").

## Example 1.2   Creating a Multi-owner (or Shared) Diskset

Assume that the root replicas already exist so that you just need to create the new multi-owner set.

Note: You must have a RAC framework resource and a RAC Solaris Volume Manager resource configured in a RAC framework resource group to be able to perform this command. The RAC framework resource group must also be online.

```
phys-earth1# metaset -s multiset -M -a -h phys-earth1 phys-earth2
```
Disks are added at this point.

### Solaris Volume Manager's State Replica Majority

Solaris Volume Manager uses replica databases to store information about the RAID devices that are configured on the system. Data integrity is established by requiring a majority of these replicas to be available when you make changes, take control, or release a diskset. Although this approach is robust and provides strong protection against data corruption, it can result in your data being accessible in read-only mode if 50 percent or more of the state replicas are unavailable when the diskset is imported.

When you configure your system such that storage is evenly split between two locations, the resulting configuration will have the Solaris Volume Manager state replicas evenly distributed, too. Any event that causes the instantaneous loss of half of your cluster nodes and half of your storage will cause the metasets currently held on the failed nodes to be imported read-only on the remaining working nodes. Their lack of state replica majority means that the system cannot risk importing them read-write because of concerns about data corruption.

Solaris Volume Manager does allow you to add what are known as *mediators* to each diskset. Mediators are in-memory copies of the state replica database that are held on a per-node basis and used when there is a reasonably long time gap (of the order of tens of seconds) between the failure of the storage and the failure of the node as in the preceding scenario. When Solaris Volume Manager detects the loss of the state replicas on the storage, it marks the additional mediator copies as "golden." If a server then fails, the remaining server has a guarantee, from the "golden" state of the mediator, that it is safe to import the diskset read-write.

**Note**

If you reboot the remaining node or nodes without removing the stale state replicas related to the inaccessible array, then you will lose the "golden" characteristic of the in-memory mediator and no longer be able to re-import the diskset read-write.

One way you can avoid this problem is by distributing your Solaris Volume Manager storage across an odd number of arrays such that no single failure can make exactly half of the cluster nodes and half of the storage used inaccessible. However, it is unlikely that you can achieve this solution cost effectively, particularly when it involves laying or renting fiber connectivity between widely separated data centers, purely for the purpose of housing a single LUN.

The Solaris 10 10/09 release offers an alternative solution to the problem with an even number of mediators. You can now add an extra mediator to a diskset that is held on a node that is not part of the cluster. This remote node needs only IP connectivity. This node could be in a remote location that is not likely to be subject to the same failure that could occur at either of the two main sites. Indeed, you can even use a node within the same data center to avoid failures that simultaneously take out exactly half of your storage and half of your cluster nodes. The following example shows how this feature is used.

## Example 1.3  Adding a Third-Site Mediator to a Diskset

This example builds on Example 1.1, "Creating a Single-Owner (Nonshared) Diskset."

Assume that the set will consist of just two arrays and thus will require a remote mediator as well.

Check that `root` is in group 14 on the remote node.

```
phys-spring1# grep sysadmin /etc/group
sysadmin::14:root
```

Add mediators for all the cluster nodes (`phys-winter1`, `phys-winter2`) and the additional node (`phys-spring1`).

```
phys-winter1# metaset -s myset -a -m phys-winter1 phys-winter2 \
> phys-spring1
```

Check the status of the set.

```
phys-winter1# metaset -s myset

Set name = myset, Set number = 2

Host              Owner
phys-winter1
phys-winter2

Mediator Host(s)   Aliases
phys-winter1
phys-winter2
phys-spring1
```

Check the mediator status.

```
phys-winter1# medstat -s myset
Mediator          Status  Golden
phys-winter1        Ok    No
phys-winter2        Ok    No
phys-spring1        Ok    No
```

Disks are added at this point.

Multi-owner metasets do not need mediators because the control of the metasets is not passed between nodes as single-owner metasets are. However, if all the nodes that own a metaset fail and half of the replicas are unavailable, then the metaset cannot be imported until sufficient stale state replica databases are removed to reestablish a majority of good replicas.

## Built-In Oracle Solaris ZFS Storage Pool RAID Protection

If you plan to store your data in an Oracle Solaris ZFS file system, then the underlying *zpool* can be mirrored or *RAIDZ*-protected. The advantage of these built-in capabilities is that if the protection needs to be repaired for any reason, for example, a disk failed completely or transiently, only the data blocks in use are considered for repair and only the data blocks that have changed are fixed. This approach makes the entire resilvering process, as it is known, far quicker [ZFSMirror]. Consequently, this approach has less of an impact on your services.

## Data Protection Using Storage-Based Replication

Originally, the Solaris Cluster software restricted you to using host-based mirroring to protect your data from disk failures. Subsequent releases have provided another option to protect your data: storage-based replication.

With host-based mirroring, a cluster node writes data to all of the underlying devices that constitute the metadevice before returning control to the kernel or even to your application if it is writing data synchronously. As described in the section "Performance Impact of Separating Data Centers," large separations between cluster nodes and associated storage arrays can have a significant impact on your application's performance. When the host needs to read data, it can read from any one of the mirror components in the diskset or disk group. If you have a configuration in which cluster nodes and their associated portions of the shared storage are widely separated, you can configure the diskset or disk group to read from a preferred metadevice or *plex*.

In contrast, storage-based replication handles the I/O operation at a completely different level. The Solaris kernel makes an I/O request through the disk device driver, and the data is written to the primary array. The array firmware then replicates your data to the secondary storage array at the remote site. The storage array can be configured to perform this replication either synchronously or asynchronously, on a per-disk grouping basis. The difference between these two approaches is that in the synchronous option, the array does not acknowledge that the write is complete until it has committed your data to the remote array. In the asynchronous option, the array acknowledges the write immediately and manages the transfer of your data between the arrays at a later date. Of course, in the latter case, you lose the guarantee that your data has been stored on the remote array because the possibility exists that the local array might fail before the remote array has received the latest changes to your data. However, if service levels dictate that you require application performance over data currency, then you have to make this trade-off.

With the Solaris Cluster 3.2 11/09 release, you can use EMC Symmetrix Remote Data Facility or Hitachi TrueCopy and Universal Replicator storage replication products as a replacement for host-based mirroring. You can configure these products to replicate your data synchronously or asynchronously, as determined by your recovery point objective (RPO).

### Note

When you use asynchronous replication, some failure scenarios might require manual intervention to recover the configuration.

### Ensuring Data Consistency after a Rolling Failure

A *rolling failure* is defined as a second failure occurring while a system is in the process of recovering from an initial failure. Rolling failures can have important consequences for data consistency, as explained next.

When an application writes data to a file system or a raw-disk partition, it does so with the expectation that the order in which the writes are issued is the order in which they are committed to storage. This expectation is guaranteed by host-based mirroring. For storage-based replication, the order in which writes are made to the remote array has a greater dependency on both the product and the configuration that you use. The features and capabilities of Hitachi's TrueCopy software illustrate the necessary considerations.

TrueCopy manages the replication between pairs of local and remote LUNs in groups. A single group can be replicated either synchronously or asynchronously (the `async` fence level). The synchronous option itself has three fence levels named `data`, `status`, and `never`, which enable you to specify how the local array should react if the local storage array cannot communicate with or update the status of the remote storage array.

Under normal operating conditions, data is replicated between the two arrays as defined by the replication policy for each group. The order in which the writes are committed to the secondary array is the order in which the application writes them to the primary array. Consider what happens when the link between the primary and remote secondary array fails, and no updates can be made. For fence levels `data` and `status` the outcome is that the application receives an I/O error. However, for the `never` and `async` fence levels, the changes are stored on the local array so that the remote array can be updated later. These changes are stored using a bitmap that records the blocks that need to be forwarded. Unfortunately, the bitmap contains no record of the order in which these blocks were changed. After you have fixed your communication problem, these blocks are propagated to the remote array. If the local primary array experiences a catastrophic failure before it can complete the catch-up process, then the data that you have on the remote array will almost certainly be inconsistent. The extent to which the data is unusable depends on the data structures it contains. For a database, it could mean that indexes are pointing to incorrect or partially populated blocks. For file systems, it could result in a file system with potentially some degree of data loss that needs checking before it can be mounted.

How can you avoid this problem? The Hitachi Data Systems Universal Replicator software, a complementary product to TrueCopy, has a configurable feature that virtually eliminates this problem. Journal devices are LUNs that are set aside within both local and remote arrays to record details of the I/O transactions that are made by an application against that array. Each group can have a journal device that is associated with it. Furthermore, a property called a *consistency group ID* can be assigned to one or more groups to indicate that the arrays will guarantee I/O consistency across their constituent LUN pairs as a whole and not just as individual groups. This combination of journal devices and consistency group IDs means that the remote array can pull from the primary array any pending changes in the correct chronological order. Thus, even if a rolling failure occurs, the changes brought over will leave the application data consistent, but you will suffer some level of data loss.

### Restriction on Parallel Applications

Another significant difference between host-based mirroring and storage-based replication is that the copy of your data on the secondary site is read-only in the case of storage-based replication. The copy of your data at this secondary site cannot be written to by any of the cluster nodes until it is promoted from being the secondary copy of your data to being the primary copy as part of a controlled switchover or takeover process (see the section "Switchover and Takeover" in Chapter 6, "Oracle Solaris Cluster Geographic Edition: Features and Architecture"). This limitation places the following restriction on the use of storage-based replication with parallel applications such as Oracle RAC because these applications require continuous read and write access to the underlying storage volumes from all database instances concurrently. At the point of failure, the promotion of secondary volumes to primary volumes necessitates a shutdown of all services accessing that volume, which is clearly contrary to the goals of such applications. The best that can be achieved is a failover Oracle service, which can be implemented without resorting to a full-blown Oracle RAC implementation.

> **Note**
>
> You cannot use storage-based replication to support parallel applications such as Oracle RAC.

### Reasons to Use Storage-Based Replication within a Cluster

Why would you choose to use storage-based replication over host-based mirroring? The answer is often that organizations have standardized on these storage replication products because the software provides them with a central point of control for data replication regardless of the server platforms attached to the storage array. Furthermore, organizations prefer to avoid the cost of additional software licenses or the training that is needed to support a host-based mirroring product.

Because storage-based replication is commonly used for deployments where the cluster nodes and storage arrays have been split across two data centers, two more reasons are often cited for using this approach. The first reason is that storage-based replication does not require the storage array networks at each site to be bridged. Instead, storage-based replication occurs out-of-band on a private Fibre Channel, ESCON, or Gigabit Ethernet network. The second but less commonly cited reason is that storage-based replication offers the use of asynchronous replication, thus freeing applications from the constraints that campus clusters bring (see "Campus and Metro Clusters").

## Public Networking

Every node in a cluster is connected to one or more public networks through which client applications access the services of the cluster. As with most hardware components, these networks can fail. If they are the sole means by which client systems access an application, any user connections are lost. To guard against this problem, you can connect the cluster to a resilient corporate network infrastructure and have multiple switches and routers between the client system and the cluster. In other words, there should be at least two completely independent paths from the cluster to the external public network. Thus, you would have a minimum of two network ports, preferably with one port on each of two network interface cards (NICs), for each public subnet connection in order to avoid a single point of failure.

With this level of resiliency, the cluster can survive the failure of a local NIC, switch, or hub. Then, rather than switching an entire service over from one node to another node with all the delays and disruption to user connectivity that this process entails, the service can continue to communicate with its clients through the alternative NIC. The Solaris IP network multipathing (IPMP) software migrates all of the logical host IP addresses (see the section "SUNW.LogicalHostname" in Chapter 2, "Oracle Solaris Cluster: Features and Architecture") from the failed NIC to the standby NIC.

Although you can configure a backup NIC that runs at a different speed from the primary NIC, it is not considered best practice. If an application is forced to use the lower-speed NIC and it is a network-intensive application, then the performance of the application could be degraded.

One other requirement for a supported cluster configuration is that all cluster nodes must connect to the same public subnets. Although not usually an issue in a single data center, this requirement can add complexity and require special consideration when your cluster spans multiple sites, especially if your organization's network policy does not allow your network administrators to configure a suitable spanning tree architecture to bridge the public networks of sites (see "Campus and Metro Clusters"). The technical issues that would require resolution if you do not connect all the nodes in your cluster to the same subnet include

- Requiring your client applications to be configured to handle two possible IP addresses for each service that the cluster hosts.

- Requiring your name service to be updated after any service failover occurs. The name service update is needed to allow clients to receive the new host-name-to-IP address mapping. Applications, such as network file system (NFS), depend on a fixed hostname and path name combination to mount a remote directory.

## Configuring IPMP for Your Public Networks

The Solaris Cluster software requires public NICs to be placed in IPMP groups, which, in turn, requires that you set `local-mac-address?=true` in the cluster node's `eeprom`. If you have not configured an IPMP group for your public subnet, when you install the Solaris Cluster software, the installation process will create a minimal configuration for you.

When you configure IPMP manually, you can use link failure detection alone, or you can choose to use a test address. The latter gives you a greater degree of end-to-end connectivity testing because it relies on the IPMP probe packets being able to traverse your network all the way to the probe target host and back.

The operation of IPMP (the `in.mpathd` daemon) depends on your routing configuration. Therefore, `in.mpathd` always refers to the routing table (`IRE-cache`) to distinguish which test partner or test partners will be used. Test partners are required for determining whether your interface is working properly.

By default, `in.mpathd` chooses your cluster's default router as a single test target for probing. If no default router exists for the test interface IP address (or if your network security group has disabled ICMP replies), arbitrary hosts are discovered by sending `icmp-echo` "all hosts" multicast packets (`224.0.0.1`) on the subnet to detect potential test partners. (An "all routers" multicast packet [`224.0.0.2`] will never be sent.) The first five hosts that respond to the `icmp-echo` packets are chosen as targets for probing. In such a non-default router environment, `in.mpathd` always tries to find five probe targets through an "all hosts" multicast packet. If this method cannot find any potential targets, you must provide some targets yourself using a script similar to the following one.

## Example 1.4   Sample Shell Script to Add Static IPMP Probe Targets

```
#!/bin/ksh
# This script assumes that the public network is on the 192.168.1.0/24 subnet.
# If you use the latest versions of Solaris 10 OS, you can use the
```

```
# "route -p .." option to make the additional routes persistent.
IPMP_TEST_TARGETS="192.168.1.41 192.168.1.42 192.168.1.43"
for target in ${IPMP_TEST_TARGETS}
do
        /usr/sbin/route add -host $target $target
done
```

The `in.mpathd` daemon detects failures and repairs them by sending `icmp-echo` probes (similar to pinging) from all interfaces that are part of the IPMP group. If there are no replies to five consecutive probes, the interface is considered to have failed, and the daemon performs a failover of the network address to another interface in the IPMP group. The probing rate depends on the failure detection time, which is defined in `/etc/default/mpathd`. By default, the failure detection time is 10 seconds. Thus, the five probes will be sent within the failure detection time [IPMP].

## Solaris Cluster Public Network Monitoring Daemon

Whereas the IPMP multipathing daemon (`in.mpathd`) is responsible for failing over network addresses between NICs within a cluster node, the Solaris Cluster public network monitoring daemon `cl_pnmd` (see the `cl_pnmd`(1m) man page) tracks the status of the IPMP groups and facilitates internode failover for all IPMP groups.

When the `prenet_start` method of a logical or shared address resource (see the section "Resource Types" in Chapter 2, "Oracle Solaris Cluster: Features and Architecture," for a description of these entities) is called by the Resource Group Manager (see the section "Resource Group Manager Daemon" in Chapter 2), the method plumbs in your chosen IP address on the appropriate NIC. The method also registers callbacks with `cl_pmnd`. Consequently, when `cl_pmnd` detects that a relevant IPMP group has failed, it calls the callbacks that were registered by the logical host/shared address resources. These callbacks, in turn, make calls to the Resource Group Manager, through interfaces such as `scha_control`(1HA), to have the resource group containing this resource moved to a healthy node.

When a logical or shared IP address is plumbed on the new cluster node, the Oracle Solaris OS sends several gratuitous Address Resolution Protocol (ARP) packets to alert other devices on the subnet to the new MAC-to-IP address mapping. The Solaris Cluster software does not migrate the MAC address with the logical or shared IP address. Consequently, if your network security administrator is creating firewall rules, these rules should not rely on a consistent mapping for the MAC-to-IP address for these entities.

## Limiting Network Interface Requirements Using VLAN Tagging

Having separate NICs for each subnet can place an excessive demand for expansion slots on your cluster nodes. This demand can be particularly problematic for low-end servers where expansion slots are limited or if suitable multi-NIC cards are not available. Fortunately, VLAN tagging (IEEE standard 802.1q [VlanTag]) enables you to configure NICs to multiple subnets, assuming that they and the switch to which they connect support this capability. The following example shows how this feature is used.

### Example 1.5   Creating Two Tagged VLANs on the Same NIC

Check that `e1000g4` exists.

```
# dladm show-link | grep e1000g4
e1000g4          type: non-vlan  mtu: 1500       device: e1000g4
```

It does exist and it does not have any tagged VLANs yet.

Configure your network switch to handle VLAN tags 12 and 13.

Plumb in VLAN tags 12 and 13.

The interface number is calculated using the following formula:

```
    1000 * VLAN tag + adapter instance number
```

In this example, the calculation for VLAN tag 13 results in the following:

```
    1000 * 13 + 4 = 13004
# ifconfig e1000g12004 plumb 192.168.1.42 netmask + broadcast + up
# ifconfig e1000g13004 plumb 172.20.1.42 netmask + broadcast + up
# ifconfig e1000g12004
e1000g12004: flags=201000843<UP,BROADCAST,RUNNING,MULTICAST,IPv4,CoS> mtu 1500 index
10
        inet 192.168.1.42 netmask ffffff00 broadcast 192.168.1.255
        ether 0:15:17:b:72:4e
# ifconfig e1000g13004
e1000g13004: flags=201000843<UP,BROADCAST,RUNNING,MULTICAST,IPv4,CoS> mtu 1500 index
11
        inet 172.20.1.42 netmask ffff0000 broadcast 172.20.255.255
        ether 0:15:17:b:72:4e
# dladm show-link | grep e1000g4
e1000g4          type: non-vlan  mtu: 1500       device: e1000g4
e1000g12004      type: vlan 12   mtu: 1500       device: e1000g4
e1000g13004      type: vlan 13   mtu: 1500       device: e1000g4
```

## Network Performance: Jumbo Frames and Link Aggregation

The Solaris Cluster software supports a wide range of Ethernet adapter cards with speeds ranging from 10 megabits per second to 10 gigabits per second. Despite this wide range of speeds, you might still want to maximize your cluster nodes' networking performance.

One option for increasing network performance is called *jumbo frames*. The Oracle Solaris OS transmits your data through your NICs and across your networks in packets that are limited to no more than the maximum transmission unit (MTU) number of bytes. By default, Solaris Cluster public NICs are configured to use the standard Solaris MTU size of 1500 bytes. For some workloads, it can be more efficient to batch the work that the Solaris kernel network drivers perform into larger chunks. You can do so by increasing the MTU size that is configured on the NIC with the condition that both the NIC and the switch are capable of handling this increased packet size. For scalable services (see the section "Failover, Scalable, and Multi-Master Resources" in Chapter 2, "Oracle Solaris Cluster: Features and Architecture"), an additional requirement is that the MTU of the private network must be the same size as or larger than the MTU of your public network.

The other option you can use to increase the potential bandwidth between a cluster node and public subnets is called *link aggregation*, also known as *trunking* or *interface bonding*. Link aggregation combines multiple physical NICs into a single logical link with the potential aggregate throughput of the sum of those combined links. Link aggregation must also be supported by the switches to which you connect the aggregated network links.

The Solaris 10 OS supports native link aggregation (IEEE standard 802.3ad) capabilities through the `dladm` command (see the `dladm`(1m) man page). The Sun Trunking software provides link aggregation capabilities to a limited set of NICs for clusters that run the Solaris 9 OS. However, regardless of which product you use, you still need to put the resulting aggregated link into an IPMP group to enable its use within the Solaris Cluster software. The following example shows how to create an aggregation using `dladm`.

## Example 1.6  Creating an Aggregated Link from Two Physical Network Interfaces

Check what links are on the system.

```
# dladm show-link
e1000g0         type: non-vlan   mtu: 1500    device: e1000g0
e1000g1         type: non-vlan   mtu: 1500    device: e1000g1
e1000g2         type: non-vlan   mtu: 1500    device: e1000g2
e1000g3         type: non-vlan   mtu: 1500    device: e1000g3
e1000g4         type: non-vlan   mtu: 1500    device: e1000g4
e1000g5         type: non-vlan   mtu: 1500    device: e1000g5
clprivnet0      type: legacy     mtu: 1486    device: clprivnet0
```

Create an aggregation from `e1000g4` and `e1000g5`.

```
# dladm create-aggr -d e1000g4 -d e1000g5 1
# dladm show-link
e1000g0        type: non-vlan  mtu: 1500    device: e1000g0
e1000g1        type: non-vlan  mtu: 1500    device: e1000g1
e1000g2        type: non-vlan  mtu: 1500    device: e1000g2
e1000g3        type: non-vlan  mtu: 1500    device: e1000g3
e1000g4        type: non-vlan  mtu: 1500    device: e1000g4
e1000g5        type: non-vlan  mtu: 1500    device: e1000g5
aggr1          type: non-vlan  mtu: 1500    aggregation: key 1
clprivnet0     type: legacy    mtu: 1486    device: clprivnet0
```

Plumb the aggregation with an IP address.

```
# ifconfig aggr1 plumb 192.168.1.42 netmask + broadcast + up
# ifconfig aggr1
aggr1: flags=1000843<UP,BROADCAST,RUNNING,MULTICAST,IPv4> mtu 1500 index 12
        inet 192.168.1.42 netmask ffffff00 broadcast 192.168.1.255
        ether 0:15:17:b:72:4e
```

Finally, create a `/etc/hostname.aggr1` file so that the IPMP group is configured on reboot.

```
# cat /etc/hostname.aggr1
myhost group sc_ipmp1 -failover
```

# Private Networking

A cluster uses a private interconnect for communications between cluster machines. The private interconnect consists of one or more networks that support communications between cluster machines. For purposes of high availability, you ideally use at least two separate private networks for the private interconnects. More than two private networks can be configured, but two networks typically provide more than adequate network bandwidth. The Solaris Cluster software uses the private interconnect for all communications between cluster machines. Data services can also use the private interconnect for communications between cluster machines. Parallel database software typically makes heavy use of the private interconnect, whereas failover data services typically do not use the private interconnect, because all of the components of a failover data service reside on the same machine.

The cluster exchanges *heartbeat messages* across each path between each pair of cluster machines. The cluster uses heartbeat messages for two purposes. When heartbeat messages cannot be successfully exchanged across a path, the cluster closes that communication path. The cluster automatically reroutes communications across surviving paths between the pair of cluster machines. If all of the paths between a pair of nodes fail, the local node declares that the local node can no longer communicate with the other node, and the system initiates a cluster reconfiguration process in order to recover. Refer to the section "Cluster Membership" in Chapter 2, "Oracle Solaris Cluster: Features and Architecture," for more information.

Figure 1.5 shows the two ways in which you can connect the private networks to the cluster nodes: either back-to-back, directly connecting one network port on one node to its peer, or in a switch-connected configuration. Although the former is obviously lower in cost, it is less flexible and requires that you add switches if you need to add a third node to your cluster. Furthermore, although you are allowed to create a cluster with just one private network, you should do so only for development clusters because this approach represents an obvious single point of failure, the results of which are described in the section "Cluster Membership" in Chapter 2, "Oracle Solaris Cluster: Features and Architecture." Similarly, you should exercise caution when using VLAN tagging (see "Limiting Network Interface Requirements Using VLAN Tagging") to enable you to use a single NIC for both public and private networks. Excessive traffic on the public network could prevent packets from being sent and received on the private network.

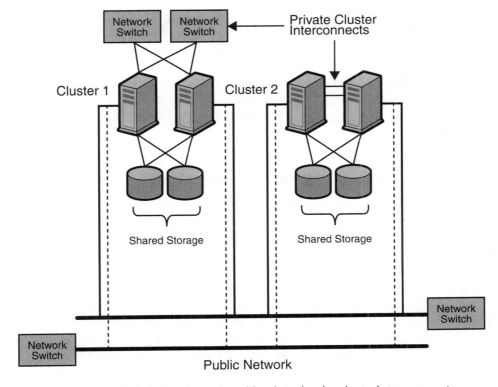

**Figure 1.5** Switch-connected and back-to-back private interconnects

Where several clusters share a common set of network switches, it is ideal to use separate VLANs (or separate partitions, in the case of InfiniBand switches, where InfiniBand is used for the private networks) to isolate the private networks of each cluster.

Heartbeat messages are implemented as low-level packets that are sent over a high-priority, dedicated "STREAM." This implementation isolates the handling of the heartbeat packets from the handling of all other IP-based traffic. The low-level implementation of the heartbeat packet means that the heartbeat packets cannot be routed.

## Campus and Metro Clusters

Most Solaris Cluster installations are contained within a single data center. To follow industry best practice, you must locate individual cluster nodes (or the cabinets containing them) in different areas of the same room to ensure that a single problem, such as a water sprinkler accidentally activating, does not result in the failure of all cluster nodes. The increased cabling lengths of technologies, such as Fibre Channel storage, have facilitated this approach. Although this approach protects against localized disasters to some extent, it still means that any events that result in a complete data center failure will cause a service outage. This possibility exists even when you consider the points made in "Solaris Volume Manager's State Replica Majority" and in the section "Handling Quorum in Campus and Metro Cluster Configurations" in Chapter 2, "Oracle Solaris Cluster: Features and Architecture."

### Stretching Cluster Node Separation to the Limit

Improvements in optical technology have decreased the cost of long-distance, high-bandwidth connectivity. Initially, these improvements enabled you to create campus clusters where your cluster nodes were separated by a maximum of 10 kilometers. As technology improved still further, this distance increased to 400 kilometers to create what are called *metropolitan clusters*, or *metro clusters* for short. Thus, the capability to cluster systems across hundreds of kilometers using dense wave division multiplexors (DWDMs) and SAN-connected Fibre Channel storage devices is now both technically and financially feasible. Figure 1.6 outlines how you would use DWDMs with either dark fiber or connectivity services that are rented from an Internet service provider (ISP) to extend both your SAN and LAN configurations. The number of channels or ports that you need on your DWDM depends on the number of SAN interswitch links (ISLs) and LAN subnets that you need to connect.

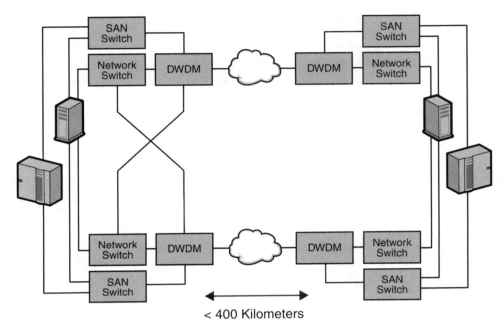

**Figure 1.6** Using dense wave division multiplexors to create a metro cluster

The only restrictions on such configurations are the following:

- The networks connecting the DWDMs must follow diverse routes for redundancy purposes.
- The latency of the links cannot exceed 15 milliseconds for a one-way trip.

This latency figure is a practical limit that was determined by Oracle's product-testing efforts rather than a technological limit. Regardless of how far you separate your cluster nodes, your public and private networks must still conform to the requirements that are described in the respective sections covering those areas.

When correctly architected, such configurations can provide some level of protection against localized disasters. However, do not view such a configuration as a complete disaster recovery solution. Despite the node separation, there is still only one logical copy of the data. As such, any corruption, deletion, or administrative error could render your services inoperable. Furthermore, separating your cluster nodes in this way is not without its consequences, as explained in the next section.

## Performance Impact of Separating Data Centers

Using geographically separated data centers to provide an additional level of disaster protection comes at a price, regardless of whether you use host-based mirroring or synchronous storage-based replication to avoid data loss if a disaster occurs. The reason is that each additional meter of separation results in a minimum of 5 nanoseconds of extra I/O latency. Every physical storage I/O requires two SCSI transactions that must be completed serially and acknowledged before the I/O is considered complete. One transaction establishes the command and the other transaction sends the data. Although some SAN switches allow the SCSI setup command to be acknowledged locally, the data transfer and acknowledgment must physically occur before the I/O returns as complete in the operating system.

Bandwidth bottlenecks can be removed to a great extent. Unfortunately, latency bottlenecks can be overcome only to a point. The speed of light in glass is 5 nanoseconds per meter. As an example, attempting to replicate transactions synchronously over 1000 kilometers inevitably adds a delay of a minimum of 20 milliseconds to the transaction.

> Additional latency = (distance in meters) multiplied by (the time taken to travel 1 meter) multiplied by (number of trips) multiplied by (number of parts to a trip)

> Additional latency = (1000 * 1000) * 5 * 2 * 2 = 20,000,000 nanoseconds (or 20 milliseconds)

If you rent bandwidth from an ISP, rather than having dark fiber between your data centers, then the terms of the service-level agreement for the communications infrastructure are important. Factors such as other traffic on the communications link, forwarding delays through any intermediate communications equipment, and the possibility that the communications links follow an indirect route could increase the latency to 50 to 100 milliseconds. At the standby site data needs to be written to cache (assuming the array has a cache) or physical disk (if it does not have a cache). The extra time taken to write the data to the remote array can add precious milliseconds to the overall time taken. Given these facts, a delay of approximately 0.1 second might be more realistic. However, the absolute number is not that important. Instead, the relative increase in the time taken to write the application data determines the perceived performance penalty.

For example, suppose your database service performs well on a system with locally attached storage. However, the service is known to be sensitive to the response time of single-threaded, sequential writes to its online redo logs. If the typical response time for your locally attached LUN is 2 milliseconds, then configuring a mirror 100 kilometers away adds a minimum of 2 milliseconds to your service time, or a 100 percent increase. This increase can result in a substantial, and unavoidable, drop in database performance. Here, the underlying technology makes no difference. Both host-based mirroring and synchronous storage-based replication are subject to the same laws of physics. Naturally, you could replicate data asynchronously, but that could potentially result in data loss, which is most likely undesirable.

These characteristics have been demonstrated by tests that were run on the configuration shown in Figure 1.7.

The interswitch link ports on the SAN switches are configured with sufficient buffer credits to help ensure that the switch is not the limiting factor. When insufficient buffer credits are configured, the poor performance over the extended distance degrades even further.

The throughput is then measured for both local (0 kilometers) I/O and remote (80 kilometers) I/O, the results of which are illustrated in Figure 1.8. The tests measure throughput to raw disk (/dev/rdsk/cXtYdZs0), as opposed to the file

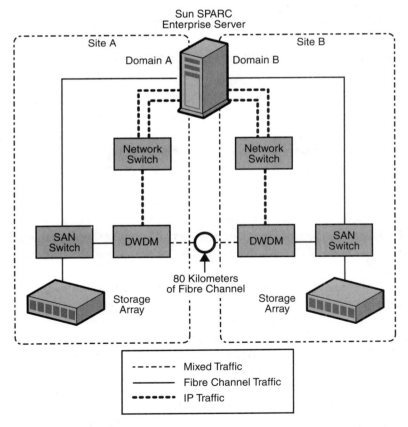

**Figure 1.7** Configuration for testing I/O throughput over extended distances

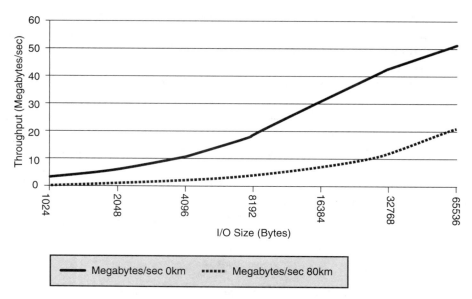

**Figure 1.8** Raw, single-threaded, sequential write I/O throughput

system, to avoid the effects of the Oracle Solaris OS file system page cache that can distort the results. This approach equates to applications that open file system data files using the O_SYNC flag. For example, the Oracle database software opens its online redo logs with this flag. Although the latest storage arrays might achieve higher I/O throughput results than the arrays used in the tests, the newer arrays would still demonstrate the same performance degradation characteristics when they are connected over 80 kilometers of fiber cable.

Raw, single-threaded, sequential writes show significant degradation at 80 kilometers. The reason is that the local storage array has a response time of 1 millisecond, whereas the remote operations consume a minimum of 2.6 milliseconds. If the array can (asynchronously) destage the data from cache faster than the requests are sent, then the cache never becomes full, and the additional latency I/O remains the dominant factor.

In contrast, single-threaded, random writes do not degrade nearly as much, as shown in Figure 1.9. Under load, the array has a service time of approximately 5 milliseconds. The extra 1.6-millisecond latency (80 × 1000 × 2 × 2 × 5 nanoseconds) is masked by the time it takes to destage the data from cache to disk. The capability to mask this extra latency is heavily dependent on any cache the storage subsystem contains and how effectively the storage subsystem can sustain the flow of data through the cache. If the cache is unable to keep up with the write request rate, then random write degradation might tend toward that of sequential

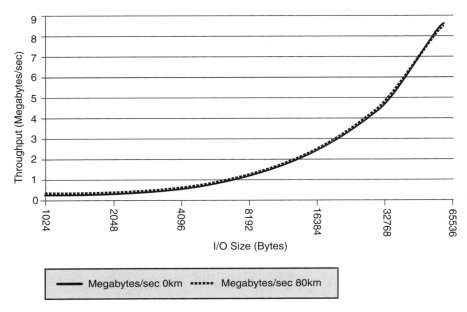

**Figure 1.9** Raw, single-threaded, random write I/O throughput

writes. The exact amount of degradation depends on how much extra latency, caused by the extended distance, is passed on to the write. Furthermore, the performance of multithreaded, random writes is again determined by whether the storage array's cache can keep up with the I/O demand. When the array is driven to its saturation point, the additional latency is once again masked by the destaging time because it is typically substantially larger (8 to 10 milliseconds) than the extra latency (1 to 2 milliseconds) that is caused by the extended distance.

These issues also place a practical limit on the node separation of systems that are part of a three-data-center architecture. For more information see the section "Three-Data-Center Architectures: Combining Campus and Geographic Options" in Chapter 5, "Oracle Solaris Cluster Geographic Edition: Overview."

Performance characteristics for single-threaded sequential writes and multithreaded random writes are important when considering the processes that databases use to record transactions and checkpoint (or flush) their buffer cache. Single-threaded write performance is the factor that determines write performance to a transaction log file, for example, Oracle's online redo log. The performance of write I/Os, in turn, governs the transaction commit time and thus the perceived application performance. Multithreaded random write performance governs the time it takes to flush a database's buffer cache. Increasing the time for a flush can result in greater contention for free buffer pages, thus lowering application performance even more.

Note that remote reads are never performed by a system that is correctly configured. Reads should always be fulfilled from a preferred (local) mirror, unless a fault occurs on this component.

**2**

# Oracle Solaris Cluster: Features and Architecture

This chapter provides technical details on Oracle Solaris Cluster features and commentary on the ramifications these features might have for system design and implementation. It begins by examining the core Solaris Cluster capabilities. The chapter then discusses the most critical component of the cluster: its management of configuration information. Next comes information about how the cluster determines cluster membership and protects data integrity. The remaining sections follow a roughly logical ordering of devices, file systems, networking, and finally, the resource types, resources, and resource groups that are used to encapsulate your services.

## Cluster Architecture

The Solaris Cluster software extends the Solaris operating environment into a cluster operating system through several kernel and non-kernel components. The Solaris Cluster software

- Supports a variety of file systems, including both cluster file systems and highly available file systems
- Manages storage devices
- Provides a cluster-wide unique address space for storage devices
- Manages volume manager devices

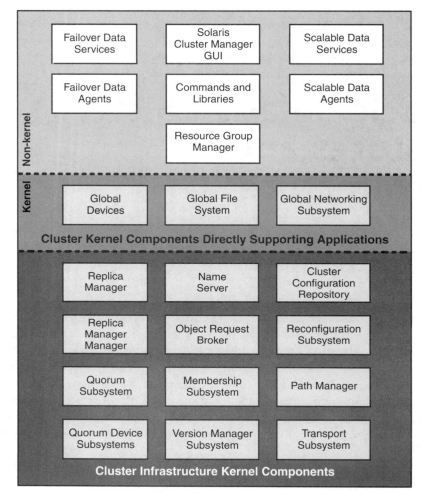

**Figure 2.1** Relationships among the Solaris Cluster components

This section describes the high-level architecture for a Solaris Cluster system. Figure 2.1 identifies the major subsystems of the Solaris Cluster software. The goal of this section is to identify the major components and how they fit together to form a cluster. Subsequent sections provide more details on each major subsystem.

The discussion begins with the cluster infrastructure and ends with the management of data services.

- The Name Server provides the means by which cluster components can dynamically connect with other cluster components.

- The Object Request Broker subsystem provides reliable communications between cluster components regardless of which node the components reside upon and regardless of whether the components reside in the kernel or a user process.

- The HA Framework supports highly available services, including the management of primary and secondary components and general checkpoint support.

- The Membership subsystem determines whether the nodes that can communicate should be allowed to form the one and only cluster.

- The Quorum subsystem supports any configured quorum devices. The Solaris Cluster software supports a wide variety of quorum devices: shared disks, quorum servers, and NAS devices.

- The Transport subsystem manages the private interconnect and provides the capability to communicate across the private interconnect. This subsystem uses heartbeats to monitor the status of communication paths between nodes. The Transport subsystem notifies the Membership subsystem when a cluster node becomes reachable through the private network or when a cluster node becomes unreachable.

- The Reconfiguration subsystem drives the process by which a cluster readjusts itself after a change in cluster membership. A cluster reconfiguration involves many cluster subsystems because many of them utilize cluster membership.

- The Version Manager subsystem determines whether a joining node has the appropriate version of software. This subsystem also orchestrates the activation of new software when an administrator commits the cluster to using new software.

- The Storage Fencing subsystem ensures that data is protected from corruption by nodes that are not part of the current cluster membership.

- The Global Networking subsystem delivers communications across the cluster based on an administrator-specified load-balancing policy. The Private Networking feature is actually provided by the Transport subsystem. This feature enables applications to communicate across the private interconnect. The `clprivnet` software stripes communications across the private interconnect and transparently handles communication path failures as long as at least one communication path remains operational.

- The Resource Group Manager (RGM) subsystem manages applications and the resources used by cluster applications. More specifically, the RGM ensures that cluster applications run on a cluster node where needed resources are available. A cluster application is called a *data service*, often abbreviated to just a *service*. A cluster application that runs on only one node at a time is a *failover application*, and a cluster application that runs an instance on multiple nodes at a time is a scalable or multi-master application. The RGM uses individual agents to manage each data service.

These subsystems all reside in the kernel and are not directly visible to cluster applications.

Solaris Cluster Manager (formerly Sun Cluster Manager) provides a graphical user interface for observing and controlling the cluster.

## Object Request Broker Subsystem

The Object Request Broker (ORB) subsystem connects the cluster components. The client software in the Solaris Cluster framework can access the server software using a form of a procedure call referred to as an *invocation*. The server component exists in the form of an object, more specifically a C++ object. A server object can publish a reference in the Name Server. A client can obtain a reference to the server object through *lookups* in the Name Server. The client makes invocations to the server object using the reference to determine the server location. There are no restrictions on the locations of the client and the server. Components can reside in the kernel or in a user process. In addition, they can reside on the same or different machines.

The ORB provides the following functionality:

- Converts invocations in the same address space into C++ procedure calls
- Supports the marshaling and unmarshaling of information for invocations across different address spaces
- Provides reliable remote procedure calls that handle cluster membership for internode invocations
- Implements flow control of invocations to ensure that invocations going to a node do not overwhelm the target node

The ORB uses Solaris doors (see the libdoor(3LIB) man page) to optimize communication costs for invocations crossing the kernel/user-process boundary, and also for communications between two separate user processes on the same machine.

The ORB design had its antecedents in the Common Object Request Broker Architecture (CORBA) model. However, the ORB design has diverged significantly from the current CORBA standard. In the ORB implementation, performance is an important consideration, and nonessential CORBA features are not part of the

ORB design. The primary goal of the ORB design is location-transparent, reliable communications.

## High-Availability Framework

A primary goal of the Solaris Cluster software is to provide high availability. More specifically, a cluster application should not be negatively impacted by the failure of a cluster machine that is not hosting the cluster application. In multiple cases, a cluster service can run on a different machine from the machine hosting the cluster application. The solution is to implement these services as high-availability (HA) services. The HA framework provides a set of features that support HA services. At this time, all HA services run in the kernel. Note that the HA framework does not hide the failure of the machine hosting the application.

The HA service uses the *primary/secondary/spare* model. One machine hosts the one and only primary, which responds to all requests for that particular HA service. The primary keeps the secondaries informed about the state of the HA service. The number of secondaries can range from one up to the number of nodes in the cluster minus one (for the primary node). When the machine hosting the primary fails, the system promotes one of the secondaries to become the new primary. Using information about the state of the HA service, the new primary completes requests that are outstanding at the time of the failover, and this failover is transparent to clients of the HA service. There is a cost associated with maintaining state information on a secondary. In some cases, the choice is made to limit the number of secondaries to one. A spare is a node that can support the HA service, but it is not currently acting as either a primary or secondary. A spare has no information about the state of the HA service. When the system promotes a secondary to become a primary, the system promotes a spare to become a secondary when a spare is available. The primary takes a snapshot of the state of the HA service and ships that information to a newly promoted secondary. The term *provider* is used for the software on a machine that can become a primary, secondary, or spare.

The Replica Manager manages all of the HA services, with one exception. The Replica Manager learns about machine failures from the Membership subsystem. Each HA service provider registers with the Replica Manager. The Replica Manager assigns the role of primary, secondary, or spare to each provider. This role can change as a result of machine failure or administrator commands.

The Replica Manager is itself an HA service. The Replica Manager cannot manage itself. The Replica Manager Manager determines which Replica Manager provider will be the primary, and all other Replica Manager providers are secondaries. The Replica Manager Manager chooses the Replica Manager primary as part of the cluster reconfiguration process.

The `replctl` command can display a list of all HA services. This list identifies the location of each provider for that HA service along with the role: primary, secondary, or spare. The administrator can use the `replctl` command to change the role of a provider. Usually, the administrator will not manually change provider roles.

Each HA service primary is a collection of one or more objects all colocated on the same machine. The primary object publishes one or more references in the Name Server. Clients look up the reference in the Name Server. The reference to an HA service object has a special property. The reference always refers to the location of the HA service primary, regardless of the actual location of the HA service primary. Clients do not need new references when the HA service primary moves.

An invocation to an HA service is called an HA invocation. The HA invocation supports *at most once* semantics. The HA invocation does not support *exactly once* semantics because all of the machines hosting primary and secondary providers could fail during the invocation, and thus the machine could not complete the HA invocation. As long as the machine hosting the client keeps running and at least one machine is running with state information about the HA service (which means either a primary or a secondary that can become a primary), the HA invocation will complete without machine failures being visible to the client.

Several features are required to support an HA invocation. The machine hosting the primary could fail before completing the HA invocation. The machine failure triggers a cluster reconfiguration, during which time the Replica Manager promotes a secondary to become the new primary and the HA framework changes all references to the affected HA service to refer to the new primary. After the cluster reconfiguration completes, the HA framework sends the invocation to the new primary without requiring the client to do anything.

Some HA invocations are not idempotent. The old primary might have performed the requested operation and the machine failed just prior to sending the reply, in which case the HA invocation cannot simply be replayed. To deal with this situation, the HA service primary uses one or more checkpoints. A checkpoint must contain sufficient information so that a newly promoted primary could determine whether the HA invocation has already completed and, if not, provide sufficient information to complete the HA invocation. This means that the primary sends any checkpoint notification prior to making changes related to that checkpoint. The HA services are generally multithreaded, which means that multiple HA invocations can be active concurrently. The secondary records checkpoint information about a specific HA invocation in a `transaction_state` data structure. When the primary completes the HA invocation, the primary *commits* the transaction, which alerts all of the secondaries that they can discard the information about the completed transaction. There are provisions for dealing with the case where the primary fails after completing the transaction but before committing the transaction.

The behavior of an HA invocation is illustrated with an example from the Proxy file system (PxFS) (see Figure 2.2). The file system operation to delete a file is not idempotent. Consider the case where the file to be deleted exists prior to the HA invocation. The first attempt to delete the file would return success, whereas a replay would return an error indicating that the file did not exist. Thus, this request needs checkpoints.

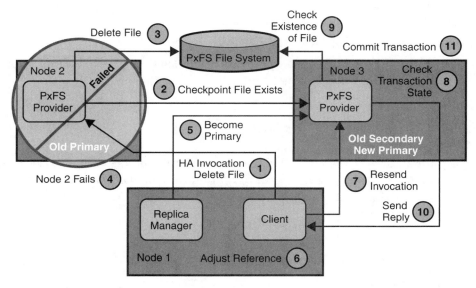

**Figure 2.2** Surviving a PxFS primary node failure during a file deletion operation

For this example, consider a three-node cluster. The client is on node 1. The PxFS primary is on node 2 and the PxFS secondary is on node 3. Node 1 cannot host a PxFS provider, because node 1 does not have a direct path to the storage device.

The following describes the behavior of the HA invocation for this example:

1. The client sends an invocation to the PxFS primary.
2. The PxFS primary checkpoints information to the PxFS secondary, and that information includes whether the file to be deleted exists.
3. The PxFS primary deletes the file.
4. The machine hosting the PxFS primary fails before the PxFS primary sends the reply.

5. The node failure results in a cluster reconfiguration. The Replica Manager promotes the PxFS secondary on node 3 to become the PxFS primary.

6. The HA framework adjusts all references to the PxFS HA service to refer to the new PxFS primary.

7. The HA framework, and not the client, sends the HA invocation from node 1 to node 3.

8. The new PxFS primary looks at the `transaction_state` information for this HA invocation.

9. The new PxFS primary checks for the file that is supposed to be deleted and finds that the file has already been deleted.

10. The new PxFS primary returns success.

11. The new PxFS primary then commits the transaction, which does nothing because there is no secondary to inform.

## Cluster Configuration Control

To maintain an accurate and up-to-date representation of a Solaris Cluster configuration, clustered systems require configuration control. The Solaris Cluster software uses a cluster configuration repository (CCR) to store the current cluster configuration information.

## Cluster Configuration Repository

The Solaris Cluster software automatically stores details of your cluster's global configuration in the CCR. It also maintains a separate repository for each zone cluster (see the section "Zone Clusters" in Chapter 3, "Combining Virtualization Technologies with Oracle Solaris Cluster Software") that you have configured.

These repositories consist of a set of ASCII files that reside in the root (/) file system of each physical cluster node. For the global cluster, they are stored in the `/etc/cluster/ccr/global` directory. Each zone-cluster repository is stored in a subdirectory of `/etc/cluster/ccr/` that is named after the container cluster, for example, `/etc/cluster/ccr/zone_cluster_foo`. The storage requirement for the CCR is relatively modest. Even in the largest possible cluster configuration the CCR uses less than 1 megabyte.

The CCR files for the global cluster contain all of the information needed to manage the global cluster. The following is a list of some of the configuration information that is stored:

- Cluster name
- Cluster nodes
- Global node IP addresses
- Private interconnect topology
- Details of quorum devices
- Details of resource groups, resource types, and resources
- Device ID (DID) instances
- Details of device groups

The CCR files for each zone cluster contain a subset of this information. For example, these files do not have information about quorum devices, interconnect topology, or device groups.

At boot time, the system requires some of the information in the CCR files, for example, the node's registration key for the persistent group reservation and persistent group reservation emulation protocols, the cluster name, transport information, and so forth. This information cannot be placed on shared storage because the local node must be able to access CCR information before shared storage is accessible. Each node has a local copy of all CCR information. The local node accesses this CCR information in read-only mode until the cluster forms. The cluster reconfiguration process propagates the latest CCR information to all nodes that need to be updated. After that operation completes, the cluster permits both read and write access to CCR information.

## CCR File Consistency

The cluster framework maintains the consistency of the CCR files by using a distributed two-phase commit protocol, implemented as an HA service. See "High-Availability Framework."

The CCR files include information supporting a wide range of cluster subsystems. The administrator can change cluster configuration information by using any of the appropriate cluster commands. For example, the clresource command changes the RGM resource information. The clresourcegroup command changes the RGM resource group information (see the respective man pages for more details).

Each CCR file contains a generation (or version) number and a checksum that allow the Solaris Cluster software to ensure that the information the file contains is the latest version and that the contents have not been corrupted. When the configuration of a cluster is changed, through either the command-line interface or the browser interface, the generation number and checksum are automatically updated.

> **Warning**
>
> Do not manually edit the CCR files. Inconsistent changes made manually can lead to a cluster-wide failure and the failure of cluster nodes to boot successfully. The recovery procedure will then require one or more nodes to be booted in non-cluster mode.

## Cluster Membership

The Solaris Cluster software defines the *active membership* as a group of nodes that can successfully communicate with every other node in the group through the private interconnect. This concept is critical to the success of a cluster product performing distributed computing operations. The Cluster Membership Monitor (CMM) must ensure that only one cluster incarnation is in progress at a time.

### Split-Brain Condition

A split-brain condition occurs when a single cluster has a failure that divides the cluster into multiple partitions, where each partition is unaware of any other partition. Because each new cluster is unaware of other partitions, a collision in shared resources could occur. Network addresses can be duplicated because each new cluster partition determines that it should own the logical network addresses of the services that the cluster hosts. Shared storage could also be affected because each cluster erroneously determines that it owns the shared storage. The result is *severe data corruption*.

### Membership

To determine membership and, more important, to ensure data integrity, the CMM must achieve the following:

- Account for a change in cluster membership, such as a node joining or leaving the cluster
- Ensure that a faulty node leaves the cluster
- Ensure that a faulty node stays out of the cluster until it is repaired
- Ensure that only one cluster remains active

Given these requirements, the CMM protects a cluster against these failures:

- *Split-brain conditions*: All communication between a set of nodes is lost and the cluster becomes partitioned into subclusters, each of which determines that it is the only partition.

- *Amnesia conditions*: The cluster restarts after a shutdown with cluster configuration data that is older than the time of the shutdown. See "Amnesia Condition" for more information, including the solution for this problem.

The Solaris Cluster software avoids split-brain conditions by using the majority vote principle (see "Majority Voting") to circumvent undesirable situations that would otherwise compromise cluster availability.

Maintaining correct membership is vital to a wide range of cluster subsystems. When membership changes, the CMM initiates a cluster reconfiguration. The first part of the cluster reconfiguration determines the current membership. Later parts of the cluster reconfiguration involve a wide range of cluster subsystems. For more information, see "Reconfiguration."

### CMM Implementation

The Solaris Cluster software implements the CMM as kernel modules on each cluster node using high-priority threads. Therefore, resource starvation is much less likely to affect the CMM than a user-level daemon would. Consequently, the Solaris Cluster software supports faster failure detection and recovery. Note that these failure detection and recovery times are typically small relative to the time taken for an application to recover, which tends to dominate failover times. The Transport subsystem monitors connectivity between cluster nodes and notifies the CMM when a node becomes reachable or unreachable. A node is reachable across the private interconnect as long as at least one path is operational between a pair of nodes.

## Majority Voting

The cluster membership model is independent of the cluster storage topology and the volume manager you use. The basic principle relies on the concept of a majority, that is, more than half of a particular quantity. Although cluster installation has special rules relating to quorum, the following discussion covers only the normal operational conditions of a cluster.

Each node within the cluster is given one "vote." The quantity $V_n$ represents the total number of node votes. For a cluster with no quorum devices configured, a majority of nodes must be able to communicate with each other over the private interconnect. A majority is calculated as $\text{int}[V_n*0.5] + 1$, in which the int function computes the integer portion of its operand. If this condition is not met, nodes in the particular subcluster panic because they lose majority. A subcluster is any subset of nodes that constitute the entire cluster.

This algorithm has undesirable consequences for a two-node cluster because shutting down one node automatically shuts down the other node. You can overcome this behavior by using a quorum device. The Solaris Cluster software supports multiple kinds of quorum devices:

- A *quorum disk*: a nominated disk in the shared storage of your cluster
- A *quorum server*: a Solaris server on the network
- A network-attached storage device

When a quorum device is multihosted to N nodes, it is given N − 1 votes. A dual-hosted quorum device receives only one vote. Quorum servers and NAS quorum devices are connected to all N nodes in the cluster, and such a quorum device has N − 1 votes.

Defining the total number of votes contributed by quorum devices as $V_q$, the total number of votes now available to the cluster (defined as $V_t$) is, therefore, $V_t = V_n + V_q$. A subcluster must still gain a majority of the available votes to continue. However, this calculation is now int$[V_t * 0.5] + 1$.

A quorum device must be defined for a two-node cluster during normal operations. In some cases, a two-node cluster can operate without a quorum device during emergency repair procedures. This arrangement enables any single node that obtains the vote of the quorum device to maintain majority and continue as a viable cluster. The CMM forces the losing node to halt.

A quorum device can be used in a cluster with more than two nodes. Consider the example of a cluster with four nodes and a quorum device that connects to all cluster nodes. Because each node has one vote, the total node vote count, $V_n$, is 4. The vote count for the quorum device $V_q$ is (4 − 1 = 3) 3 votes. The total number of possible votes, $V_t$, is 7. A cluster partition needs 4 votes for that partition to survive. If all four nodes keep running and the quorum device fails, the cluster partition has 4 votes and can survive. If three nodes fail and the remaining node gains the votes held by the quorum device, then that cluster partition has 4 votes and that partition can survive.

If one quorum device is beneficial, you might think that more quorum devices are even better. That is not always the case. Consider a four-node cluster with two fully connected quorum devices. The nodes have a total, $V_n$, of 4 votes. Each quorum device has 3 votes. The total possible quorum votes, $V_q$, is 10 votes. In the case where all four nodes survive and both quorum devices fail, the cluster partition does not have sufficient votes to survive. This lack of quorum happens even when all of the nodes are still running.

Finally, if your cluster does not have any shared storage, or if your cluster uses storage-based replication instead of host-based mirroring, then you might have to use a quorum server rather than a quorum device.

## Quorum Device General Behavior

All of these quorum devices conform to a Solaris Cluster standard for quorum device behavior. Where the following text describes a quorum device as being "owned" by a cluster node, "ownership" simply implies that the cluster partition containing the "owning" node has gained exclusive rights to the votes held by the quorum device. This section describes this common behavior for quorum devices.

All quorum devices

- Support the capability to persistently record a unique registration key for each cluster node.

- Support the capability to persistently record a reservation key that identifies the owner of the quorum device. The reservation key value is either zero, which represents no owner, or a value equal to the registration key of a cluster node.

- Support the capability to have an exclusive owner node.

- Always allow any cluster node to read the registration keys regardless of whether the registration key of the requesting node is present on that quorum device.

As nodes join the cluster, their registration keys are written to the quorum device by the Solaris Cluster software. When a node leaves the cluster, the registration key of the departing node is removed from the device by one of the remaining cluster nodes. The node performing this operation reserves the device using its own registration key as the reservation key. The registration keys of current cluster nodes remain on the quorum device until the node departs the cluster. The cluster partition that retains ownership of the quorum device obtains the quorum votes of that quorum device. This behavior is critical to the survival of the cluster partition because the total quorum votes, $V_t$, held by a cluster partition determine whether the partition survives.

If a node panics while removing the key of a departing node, the CMM attempts another reconfiguration. If the remaining nodes can still form a cluster, they proceed to remove the key of the previously departing node as well as the node that just panicked. If the remaining nodes do not form a majority, the cluster aborts. In this instance, the quorum device has the registration keys of these remaining nodes, the node that panicked, and the ousted node, because the last successful reconfiguration had exactly those members.

Because all quorum devices retain registration keys persistently, the quorum device has the registration keys of all the members in the last cluster reconfiguration. This behavior supports the amnesia feature (see "Amnesia Condition"). If the last cluster configuration had just one member, that registration key is the only key on the quorum device. An amnesiac node cannot become the owner of a quorum device until after successfully joining a cluster because the registration key of the amnesiac node is not on the quorum device.

### Quorum Disk Device Reservation Mechanisms

The storage devices shared by a cluster can be divided into three categories:

- Devices that support the SCSI-3 Persistent Group Reservation (PGR) protocol
- Devices that support only the SCSI-2 Reservation protocol
- Devices that support neither protocol but use the software quorum protocol, for example, Serial Advanced Technology Attachment (SATA) disks and solid-state disks (SSD)

When a storage device is configured as a quorum device, the Quorum subsystem is responsible for fencing the configured quorum device. The storage device fencing (see "Storage Device Fencing Subsystem") subsystem ignores configured quorum devices.

**SCSI-3 PGR**    The SCSI-3 Persistent Group Reservation (PGR) protocol has operations supported by `ioctl` system calls that closely map to the operations needed by the generic Solaris Cluster quorum device. PGR persistently supports both per-host registration keys and a reservation key. The Solaris Cluster software uses the PGR option that always allows read operations but disallows write operations from nodes that do not have their registration key on the device. Any node that attempts a write operation after its own registration key has been removed from the device will encounter a reservation conflict and panic. The SCSI-3 PGR protocol can be used only on devices that have the software to support this protocol.

**SCSI-2 and PGRe**    The SCSI-2 Reservation protocol is less feature-rich than the SCSI-3 PGR protocol. The SCSI-2 Reservation protocol can be used only by disks that are connected to precisely two nodes, because the SCSI-2 Reservation protocol either allows or disallows access to a node, rather than working at a group level. Furthermore, unlike the persistent reservations of SCSI-3 PGR, SCSI-2 reservations are lost if the node or disk is reset.

The Solaris Cluster software builds on the SCSI-2 protocol to emulate some of the features of the SCSI-3 PGR protocol. This extension is called PGRe, where the *e* stands for "emulation." In particular, the PGRe extension emulates the registration and reservation keys of the SCSI-3 PGR protocol.

When a *split-brain* condition occurs (see "Split-Brain Condition"), the node that owns the shared disk issues the SCSI-2 take ownership operation and ensures that the SCSI-2 reservation remains in effect for at least 6 seconds. Each node probes the shared disk within the 6-second time period. When a node ejected from the cluster encounters the SCSI-2 reservation, the node receives an error and self-terminates. When a split-brain condition occurs, the node that becomes the owner adds the quorum device vote count to the cluster partition to which the owning node belongs.

SCSI-2 PGRe includes the following features:

- Solaris disk drive handlers reserve a relatively small amount of space on each disk for disks with either a volume table of contents (VTOC) or an extensible firmware interface (EFI) label. The Solaris Cluster software has exclusive use of 65 blocks in this reserved area. The PGRe uses one block for each of the 64 possible nodes and an extra block for the reservation owner. The same disk can be used for other purposes, such as hosting a file system.

- PGRe emulates the SCSI-3 PGR `ioctl` system calls. The emulation of `PreemptAndAbort` uses Lamport's algorithm [Lamport].

- PGRe uses SCSI-2 `Tkown` and `Release` `ioctl` system calls in conjunction with the emulation of SCSI-3 PGR `ioctl` system calls to ensure that the loser in the quorum race is removed from the cluster and encounters a reservation conflict.

**Software Quorum**     The Solaris Cluster software also supports the software quorum protocol. This protocol emulates SCSI-3 PGR completely in software. The software quorum only needs the device to support read and write operations, but neither SCSI-2 nor SCSI-3 reservation-related operations. Consequently, you can use any kind of shared disk as a quorum device with the Solaris Cluster software. For example, you can now use SATA devices as well as solid-state disk (SSD) devices as quorum devices.

The protocol uses the same approach as SCSI-3 PGR to place registration keys on the quorum device and use the registration key as the reservation key when removing the registration keys of departing cluster nodes.

Each node probes the shared device every 2 seconds (assume that this configurable time period is called T) to check if the node's registration key is still present on the disk. When a *split-brain* event occurs (see "Split-Brain Condition"), the node that owns the shared disk (or that will become the new owner) removes the registration key of the departing node and then delays the cluster reconfiguration for twice the probe period (T * 2). This delay ensures that the departing node will probe the disk, determine that its registration key has been removed from the device, and thus self-terminate. The node that becomes the owner of the quorum device adds the quorum device vote count to the cluster partition to which the owning node belongs.

To use a shared device with the software quorum protocol, you first need to turn off SCSI fencing for that device (see "Storage Device Fencing Subsystem"). When you subsequently configure the shared device as a quorum device, the Solaris Cluster software determines that SCSI fencing for the device is turned off and automatically uses the software quorum protocol. The SCSI-2 take ownership `ioctl` system calls are not used on software quorum devices.

The software quorum provides a level of data-integrity protection comparable to SCSI-2-based fencing.

**iSCSI**    An iSCSI device appears to the Solaris Cluster software as if it were a directly connected storage device. The Solaris Cluster software is currently not aware that an iSCSI device is not a SCSI device. If the iSCSI device can support SCSI-3 PGR, the iSCSI device can be configured as a shared disk quorum device using SCSI-3 PGR. Similarly, if the iSCSI device can support SCSI-2 Reservations, the iSCSI device can be configured as a shared disk quorum device using SCSI-2 Reservations. An iSCSI device can always be configured as a shared disk quorum device using the software quorum protocol. In the Solaris 10 OS, an iSCSI device must be on the same subnet as the cluster in order to be configured as a quorum device.

### Quorum Server

The *quorum server* is a daemon process (`/usr/cluster/lib/sc/scqsd`) that acts as a quorum device. The quorum server daemon can be started and stopped using the `clquorumserver` command (see the `clquorumserver`(1M) man page).

The quorum server daemon must run on either a SPARC-based system that is running either the Solaris 9 OS or the Solaris 10 OS, or it must run on an x64-based system that is running the Solaris 10 OS. In addition, the host must have the Solaris Cluster quorum server packages (`SUNWscqsr` and `SUNWscqsu`) loaded.

The quorum server daemon cannot reside on a node of a cluster to which the quorum server daemon is providing quorum services. The machine architecture (SPARC or x64) that hosts the quorum server does not have to match that of the cluster nodes. The quorum server emulates PGR in a manner similar to the software quorum protocol.

Unlike a quorum disk, which is used only by a single cluster, a single quorum server daemon can support many clusters. Alternatively, you can run multiple quorum server daemons on the same Solaris system, and each quorum server daemon would use a different IP address/port combination.

It is considered best practice to assign each client cluster to its own quorum server daemon processes, such that each cluster communicates with its own quorum server daemon. However, you can configure your client clusters to share a common quorum server daemon on a single, common IP address/port. Using several separate quorum server daemons provides greater maintenance flexibility and lowers the likelihood that a single failure will affect more than one cluster. If you want to maintain separate copies of the quorum server software, then place each instance in its own Oracle Solaris zone. A *non-global zone* is a virtualized operating system environment created within a single instance of the Oracle Solaris OS, known as the *global zone*. Oracle Solaris Zones (also called Oracle Solaris Containers) is a feature of the Solaris 10 OS (see the section "Oracle Solaris Zones" in Chapter 3, "Combining Virtualization Technologies with Oracle Solaris Cluster Software"). If your organization has very large numbers of clusters that require quorum server services, it is considered best practice to use several machines, each with one or more quorum server daemons configured.

When using a quorum server as the quorum device, operations (such as reading, registering, or removing keys) have a 5-second communication timeout before they are retried. This timeout period ensures that the quorum algorithm quickly reaches a conclusion.

### Network-Attached Storage

Network Appliance network-attached storage (NAS) devices can be configured as quorum devices. The Network Appliance quorum device can be located on either the local subnet or a remote network.

Oracle NAS devices can also be configured as quorum devices. The administrator creates a LUN on the Oracle NAS device and exports the LUN through iSCSI to all of the iSCSI cluster machines. The LUN on the Oracle NAS device is used the same way as any other iSCSI shared storage device, and the same restrictions apply.

### Amnesia Condition

*Amnesia* is a failure mode in which a node starts with stale cluster configuration information. Amnesia is a synchronization error that occurs when the cluster configuration information was not propagated to all of the nodes. For example, consider the case of a two-node cluster with node X and node Y. When node X is shut down and the administrator reconfigures the cluster from node Y, the cluster configuration information of node X is now stale. Then node Y shuts down. If node X now boots and attempts to form a cluster, the cluster consisting of node X still has stale, incorrect information.

The cluster has rules that guarantee that a cluster cannot form without the latest CCR information. One rule is that CCR changes can be made only in cluster mode, except during emergency repair procedures.

Consider a cluster with no quorum device. The cluster can form only if a majority of cluster nodes is present. It is impossible to have a majority vote unless at least one node was present in the previous cluster. The system will propagate the CCR information to other nodes as needed when the cluster forms.

Next, consider a cluster with a quorum device. In this configuration, a cluster can form without a majority of nodes, so simply having a majority of quorum votes does not guarantee that at least one node was a member of the previous cluster. Another rule covers this situation. When a cluster partition attempts to take ownership of a quorum device, the node attempting to take ownership must have its own registration key on the quorum device. If the node was not a member of the previous cluster, then the surviving nodes of that cluster would have removed the registration key of the departed node. Thus, a node that was not a member of the previous cluster cannot become the owner of the quorum device. The result is that a cluster cannot acquire sufficient quorum votes to form a cluster, unless at least one node was a member of the previous cluster. Again, if the cluster forms, then the system propagates the CCR information to nodes as needed.

## Uneven Cluster Partitions

Multinode clusters can be the subject of numerous failure scenarios, each of which ideally results in the safe reconfiguration of the cluster to provide continued service on the remaining nodes. With some failures, it is difficult for the cluster to determine the optimal outcome. For example, when a four-node, pair+M cluster partitions 3 to 1, it is preferable that the three-node partition acquire the three nominated quorum disk votes and survive. However, a single node could obtain the quorum disk votes first and attain the majority vote, even though this outcome might not be desirable. In an alternative scenario, in which the three nodes instantaneously lose communication with the single node (through some bizarre interconnect failure), leading to a 1:1:1:1 split, the single node could obtain the quorum disk votes and continue as the remaining cluster member.

The Solaris Cluster software has heuristics that significantly increase the possibility that the most desirable partition survives to become the active cluster. The CMM delays unhealthy nodes acquiring the quorum device or devices. The CMM also has a small delay that is proportional to the number of nodes that are not in the current cluster partition. A partition with all nodes present does not have a delay. In some instances, the cluster partition with fewer nodes is the only partition still running. Thus, it is undesirable to use long delays. The delays are just long enough to be effective, as shown by empirical testing.

If the nodes in a minority partition cannot achieve majority, even with the addition of all of the quorum votes, these nodes decline to participate in the race and panic out of the cluster.

## Quorum Monitoring

Quorum devices are passive and are required to maintain cluster stability only when the membership of the cluster changes. It is undesirable for your cluster to fail simply because the quorum device is faulty during a critical membership transition. Adding more quorum devices does not help because the likelihood that one or more of these devices is faulty increases as you add them. Consequently, you should configure only the minimum number of quorum devices that are required for cluster stability. In the case of a scalable storage topology, you need one quorum device.

The quorum-monitoring feature periodically checks the status of all configured quorum devices and initiates the following actions:

- Takes offline any quorum device that is not working properly
- Brings online any formerly nonfunctional quorum device whose problem is resolved and loads the quorum device with the appropriate information

You must monitor the `syslogd` output (see the `syslogd`(1M) man page) for any problems with your quorum devices and take the appropriate action to replace them. In some cases, a quorum device works intermittently. For example, a router between the cluster nodes and a quorum server might be unreliable. Quorum monitoring will detect failures when the router fails and bring the quorum server back online when the router starts working again. When you notice an intermittent problem, you should replace that quorum device at least until the intermittent problem can be diagnosed and repaired.

## Handling Quorum in Campus and Metro Cluster Configurations

You might decide to implement a campus or metro cluster to provide some level of protection against the failure of a single data center. If you use Solaris Volume Manager, then you must address the issue of the Solaris Volume Manager state replica quorum that is discussed in the section "Solaris Volume Manager's State Replica Majority" in Chapter 1, "Oracle Solaris Cluster: Overview." However, the more general problem of how to maintain cluster quorum must also be addressed. If you choose a quorum device that is located in either campus cluster data center, then loss of that data center results in the cluster becoming unavailable. The remaining cluster nodes are panicked out of the cluster because they cannot access the quorum device in the failed data center.

One way to overcome this problem is to have a quorum device located in a third data center that is connected to the same SAN infrastructure used by your main cluster nodes. Usually, this solution is prohibitively expensive because of the cost of the fiber infrastructure required for implementation. Fortunately, the Solaris Cluster software provides a quorum server feature that helps reduce the cost of such an implementation. Rather than requiring full SAN connectivity to this remote site, a quorum server is simply a system running the Solaris 9 OS, or the Solaris 10 OS, that can be accessed through TCP/IP over the network.

It is not even necessary for this server to be on the same subnet as the cluster it is serving. Moreover, a single quorum server can simultaneously perform this service for multiple clusters. Last, this server has precisely the same characteristics as quorum disks; that is, it is actively used only when cluster membership changes occur.

### Quorum Device Recommendations

The Solaris Cluster software supports several quorum device options in order to meet diverse data center requirements. Though all of the quorum device protocols work, the following guidelines explain which quorum device to use under certain circumstances:

1. To save money, use the devices connected to your system.
2. Use a fully connected quorum device when possible with existing hardware. The availability characteristics are easiest to understand and more often than not most closely match the desired availability behavior.
3. Because of cost considerations, use a quorum server for configurations with nodes located in different physical locations. No extra wires are needed.
4. Small differences in performance exist between the various quorum devices. When recovery time differences of 1 to 2 seconds matter, consider the performance time characteristics of the various quorum devices.
5. If you have any concerns about the SCSI-2 and SCSI-3 feature sets on your shared disks, use the software quorum protocol.

### Membership Programming Interface

The CMM provides a programming interface for membership information. Clients of the programming interface can request a snapshot of the current membership. Interfaces for learning about membership changes are also available. A client can register to receive a callback whenever membership changes. Each membership callback includes a snapshot of the membership at the time of the callback. The clients can be in either a kernel or a non-kernel process.

The CMM programming interface supports the following forms of membership:

- *Cluster node membership*: The membership information relates to either the global cluster or a specific zone cluster. The client specifies the desired cluster.
- *Process membership*: The membership information reports a node as running when both the cluster node and the specified process are running.
- *Process up / zone down*: The membership information reports a node as "up" when both the process is running and the zone-cluster node is running, and reporting the node as "down" only when the zone-cluster node is not running.

Several Solaris Cluster subsystems are clients of this membership programming interface, including the RGM, the UNIX Cluster Membership Monitor (UCMM), and the Volume Manager UNIX Cluster Membership Monitor (VUCMM). This programming interface is not currently available to applications.

## Reconfiguration

The cluster reconfiguration process is an important part of the Solaris Cluster software. Whenever membership changes, the cluster performs a cluster reconfiguration to adjust to the new configuration. The cluster reconfiguration process is an activity that involves a wide range of cluster subsystems. The Solaris Cluster software performs cluster reconfigurations for both global-cluster membership changes and zone-cluster membership changes.

In this section, global-cluster membership is discussed in more detail. The Transport subsystem monitors whether cluster nodes can communicate with each other. When a node successfully establishes a communication path with another node, the Transport subsystem on that node declares that the other node is now reachable. The Transport subsystem monitors the health of each communication path between nodes. Whenever a path fails or the Transport subsystem can no longer exchange heartbeat messages over a communication path, the Transport subsystem marks that path as being "down." When the last communication path fails, the Transport subsystem on a node declares that the other node is unreachable.

Upon receiving notification from the Transport subsystem that a node is reachable or unreachable, the CMM initiates a cluster reconfiguration. The CMM exchanges information about connectivity between nodes in the current partition and prunes membership to a fully connected subset. The CMM on each node in the partition determines whether the local node should be the owner of a configured quorum device. If so, the CMM attempts to acquire ownership of the quorum device. The CMM tallies the quorum votes of the cluster partition and determines whether the partition can survive.

The reconfiguration process on the surviving partition then performs a recovery that involves many subsystems:

- The reconfiguration process fences nodes that are no longer in the cluster.
- The reconfiguration process terminates requests to any departed nodes.
- The reconfiguration process reallocates resources among surviving nodes.
- The reconfiguration process ensures that a Replica Manager primary is now active and that that Replica Manager will drive failovers needed by HA services.

Eventually, the cluster reconfiguration results in the cluster moving data services and their associated resources to surviving nodes.

A membership change could happen in the middle of a cluster reconfiguration. In some instances, the cluster reconfiguration restarts.

## Version Manager

The Solaris Cluster software has configuration files on each machine that identify which software versions the various cluster subsystems can support on that machine. The Version Manager subsystem examines all of the version information across the cluster and determines which versions can be supported and which version should be currently active. The Version Manager subsystem also determines during the course of a rolling upgrade when the cluster can support the version of the Solaris Cluster software. However, the administrator decides when to commit to using the new software. After the cluster has committed to using a version of the Solaris Cluster software, the Version Manager will not allow any machine to join the cluster when the joining node cannot support the version that is active in the current cluster.

The Version Manager supports the following version protocols:

- *Boot protocol*: a protocol that is used at boot time
- *Node pair protocol*: a pair of nodes that use a protocol based on what the two nodes can support
- *Cluster protocol*: a protocol that can be used only when all nodes in the cluster can support a specific version of the protocol

## Storage Device Fencing Subsystem

*Fencing* protects the data on storage devices against undesired write access. The cluster must prevent non-cluster members from writing to any shared data storage devices to which they might be connected.

When a node departs or joins the cluster, the cluster responds by initiating a cluster reconfiguration. After the CMM determines the new membership, the cluster reconfiguration reaches the point where the system addresses fencing. The reconfiguration process notifies the Device Configuration Service (DCS) about the nodes that have left or joined the cluster since the last time fencing was performed. The DCS uses the presence or absence of entries in the Name Server to show whether fencing is under way. The DCS submits the work to a separate thread or threads to enable the cluster reconfiguration process to continue. The cluster reconfiguration process continues with work in other cluster subsystems. The reconfiguration process completes only after the fencing operations are guaranteed to be complete, and then the Solaris Cluster software publishes a new membership.

### Disk Fencing

By default, the DCS uses the number of paths to a device to determine which fencing method to use with disks and storage arrays. If the Solaris I/O multipathing software is used, the fencing method is SCSI-3 PGR for multihosted devices and SCSI-2 Reservation operations for dual-hosted devices. In contrast, the quorum algorithm uses SCSI-3 PGR for multihosted devices and SCSI-2 Reservation operations combined with PGRe for dual-hosted devices. As part of the fencing process, the `MHIOCENFAILFAST` is enabled on all disks through an `ioctl` system call. Any non-cluster member trying to access a disk with this parameter set is forced to perform a *failfast* panic with a reservation conflict panic message; see "Disk Failfast Driver."

The global fencing policy can be changed to always use SCSI-3, which should be faster if the storage device is capable of handling this correctly, by using the `cluster` command (see the `cluster`(1M) man page). Alternatively, fencing policy can be set on a per-device basis using the `cldevice` command (see the `cldevice`(1M) man page). To completely disable SCSI fencing on a device, you can use the `nofencing` setting. Only disable SCSI fencing if you must, for example, when the storage does not support SCSI reservations.

The fencing subsystem ignores any disk configured as a quorum device, as the quorum subsystem has responsibility for such devices. Only one subsystem can manage SCSI-2 Reservation operations or SCSI-3 PGR operations on any particular device.

The following example shows you how to set the global fencing policy to `scsi3`. The example also shows you how to set the default fencing policy for an individual disk.

---

### Example 2.1  Setting the Cluster Device Fencing Options

Set the global fencing policy to `scsi3` with the `cluster` command.

```
# cluster set -p global_fencing=scsi3
```

Set the fencing policy on individual devices using the `cldevice` command.

In this example, disk `d8` has its fencing policy set to `scsi3`.

```
# cldevice set -p default_fencing=scsi3 d8
```

---

If your cluster runs Oracle Real Application Clusters (Oracle RAC), you might use the clustered version of either Solaris Volume Manager or Veritas Volume Manager. This product feature enables concurrent access to raw-disk devices from more than one cluster node. If a cluster node fails, it is fenced off from all disks in a shared Solaris Volume Manager/Veritas Volume Manager diskset or disk group either through SCSI-2 Reservation operations for dual-hosted SCSI-2 disks, or through SCSI-3 PGR for multihosted devices. Thus, Oracle RAC with more than two nodes requires shared storage that implements SCSI-3 PGR.

---

**Warning**

Do not attempt to manually alter any reservations placed on shared storage. If you do, you risk data corruption.

---

## Disk Failfast Driver

The appropriate Solaris disk driver, either `sd` or `ssd`, handles the *failfast* process for reservation conflicts. If a device access returns a reservation conflict error when the failfast parameter is enabled, the driver panics the node. With the failfast driver, you can also set up a polling thread that periodically accesses the device. The driver panics the node if the disk driver receives a reservation conflict error from the device.

## NAS Device Fencing

This kind of fencing protects data on a NAS device that is accessed through the network file system (NFS). The administrator must specify each file system on the NAS device that will be accessed by cluster nodes by using the `clnasdevice` command. The Fencing subsystem manages the read-only or read-write access privileges for each file system on the NAS device on a per-cluster-node basis. When a cluster node joins the cluster, the Fencing subsystem contacts the NAS device and grants read-write access to the joining cluster node for each file system on the NAS device. When a cluster node departs the cluster, the Fencing subsystem sets the access to read-only for each file system on the NAS device for that departing cluster node. This approach blocks write access but does not restrict read access for departed cluster nodes. Fencing is about data integrity, not security, so this approach satisfies the fencing requirement.

The fencing of data in NFS file systems on a NAS device never conflicts with quorum operations. So the fencing subsystem will fence NFS file systems on a NAS device, regardless of whether that NAS device is also configured as a quorum device.

When the cluster nodes access a LUN on a NAS device exported via iSCSI, the LUN appears to the cluster as a disk. The cluster fences such a LUN as if it were a disk.

# Devices

The tight integration of the Solaris Cluster software and the Solaris kernel enables the cluster nodes to seamlessly share devices across the cluster. The ubiquity of the global services implemented at the operating system level enables all cluster nodes to share devices and network interfaces. A global namespace enables devices to be uniquely identified and accessed. The result is a consistent, highly available environment upon which you can easily implement data services. The following sections describe these features in more detail.

## Global Devices

The Solaris Cluster software introduces the concept of a global device in which a specific device has a consistent name and a unique minor device number across the entire cluster. Using this name, a global device is accessible from all nodes. All disks, Solaris Volume Manager disksets, Veritas Volume Manager disk groups, tape, and CD-ROM devices are global, regardless of whether the devices are single or multihosted devices, and regardless of the node to which you connect them. Applications access them the same way they would in a normal single-server environment, that is, through `open`, `close`, `read`, and `write` system calls. This namespace consistency enables your system administrator to move applications from node to node within the cluster, without changing paths to data files or configuration information.

### Primary and Secondary I/O Paths

When a device is connected to two or more cluster nodes, the cluster framework designates one connection as an active *primary* I/O path and the other connections as passive *secondary* paths. This designation is in addition to any active and passive I/O path designations associated with a device that is attached to a single node through multiple connections and that uses the Solaris I/O multipathing feature. A passive secondary path can, transparently, become the active primary path in response to the failure of the node that hosts the primary path or by the cluster administrator manually migrating control with the `cldevicegroup` command (see the `cldevicegroup` (1M) man page). The HA invocation mechanism described in "High-Availability Framework" replicates any significant state in the primary to the secondary. Your applications will attain the best performance when they are colocated with the node that hosts the primary I/O path. You can do so through the use of a `SUNW.HAStoragePlus` resource (see "`SUNW.HAStoragePlus`").

The generic term that the Solaris Cluster software uses for either Solaris Volume Manager disksets, Veritas Volume Manager disk groups, and disks collected in `rawdisk`-type groupings is a *device group*. The Solaris Cluster software manages primary and secondary I/O path control for Solaris Volume Manager disksets, Veritas Volume Manager disk groups, and the default raw-disk device groups of `/dev/global/rdsk/dXsY` disks.

Therefore, multiported devices are available to an application continuously, even if the primary path fails. Applications are unaware of the failure until the final path becomes unavailable. When a device is connected to only one node, the failure of that node makes the device unavailable, and the system returns an `EIO` error to the application. However, this increased availability comes at a cost because the underlying HA framework subsystem (see "High-Availability Framework") has more work to do. By default, a device group is configured to have one primary path and one secondary path. All the remaining paths, through which the device group connects to the cluster nodes, are configured as *spares*.

You can modify the number of secondaries maintained by using the `cldevicegroup` command. However, if you simultaneously lose the primary I/O path and all the nominated secondary paths, your application will receive an `EIO` error and will be unable to transparently use any remaining unconfigured secondary paths.

## Device ID

To provide the required uniformity of the namespace, every node in the cluster must be able to refer to a single device by a common unique name and a minor number. The Solaris Cluster software implements a device ID (DID) pseudo driver to achieve this capability. During installation or under the system administrator's control, this driver searches for devices that are attached to any of the cluster nodes and assigns them unique DID numbers. The Solaris Cluster software assigns a single common name, of the form dX (where X is a number), to a multi-hosted device, even if it is hosted on different controllers in the two nodes. Figure 2.3 shows an example of the DID numbering for a three-node cluster.

The system can access device slices either locally through a /dev/did/{r}dsk/ dXsY entry or globally through a /dev/global/{r}dsk/dXsY entry. X and Y indi-

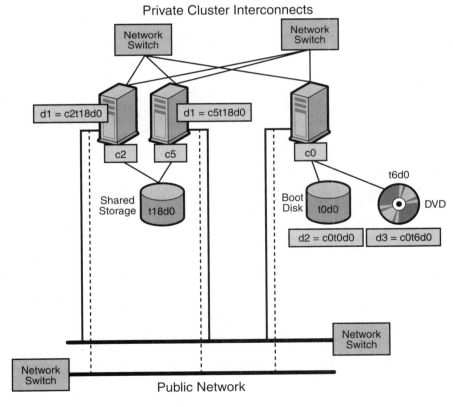

**Figure 2.3** Device ID numbering for a three-node cluster

cate the DID and slice numbers, respectively. The two entries differ subtly because the local entry is a symbolic link to an entry in the /devices/pseudo directory. However, the global entry links into the /global/.devices/node@X/devices/pseudo hierarchy.

The following example shows how the device entries for the /dev/did/dsk/d3s0 and /dev/global/dsk/d3s0 differ. The device /dev/did/dsk/d3s0 links to

### Example 2.2  How /dev/did and /dev/global Devices Differ

DID device d3 is used as an example. Compare where the symbolic links for the /dev/did and /dev/global device entries lead.

```
# cd /dev/did/dsk
# ls -l d3s0
lrwxrwxrwx   1 root        root            39 Aug 11 03:37 d3s0 -> ../../../devices/
pseudo/
did@3:3,3s0,blk
# cd ../../../devices/pseudo
# pwd
/devices/pseudo
# ls -l did@3:3,3s0,blk
brw-------   1 root        sys        239, 96 Nov  3 02:03 did@3:3,3s0,blk
# cd /dev/global/dsk
# ls -l d3s0
lrwxrwxrwx   1 root        root            39 Aug 11 03:37 d3s0 -> ../../../devices/
pseudo/
did@3:3,3s0,blk
# cd ../../../devices/pseudo
# pwd
/global/.devices/node@1/devices/pseudo
# ls -l did@3:3,3s0,blk
brw-------   1 root        root       239, 96 Aug 11 03:37 did@3:3,3s0,blk
```

/devices/pseudo/did@3:3,3s0,blk, whereas the device /dev/global/dsk/d3s0 links to /global/.devices/node@1/devices/pseudo/did@3:3,3s0,blk.

The global entry properties differ from the properties of the local entry. When a global device is accessed for the first time through a /dev/global name, the device group is placed online. The device group is assigned primary and secondary nodes by the Solaris Cluster framework. You can use the cldevicegroup command (shown in the following example) to check this assignment. The system then routes all I/O through the primary node, providing some degree of synchronization.

## Example 2.3   Checking the Primary and Secondary Paths to a Device Group

In this example the `cldevicegroup` command is used to list the primary and secondary I/O paths to all the device groups in the cluster.

```
# cldevicegroup list -v
Device group       Type        Node list
------------       ----        ---------
dsk/d18            Disk        phys-earth2
dsk/d17            Disk        phys-earth2
dsk/d13            Disk        phys-earth1
dsk/d15            Disk        phys-earth2, phys-earth1
dsk/d14            Disk        phys-earth2, phys-earth1
dsk/d12            Disk        phys-earth2, phys-earth1
dsk/d9             Disk        phys-earth1
dsk/d10            Disk        phys-earth2, phys-earth1
dsk/d8             Disk        phys-earth2, phys-earth1
dsk/d7             Disk        phys-earth2, phys-earth1
dsk/d6             Disk        phys-earth2, phys-earth1
dsk/d5             Disk        phys-earth2, phys-earth1
dsk/d4             Disk        phys-earth2, phys-earth1
dsk/d3             Disk        phys-earth2, phys-earth1
dsk/d2             Disk        phys-earth2, phys-earth1
dsk/d1             Disk        phys-earth2, phys-earth1
dsk/d16            Disk        phys-earth2
dsk/d11            Disk        phys-earth1
```

In contrast, the device group is not placed online when a device is accessed through the /dev/did device name, and no primary or secondary I/O paths are assigned. Thus, when multiple nodes access a single device through the /dev/did names, the accesses are not synchronized. Oracle RAC is the only supported application capable of coordinating concurrent access to these shared devices. In practice, shared disks are more often encapsulated in Solaris Volume Manager metasets or Veritas Volume Manager disk groups. Consequently, the applications running on the cluster access the shared storage through the metadevices that the volume managers present rather than through the /dev/did device name.

Attempting to access a /dev/did device that is not attached to the local machine generates an error. However, the device can be accessed by its /dev/global name. Solaris Volume Manager metasets and Veritas Volume Manager disk groups are initialized by different disk device names.

Solaris Volume Manager diskset devices must be constructed with the DID device names, whereas the standard control, target, device references (c2t5d4, for example) are used when disks are placed under Veritas Volume Manager or ZFS *zpool* control. Zpools can also be constructed from DID devices. Regardless of the volume management product used, the Solaris Volume Manager diskset devices or Veritas Volume Manager disk group volumes have unique name and minor number combinations across the cluster. Therefore, regardless of whether an application uses a raw-disk /dev/global or /dev/did device or a metadevice presented by Solaris Volume Manager or Veritas Volume Manager, the naming is always consistent.

You can also group multiple DID devices into what are known as rawdisk-type device groups. These device groups are not controlled by volume management products, but they can still be acted on as a whole rather than as single entities. For example, you can bring the device group online on a particular node or switch it to another node with a single cldevicegroup command. To create the rawdisk-type device group, you must first remove the default, individual dsk/dX device group entries before combining them in the new group (see Chapter 6, "Oracle Solaris Cluster Geographic Edition: Features and Architecture," Example 6.14). These rawdisk-type device groups are important for managing devices that are replicated by storage-based replication products such as EMC Symmetrix Remote Data Facility, or Hitachi TrueCopy and Universal Replicator.

## Device Namespace

For applications to operate on the global devices (see "Global Devices" and "Device ID"), they must be located in a directory somewhere in the UNIX hierarchy. The Solaris Cluster software implements a /global/.devices/node@X structure, where X represents a node number within the cluster. The Solaris Cluster software supports 64 nodes, so X can be 1 to 64. All disks represented in /dev/global, as well as all Solaris Volume Manager /dev/md metadevices and Veritas Volume Manager /dev/vx disk group volumes, are ultimately symbolically linked to a /global/.devices/node@X/devices/ pseudo entry. This directory differs from the /devices/pseudo directory because the file system on which it resides, and which the system allocates specifically at installation time, is mounted globally.

Because the /global/.devices/node@X directory hierarchies are mounted globally, the devices within them that are opened by an application inherit the highly available semantics that the global mount option confers on the file system.

When you install a Solaris Cluster system, you can use either UFS or ZFS as the root (/) file system. With UFS, you can choose to set aside a separate disk slice to hold the /global/.devices/node@X file system. Alternatively, you can allow the installation process to create a lofi-based UFS file system to fulfill this requirement. When you use the ZFS file system, the installation process always utilizes the lofi approach.

## Disk Path Monitoring

Losing all the I/O paths to your shared storage from a cluster node is considered a multiple failure. Such failures are very unusual in a properly configured cluster. As such, manually disconnecting storage cables from a cluster node should not be considered a realistic failure scenario that warrants testing. However, to accommodate such rare events, the Solaris Cluster software provides the Disk Path Monitoring (DPM) facility.

Without the DPM facility, losing all I/O connectivity between your shared storage and a cluster node might not result in your application being failed over to another cluster node with full I/O connectivity. Although the fault monitor for the application might detect that the service is not responsive, because it cannot perform any I/O, the cluster might be unable to stop the application for precisely the same reason. For data integrity reasons, it is critical that the cluster be able to completely stop the application before restarting it, anywhere within the cluster. Thus, depending on retry and timeout settings used by the cluster as part of the application's start and stop methods, the application might end up in either a STOP_FAILED or START_FAILED state on the same cluster node.

Even with the DPM facility, the cluster's response to such a loss of storage connectivity is drastic. Because an application might well have I/Os to the inaccessible shared storage still present in the device driver queue, the only realistic option for the DPM facility is to panic the cluster node. When the node panics, the reconfiguration process will result in the application being migrated to another cluster node in its node list (see "Resource Group Manager Daemon"). To satisfy the conditions for this extreme response, the cluster node must have lost access to all monitored disks from the node encountering the failure and still have another node on which the disks are accessible. Rebooting the node restarts all the resource groups and device groups that are mastered on that node on another node.

If all monitored disk paths on a node remain inaccessible after the node automatically reboots, the node does not automatically reboot again. However, if any disk paths become available after the node reboots, but then they later fail, the node automatically reboots again.

You must configure this option carefully because any node reboot will impact all services hosted on that cluster node at the point of failure.

The DPM facility can be enabled using a combination of the cldevice and clnode commands (see the clnode(1M) man page).

## Example 2.4   How to Enable Disk Path Monitoring on a Device

Enable monitoring on DID device d1.

```
# cldevice monitor -n phys-earth1,phys-earth2 /dev/did/dsk/d1
```

Set the machine to reboot when the path to any device fails completely.

```
# clnode set -p reboot_on_path_failure=enabled +
```

## Choosing the Correct Device to Use

Now that you have been introduced to all the devices types available within the Solaris Cluster software, you need to know which device to use for a particular purpose. The following brief sections list the uses for each device type.

### Standard Solaris /dev/rdsk Devices

Standard Solaris devices, with names such as /dev/rdsk/c2t4d3s2, can be used for the following:

- Oracle Solaris ZFS storage pools (zpools)
- Nonshared Veritas Volume Manager disk groups
- Shared Veritas Volume Manager disk groups

### Solaris Cluster /dev/did DID Devices

Solaris Cluster software DID devices, with names such as /dev/did/rdsk/d5s6, can be used for the following:

- Solaris Cluster quorum devices
- Oracle Solaris ZFS storage pools (zpools)
- Raw-disk storage for parallel databases, such as Oracle RAC
- Oracle Automatic Storage Management (ASM) that can provide data storage to Oracle 10*g* and 11*g* databases
- Single-owner Solaris Volume Manager disksets
- Multi-owner Solaris Volume Manager for Sun Cluster disksets

## Solaris Cluster `/dev/global` Global Devices

Solaris Cluster software global devices, with names such as `/dev/global/rdsk/`
`d5s6`, can be used for the following:

- Oracle Solaris ZFS storage pools (zpools). When using Oracle's StorageTek
  Availability Suite (AVS) software with the ZFS file system on a Solaris Cluster system, you must construct your zpool from `/dev/global` devices.
- Failover file systems or global file systems when an additional volume manager is not required.
- Raw-disk storage for failover databases, such as highly available (HA) Oracle,
  but not Oracle RAC.

## Solaris Cluster `/dev/md/diskset` Global Devices

Solaris Cluster global devices resulting from the creation of Solaris Volume Manager metadevices, with names such as `/dev/md/`*diskset*`/rdsk/d100`, can be
used for the following:

- Failover file systems or global file systems when Solaris Volume Manager is
  required. The diskset must be a single-owner diskset.
- Raw-disk storage for highly available databases, such as highly available
  (HA) Oracle. The diskset must be a single-owner diskset.
- Raw-disk storage for parallel databases, such as Oracle RAC. The diskset
  must be a multi-owner diskset.
- The devices used by a shared QFS file system. The diskset must be a multi-
  owner diskset.

## Solaris Cluster `/dev/vx/rdsk/disk_group` Global Devices

Solaris Cluster software global devices resulting from the creation of Veritas Volume
Manager volumes, with names such as `/dev/vx/rdsk/`*disk_group*`/`*volume_*
*name*, can be used for the following:

- Failover file systems or global file systems when Veritas Volume Manager is
  required. The disk group must be a nonshared disk group.
- Raw-disk storage for highly available databases, such as highly available
  (HA) Oracle. The disk group must be a nonshared disk group.
- Raw-disk storage for parallel databases, such as Oracle RAC. The disk group
  must be a shared disk group.

# File Systems on a Solaris Cluster System

The Solaris Cluster supports a wide range of file systems. The following list provides some information about when to use which kind of file system. Later subsections provide more information about each of these file systems.

- *Cluster file system*: Use this kind of file system to support cluster applications, other than Oracle RAC, that need the capability to read and write the same file system from multiple machines concurrently.
- *Shared QFS file system*: Use only this kind of file system to support Oracle RAC.
- *Failover file system*: Use this kind of file system to support failover applications.

## The Cluster File System

The terms *cluster file system* and *global file system* both refer to a file system that supports concurrent file system access from multiple nodes of the cluster. The specific implementation of a cluster file system in the Solaris Cluster software is the Proxy file system (PxFS). PxFS is a highly available, distributed, cache-coherent file system that is POSIX-compliant. The most common use case for PxFS is to support general-purpose file system workloads. PxFS extends a single-machine file system to work across the cluster.

Another primary goal of a cluster file system is to simplify administration by keeping the administration of this cluster file system as close as possible to that of a single-machine file system. Another primary function of this cluster file system is to provide a cluster-wide namespace for files.

The following subsections describe the PxFS architecture and the major features of PxFS and identify its strengths and weaknesses. A comparison with NFS is included.

### Application Access

One design goal for the Solaris Cluster software was to ensure that no changes to applications are needed for them to access PxFS file systems, and that has been achieved. PxFS presents the underlying file system to the application.

**Notes**

You must not store Oracle RAC data files in PxFS. This configuration is not supported.

Some nonstandard options might not be supported for a file system.

## PxFS Architecture

The Oracle Solaris OS supports multiple file systems. When an application issues a file system request, the system call accesses the core Oracle Solaris OS, more specifically in a subsystem that supports a generic file system interface. After performing some general tasks, this generic file system interface passes the work to the software for the specific file system. The `Solaris Vnode/VFS interface` [JMRM] defines the kernel interface between the Solaris generic file system subsystem and specific file systems, such as UFS. All standard file systems in the Oracle Solaris OS comply with the `vnode/VFS` interface. The `vnode` defines operations on individual files. The `VFS` defines operations at the file system level.

PxFS interposes between the Solaris generic file system subsystem and a single machine's file system, meaning that Oracle Solaris OS calls PxFS, instead of the underlying file system. PxFS performs various tasks needed to make the file system operation work across the cluster. In some cases, PxFS can satisfy a file system request using cached information. In other cases, PxFS eventually transfers the file system request to the underlying file system using the `vnode/VFS` interface. The underlying file system is unable to detect that the PxFS has interposed between the application and the underlying file system.

PxFS currently supports UFS, VxFS, and HSFS file systems as the underlying file system. No modifications were made to VxFS or HSFS file systems to enable this support. To enhance performance, a limited number of additional interfaces were added to UFS.

Internally, PxFS is organized using a client-server model. Every node in the cluster has a PxFS client subsystem. The PxFS client subsystem presents a proxy file system to file system clients. Thus, all client file system requests are transferred by the Solaris generic file system subsystem to the PxFS client subsystem. The PxFS client subsystem caches some information. When the PxFS client subsystem can satisfy a file system request using cached information, the PxFS client does so.

Otherwise, the PxFS file system passes the file system request using an HA invocation to the PxFS server subsystem. The ORB converts the HA invocation into a C++ call when the PxFS client and server subsystems are colocated. The ORB handles the marshaling and unmarshaling of information, as well as the transmission of the HA invocation request and reply. The location of the PxFS server subsystem does not matter to the PxFS client.

The PxFS server subsystem is an HA service. The PxFS server is the subsystem that connects the underlying file system to the PxFS client subsystem. When the PxFS server subsystem receives a file system request from a PxFS client subsystem, the PxFS server subsystem passes the file system request to the underlying file system and then returns the reply from the underlying file system to the PxFS client subsystem.

The PxFS file system must be mounted on a global device. The Device Configuration Service (DCS) manages global devices, including supplying PxFS with information about which machines can directly access storage for any particular global device. The PxFS server subsystem must be located on a machine that can directly access storage.

### PxFS at File System Level

The VFS interface defines a set of operations that are applicable to the overall file system. PxFS implements these VFS operations with a file system component on both the server and client sides. On the PxFS client side, PxFS implements a separate proxy file system with its own proxy VFS on each node as shown in Figure 2.4. The proxy file system appears to be an underlying file system. The underlying file system, such as UFS, is mounted only on the primary node. The Solaris Cluster software uses a special mount option that causes the Oracle Solaris OS to make the mount of the underlying file system invisible to the users' applications. This ensures that applications access the file system only through PxFS. When the pri-

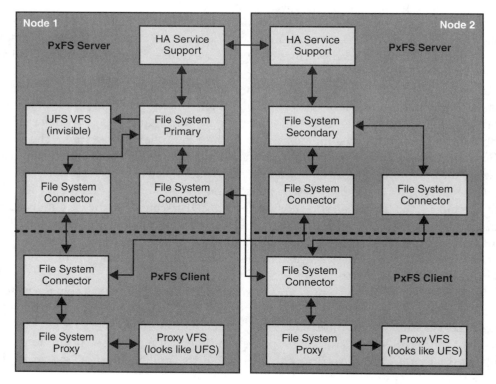

**Figure 2.4** PxFS architecture for file-system-level support

mary moves to a different node, PxFS moves the mount of the underlying file system to that node.

## PxFS Files

PxFS supports data files, directory files, symbolic links, and devices. Global devices work only when placed in a cluster file system. PxFS does not make other kinds of files, such as pipes and doors, work across the cluster. Figure 2.5 shows the PxFS architecture for supporting regular data files. The architecture for directories and symbolic links is similar, with a separate set of components for each active file. The client component exists only on those nodes where the file is active. PxFS server components do not need to be colocated on the same nodes.

## PxFS High Availability

The PxFS server subsystem is implemented as an HA service, and there is a separate PxFS server HA service for each file system. PxFS uses multiple techniques to

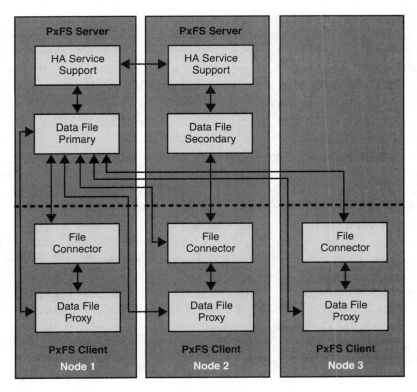

**Figure 2.5** PxFS architecture for file support

implement high availability. PxFS uses intention-based checkpoints with a variety of HA invocations. The PxFS server component collects information about the current status along with information about the requested operation and transfers this information to the secondaries. The HA service support components, shown in Figure 2.4 and Figure 2.5, distribute the checkpoint information to all of the current secondaries. If a secondary is promoted to become a primary, the newly promoted primary uses the checkpointed information to determine whether a replayed HA invocation has already completed, and it completes any partially completed operations. The checkpoints are always relatively small and primarily consist of meta-information. PxFS does not checkpoint file data.

Another technique for high availability is *state reconstruction*. This overcomes single failures by replicating information. The PxFS client subsystems have copies of a variety of information. After a node failure, the new PxFS primary queries the surviving PxFS clients in order to reconstitute their state. The software uses reference information from the ORB in order to reduce queries by skipping nodes that could not possibly have any state. This technique has enabled PxFS to eliminate a wide range of frequent checkpoints. State reconstruction happens only when a new primary is promoted, which significantly improves performance over the initial PxFS product.

PxFS uses the UFS log when working with UFS. The UFS log journals file system metadata changes. PxFS performs a `sync` of the UFS log to persistent storage to guarantee that metadata will not be lost after certain file system operations complete. The UFS log `sync` is expensive, and PxFS has become more selective about when to do a UFS log `sync`.

## PxFS Cache Coherence

All of the caches in PxFS follow a *single writer–multiple reader* model. The primary decides which PxFS client or clients can cache information and whether the client has read or write privileges. The primary can recall a caching privilege to satisfy requests from other nodes. Clients push cached information to persistent storage before relinquishing cache privileges.

PxFS caches `vnode` attributes for data files, directories, and symbolic links. It caches the results of access checks for data files, directories, and symbolic links, and it caches file data in the Solaris virtual memory page cache. These caches enable PxFS to significantly improve performance by satisfying file system requests from within the PxFS client subsystem without even contacting the PxFS server or underlying file system.

## PxFS I/O Support

POSIX semantics require that an asynchronous write operation return only after the file system can guarantee that the write request will not fail because the file system is full. To satisfy this requirement, many file systems, including an early version of PxFS, would allocate space on persistent storage prior to returning success for an asynchronous write. This process used to involve one invocation from the PxFS client to the PxFS server that allocated space on the underlying file system, and then later a second invocation from the PxFS client to the PxFS server would write to the underlying file system. Thus, a single asynchronous write could involve two traversals of the private interconnect and accessing storage twice. PxFS now vastly improves asynchronous writes by using a different design while still satisfying POSIX semantic requirements. When PxFS works with UFS, PxFS keeps track of how much space is available on storage and how much space is needed for already committed asynchronous writes. PxFS uses this accounting information to determine whether the system can guarantee that the asynchronous write will complete without encountering a *no space* error. This design eliminates the need to preallocate space for asynchronous writes. The result is a large improvement in asynchronous write performance. PxFS reverts to the old approach when the disk becomes almost full (currently 90 percent).

Solaris I/O performance drops dramatically when the number of queued I/O requests becomes large. PxFS now controls the flow of asynchronous writes, thus avoiding this issue. This control enables PxFS to support much higher peak bandwidth performance. Numerous storage products use large memory caches on the order of gigabytes. These devices can sustain high bandwidth while cache space remains available. After the cache fills, the storage product can accept more data only at a rate at which data can be written to disks, and that is a much lower bandwidth. The PxFS flow control dynamically adapts to both when the cache has free space and when the cache is full.

PxFS has been enhanced to support data transfer sizes up to 512 kilobytes. This enhancement reduces the number of communications across the private interconnect and the number of I/Os to storage. The result is much better performance.

PxFS uses two communication techniques for data transfers across the private interconnect. For small data writes, PxFS sends the data and information describing the request in one communication using a technique called *client push*. For large data writes, PxFS uses a technique called *server pull*. The PxFS client sends the request to the PxFS server, which then reads the data from the client. The big advantage in a server pull is that the PxFS server knows where to put the data and can avoid a data copy, thus improving performance.

PxFS has private interfaces with UFS that enable PxFS to allocate space and read/write data without UFS placing file data in the Solaris virtual memory page cache. This interface eliminates double caching of data and improves performance.

## Mount

Cluster file systems are mounted with the standard UNIX mount command. The global nature of the mount is distinguished through the use of the global flag in /etc/vfstab or by specifying the -g or -o global options on the mount command line. In all other respects, the mount command line for a PxFS on a UFS file system looks just like a UFS mount command line. If all nodes have mount points that can accept the mount, you can issue the mount command from any node, and the mount occurs on every cluster node. This feature is very powerful because you only need to execute the mount command from any one cluster node to make that file system globally available to all nodes.

The system replays all of the current active mounts on nodes that subsequently join the cluster. This replay allows nodes to become synchronized with the active mounts as soon as they join the cluster. If the mount fails, for example, because a mount point does not exist, the booting node drops into single-user mode so you can correct the error. Careful change management procedures can help to ensure that the booting node does not drop into single-user mode. The Mount subsystem in the Solaris Cluster software is an HA service and is thus resilient with respect to node failures.

Both PxFS on UFS and PxFS on VxFS require that the logging option be used. The system will automatically supply the logging option if it is not already supplied for PxFS on UFS. The administrator must specify the logging option for PxFS on VxFS. The use of logging avoids the need for file system check (fsck) operations, which can take a long time. This feature is important for recovery purposes because cluster applications cannot start until after the needed file systems finish mounting. The logging option is also important for making directory operations highly available.

The UFS syncdir mount option is not required. Using the syncdir mount option with PxFS on UFS will needlessly and enormously degrade performance.

The UFS forcedirectio mount option, as its name suggests, forces the system to transfer I/O operations directly from the user address space to disk, bypassing the kernel virtual memory page cache. This option is highly beneficial to applications that perform their own caching, such as Oracle database software, in which recently used data is held in the system global area (SGA). It is possible to turn on directio behavior for an individual file in a PxFS on a UFS file system not mounted with the forcedirectio option by executing the _FIODIRECTIO ioctl.

Note that the forcedirectio mount option applies to all files opened on the specified file system, so it can have a negative performance impact on other applications using the file system if those applications do not cache data themselves.

Application binaries should not be installed on cluster file systems that are mounted with the forcedirectio option set. Program binary text pages will not be cached in memory and might have to be reread from disk.

## Application Binaries, Data, and Logs

The placement of executables in a cluster file system means that the administrator has to install the executables only once for all nodes. However, this placement negatively impacts upgrade possibilities. A dual-partition upgrade cannot be used to upgrade any software that resides on shared storage, and a cluster file system is shared storage. A dual-partition upgrade can be used for minimal downtime upgrades of application software as well as other software.

Data and log files can be placed in a global file system. Failover applications run on only one node at a time, and thus there is no access contention. Scalable applications run instances on multiple nodes concurrently. The data and log files for a scalable application can be placed in a global file system only when the scalable application uses some form of synchronization, such as file locking, to control file access.

Some applications, such as Oracle RAC, are designed as cluster applications. These applications already have the necessary controls to manage access to their raw control and log files. Therefore, you can safely install application binaries on the cluster file system without making additional changes to their configuration files.

Table 2.1 compares using a cluster file system for application executables to placing them on a local file system.

**Table 2.1** Cluster File System Benefits for Application Executables

| Cluster File System | Local File Systems |
| --- | --- |
| Application patches and upgrades are done only once but cannot be done using dual-partition upgrade. The application must be stopped on the entire cluster in order to apply application patches or upgrades. | Application patches and upgrades are done multiple times. The administrator can use dual-partition upgrade to apply application patches and upgrades. |
| Changes to configuration files are done only once. | Consistent changes must be made to multiple copies of the configuration files. |
| Accidental deletion of program or configuration files can stop the application from working on every cluster node. | Accidental deletion of program or configuration files can prevent the application from working on a particular node. |
| Upgrades that overwrite the original executables can interfere with the correct operation of the running application. | When the application is not running on that node, upgrades can overwrite local copies of application executables without affecting the original version of the application running on an alternative node. |

*continues*

**Table 2.1** Cluster File System Benefits for Application Executables (*Continued*)

| Cluster File System | Local File Systems |
|---|---|
| Software that resides on a cluster file system cannot be upgraded during a dual-partition upgrade. | Software that resides on a local file system that in turn resides on shared storage (highly available local file system) cannot be upgraded during a dual-partition upgrade. |
| | Software that resides on a local file system that is private to the local node can be upgraded during a dual-partition upgrade. |

## PxFS Performance

PxFS does perform file system operations correctly.

The high-availability feature of PxFS does come at a price. Each checkpoint requires a round trip across the private interconnect because confirmation that the checkpoint has safely arrived is required. The PxFS primary does not wait for the checkpoint to be processed on the secondary node. A round trip across the private interconnect is relatively expensive. That is why other mechanisms have been substituted to improve performance. The high-availability feature also needs additional sync calls for the UFS log, which adds costs. Because PxFS is used to support high-availability clustering, this is considered a reasonable trade-off for a desired feature.

When the application is not colocated with the PxFS primary, the data being written or read must traverse the private interconnect once. Subsequent access to the same data can be satisfied from the Solaris virtual memory page cache as long as that data remains cached.

Although PxFS performance has improved significantly since PxFS was first introduced many years ago, PxFS on UFS has not reached the level of UFS on a single-machine system because of the two aforementioned issues. PxFS on UFS performance is now more of a useful workhorse but not a racehorse.

Several performance enhancements for PxFS on UFS are not available for PxFS on VxFS, which significantly reduces performance.

When using the cluster file system to support a failover application, the administrator can request that the Solaris Cluster software place the PxFS primary on the same node as the application through the use of a specialized resource type called SUNW.HAStoragePlus (see "Resource Types"). When the resource starts, the AffinityOn property ensures that the system switches its specified device groups, where possible, so that their primary path is through the local node. The system cannot start application resources that depend on SUNW.HAStoragePlus resource device groups and file systems until this initialization is complete. This approach will generally improve performance.

Better PxFS performance can be achieved by dividing the data among multiple file systems as well as by using techniques such as circular logs that increase the cache hit rate in the PxFS client subsystem.

The primary use case for PxFS is to support concurrent read/write access from multiple nodes. This use case is ideal for PxFS on UFS.

## Campus Cluster and PxFS

Given the information in "PxFS Performance" and the section "Performance Impact of Separating Data Centers" in Chapter 1, "Oracle Solaris Cluster: Overview," it is clear that a cluster file system implementation across two widely separated data centers, such as a campus cluster, is unlikely to perform well. Not only do you have the additional cost of writing data to the storage arrays on both sites, but you also have the extra overhead of the communication needed to support the internal client-server model. Consequently, in such configurations use a cluster file system only for read-mostly workloads, for example, for scalable web servers.

## PxFS Compared to NFS

At first glance, PxFS and NFS seem to have similarities. Both PxFS and NFS enable an application on one machine to access file system data on a different machine. However, upon closer examination, PxFS and NFS are significantly different. Both PxFS and NFS solve real-world problems and provide useful services, yet PxFS and NFS solve different problems.

PxFS is for the case where the supplier of file system information and file system clients are on the same machines. NFS does not support the case where the NFS server and client are on the same machine. Although it is possible to run both the NFS server and the client on the same machine for a limited time, this configuration is subject to a fatal deadlock. Given that NFS does not support a colocated NFS server and client, there are no performance optimizations for the colocated case. PxFS does support the case where the server and client are colocated and has important performance optimizations for that case.

PxFS operates on a local network, which is usually much more reliable than a wide-area network. NFS was initially for wide-area networks and its different characteristics. However, it is important to note that the use of NFS to access NAS units on the local network is now common.

PxFS and NFS use different semantics. PxFS is POSIX-compliant, whereas NFS is not.

PxFS has a special Mount subsystem that ensures consistent and automatic mounts on all nodes of the cluster. NFS has different requirements and uses the automounter facility to automatically mount file systems for remote access.

The administrator can export a PxFS file system to clients outside the cluster using NFS.

Table 2.2 contrasts the two approaches.

**Table 2.2** Cluster File System and Network File System (NFS) Differences

| PxFS | NFS |
|---|---|
| PxFS uses the Solaris Cluster Mount sub-system to provide consistent mounts across the cluster automatically. | NFS uses the automounter facility to support automatic mounts. |
| Has a global namespace. Only one mount command is needed, with all nodes having equal access. | Multiple mount commands are needed, one per node. Access characteristics can differ from node to node and depend on the share options. A globally consistent namespace can be implemented by using automounter (AutoFS) and a distributed name service, but uniformity is not enforced. |
| Data caching is fully consistent. | Applications can read stale data for a short period of time. |
| Attribute caching is fully consistent. | Applications can read stale attributes for a short period of time. |
| PxFS is highly available because it uses intention-based checkpointing for metadata. | NFS is not truly highly available because it does not guarantee that in-flight operations are correctly handled. Incorrect responses can occur when the NFS server fails between completing the operation and replying to the client. Examples include file creation and file removal. |
| File-locking semantics are maintained across failover boundaries. Lock recovery is tied to cluster membership. | If an NFSv3 client fails holding a file lock, no other client can lock the file. If an NFSv4 client fails holding a file lock, no other client can lock the file until the lease expires. |
| A cluster file system is POSIX-compliant. | NFS is not POSIX-compliant. |
| Usage is possible only within the cluster. | The NFS server and client must be on different machines. |
| Writes are cached until the standard Oracle Solaris OS mechanisms flush out dirty pages, or until the application synchronizes data with sync. | Writes are written through more aggressively to the NFS server. |

*continues*

**Table 2.2** Cluster File System and Network File System (NFS) Differences (*Continued*)

| PxFS | NFS |
|------|-----|
| The PxFS client caches data pages, not the underlying file system on the PxFS server node. | Both the NFS client and the underlying file system on the NFS server node cache data pages. |
| PxFS supports seamless failover. Failover is faster. | Seamless failover in the non-clustered case is available only for read-only services. |
| PxFS provides a mechanism to support global devices. | NFS does not support remote devices. |

## SAM-QFS Software

The Sun QFS software [QFSDoc] can be configured for use with the Solaris Cluster software in one of two ways: as a highly available local (failover) file system (see "Highly Available Local (Failover) File Systems") or as a distributed file system (such as a shared QFS file system) that can be mounted on multiple host systems. When using SAM-QFS, you can take advantage of the advanced file system features in the Sun QFS software as well as its storage and archive management features.

### Volume Management

Sun QFS file systems support both striped and round-robin disk access. The master configuration file (`/etc/opt/SUNWsamfs/mcf`) and the `mount` options specify the volume management features and enable the file system to recognize the relationships between the devices it controls. Sun QFS file systems do not require additional volume management applications. However, to use mirroring for devices in a Sun QFS environment, you can use Solaris Volume Manager.

The Sun QFS integrated volume management features use the standard Oracle Solaris OS device driver interface to pass I/O requests to and from the underlying devices. The Sun QFS software groups storage devices into family sets upon which each file system resides.

### Support for Paged and Direct I/O

The Sun QFS file system supports two different types of I/O: paged (also called *cached* or *buffered* I/O) and direct. These I/O types perform as follows:

- When *paged I/O* is used, user data is cached in virtual memory pages and the kernel writes the data to disk. The standard Oracle Solaris OS interfaces manage paged I/O. This is the default type of I/O for the Sun QFS software.

- When *direct I/O* is used, user data is written directly from user memory to disk. You can specify direct I/O by using the Oracle Solaris OS `directio` function call or the `setfa` command with its `-D` option. By using direct I/O, you can realize substantial performance improvements for large block, sequential, aligned I/O.

## High Capacity

The Sun QFS software supports files of up to $2^{63}$ bytes in length. Such very large files can be striped across many disks or RAID devices, even within a single file system. This high capacity is possible because Sun QFS file systems use true 64-bit addressing.

The number of file systems that you can configure is virtually unlimited. The volume manager enables each file system to include up to 252 device partitions, typically disk. Each partition can include up to 16 terabytes of data. This configuration offers virtually unlimited storage capacity.

There is no predefined limit on the number of files in a Sun QFS file system. Because the inode space (which holds information about the files) is dynamically allocated, the maximum number of files is limited only by the amount of disk storage available. The inodes are cataloged in the `.inodes` file under the mount point. The `.inodes` file requires 512 bytes of storage per file.

In a Sun QFS file system, the inodes are located on the metadata devices and are separated from the file data devices. In practice, the size of your metadata (mm) devices limits the number of files in a Sun QFS file system, but you can increase the maximum number of files by adding more metadata devices. The hard limit on the number of files is $2^{32} - 1$ files, and the recommended limit is $10^7$ files.

## Fast File System Recovery

A key function of a file system is its ability to recover quickly after an unscheduled outage. A Sun QFS file system often does not require a file system check after a disruption that prevents the file system from being written to disk (using `sync`). In addition, Sun QFS file systems recover from system failures without using journaling. They do so dynamically by using identification records, serial writes, and error checking for all critical I/O operations. After a system failure, even multi-terabyte-sized Sun QFS file systems can be remounted immediately.

## Metadata Storage

File systems use metadata to reference file and directory information. Typically, metadata resides on the same device as the file data. However, the Sun QFS file system has the option of separating the file system metadata from the file data by storing them on separate devices. The Sun QFS file system enables you to define one or more separate metadata devices in order to reduce device head movement and rotational latency, improve RAID cache utilization, or mirror metadata without mirroring file data.

Sun QFS file systems store inode metadata information in a separate file. This enables the number of files, and the file system as a whole, to be enlarged dynamically.

### vnode Interface

The Sun QFS file system is implemented through the standard Oracle Solaris OS virtual file system (vnode/VFS) interface.

The kernel intercepts all requests for files, including those that reside in Sun QFS file systems. If a file is identified as a Sun QFS file, the kernel passes the request to the appropriate file system for handling. Sun QFS file systems are identified as type samfs in the /etc/vfstab file and through the mount command.

### Shared File System Support

A Sun QFS shared file system is a distributed file system that can be mounted on multiple Oracle Solaris OS host systems. In a Sun QFS shared file system environment, one Oracle Solaris OS host acts as the metadata server for the file system, and additional hosts can be configured as clients. You can configure more than one host as a potential metadata server, but only one host can be the metadata server at any one time. There is no limit to the number of mount points for a Sun QFS shared file system.

The advantage of the Sun QFS shared file system is that file data passes directly from the Fibre Channel disks to the hosts. Data travels through local path I/O (also known as *direct access* I/O). In contrast, NFS transfers data over the network, and a cluster file system transfers data through the cluster private networks.

The shared file system can be implemented either as a Sun QFS shared file system or as a SAM-QFS shared file system. The file system can use either the ms file system type (Sun QFS disk cache family set) or the ma file system type (Sun QFS or SAM-QFS disk cache family set with one or more metadevices).

Sun QFS shared file systems do not support the following:

- These file types:
  - b: block special files
  - c: character special files
  - p: FIFO (named pipe) special files
- *Segmented files*: You cannot implement a SAM-QFS shared file system in a segmented-file environment.

- *Mandatory locks*: An EACCESS error is returned if the mandatory lock is set. Advisory locks are supported, however. For more information about advisory locks, see the fcntl system call.

### Benefits of Using a Shared QFS File System

Using shared QFS file systems within a Solaris Cluster implementation gives you another option for storing your Oracle RAC data and binaries. Unlike raw-disk volumes or Oracle's Automated Storage Management (ASM) software, a shared QFS file system gives your system and database administrators visibility and access to the data held within it using the standard Solaris commands, such as ls, df, du, tar, and cpio.

You can use a shared QFS file system for purposes other than just storing Oracle data. For example, you can use it for storing the Oracle binaries, too.

### Implementing a Shared QFS File System on a Solaris Cluster System

You can implement a shared QFS file system on a Solaris Cluster system in one of two ways: directly on hardware RAID-protected LUNs using /dev/did/dsk/dXsY devices (see Example 2.5), or with Solaris Volume Manager for Sun Cluster (/dev/md/*diskset*/dsk/dX) metadevices. To mirror shared QFS file system data across two storage arrays, you must use Solaris Volume Manager for Sun Cluster because a shared QFS file system does not have any built-in mirroring capabilities.

You must add an entry for the file system to the samfs.cmd file (see the samfs.cmd(4) man page) in the /etc/opt/SUNWsamfs directory. In particular, when you use a file system for Oracle RAC data, you must enable qwrite, mh_write, and forcedirectio. These flags enable multiple threads on multiple nodes to read and write to the same files simultaneously in a nonbuffered fashion. For file systems that store binaries, do not use forcedirectio.

To ensure that the shared QFS metadata server is not a single point of failure for the file system, you must also create a resource group (see "Resource Groups") containing a SUNW.qfs resource (see "Resources"). To ensure that the shared QFS file system is mounted and unmounted in the correct sequence, you must create another resource group with a scalable mount-point resource. However, rather than doing all this manually, you can use one of the Solaris Cluster configuration wizards (see the section "Solaris Cluster Wizards" in Chapter 4, "Managing Your Oracle Solaris Cluster Environment").

When correctly implemented, a shared QFS file system used for Oracle RAC data files performs almost identically to an equivalent raw-disk or Oracle ASM configuration.

## Example 2.5  Configuring and Mounting a Shared QFS File System

Go to the `/etc/opt/SUNWsamfs` directory.

```
# cd /etc/opt/SUNWsamfs
```

Here is the `mcf` file with `rac_data` striped over three LUNs:

```
# cat mcf
rac_data                    100     ms      rac_data        on      shared
/dev/did/dsk/d10s0          101     md      rac_data        on
/dev/did/dsk/d3s0           102     md      rac_data        on
/dev/did/dsk/d5s0           103     md      rac_data        on
```

This file system will be used for Oracle Real Application Clusters (RAC) data, so mount the `rac_data` file system with `forcedirectio` and `qwrite`.

```
# cat samfs.cmd
fs=rac_data
        stripe=1
        mh_write
        qwrite
        forcedirectio
```

The hosts used for metadata access are the cluster private interface hostnames.

```
# cat hosts.rac_data
phys-earth1 clusternode1-priv 1 0 server
phys-earth2 clusternode2-priv 2 0
```

Configure the file system (do this on all nodes).

```
# /opt/SUNWsamfs/sbin/samd config
Configuring SAM-FS
```

Set up an entry in `/etc/vfstab`.

```
# cat /etc/vfstab | grep rac_data
rac_data          -         /oradata        samfs   -       no      shared
```

Make the file system.

```
# /opt/SUNWsamfs/sbin/sammkfs -S rac_data
Building 'rac_data' will destroy the contents of devices:
                /dev/did/dsk/d10s0
                /dev/did/dsk/d3s0
                /dev/did/dsk/d5s0
Do you wish to continue? [y/N]y
total data kilobytes        = 41886720
total data kilobytes free   = 41884800
```

Mount the file system on this node (repeat on the other node).

```
# mount rac_data
# df -h rac_data
Filesystem            size   used  avail capacity  Mounted on
rac_data              40G    4.2G   36G    11%     /oradata
```

### Supporting Sun QFS Clients Outside the Cluster

Clients outside the cluster are used when you want your applications running on hosts external to the cluster to access data stored on one or more cluster file systems. Cluster device fencing (see "Storage Device Fencing Subsystem") is lowered so that clients outside of the cluster can access the data stored on the storage managed by the cluster.

If you implement this option, you must ensure that no other data service inside the cluster uses the data that applications access from outside the cluster. Additionally, this option requires that a logical hostname be used for communications between the shared QFS metadata server and metadata clients that exist outside the cluster. (This requires extra configuration within the cluster setup.) Ideally, you use a dedicated network for communications between the cluster nodes and the nodes that exist outside the cluster.

You must use a direct-attached Fibre Channel storage topology, but you can use any supported hardware RAID storage array.

Finally, this option offers shared QFS file system features but without archiving capabilities. The cluster nodes provide automated failover of the metadata server. Your configuration options are limited to a maximum of 4 nodes inside the cluster and up to 16 nodes outside the cluster.

## Highly Available Local (Failover) File Systems

In general, when creating a failover service, you should configure one or more highly available local (failover) file systems to hold the data associated with the service. The Solaris Cluster software supports the following as failover file systems:

- ZFS
- UFS
- QFS (not a shared QFS file system)
- VxFS

A failover file system, such as UFS, has the same performance characteristics as when used on a non-clustered Solaris system. A failover file system introduces no cluster overhead during file system operations. The only difference for a failover file system is that the Solaris Cluster software adds support for moving the failover file system from one machine with a direct path to storage to another machine with a direct path to storage. The Solaris Cluster software also monitors the failover file system and can detect when it malfunctions.

The process of failing over a file system from one cluster node to another involves the following steps:

1.  Unmounting the file system, which might require terminating any processes that are still using subdirectories of the mount point
2.  Relinquishing control of any associated Solaris Volume Manager diskset, Veritas Volume Manager device group, or zpool by the current mastering node
3.  Taking control of the same Solaris Volume Manager diskset, Veritas Volume Manager device group, or zpool by the new mastering node
4.  Running a file system check for some file systems, but `fsck` is not needed for UFS with UFS logging enabled or for the Oracle Solaris ZFS file system
5.  Mounting the file system

These steps are performed for you when you configure a `SUNW.HAStoragePlus` resource (see "`SUNW.HAStoragePlus`").

If you split your cluster nodes between data centers, in a campus or metro cluster, you will incur a performance penalty for writing data to a remote storage array. Although the performance penalty is less than the penalty you would incur for a cluster file system, it might still result in unacceptably poor application performance.

## Oracle Solaris ZFS File System

The Oracle Solaris ZFS file system contains both file system and volume manager features. The *zpool* is the ZFS volume manager component, and a single zpool can support multiple file systems. A zpool can be active on only one machine at a time, meaning that the ZFS file systems residing on one zpool cannot be active on different machines at the same time. Whenever two ZFS file systems support two different applications that might at some point run on two different machines, these two ZFS file systems must reside on separate zpools. The `SUNW.HAStoragePlus` feature works a little differently for ZFS in that it operates at the granularity of the zpool. In other words, `SUNW.HAStoragePlus` manages the location of the zpool.

# Cluster Public Networking

The Solaris Cluster software provides two mechanisms through which your client applications can access services on the cluster: logical IP addresses and global IP addresses. You cannot use these addresses arbitrarily as they are designed for specific types of service. Logical IP addresses are used by failover services such as highly available (HA) NFS and highly available (HA) Oracle. Global IP addresses are for scalable services that can run on more than one node concurrently without corrupting their data, for example, Sun Java System Web Server. The section concludes with a discussion of how these mechanisms affect the way you configure firewalls that are present in your network topology.

## Logical (Virtual) Hosts

To move your services between nodes without having to change the way in which your client applications access those services, you need a mechanism to virtualize their location. Usually, your client applications would use the physical IP address of the server on which your service is located. Obviously, this cannot be used if your service could reside on another cluster node. Instead, you use a logical or virtual IP address that moves between cluster nodes with your service.

The cluster framework controls the migration of this address, unplumbing it from its original NIC and plumbing it on a suitable NIC on the new host. As a result, your logical IP address is plumbed on a logical interface. In the following example, the chosen address is plumbed on `e1000g0:1`. When you create your logical host resource, you must ensure that the logical IP address it represents can be hosted on one of the cluster's public subnets. If it cannot, you will receive an error message.

---

### Example 2.6   Creating a Resource Group Containing a Logical Host Resource and Bringing It Online

Ensure that the hostname can be resolved.

```
# getent hosts earth
10.11.195.119    earth
```

Create a resource group called `example-rg`.

```
# clresourcegroup create example-rg
```

Add a logical hostname resource to it.

```
# clreslogicalhostname create -g example-rg \
>       -h earth example-lh-rs
```

Bring the resource group online.

```
# clresourcegroup manage example-rg
# clresourcegroup online example-rg
```

List the IP addresses that are plumbed on the system.

```
# ifconfig -a
lo0: flags=2001000849<UP,LOOPBACK,RUNNING,MULTICAST,IPv4,VIRTUAL> mtu 8232 index 1
        inet 127.0.0.1 netmask ff000000
e1000g0: flags=9000843<UP,BROADCAST,RUNNING,MULTICAST,IPv4,NOFAILOVER> mtu 1500
index 3
        inet 10.11.195.116 netmask ffffff00 broadcast 10.11.195.255
        groupname sc_ipmp0
        ether 0:14:4f:e:b2:fa
e1000g0:1: flags=1001040843<UP,BROADCAST,RUNNING,MULTICAST,DEPRECATED,IPv4,FIXEDMTU>
mtu 1500 index 3
        inet 10.11.195.119 netmask ffffff00 broadcast 10.11.195.255
e1000g1: flags=1008843<UP,BROADCAST,RUNNING,MULTICAST,PRIVATE,IPv4> mtu 1500 index 5
        inet 172.16.0.129 netmask ffffff80 broadcast 172.16.0.255
        ether 0:14:4f:e:b2:fb
e1000g2: flags=4001008842<BROADCAST,RUNNING,MULTICAST,PRIVATE,IPv4,DUPLICATE> mtu
1500 index 4
        inet 172.16.1.1 netmask ffffff80 broadcast 172.16.1.127
        ether 0:14:4f:e:b2:fc
clprivnet0: flags=1009843<UP,BROADCAST,RUNNING,MULTICAST,MULTI_BCAST,PRIVATE,IPv4>
mtu 1500 index 6
        inet 172.16.4.1 netmask fffffe00 broadcast 172.16.5.255
        ether 0:0:0:0:0:1
```

## Configuring Your Firewall for Outbound Network Traffic

To understand how your logical hosts interact with the firewall rules, you need to understand how address selection is made for an outgoing packet. First, you must distinguish between TCP [RFC793] and UDP [RFC768]. TCP is a connection-oriented protocol; that is, a connection is established between a client and a service. Using this connection, source and target addresses are always used appropriately. In a Solaris Cluster environment, the source address of a packet sent by the service to a client is usually the logical IP address of that HA service, but only if the client used the logical service address to send its request to the service. Consequently, this address will not cause any problems with firewalls because you know exactly which IP addresses will be used as source addresses for outgoing IP addresses.

In contrast, UDP is a connectionless protocol; that is, there is no established connection between a client and a server (service). A UDP-based service can choose its source address for outgoing packets by binding itself to a fixed address, but most services don't. Instead, they accept incoming packets from all configured network addresses. The following code segment will be familiar if you have done any network programming.

## Example 2.7  Code for Binding to Any Network Address Hosted by the Server

The following C code fragment shows how a server process can be written to bind to all the configured IP addresses:

```
struct sockaddr_in address;
...
address.sin_addr.s_addr = INADDR_ANY;
...
if (bind (..., (struct sockaddr *) &address, ...) == 0
```

Using this typical segment of code, the UDP service listens on all configured IP addresses. The outbound source address is set by the IP layer. The algorithm that chooses which source address to use is complex and cannot be influenced [SourceAddr]. If an IP address is marked DEPRECATED, as it is in Example 2.6, then it is not used as a source address unless only deprecated interfaces are available.

The Solaris Cluster software marks these interfaces as DEPRECATED to stop applications that make outbound connections from using them as a source IP address. This prevents the application from failing when that address is moved from the current cluster node to another cluster node.

You can use the following options to enable your firewall to pass UDP traffic generated by highly available services on your cluster:

- Configure your firewall rules to accept packets that originate from any IP address configured on the nodes where your service can be hosted.

- Change your service so that it binds only to the highly available service IP address rather than to all the IP addresses configured on the node. This option is possible only if the software configuration lets you make this change, or if you have access to the source code.

One other less desirable option is to move your service into a highly available (HA) container (see the section "HA Containers" in Chapter 3, "Combining Virtualization Technologies with Oracle Solaris Cluster Software"). However, doing so makes upgrades more disruptive and can limit the usage of the Solaris Cluster agents.

## Global Networking Service

Another valuable feature built into the Solaris Cluster software is the global networking service. On a single server, you can assign IP addresses to ports on network interface cards (NICs) with the `ifconfig` command. A single NIC can host multiple addresses, but typically most servers present one IP address per subnet to which they are connected. Applications running on that server can then issue `bind` system calls to bind to those addresses. The Solaris Cluster software extends this concept to create a global IP address visible to all nodes within the cluster hosting applications that are dependent on these specific addresses.

Global IP addresses, also known as *global interfaces* (GIFs), are installed on the appropriate NICs for the subnets to which the cluster is connected. The GIF is configured as a highly available, rather than scalable, resource (see "Resources"). The node hosting the GIF is known as the *GIF node* or GIN.

Figure 2.6 shows a four-node cluster that hosts a scalable web service on three of the cluster nodes. The global IP address for the web service is usually hosted on the fourth node but can fail over to the third node, if required.

Nodes defined by the union of the resource group `nodelist` standard property and the resource group `auxnodelist` extension property have the global IP address configured on their loopback interface (`lo0:2`, `lo0:3`, and so forth), enabling local cluster applications to bind to it. Hosting the global IP address on the loopback interface prevents the node from accepting incoming packets directly from the network while forcing TCP/IP to adopt the address as local.

When a network packet destined for the global IP address arrives at the GIN, it is distributed through the private network to one of the cluster nodes. The node receiving the forwarded packet acknowledges the destination address as internal and processes it. The system then responds by sending out one or more packets with the global IP address as the source address, assuming the connection was made through TCP (see "Configuring Your Firewall for Outbound Network Traffic") directly to the network, rather than sending the packets back across the private network and through the GIF.

This feature allows services to be started on multiple cluster nodes and bound to the global IP address. Scalable services, such as the Sun Java System Web Server, are described in more detail in the following sections.

### Packet Distribution Mechanisms

The Solaris Cluster software provides two classes of scalable service:

- *Pure service*: This class of scalable service is identified by the `LB_WEIGHTED` policy. Under this load-balancing policy, client requests, which are identified

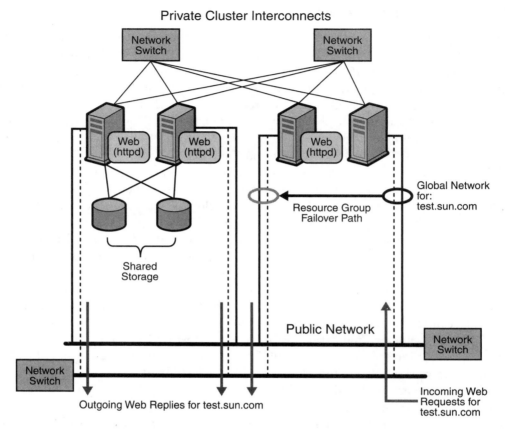

**Figure 2.6** A four-node cluster configured with a global IP address

by the client IP address and port, are distributed according to the weighting given to the cluster nodes. By default, each participating node is given the same weighting and has an equal chance of being selected for a given client IP-port combination. A hash function is used to select the actual node from a vector, randomly populated with the node IDs. The distribution of the node IDs is proportional to the weights. Thus, it is not predictable, on an individual basis, what the selection would be.

- *Sticky service*: This class of scalable service is identified by the LB_STICKY or LB_STICKY_WILD policy. In this policy, a given client of the scalable service, which is identified by the client IP address, is always sent to the same node.

The Solaris Cluster releases prior to 3.2 11/09 provided IP affinity only for TCP services. The selection of server nodes for UDP packets was based on the binding relationships that are established by TCP connections to services in the same service group. No IP affinity was guaranteed if a service group had only the UDP service.

**Generic Affinity and Affinity Timeout**     The Solaris Cluster 3.2 11/09 release has a generic affinity feature that solves this issue and provides IP affinity to the client, regardless of the protocol. When the `generic_affinity` property is set to `true`, this feature guarantees that a client that has existing connections (TCP, UDP, or SCTP) and is "sticky" (`LB_STICKY` or `LB_STICKY_WILD`) with respect to the instance will remain sticky. When enabled, all packets from the client to the scalable service follow the first packet from the client, regardless of the protocol that is used by the connection.

The `Affinity_timeout` resource property controls the number of seconds that IP affinity lasts after a client closes all its connections to the sticky scalable service. Because the UDP protocol does not support "open connection" or "close connection," the `Affinity_timeout` property controls the following timeout limits:

- Service group with UDP service only: the number of seconds that IP affinity lasts after the last packet is received from the client
- Service group with UDP and TCP/SCTP services: the number of seconds that IP affinity lasts after the client closes all its connections or after the last packet is received from the client, whichever is later

The weighting policies can also be combined with the `round_robin` and `conn_threshold` resource property, described next, to provide deterministic distribution based on fixed ordering.

**Packet Distribution without Using the `round_robin` Property**     When the `round_robin` property is set to `false`, the distribution mechanism works as follows: The GIN accepts the packet from the network. The appropriate combination of source IP address and port number for the policy is used by its packet dispatch table (PDT) to calculate the target node for the packet. By default, each node is given equal weight, so for a three-node cluster with all nodes running a scalable resource, each node would receive one-third of the overall traffic.

The GIN then transfers the packets to the target node over the private interconnect to present them for use by the application on the loopback interface. When the application responds, the system transmits the outgoing packets using the relevant local NIC.

You can dynamically change load-balancing weights at any time with the clresource command without shutting down dependent applications. For example, in a three-node system, the nodes A, B, and C have weights of 10, 30, and 40 (note that the weights do not need to add up to 100). In this case, the nodes receive one-eighth, three-eighths, and one-half of the total traffic, respectively.

Packets sent from a fixed port on a client node are always sent to the same destination node. Only a change in the weighting policy or the failure of one of the target nodes would alter the distribution by changing the result of the PDT calculation. In the preceding example, if node B fails, node A would receive one-fifth of the packets, and node C would receive four-fifths of the packets.

The LB_STICKY policy ensures that requests from a given client IP address to a particular destination port are always directed to the same node hosting the target scalable service. This policy enables concurrent client connections to target nodes to share in-memory state. This capability is especially useful, for example, for an e-commerce site. The shopper can browse through the goods available and fill the shopping cart through one connection and service (HTTP on port 80) and then use a second connection and service (SSL on port 443) to pay for the goods. E-commerce applications that use the concept of a shopping cart often use session state information to link the user with details of the contents of his or her shopping cart. If the session state information is available only on the cluster node through which the user is browsing for items to purchase, then directing the shopper to a separate node for payment might result in the cart's details being inaccessible.

For application services that dynamically allocate ports, such as a passive mode FTP service, the initial connection on port 21 must be redirected to another port chosen by the service. This type of service must use the wildcard sticky policy. Under the LB_STICKY_WILD policy, all packets from a client IP address are directed to the same target node, regardless of their destination port.

The Solaris Cluster software allows both many-to-many and one-to-many relationships between services and global IP addresses. For example, a four-node cluster, with nodes A, B, C, and D, can host the global IP address test.sun.com on the public network interface of node D. The system can also be configured with a scalable web service on port 80 on nodes A, B, and C and with another scalable web service on port 90 on nodes A and B only. In contrast, the same cluster could host two global IP addresses: uat.sun.com and dev.sun.com on nodes A and B respectively, both with scalable web services on port 80 running on all four nodes. Furthermore, either configuration could be combined with additional failover services as required or as resources allow.

**Deterministic Distribution Using round_robin, conn_threshold, and udp_session_timeout Properties**    In the round-robin load-balancing mechanism, server nodes are assigned to requests that are deterministically based on a fixed ordering of the nodes according to the weight assignments. The advantage of this mechanism is that it provides a balanced distribution of load, regardless of the number of requests and clients. To enable this mechanism, the round_robin resource property must be set to true.

The round-robin load-balancing mechanism uses a node-assignment vector, which is built on the weights and utilization of the node. The node-assignment vector gives the order in which requests are distributed as they are received. Requests return to the beginning of the node-assignment vector after the end of the vector is reached.

The node-assignment vector is built as shown in the following algorithm. In this algorithm, W[ I ] represents the weight vector, where I is the node ID number. C[ I ] represents the number of connections that are assigned to a node. The ID node number (I) can take a value from 1 to N, where N is the highest number of node IDs that have been created in the cluster. U[ I ] represents the utilization of the node.

1. Initialize C[ I ] to all zeros for all I.
2. Calculate U[ I ] = C[ I ]/W[ I ].
3. Give the next connection to the node with the smallest U[ I ]. If more than one node has the same U[ I ], the node with the largest W[ ] is selected. Increment C[ ] for the selected node by one. This sequence becomes the node assignment sequence.
4. Repeat steps 2 and 3 for all nodes where C[ I ] is not equal to W[ I ].

For example, the node assignment for a scalable service that is hosted on two nodes with weights 2 and 7 is 2,1,2,2,2,1,2,2,2, where each numeral represents the node ID for which the request is dispatched. After requests reach the end of the vector, they return to the beginning of the vector and repeat the sequence.

The load-balancing mechanism would provide a typical round-robin distribution if the weights that are assigned to all nodes were the same.

The conn_threshold resource property controls the number of connections after which the cleanup thread will be started. The *cleanup thread* cleans all TCP connections that have not completed the three-way TCP handshake. No new connections are accepted until the number of connections drops below the number defined by the value of conn_threshold.

Because the UDP protocol does not have the concept of an "open connection" or "close connection," the UDP service does not provide session timeouts. To manage UDP session timeouts, a new cluster-wide property, udp_session_timeout, is defined for the round-robin load-balancing mechanism. The udp_session_timeout property is used only for weighted scalable services. This causes the removal of the forwarding entries that are created when a UDP client connects to the scalable service. For sticky and sticky wildcard services, the `affinity_timeout` property is used (see "Packet Distribution Mechanisms").

> **Note**
>
> Changing the value of the `udp_session_timeout` property requires a cluster reboot.

### Solaris Cluster Scalable Service Support for SCTP

The Solaris Cluster 3.2 software supports a new transport protocol called *Stream Control Transmission Protocol* (SCTP). SCTP is a transport protocol that has similarities to both TCP and UDP but with many added features. The Solaris Cluster software's SCTP feature works with the Solaris 10 6/06 OS or later release.

Most SCTP features are directly supported in the Solaris Cluster environment. Therefore, they work in a Solaris Cluster environment similarly to the way they work in a non–Solaris Cluster environment without application code changes. The exception is when SCTP is used with a sticky wildcard load-balancing policy. The different approach to binding for the sticky wildcard policy is described in "Case 2: SCTP Binding with a Sticky Policy."

The following are the Solaris Cluster scalable service features that are related to SCTP. All other SCTP features are supported in the Solaris Cluster environment.

- *Load-balancing policies*: In the Solaris Cluster software, weighted, sticky, and sticky wildcard load-balancing policies are supported for SCTP services.
- *Multihoming*: This SCTP feature is supported for Solaris Cluster scalable services. With this feature, a single association can use multiple IP addresses, for both the server and the client, and can send a packet with any combination of source and destination addresses.

The behavior of the `bind` system calls changes somewhat in the Solaris Cluster environment. In stand-alone systems, applications generally bind in two different ways:

- *Explicit* binding, where an explicit list of IP addresses is passed in the `bind` system call
- *Implicit* binding, where the `INADDR_ANY` keyword is supplied as the binding address

In the latter case, the listener is bound to a wildcard address. If the host contains multiple addresses, a client can potentially connect to the listener with any available address. Up to this point, this capability is applicable to both TCP and SCTP.

- With TCP, a connection is established with only one IP address, in other words, the destination IP address of the first SYN packet.
- With SCTP, all available addresses are used to construct an association.

In a Solaris Cluster environment, there are two classifications of addresses:

- *Local addresses*: This classification includes transport addresses used by the private interconnect, logical hostnames, and other local addresses.
- *Shared addresses*: See "Global Networking Service."

In a Solaris Cluster environment, address short-listing is performed automatically during implicit binding. If the address short-listing is not done internally, then if an application uses INADDR_ANY during binding, it will eventually use a mixture of local and shared addresses in an association. The mixing of different classifications of addresses within an association is risky and might cause association abort. This behavior exists only for the SCTP protocol, as SCTP uses all the available bound addresses in an association. Also, the application developers are not supposed to handle these address classifications during binding, as the concept of local and shared addresses is not present in a non–Solaris Cluster environment.

Automatic address short-listing is performed during binding with SCTP in a Solaris Cluster environment. The Solaris Cluster software automatically identifies an application as a scalable application by matching the port number of the application with the port number of the registered services. The registered services are those services that were created with the clresource command as scalable services. If the service is a scalable service, only the corresponding shared addresses are used for binding. Otherwise, local addresses are used for binding.

Similarly, for explicit binding, if a mixture of addresses is passed, then other address classifications are excluded from the list.

A client program that does not use the bind system call follows the same rule as INADDR_ANY.

**Case 1: SCTP Binding with a Weighted or Sticky Policy**     This case assumes that no other scalable services are registered in the cluster.

- A1 and B1 are the shared addresses for a scalable service S1 with port P1.
- A2 and B2 are the shared addresses for a scalable service S2 with port P2.
- A3 and B3 are local addresses.

The following are the behaviors of one form of the `bind` system call:

- `bind(INADDR_ANY, P1, ...)` will bind with A1 and B1.
- `bind(INADDR_ANY, P2, ...)` will bind with A2 and B2.
- `bind(INADDR_ANY, P3, ...)` will bind with A3 and B3.

Similarly, the following are the behaviors of another form of the `bind` system call:

- `bind({A1, A2}, P1, ...)` will bind with A1.
- `bind({A2, A3}, P1, ...)` will fail.
- `bind({A2, A3, B3}, P3, ...)` will bind with A3 and B3.

**Case 2: SCTP Binding with a Sticky Policy**      The exception to the algorithm in Case 1 is when you use a sticky wildcard service. With TCP, the applications that serve on multiple ports, which are dynamically determined at runtime, generally use the sticky wildcard policy. This policy guarantees that all packets that come from a single client are forwarded to the same cluster node, regardless of the destination port number. Usually, sticky wildcard services are not registered with a particular port number.

If the algorithm in Case 1 is applied for SCTP bind address manipulation, the algorithm might treat a sticky wildcard address as a local address because a matching port number might not be registered for it.

Therefore, if the cluster contains any sticky wildcard services and if the binding port number does not match any registered service, then the `bind` system call will bind with the addresses as it usually does in the default case. In addition, it will not perform any kind of address short-listing.

In contrast to the examples in Case 1, if S1 is a sticky wildcard service, then the following are the behaviors of one form of the `bind` system call:

- `bind(INADDR_ANY, P1, ...)` will bind with A1 and B1.
- `bind(INADDR_ANY, P2, ...)` will bind with A2 and B2.
- `bind(INADDR_ANY, P3, ...)` will bind with A1, B1, A2, B2, A3, and B3.

Similarly, the following are the behaviors of another form of `bind` system call:

- `bind({A1, A2}, P1, ...)` will bind with A1.
- `bind({A2, A3}, P1, ...)` will fail.
- `bind({A2, A3, B3}, P3, ...)` will bind with A2, A3, and B3.

Therefore, sticky wildcard service developers are advised not to use INADDR_ANY binding. Rather, they should bind explicitly to the correct set of addresses. Otherwise, associations might become disconnected.

With the bindx system call, address-filtering logic works similarly to the explicit binding case.

## Outgoing Connection Support for Scalable Services

Traditional scalable services handle requests originating from clients outside the cluster. Outgoing requests originating from the scalable service carry the IP address of the cluster node but not the virtual IP address provided by the SUNW.SharedAddress resource. If you set the Outgoing_Connection resource property to true when Generic_Affinity is set to true and Load_balancing_policy is set to LB_STICKY_WILD, then a scalable service can initiate requests to a server outside the cluster and use the virtual IP address of the Network_resources_used property as the source address. The load balancer ensures that any incoming replies are forwarded to the initiating node. This hides the IP addresses of each cluster node and allows for better abstraction of network topology and more flexible setup (such as filtering and security) between clusters that belong to different organizations.

### Notes

Only one node of the cluster might initiate requests to a given server at a time.

The resource configured for the application with the outgoing_connection property enabled cannot have a dependency on more than one failover resource group that contains the scalable addresses used by the application. Thus, for the outgoing connections feature, all scalable addresses used by the application need to be configured in one failover resource group.

## IPsec Security Association Failover for Scalable Services

In a scalable service setup using IP Security Architecture (IPsec), clients must renegotiate the IPsec security association (SA) state after a failover because all SA session states are specific to a node. This increases the recovery time perceived by the clients and places an unnecessary processing load on the cluster.

If you set the following resource properties on your scalable resource and IPsec is enabled on the cluster private network, then some of the IPsec association states pertaining to the scalable service are replicated over the interconnect to all other cluster nodes, eliminating the need for SA renegotiation after a failover. This improves client failover time.

- `Ipsec_Session_Failover=true`
- `Generic_Affinity=true`
- `CheckActivePortInstance=true`
- `Load_balancing_policy=LB_STICKY_WILD`

---

**Notes**

IPsec associations that are actively used are not replicated because of the extremely high load that doing so would impose on the cluster interconnect. By default, only associations that are idle for over 2 minutes are replicated.

To ensure protection of the IPsec state, including keying material during replication, you must deploy IPsec on the interconnect.

Internet Key Exchange (IKE) must be used for the scalable service in order to support the replication of IPsec associations.

---

### Advantages of the Global Network Service

The global networking service enables the cluster to provide scalable outbound IP traffic. This increases both throughput and response time without requiring any additional load-balancing hardware or software. Typically, inbound client network traffic is much lighter than the outbound network traffic it generates. Because of its tight integration with the cluster framework, this mechanism also ensures that the PDT driver does not distribute packets to nodes that are not currently participating in a cluster.

At first it might seem that the GIF is a system bottleneck. However, most workloads that are amenable to becoming scalable services have traffic profiles in which outbound packets outnumber inbound packets by as much as six to one. Most web servers and streaming media services are in this category.

### Client Connection Recovery after a GIN Node Failure

A global IP address is defined as an instance of a `SUNW.SharedAddress` resource and placed in a failover resource group; see "Data Service and Application Agents." If the node that is hosting one or more GIFs fails, the system reconfigures the address or addresses onto an appropriate public network interface of another cluster node, defined in the resource group as a potential host for the GIF. IP packets reestablish their flow through the new GIN and are forwarded to the subscribing services as before. IPMP and the public network-monitoring facility (see the section "Solaris Cluster Public Network Monitoring Daemon" in Chapter 1, "Oracle Solaris Cluster: Overview") protect the GIF against NIC or network failure on the GIN.

From a client IP perspective, the global networking service is available continuously. As part of the standard TCP/IP recovery mechanisms, the system retransmits packets that are dropped while the interface is being moved. If the application is UDP-based, it retransmits lost packets. To applications on both the client and the cluster, the global IP address functions the same as IP addresses on a single server. No application changes are required. You can migrate the global IP addresses with the `clresourcegroup` command.

## Cluster Private Interconnect

The Solaris Cluster software uses one or more networks to connect the cluster machines. To avoid a *single point of failure*, you must deploy multiple, completely independent networks. The collection of all of the networks connecting the cluster machines is called the *private interconnect*. Although there is no inherent limitation on the number of interconnects that a machine can support, the Solaris Cluster software imposes a practical limit of six private interconnects on cluster configurations.

The Solaris Cluster software communicates regularly between nodes across the private interconnect in order to turn a collection of machines into a cluster. Many different cluster subsystems make use of the private interconnect. The Solaris Cluster software requires that all of the machines in the cluster be able to communicate directly. The private interconnect is so essential that the Solaris Cluster software exchanges heartbeats across each communication path between a pair of nodes to monitor the proper functioning of these communication links.

Cluster applications, typically just scalable applications, also use the private interconnect for communications.

### Private Interconnect Heartbeats

Heartbeat messages use a low-level Data Link Provider Interface (DLPI) mechanism to determine cluster connectivity. A message is sent as raw Ethernet packets that contain the node IDs of the sender and receiver, the cluster incarnation number, and two time stamps. The cluster node sending the message adds a time stamp based on its current system clock and the last time stamp it received from the peer node. Because the DLPI interface uses the Medium Access Control (MAC) layer and not IP addresses, the heartbeat cannot be routed.

### Private Interconnect Topology

For clusters with only two nodes, simple back-to-back (direct connection) cabling suffices. However, with larger clusters you should ideally configure multiple switches, one for each private connection, thus avoiding any single points of failure. Multiple clusters can share one or more network switches, but it is best practice to separate individual cluster heartbeat networks into isolated VLANs. This practice ensures that there is no competition for the networks, and it limits the risk of misconfiguration affecting more than one cluster. However, you can consolidate your cluster heartbeat traffic onto fewer VLANs, but there is a finite possibility that excessive traffic generated across one cluster's private networks could affect others sharing the link.

Regardless of the number of nodes in your cluster, you must ensure that every cluster node is connected to each of the private interconnect networks. When the cluster node count is greater than two, the network connectivity becomes a "star" topology.

Configuring multiple private networks is particularly beneficial when the global features described (see "The Cluster File System" and "Global Networking Service") are heavily used. Figure 1.5 shows back-to-back and switch-connected private interconnects.

The Solaris Cluster software allows you to dynamically add and remove private interconnects without shutting down the cluster or stopping the applications. In addition, it supports arbitrary interconnect topologies, allowing some node pairs to have more shared interconnect bandwidth than others. For example, a three-node pair+M topology, with nodes A, B, and C, could have an additional private interconnect between B and C only, over and above the minimum connectivity between all the hosts.

## Private Interconnect Traffic

The Solaris Cluster software uses the private interconnects to transmit a variety of information. The most important are the regular cluster heartbeat messages. Each node sends a message to its cluster peers every `heartbeat_quantum` milliseconds (the default value is 1000), as defined in the CCR. The message contains a time stamp and an echo of the last time-stamp value it received from that peer. If the last echoed time stamp is older than `heartbeat_timeout` milliseconds (the default value is 10,000) when a node receives a message, the path is declared `faulted`. For example, if node A receives regular heartbeats from node B, but they have old time stamps (because node B has not received a message from node A recently), node A declares the path `faulted` despite receiving heartbeats. If all paths between a pair of nodes are lost, the Cluster Membership Monitor (see "Cluster Membership") maintains cluster integrity by executing a cluster reconfiguration because of the network partition.

> **Warning**
>
> Although you can tune both the `heartbeat_quantum` and `heartbeat_timeout` prop-
> erties, you must do so with care. Making the timeouts too small might make your cluster
> unstable.

To handle situations in which the nodes are receiving DLPI heartbeats but no
TCP/IP messages are getting through, the private interconnect also uses a TCP/IP
timeout. If the cluster cannot send a message queued for a particular path within
90 seconds, it declares that path `faulted`. The cluster then shuts down the path
and attempts to reestablish it. Meanwhile, the system independently sends the
message again through an alternate path.

Failover applications that access global devices, such as relational database
management systems (RDBMSs) implemented on global raw-disk disk slices, rely
indirectly on the private interconnect. The replica framework must send messages
over the private interconnect to ensure that the primary and secondary I/O paths
remain synchronized. If the application and the primary I/O path are not colocated,
the private interconnect is used to transfer bulk data, too. Similarly, if an application
relies on the cluster file system and the application is not colocated with the primary I/O path, a corresponding amount of private interconnect traffic is generated.

Scalable applications, such as the Sun Java System and Apache web servers,
also require the private interconnect to mediate global IP traffic distribution
because the system forwards packets over the interconnects after the PDT establishes the target node.

Finally, the default network time protocol (NTP) setup created as part of the
Solaris Cluster configuration process uses the private interconnect networks to
synchronize the clocks on the cluster nodes.

## `clprivnet0` Virtual Network Interface

When the Solaris Cluster software is installed, it automatically creates a virtual
network interface called `clprivnet0`. This virtual interface can be supplied
directly to applications such as Oracle RAC, MySQL Cluster, or clustered Apache
Tomcat. Indeed, this virtual interface benefits any application that needs a highly
available trunked network between the constituent cluster nodes.

The virtual interface provides transparent aggregation of all the underlying
cluster private interconnect interfaces. If a path between cluster nodes fails, that
path is automatically removed from the trunk until such time as the path is found
to be working again. If private interconnects are added or removed, this task can
be performed online, and `clprivnet0` automatically takes account of the change.

The combination of `clprivnet` and Solaris Cluster heartbeats provides an end-to-end test of the health of the intercluster node communications link. If you tried to implement a similar private interconnect using IPMP, it would only test the capability of a network adapter to communicate with a remote "pingable" target and not necessarily the host that is the recipient of the application messages.

The `clprivnet0` interface supports all NICs that are qualified with the Solaris Cluster software, including 100Base-T, Gigabit Ethernet, 10 Gigabit Ethernet, and InfiniBand NICs, as well as jumbo frames. In addition, this interface does not require any special switch features, such as 802.3ad, and also supports connecting each path to a separate switch, which is actually the ideal configuration.

## Benefits of `clprivnet0` to Oracle RAC

Oracle RAC database instances use Cache Fusion to ensure data consistency for applications and on-disk data integrity. To achieve this, Cache Fusion must communicate information about data locks held between nodes and, when required, pass data pages. Depending on how the database was created, the data pages can be between 2 kilobytes and 32 kilobytes in size. As the user load level increases, contention for important data pages grows. For the application to scale, it is important that the interconnect be able to handle the level of traffic by load-balancing the requests across all the available NICs.

The Oracle Clusterware software allows the configuration of multiple cluster interconnects (through the `cluster_interconnects` parameter) to support Cache Fusion traffic, but this option comes at the cost of reducing availability if one database is configured to use multiple interfaces. If this option is chosen and an interconnect fails, instance evictions will result. Similarly, if one of the interfaces fails, the database will not start. Furthermore, using the `cluster_interconnects` parameter means that database instances dependent on it must be shut down to make changes to its value. Alternatively, if instances inherit this setting from Oracle Clusterware, the value can be changed postinstallation using the `oifcfg` command, but doing so necessitates a restart of Oracle Clusterware.

The previous section describes how Solaris Cluster software creates a `clprivnet0` virtual interface for use by Oracle Clusterware and Cache Fusion traffic. The `clprivnet0` interface can then be nominated as the private network for Oracle Clusterware to use during the Oracle Clusterware software installation process.

The `clprivnet0` interface has the following load-balancing properties:

- TCP transmission is distributed on a per-connection basis. A given TCP connection is mapped to a physical path (that is, the same path is selected for transmissions over that TCP connection). However, if the physical path is detected to be faulty, the TCP connection is transparently failed over to one of the remaining healthy paths.

- UDP transmission is round-robin on a packet basis. Fragments for the same UDP datagram go over the same link. Therefore, using `clprivnet` simplifies Oracle configuration while ensuring high availability and maximum use of available interconnect bandwidth. Changes in the underlying makeup of `clprivnet` are transparent to the Oracle software.

## Cluster Resilience to Private Network Failure

A cluster can survive multiple failures of the private interconnect infrastructure. The cluster continues to function without loss of service and without requiring any node shutdowns as long as each node has a path to connect it to every other current cluster member. The cluster transport drivers load-balance the cluster framework messages, on a simple round-robin basis, across the available interconnects. Thus, multiple requests benefit transparently from the parallelism that the multiple connections offer. A failure of all the private interconnects leads to a split-brain condition occurring (see "Split-Brain Condition" and "Cluster Membership").

## Protocols Used by the Cluster Private Network

Cluster internode communication protocols depend on the transport configured. For connections based on Ethernet or InfiniBand, the private interconnect uses DLPI and TCP/IP messages. Applications that use the `clprivnet0` virtual interface on the private networks can also take advantage of Reliable Datagram Sockets (RDS) over InfiniBand. Although TCP and UDP messages are striped over the available DLPI adapters, this is not the case with RDS over InfiniBand because TCP and UDP are not being used.

Both RDS and DLPI are implemented with optimizations to enable bulk data transfer and efficient buffer allocation with respect to the underlying hardware. The Solaris 10 OS currently supports only RDS version 1.

## TCP/IP

Despite being inexpensive, an Ethernet connection has the overhead of encapsulating each message in one or more TCP/IP packets. These packets then pass through the respective TCP/IP stacks on both the sending and receiving cluster nodes. For servers connected back-to-back over a distance of less than 10 meters, this process usually causes a packet latency of tens to hundreds of microseconds. Although this latency sounds insignificant, you must compare it with local memory accesses within a server. Typically, these accesses take tens to hundreds of nanoseconds. Thus, on average, messages that must be sent between servers take 1000 times longer to arrive than if they were written directly into local memory.

Whenever the cluster framework makes an ORB call that accesses or passes data to a remote object, it uses a TCP/IP message. Each of these messages incurs the TCP/IP packet overhead. All internal cluster communication currently uses TCP and does not take advantage of RDS over InfiniBand if it is used for the private interconnect.

## InfiniBand

InfiniBand drivers were added to the Solaris 10 1/06 release, but not all of Oracle's Sun servers support InfiniBand Host Channel Adapters (HCAs). InfiniBand is capable of running at a number of different speeds: single data rate (SDR), double data rate (DDR), or quad data rate (QDR). These speeds run at 10 gigabits per second, 20 gigabits per second, and 40 gigabits per second, respectively. Because all current InfiniBand cards have two ports, only one InfiniBand HCA is needed for minimal Solaris Cluster configurations, although separate cards are ideal. The use of InfiniBand is also restricted to private networks, so you cannot use it for public networking or storage connectivity.

Tests run with Oracle 11*g* Real Application Cluster show that the latency offered by RDS version 1 over InfiniBand is roughly one-third that of Gigabit Ethernet and half that of 10 Gigabit Ethernet (see page 19 of [11gRefArch]). Although using InfiniBand leads to better overall response times, the improvement in response times is not as large as the decrease in network latency. This is because the application response time is determined by the sum of the time taken to execute the application, database, and kernel networking code, as well as the network latency. The change in network latency is only relatively small compared to the sum of the other latency components.

## Choosing Your Subnet Allocation for the Private Network

The network interfaces that constitute the private interconnect are allocated addresses from the IP network number provided during installation. By default, on the Solaris 10 OS, the `172.16.0.0` network address is used with a netmask of `255.255.240.0`. This IP address range supports a combined maximum of 64 voting nodes and non-global zones, a maximum of 12 zone clusters (see the section "Zone Clusters" in Chapter 3, "Combining Virtualization Technologies with Oracle Solaris Cluster Software"), and a maximum of 10 private networks. However, this subnet allocation consumes a very large number of addresses for potential use by the cluster and might be considered a little excessive. You can change the allocation during installation. You can also change the allocation after your cluster has been installed. This change does not require a cluster-wide shutdown when you are increasing the number of supported zone clusters, but it does require a cluster-wide shutdown for other changes. Any subnet you choose must not be routed within your organization.

## Network Ports Used by the Solaris Cluster Software

The Solaris Cluster software uses four ports for internal communication, which are statically defined in the `tcp_transport.h` [Transport] source code file. These ports are 8059, 8060, 8061, and 8062. If your application uses one of these ports, it must be reconfigured to use another free port. Furthermore, any firewall or host-based filtering must avoid blocking these ports on the cluster private networks.

## Configuration Guidelines

When you are configuring a cluster that implements only failover services built on failover file systems, there is little need to worry about the bandwidth or latency of the private interconnects. If you are building an Oracle RAC system, then consider using either multiple Gigabit Ethernets or InfiniBand with RDS enabled (instead of IP over InfiniBand). If InfiniBand cards are not available on your target server nodes, then 10 Gigabit Ethernet is likely to be your best alternative.

Finally, if you are building systems that use a cluster file system, then Gigabit Ethernet is sufficient for low-end servers, and 10 Gigabit Ethernet can be considered for high-end servers. Because the internode communication for a cluster file system does not take advantage of RDS, do not consider InfiniBand for non–Oracle RAC configurations.

## Data Service and Application Agents

A *data service* is an application running on a cluster that is made highly available through a collection of scripts and programs that provide start, stop, and monitoring capabilities. The Solaris Cluster software supports four types of data service: failover, scalable, multi-master, and parallel. Scalable data services rely on the global networking and cluster file system functions in the Solaris Cluster software.

The Solaris Cluster software supports an extensive list of data services from Oracle and independent software vendors. The data services supported directly by Oracle include

- Agfa IMPAX
- Apache proxy server, Apache Tomcat, Apache web server
- Dynamic Host Configuration Protocol (DHCP)
- Domain name service (DNS)
- High availability database (HADB)
- IBM Informix
- IBM WebSphere Message Broker, IBM WebSphere MQ
- Sun Java System Application Server, Directory Server, Message Queue Broker, Messaging Server, Web Proxy Server, Web Server
- Kerberos
- Guest Logical Domains
- MySQL
- Oracle Grid Engine
- Sun N1 Service Provisioning System
- Veritas NetBackup
- NFS
- Oracle Application Server
- Oracle E-Business Suite
- Oracle Server, Oracle ASM, Oracle 8i OPS, Oracle RAC
- Oracle WebLogic Server
- PostgreSQL
- Samba
- SAP, SAP liveCache, SAP MaxDB
- Siebel
- Oracle Solaris Zones
- StorageTek Availability Suite
- SWIFTAlliance Access, SWIFTAlliance Gateway
- Sybase ASE

Many of these can be used with the virtualization technologies described in Chapter 3, "Combining Virtualization Technologies with Oracle Solaris Cluster Software." The one major exception to this rule is that you cannot combine these data services with failover guest domains (see the section "Failover Guest Domains" in Chapter 3).

## Data Service Constructs

The Solaris Cluster software takes an object-oriented approach to the creation of the components needed to build highly available and scalable data services. The three main constructs used are the resource type, the resource, and the resource group. The following sections describe each construct in detail. The Resource Group Manager daemon, which orchestrates these constructs within your cluster, is described first.

## Resource Group Manager Daemon

The Resource Group Manager daemon, rgmd, is the user-level program that synchronizes the control of resource groups and resources within your cluster. It uses the cluster configuration repository to discover which user-level programs it must call to invoke the relevant resource methods.

When the rgmd daemon must place a resource group online or offline on a given node, it calls the methods for the resources in the resource group to start or stop them, as appropriate.

Whenever the cluster membership changes, the Cluster Membership Monitor (CMM) drives the rgmd daemon. In turn, rgmd uses the "fork-exec" daemon, rpc.fed, to fork and execute data service method programs. These daemons communicate by using local Solaris *doors* calls on each node. The rpc.fed daemon is a multithreaded program that blocks the doors call until the execution of the program completes or times out, and then this daemon returns an exit status to the caller.

When moving a resource group between nodes, the rgmd daemon must be certain that a resource has stopped on one node before it restarts the resource on another node. If this requirement is not strictly enforced, a nonscalable application could be simultaneously run on more than one node and, therefore, corrupt its data. If rgmd cannot be certain that it stopped the application, it sets a STOP_ FAILED flag on the appropriate resource.

You must manually clear this flag before the application can be restarted. You can then ensure that the application is actually stopped before you clear the flag to restart the resource.

The rgmd daemon also enables considerable flexibility in the management of resource and resource group properties without requiring you to shut down applications or the cluster. For example, you can add extra nodes to a two-node cluster running a scalable web service, and then you can modify the scalable web resource group to allow it to run on the new node without stopping the existing web services.

Similarly, if a web service is already running three httpd instances across a four-node cluster, you can decrease the number of instances to two or increase it to four without interrupting service.

## Resource Types

The basic building block for all data services is the *resource type*, which the Solaris Cluster software also refers to as an *agent*. The Solaris Cluster software ships with the following resource types preinstalled in `/usr/cluster/lib/rgm/rtreg`:

- `SUNW.derby`
- `SUNW.Event`
- `SUNW.HAStoragePlus`
- `SUNW.LogicalHostname`
- `SUNW.ScalDeviceGroup`
- `SUNW.ScalMountPoint`
- `SUNW.scmasa`
- `SUNW.sctelemetry`
- `SUNW.SharedAddress`
- `SUNW.vucmm_cvm`
- `SUNW.vucmm_framework`
- `SUNW.vucmm_svm`
- `SUNW.wait_zc_boot`

The `SUNW.LogicalHostname`, `SUNW.SharedAddress`, `SUNW.HAStoragePlus`, and `SUNW.gds` resource types are described in more detail in the subsequent sections.

Assuming you have a license to use additional agents, you can load the Sun resource types from the Solaris Cluster agent media by using the `scinstall` command. You can then register them with the cluster framework by using the `clresourcetype` command (see the `clresourcetype`(1M) man page). If you do not register the resource type, any attempt to create a resource of that type fails and returns an error.

A Solaris package that contains a resource type has all of the methods (programs or shell scripts) needed to start, stop, and monitor the application. In addition, a resource type registration (RTR) file provides the path to methods, the names of the methods, settings for any standard resource properties, and definitions of specific resource extension properties. Registering the resource type with the cluster framework by using the `clresourcetype` command enables the `rgmd` daemon (see "Resource Group Manager Daemon") to locate the methods necessary to control applications and start them with the correct parameter settings. Thus, a general resource type can be written for use by multiple applications, rather than a specific instance of an application.

The resource types are written so you can use them with both the Solaris 9 OS and with the global zone, and with all forms and uses of non-global zones in the Solaris 10 OS. However, they cannot be used with either solaris8, solaris9, or 1x-branded zones in Solaris 10 OS (see the section "Branded Zones (BrandZ)" in Chapter 3, "Combining Virtualization Technologies with Oracle Solaris Cluster Software") because the agent packages are not installed in these environments.

Table 2.3 lists the resource type properties that define all the possible callback methods that can be used to control and monitor a target application. At a minimum, you need to define only the start method unless you use the prenet or postnet method. The methods can be either compiled programs or shell scripts. If you do not define a stop method, your application will be terminated using the kill command.

**Table 2.3** Resource Type Callback Methods

| Property | Function |
|---|---|
| START | Starts the application. |
| STOP | Stops the application. |
| UPDATE | Updates a running resource whose properties have been changed. |
| VALIDATE | Checks the property settings for a resource of this type. |
| PRENET_START | Performs start actions that must be completed before network interfaces are "configured up." It is called by the RGM before calling the start method of any network address resources on which a resource of this type depends. |
| POSTNET_STOP | Performs stop actions that must be completed after the network interfaces are "configured down." It is called by the RGM after calling the stop method of any network address resources on which a resource of this type depends. |
| MONITOR_START | Starts a fault monitor for a resource of this type. |
| MONITOR_STOP | Stops a fault monitor for a resource of this type. |
| MONITOR_CHECK | Called by the RGM on each resource in a resource group, before performing a monitor-requested failover of the group. |
| INIT | Initializes resources of this type. It is called by the RGM when a resource of this type is placed under RGM control. |
| FINI | Removes resources of this type. It is called by the RGM when a resource of this type is removed from RGM control. |
| BOOT | Initializes resources of this type similar to the init method. It is called by the RGM on a node that joins or rejoins the cluster when a resource of this type is already managed. |

### SUNW.LogicalHostname

`SUNW.LogicalHostname` is the resource type that provides the logical IP address for failover services, such as Oracle, NFS, or failover web services. This address resource is placed in a failover resource group that is instantiated on one cluster node at any one time. The logical IP address can, for example, be configured on `e1000g0:2` (see Example 2.6). Consequently, the logical IP address is available only to applications that are located on the same cluster node.

On clusters that run the Solaris 10 OS, you cannot create `SUNW.LogicalHostname` resources from within a static non-global zone (see the section "Global-Cluster Non-Voting Node" in Chapter 3, "Combining Virtualization Technologies with Oracle Solaris Cluster Software"). The `clreslogicalhostname` command can be run only from the global zone or from within a zone cluster (see the section "Zone Clusters" in Chapter 3).

### SUNW.SharedAddress

`SUNW.SharedAddress` is the resource type that provides the logical IP address for scalable services, such as the Sun Java System and Apache web servers. This address resource is placed in a failover resource group that is instantiated on one cluster node at a time. The logical IP address itself, for example, can be configured on `e1000g0:2`, but it is also configured on the loopback interfaces (`lo0`) of cluster nodes running scalable services that depend on this address.

On clusters that run the Solaris 10 OS, you cannot create `SUNW.SharedAddress` resources from within a static non-global zone. The `clressharedaddress` command can be run only from the global zone or from within a zone cluster.

---

### Example 2.8  Creating a Resource Group Containing a Shared Address Resource and Bringing It Online

Ensure that the hostname can be resolved.

```
node1# getent hosts earth
10.11.195.119    earth
```

Create a resource group called `example-rg`.

```
node1# clresourcegroup create example-rg
```

Add a shared address resource to the resource group.

```
node1# clressharedaddress create -g example-rg -h earth \
> example-sa-rs
```

Bring the resource group online.

```
node1# clresourcegroup manage example-rg
node1# clresourcegroup online example-rg
```

List the IP addresses that are plumbed on each system.

```
node1# ifconfig -a
    .
    .
    .
e1000g0:1: flags=1001040843<UP,BROADCAST,RUNNING,MULTICAST,DEPRECATED,IPv4,FIXEDMTU> mtu
1500 index 3
        inet 10.11.195.119 netmask ffffff00 broadcast 10.11.195.255
    .
    .
    .
```

Now check the other system.

```
node2# ifconfig -a
lo0: flags=20010008c9<UP,LOOPBACK,RUNNING,NOARP,MULTICAST,IPv4,VIRTUAL> mtu 8232
index 1
        inet 127.0.0.1 netmask ff000000
lo0:1: flags=20010088c9<UP,LOOPBACK,RUNNING,NOARP,MULTICAST,PRIVATE,IPv4,VIRTUAL> mtu
8232 index 1
        inet 10.11.195.119 netmask ffffffff
    .
    .
    .
```

## SUNW.HAStoragePlus

SUNW.HAStoragePlus is a resource type that enables application resources that depend on global devices, cluster file systems (UFS or VxFS), failover file systems (UFS, VxFS, or QFS), or zpool to synchronize their startup with the availability of the storage resources on which they depend. A SUNW.HAStoragePlus resource is placed in an application failover resource group, and subsequent application resource definitions are made dependent on it. To control global devices or global file systems, you can add a SUNW.HAStoragePlus resource to a scalable resource group. In either case, the relevant devices and path names are specified as extension properties of the SUNW.HAStoragePlus resource.

When you configure a SUNW.HAStoragePlus resource, you must leave the AffinityOn property set to its default value of true. This ensures that any devices or file systems listed in the GlobalDevicePaths and Filesystem-MountPoints properties of the resource have their primary I/O paths switched over with the application when it is switched or failed over to a new node. This property does not apply to the ZFS file system and is consequently ignored.

Example 6.15 in Chapter 6, "Oracle Solaris Cluster Geographic Edition: Features and Architecture," shows how to create a simple failover file system resource for a failover application. Bringing resource group `app-rg` online results in the file system being mounted. Taking this resource group offline results in the file system being unmounted.

### SUNW.gds

The `SUNW.gds`, or Generic Data Service (GDS), is a resource type that allows you to quickly create agents for applications where neither the application vendor nor Oracle provides an agent. The core of the agent contains all of the best practices required to control an application in a cluster, including how many times to try restarting the application before failing it over and how to react to network failure.

For more information about how to extend the Solaris Cluster agent support, see the section "Creating New Resource Types" in Chapter 4, "Managing Your Oracle Solaris Cluster Environment."

## Resources

*Resources* are instantiations of specific resource types. They inherit all of the methods registered for the resource type with the cluster framework. The definition of a resource provides specific values for standard and required extension properties, as defined in the RTR file. These values can include path names to application configuration files, any TCP/IP ports they listen on, timeout settings, and so on. Multiple resources of a particular resource type can exist within the cluster without modifying the original programs or shell scripts. The resource standard and extension properties enable fine-grained control of data services on a service-by-service basis. You can change the property values while the cluster is running, enabling you to manage the load on your cluster nodes.

Resources can be *enabled* or *disabled*, but enabling a resource does not necessarily start the application that the resource controls. Instead, enabling or disabling a resource sets the resource `On_off_switch` property. Table 2.4 shows the state changes that a resource undergoes in response to various Solaris Cluster commands to enable or disable the resource or to online or offline the resource group. The table cells in gray indicate that the command has no effect on the overall state of the resource or resource group.

When one resource relies on another resource, for example, when an NFS share relies on a running network interface, the Solaris Cluster software provides four types of dependency: strong, weak, restart, and offline restart. For example, when another resource, `rac-framework-rs`, must be online before the resource `rac-udlm-rs` can start successfully, you can set the `resource_dependencies` property for `rac-udlm-rs` to `rac-framework-rs` to ensure that the `rgmd` daemon honors these relationships. See the following example, which shows the resource configured in this fashion.

**Table 2.4** Resource State Changes

| Action/Initial State | Resource Group Offline, Resource Enabled | Resource Group Offline, Resource Disabled | Resource Group Online, Resource Enabled | Resource Group Online, Resource Disabled |
|---|---|---|---|---|
| **Bring the Resource Group Online**<br>`(clrg online)` | The resource group and resource are brought online. The resource remains enabled and the application is started. | The resource group is brought online, but the resource remains disabled and offline. The application is not started. | No change. The resource group and resource are already online, and the application is already started. | No change. The resource group is already online, but the resource remains disabled and offline. The application remains stopped. |
| **Bring the Resource Group Online**<br>`(clrg offline)` | No change. The resource group is already offline. The resource remains enabled, and the application remains stopped. | No change. The resource group is already offline. The resource remains disabled, and the application remains stopped. | The resource group and resource are brought offline. The resource remains enabled, but the application is stopped. | The resource group is brought offline. The resource remains disabled and offline, and the application remains stopped. |
| **Enable the Resource**<br>`(clrs enable)` | No change. The resource group remains offline. The resource is already enabled but remains offline. The application remains stopped. | The resource group remains offline. However, the resource is enabled but remains offline. The application remains stopped. | No change. The resource group remains online. The resource is already enabled and remains online. The application remains started. | The resource group remains online. The resource is enabled and brought online. The application is started. |
| **Disable the Resource**<br>`(clrs disable)` | The resource group remains offline. The resource is disabled but remains offline. The application remains stopped. | No change. The resource group and resource remain offline. The resource remains disabled, and the application remains stopped. | The resource group remains online, but the resource is disabled and brought offline. The application is stopped. | No change. The resource group remains online, and the resource remains disabled and offline. The application remains stopped. |

**Example 2.9   Showing the Strong Dependency of the Real Application Cluster UDLM Resource on the RAC Framework Resource**

List all the properties of the resource `rac-udlm-rs`.

```
# clresource show -v rac-udlm-rs

=== Resources ===

Resource:                                rac-udlm-rs
  Type:                                  SUNW.rac_udlm:3
  Type_version:                          3
  Group:                                 rac-framework-rg
  R_description:
  Resource_project_name:                 default
  Enabled{phys-earth1}:                  True
  Enabled{phys-earth2}:                  True
  Monitored{phys-earth1}:                True
  Monitored{phys-earth2}:                True
  Resource_dependencies:                 rac-framework-rs
  Resource_dependencies_weak:            <NULL>
  Resource_dependencies_restart:         <NULL>
  Resource_dependencies_offline_restart: <NULL>

  --- Standard and extension properties ---
     .
     .
     .
```

Where the dependency is weaker, the `resource_dependencies_weak` property ensures that `rgmd` calls the `start` methods of the depended-on resources before those of the dependent resource. However, although the `rgmd` waits for the `start` method of the depended-on resource to complete, there is no requirement for the `start` method of the depended-on resource to succeed or even complete within the set timeout. In either case, `rgmd` then calls the `start` method of the dependent resource. Furthermore, if the depended-on resource remains offline because it is disabled or its resource group is offline, the dependent resource will still be started.

Each resource dependency property (strong, weak, restart, and offline restart) can be scoped in one of three ways (see the `r_properties`(5) man page):

- `LOCAL_NODE`: The resource depends on another resource that is on the same local node.

- `ANY_NODE`: The resource depends on another resource that could be on another cluster node.

- `FROM_RG_AFFINITIES`: This scope is the default. If the resource group of the resource has a strong positive affinity for the resource group of the resource it depends on, then the effect equates to a LOCAL_NODE dependency. Otherwise, it equates to an ANY_NODE dependency.

In each case, the dependency is specified by enclosing one of these directives in "{ }" after the name of the depended-on resource.

The resource dependencies form what is known in mathematics as a *directed acyclic graph*. The RGM does not permit any cycles (loops) in the overall set of resource dependencies. The start and stop methods for a resource must ensure that the application actually starts or stops before returning control to the calling program.

You can then bring applications online and offline individually by enabling or disabling the resources with the clresource command. If you supply the -r (recursive) flag to the clresource command, then both the depended-on resource and the dependent resource will be disabled, even if only the depended-on resource is used in the command syntax. You can also disable a resource even if another resource is dependent on it, though doing so results in the warning shown in the following example [DepRes].

---

### Example 2.10  Disabling a Resource That Has Another Resource Dependent on It Where Both Are Initially Online

Use the clresource command to disable resource rs2.

```
psnow2# clresource disable rs2
(C782285) WARNING: Resource rs2 being disabled while its dependent resources {rs1}
remain online.
```

---

The clresourcegroup command is used to bring entire resource groups online and/or offline; see "Resource Groups." You can also enable or disable the monitoring of a specific resource by using the monitor or unmonitor options of the clresource command.

### Per-Node Resource Properties

When a resource is part of a multi-master resource group, that is, one that is online on multiple nodes at once, you can disable the resource on a per-node basis. This enables you to have your resource online on a subset of the nodes that constitute your resource group node list. Furthermore, if your resource has per-node properties, such as the Enabled or Monitored properties listed for rac-udlm-rs in Example 2.9, then you can set these properties on a per-node basis, too. One example of where these properties are needed is the RAC proxy server resource. This type of resource requires the Oracle system ID (SID) for the database instance running on each node.

### Failover, Scalable, and Multi-Master Resources

Depending on the type of application you are making highly available, you might choose to encapsulate it with either a failover, scalable, or multi-master resource. This resource then drives the type of resource group you create: failover or scalable, as expressed through the RG_mode property.

A failover resource is one in which a particular invocation of an application can execute on only one node at any one time. A standard HA-NFS service is a good example of such an application. The NFS service is stateful, such that the same file system cannot be shared from multiple nodes at once.

Some applications do not use a shared address and can run on multiple nodes at once without causing data corruption. This type of application is a multi-master service. The RAC framework resource group contains at least one multi-master resource, the RAC framework resource, which drives the reconfiguration steps after a cluster membership change. This RAC framework resource enables Oracle RAC databases to interoperate with the Solaris Cluster software (see "Parallel Services"). Other multi-master resource types include the Apache Tomcat application server, though this type of application would need to rely on an external hardware load balancer to allow user connections.

A scalable resource can be considered a special kind of multi-master resource. A scalable resource differs from a failover resource because it allows suitable applications to run instances of the application on more than one node at once and use a common shared IP address (see "SUNW.SharedAddress"). Currently, only Sun Java System and Apache web servers and Apache Tomcat can be run in this fashion. All the other Oracle-supported applications run in failover or multi-master mode.

An application must be relatively stateless to run as a scalable resource, meaning that instances must not be required to share any state or locking information between them. Because web servers simply serve web pages to a user population, they are ideal candidates for this approach. Currently, no generic mechanism exists to enable state-based applications to coordinate their data access and enable them to run as scalable services.

For resource types that can be run as a scalable service, you must set the failover property in the RTR file to false. This value enables you to set the maximum_primaries and desired_primaries resource group properties to values greater than one. By changing these values, you can dynamically vary application capacity and resilience in response to the user load and business needs.

## Resource Groups

Resource groups form the logical container for one or more resources. A failover resource group is online on only one node at a time, and that node hosts all of the resources in that group. In contrast, a scalable resource group can be online on more than one node at a time. Initially, when you create a resource group, it is in the *unmanaged* state.

The `rgmd` daemon is responsible for bringing resource groups online or offline on the appropriate nodes. When it does so, it calls the `start` or `stop` methods for the resources in that resource group.

Figure 2.7 is an example of a failover resource group configuration.

The `rgmd` daemon can initiate a resource group migration in response to a `clresourcegroup` command request to move a service, or in response to the failure of a node that is currently hosting one or more resource groups. However, this migration happens only if the resource group is in the *managed* state. You must bring your resource group into this state using the `clresourcegroup` command.

When running multiple data services, you can configure each unrelated service into its own resource group. Ideally, to maintain optimal performance, each data service must rely, when possible, on separate device groups for their file systems and global device services. This separation enables you to colocate the primary I/O path with the data service at all times. Multiple instances of an Oracle database server serve as a good example. When data services depend on one another, they generally benefit from being in the same resource group.

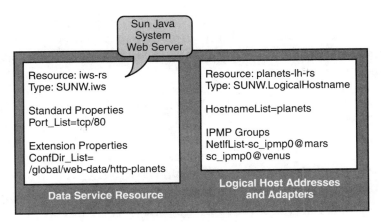

Data Service Resource Group: planets-web-svr-rg

**Figure 2.7** Example of a failover resource group configuration
for a Sun Java System Web Server

## Resource Group Dependency and Affinity Options

Resource groups have two properties that affect the way in which multiple resource groups interact: RG_dependencies and RG_affinities. You need to understand these if you want to implement more complex service stacks on a Solaris Cluster system.

RG_dependencies is a legacy property that has been superseded by the resource dependency properties. It is used to indicate a preferred order for bringing dependent resource groups online or offline on the same node. For example, if your application server needed to be brought online only after your database had started, then you would create a resource group dependency from the application server resource group to the database server resource group. However, this property has no effect if the groups are brought online on different nodes.

The other property for controlling how resource groups are brought online and offline on cluster nodes is the RG_affinities property introduced in the Sun Cluster 3.1 09/04 software. The selection of a primary node for a resource group is determined by the nodelist property that is configured for the group. The nodelist property specifies a list of nodes or zones where the resource group can be brought online, in order of preference. These nodes or zones are known as the *potential primaries* (or *masters*) of the resource group.

The node list preference order is modified by the following factors:

- *"Ping-pong" prevention*: If the resource group has recently failed to start on a given node or zone, that node or zone is given lower priority than one on which it has not yet failed.

- *Resource group affinities*: This configurable resource group property indicates a positive or negative affinity of one group for another group. The node selection algorithm always satisfies strong affinities and makes a best effort to satisfy weak affinities.

The RG_affinities property enables you to indicate that the RGM should do one of the following:

- Attempt to locate the resource group on a node that is a current master of another group, referred to as *positive affinity*.

- Attempt to locate the resource group on a node that is not a current master of a given group, referred to as *negative affinity*.

The following are the five types of resource group affinities:

- *Weak positive affinity*: denoted by "+" (one plus sign)

- *Strong positive affinity*: denoted by "++" (two plus signs)
- *Strong positive affinity with failover delegation*: denoted by "+++" (three plus signs)
- *Weak negative affinity*: denoted by "-" (one minus sign)
- *Strong negative affinity*: denoted by "--" (two minus signs)

The following examples show how these resource group affinities are used.

Example 2.11 shows how to enforce colocation of a resource group with another resource group. Assume that your cluster is running an Oracle database server controlled by a failover resource group, ora-rg. You also have an application in resource group dbmeasure-rg, which measures and logs the performance of the database. The dbmeasure application, if it runs, must run on the same node as the Oracle server. However, use of this application is not mandatory, and the Oracle database can run well without it.

You can force dbmeasure to run only on a node where the Oracle database is running by declaring a strong positive affinity, as shown in the following example.

## Example 2.11  Setting a Strong Positive Resource Group Affinity

Use the clresourcegroup command to set a strong positive affinity for resource group ora-rg.

```
# clresourcegroup set -p RG_affinities=++ora-rg dbmeasure-rg
```

When you initially bring ora-rg online, dbmeasure-rg automatically comes online on the same node. If ora-rg fails over to a different node or zone, then dbmeasure-rg follows it automatically. While ora-rg remains online you can bring dbmeasure-rg offline. However, dbmeasure-rg cannot switch over or fail over onto any node where ora-rg is *not* running.

In addition to the resource group affinities, you might also configure a dependency of the dbmeasure resource upon the Oracle server resource. This assures that the dbmeasure resource is not started until the Oracle server resource is online. Resource group affinities are enforced independently of resource dependencies. Whereas resource dependencies control the order in which resources are started and stopped, resource group affinities control the locations where resource groups are brought online across multiple nodes or zones of a cluster.

Assume that dbmeasure is a more critical application, and it is important to keep it running. In that case, you could force dbmeasure-rg to initiate a failover onto a different node, dragging ora-rg along with it. To do so, you would use the strong positive affinity with delegated failover, as shown in the following example.

## Example 2.12  Setting a Strong Positive Resource Group Affinity with Delegated Failover

Use the `clresourcegroup` command to set a strong positive affinity with delegated failover for resource group `ora-rg`.

```
# clresourcegroup set -p RG_affinities=+++ora-rg dbmeasure-rg
```

Example 2.13 shows how to specify a preferred colocation of a resource group with another resource group. Assume, again, that a cluster is running the Oracle database resource group `ora-rg`. On the same cluster, you are running a customer service application that uses the database. This application is configured in a separate failover resource group, `app-rg`. The application and the database *can* run on two different nodes, but you have discovered that the application is database-intensive and runs faster if it is hosted on the same node as the database. Therefore, you prefer to start the application on the same node as the database.

However, you want to avoid switching the application from one node to another node, even if the database changes nodes. To avoid breaking client connections or for some other reason, you would rather keep the application on its current master, even if doing so incurs some performance penalty.

To achieve this behavior, you give `app-rg` a weak positive affinity for `ora-rg`, as shown in the following example.

## Example 2.13  Setting a Weak Positive Resource Group Affinity

Use the `clresourcegroup` command to set a weak positive affinity for resource group `ora-rg`.

```
# clresourcegroup set -p RG_affinities=+ora-rg app-rg
```

With this affinity, the RGM will start `app-rg` on the same node as `ora-rg`, when possible. However, the RGM will not force `app-rg` to always run on the same node.

The following example shows you how to balance the load of a set of resource groups. Assume that a cluster is hosting three independent applications in resource groups `app1-rg`, `app2-rg`, and `app3-rg`. By giving each resource group a weak negative affinity for the other two groups, you can achieve a rudimentary form of load balancing on the cluster.

## Example 2.14   Using Weak Negative Resource Group Affinity for Rudimentary Load Balancing

Use the `clresourcegroup` command to set weak negative affinities between each of the three resource groups.

```
# clresourcegroup set -p RG_affinities=-app2-rg,-app3-rg app1-rg
# clresourcegroup set -p RG_affinities=-app1-rg,-app3-rg app2-rg
# clresourcegroup set -p RG_affinities=-app1-rg,-app2-rg app3-rg
```

With these affinities, the RGM will try to bring each resource group online on a node that is not currently hosting either of the other two groups. If three or more nodes are available, this will place each resource group onto its own node. If fewer than three nodes are available, then the RGM will "double up" or "triple up" the resource groups onto the available node or nodes. Conceptually, the resource group with weak negative affinity is trying to avoid the other resource groups, not unlike electrostatic charges that repel one another.

Example 2.15 shows how to specify that a critical service has precedence. In this example, a critical service, an Oracle database, is in the `ora-rg` resource group and is sharing the cluster with a noncritical service. This noncritical service is a prototype of a newer version of your software, which is undergoing testing and development. You have a two-node cluster, and you want `ora-rg` to start on one node, and `test-rg` to start on the other node. Assume that the first node, hosting `ora-rg`, fails, causing `ora-rg` to fail over to the second node. You want the non-critical service in `test-rg` to go offline on that node.

To achieve this behavior, you give `test-rg` a strong negative affinity for `ora-rg`.

## Example 2.15   Setting Strong Negative Resource Group Affinity

Use the `clresourcegroup` command to set a strong negative affinity for resource group `ora-rg`.

```
# clresourcegroup set -p RG_affinities=--ora-rg test-rg
```

When the first node fails and `ora-rg` fails over to the second node where `test-rg` is currently running, `test-rg` will get removed from the second node and will remain offline (assuming a two-node cluster). When the first node reboots, it takes on the role of backup node, and `test-rg` is automatically started on it.

Example 2.16 shows how to combine different flavors of the `RG_affinities` property to achieve more complex behavior. In the Solaris Cluster HA for SAP Replicated Enqueue Service, you configure the enqueue server in one resource group, `enq-rg`, and the replica server in a second resource group, `repl-rg`.

A requirement of this data service is that if the enqueue server fails on the node where it is currently running, it must fail over to the node where the replica server is running. The replica server needs to move immediately to a different node. Setting a weak positive affinity from the enqueue server resource group to the replica server resource group ensures that the enqueue server resource group will fail over to the node where the replica server is currently running.

### Example 2.16  Setting Weak Positive Resource Group Affinity for the SAP Enqueue Resource Group

Use the `clresourcegroup` command to set a weak positive affinity for resource group `repl-rg`.

```
# clresourcegroup set -p RG_affinities=+repl-rg enq-rg
```

Setting a strong negative affinity from the replica server resource group to the enqueue server resource group ensures that the replica server resource group is off-loaded from the replica server node before the enqueue server resource group is brought online on the same node.

### Example 2.17  Setting Strong Negative Resource Group Affinity for the SAP Replica Server Resource Group

Use the `clresourcegroup` command to set a strong negative affinity for resource group `enq-rg`.

```
# clresourcegroup set -p RG_affinities=--enq-rg repl-rg
```

The replica server resource group will be started up on another node, if one is available.

**Declaring Affinities between Resource Groups in Different Zones**    Although zones are not covered until the section "Oracle Solaris Zones" in Chapter 3, "Combining Virtualization Technologies with Oracle Solaris Cluster Software," it is worth noting here that you can declare affinities between resource groups in different zones. If you declare affinities between resource groups that run in different non-global zones, then the `nodelist` property of each resource group must share a common set of physical nodes. For example, if the first resource group has a node list of `node-one:zone-one,node-two:zone-two`, then the second resource group must use zones that are resident on `node-one` and `node-two`.

---

### Example 2.18  Setting Affinities between Resource Groups in Different Zones

Use the `clresourcegroup` command to set a strong positive affinity for resource group `rg2`.

```
# clresourcegroup create -n node1,node2 rg2
# clresourcegroup create -n node1:zone1,node2:zone2 rg1
# clresourcegroup set -p rg_affinities=++rg2 rg1
```

---

In Example 2.18, resource group `rg2` runs in the global zone of nodes `node1` and `node2`, and `rg1` runs in non-global zones (`zone1` and `zone2`) on those nodes. The strong positive affinity assures that `rg1` is allowed to run only on a physical node where `rg2` is currently online.

Thus, by using the simple declarative mechanism of the `RG_affinities` property, you can achieve robust recovery behavior for your data services running on a Solaris Cluster system.

## Parallel Services

Parallel applications such as Oracle RAC differ from a single-instance Oracle database running in a failover mode. An Oracle RAC consists of multiple database instances running on separate nodes, sharing a common set of data files. Although IBM DB2 is a parallel database, it does not perform concurrent I/O from multiple nodes to the same raw-disk device, and so it is not a shared disk architecture. Instead, it uses a shared-nothing architecture, moving functions and data between nodes to satisfy queries.

Under normal circumstances, an Oracle instance caches data from its data files (or tablespaces) in its system global area (SGA). Numerous in-memory latches or locks maintain the integrity of SGA by ensuring that multiple users on that server do not corrupt the data through uncontrolled simultaneous access. The latches effectively synchronize the access of users to the underlying data. When the parallel version of Oracle is running, a distributed lock manager (DLM) must keep the data in multiple SGAs coherent and synchronized. This action ensures that data cache integrity is maintained for multiuser access across multiple nodes. The DLM communicates between the nodes through the private interconnect, of which the `clprivnet0` implementation ensures resilient internode communication.

Unlike the global file service, the Oracle parallel implementations require concurrent local access to the underlying disks from each node on which they are running. This means that regular disk I/O is not being proxied across the interconnect, as is the case in which a service runs remotely from the primary I/O path. However, when the SGA on one node must share a data block that is currently cached on another node, the data is passed between the nodes through the private interconnect. This technology, called Cache Fusion, was introduced in Oracle 9*i* Real Application Clusters.

The Solaris Cluster 3.2 software includes several features specifically designed to enhance the manageability of Oracle RAC deployments. These new resource types enable better coordination of Oracle startup and shutdown in a clustered environment, avoiding any failures that might otherwise occur. The following discussion focuses on Oracle 10*g* and 11*g* Real Application Cluster, as they are the most recent releases. However, availability management integration features are also beneficial to Oracle 9*i* Real Application Cluster.

### Oracle RAC Availability Management Integration Features

Oracle Clusterware has two important components: the Oracle Cluster Registry (OCR) and a set of voting disks. These components and several daemon processes constitute the Oracle Clusterware framework.

When installing Oracle Clusterware on systems running the Solaris Cluster software, your database administrators can choose to create the OCR and voting disks on shared raw-disk hardware RAID LUNs, on raw-disk volume manager devices, on a shared QFS file system, or on a network-attached storage (NAS) file system. When running without the Solaris Cluster software, your options are reduced to raw-disk or NAS.

After Oracle Clusterware has started, it waits for the file systems or devices holding its OCR and voting disks to come online. However, if Oracle Clusterware is not stopped at the right point during a cluster or node shutdown (that is, before any file systems it might depend on are unmounted), then I/O timeouts will occur and one or more nodes will panic because their voting disks are not responding.

The Solaris Cluster software provides a mechanism to create dependencies between Oracle Clusterware, the Oracle RAC databases, and the underlying storage to ensure that both the startup and shutdown operations are correctly sequenced (described in detail in the following subsections). It should be reiterated that without Solaris Cluster software, Oracle Clusterware alone would not have any option for volume management or a shared file system other than NAS in the Oracle Solaris OS.

## Solaris Cluster Scalable Device Group Resources

Scalable device group resources are used to ensure that Solaris Volume Manager disksets or Veritas Volume Manager disk groups are correctly configured prior to allowing any dependent Solaris Cluster resources to start. The validation mechanisms contained in the resource type check that your diskset or disk group is valid, multi-owner, and hosted on the given nodes, and that your diskset or device group has at least one volume present. The resource also supports a parameter to define an additional list of logical devices to check.

The continuing health of these disksets and device groups is then checked regularly by using either the `metaset` or the `vxprint` command to ensure that no problems have arisen that might cause any dependent services to fail. If a problem is found, then the resource is placed into a disabled state on a per-node basis.

## Solaris Cluster Scalable Mount-Point Resources

Scalable mount-point resources are used to ensure that your shared QFS and NAS mounted file systems are functioning correctly. The validation mechanisms contained in the resource type check that any NAS file system is exported and that any shared QFS file system has an entry in the `/etc/vfstab` and `/etc/opt/ SUNWsamfs/mcf` files. For shared QFS file systems, these mechanisms also check that the QFS metadata server resource exists and that the scalable mount-point resource has a dependency on it.

The health of these file systems is probed by using I/O to preallocate test files created in the mount-point directory of the file system when the resource is started. If this probe succeeds, the file system is deemed to be healthy. Otherwise, the resource is placed into a disabled state on that node.

## Solaris Cluster Clusterware Framework Resource

The Solaris Cluster software Clusterware framework resource is used to allow Oracle Clusterware to be stopped before your NAS or shared QFS file systems, or the disk groups and disksets, are stopped. This is achieved by setting up strong dependencies from the Clusterware framework resource on the appropriate scalable mount-point and device-group resources.

In addition, the resource regularly probes for the existence of the `ocssd.bin` process to check whether the Oracle Clusterware framework is still healthy. The current state is reflected in the output from the `clresourcegroup` and `cluster` commands and in the Solaris Cluster Manager browser interface.

### Solaris Cluster RAC Proxy Resources

The Solaris Cluster software RAC proxy resources are used to coordinate the startup and shutdown processes of your Oracle RAC database instances, so a single cluster could contain more than one of these resource groups. An instance of the resource checks the validity of the Oracle RAC and Oracle Clusterware home directories and determines whether the Oracle database name corresponds to an existing database. If Oracle Clusterware is found to be running, the resource proceeds to start the database instances on the appropriate nodes. Conversely, if the resource is being stopped, it will shut down these instances.

The status of your Oracle instances is monitored using the Oracle Fast Application Notification (FAN) mechanism, which forwards events to the Solaris Cluster monitoring system. This mechanism allows the Solaris Cluster software to report the status of the instances in the output of commands such as `cluster status -t resource` or `clresource status` and in the Solaris Cluster Manager browser interface. As with all Solaris Cluster resources, it can be disabled to allow maintenance of your Oracle database instances.

### Oracle Clusterware Storage Proxy Resources

The resources described previously enable higher levels of integration between Oracle Clusterware resources and Solaris Cluster scalable device-group and scalable mount-point storage resources. The Solaris Cluster `clsetup` program simplifies the creation of both sets of framework resources. The Oracle Clusterware resources that `clsetup` generates include a per-node dependency on the relevant Solaris Cluster storage resource for a particular Oracle RAC database, ensuring that its instances are not started until the storage resources on which they rely are available.

## Daemon Processes

Many daemon processes are associated with the Solaris Cluster software. Additionally, several daemon processes are involved in handling the interaction between Solaris Volume Manager and the Solaris Cluster framework. In the Solaris 10 OS, these processes are started by the Service Management Facility (SMF). The following list describes each daemon and gives its corresponding SMF service:

- `clexecd` (`svc:/system/cluster/clexecd`): This daemon supports the capability to issue commands specific to devices and file systems.
- `cl_ccrad` (`svc:/system/cluster/cl-ccra`): This daemon obtains cluster configuration information.

- `cl_eventlogd` (`svc:/system/cluster/cl-eventlog`): This daemon supports the logging of cluster events. The daemon logs the entire cluster event data structure, without any conversion from the event's binary format, to a log file.

- `cl_execd` (`svc:/system/cluster/cl_execd`): This daemon supports the capability to execute a command on any machine in either a global cluster or a zone cluster. This capability is used internally by the Solaris Cluster software.

- `cl_pnmd` (`svc:/system/cluster/pnm`): This daemon is the Solaris Cluster public network monitoring daemon (see the section "Solaris Cluster Public Network Monitoring Daemon" in Chapter 1, "Oracle Solaris Cluster: Overview").

- `cznetd` (`svc:/system/cluster/cznetd`): This daemon enables the `clprivnet` network on zone-cluster nodes. It is usually started up at system boot time. When the daemon is started, it registers callbacks for zone state changes and zone-cluster membership changes. Later, based on the callback event the daemon receives, the daemon either plumbs or unplumbs the `clprivnet` network on zone-cluster nodes.

- `failfastd` (`svc:/system/cluster/sc_failfastd`): This daemon is the failfast daemon. Some cluster components register with this daemon. If the cluster component fails, the system performs a failfast. A failure in the global zone results in a machine panic. A failure in a non-global zone results in a zone reboot.

- `ifconfig_proxy_serverd` (`svc:/system/cluster/sc_ifconfig_server`): This daemon supports `ifconfig` actions for a zone cluster. The daemon checks zone-cluster configuration information to determine whether the requesting zone cluster has authorization for that NIC/IP address. The set of allowed `ifconfig` operations for a zone cluster is restricted to just a few basic ones.

- `mdmonitord` (`svc:/system/mdmonitor`): This daemon is the Solaris Volume Manager daemon that monitors and checks RAID-1 devices (mirrors), RAID-5 devices, and hot spares.

- `pmmd` (`svc:/system/cluster/sc_pmmd`): This daemon is the process membership monitoring daemon. It provides process membership to a registered process and its peers that are running on a set of cluster nodes. The `rgmd` daemon registers with `pmmd`.

- `qd_userd` (part of `svc:/system/cluster/bootcluster`): The Membership subsystem component in the kernel uses this daemon to carry out some quorum-device-related operations that must be performed in non-kernel mode.

- `rgmd` (`svc:/system/cluster/rgm_starter`): This daemon manages applications and application resources for a specific cluster (global cluster or zone cluster). The number of daemons depends on the number of clusters.

- `rpc.fed` (`svc:/system/cluster/rpc-fed`): This is the Sun RPC fork execution daemon. For example, this daemon performs tasks when service-level management is enabled on a resource group.

- `rpc.mdcommd` (`svc:/network/rpc/mdcomm`): This daemon is the Solaris Volume Manager for Sun Cluster multinode daemon process that handles the communications between the nodes in the cluster. This daemon has a partner process, `/usr/lib/lvm/mddoors`, whose job is to transfer messages from the kernel to the non-kernel `rpc.mdcommd` daemon.

- `rpc.metacld` (`svc:/network/rpc/metacld`): This daemon is the Solaris Volume Manager command-forwarding daemon for the non-multi-owner disksets. It passes commands run on one node to the node that owns the diskset.

- `rpc.metad` (`svc:/network/rpc/meta`): This daemon is the Solaris Volume Manager diskset daemon that accepts incoming requests to administer the disksets, such as adding and removing nodes, disks, and mediators.

- `rpc.metamedd` (`svc:/network/rpc/metamed`): This daemon is the Solaris Volume Manager mediator server daemon.

- `rpc.pmfd` (`svc:/system/cluster/rpc-pmf`): This daemon is the RPC process-monitoring server daemon (see the `rpc.pmfd`(1M) man page).

- `rtreg_proxy_serverd` (`svc:/system/cluster/sc_rtreg_server`): This daemon supports the capability to register an RGM resource type for a zone cluster. The daemon checks that the resource type has characteristics that are allowed for a zone cluster.

- `scprivipd` (`svc:/system/cluster/scprivipd`): This daemon enables the `clprivnet` network on global-cluster non-voting nodes (see the section "Global-Cluster Non-Voting Node" in Chapter 3, "Combining Virtualization Technologies with Oracle Solaris Cluster Software"). The daemon is usually started at system boot time. When the daemon is started, it registers the callbacks for zone state changes. Based on the event the daemon receives, it either plumbs or unplumbs the `clprivnet` on global-cluster non-voting nodes.

- `scqdmd` (`svc:/system/cluster/scqmd`): This daemon monitors all configured quorum devices and supports all types of quorum devices. When a previously healthy quorum device fails to respond correctly, the daemon brings the quorum device offline and reports the problem. When a formerly offline quorum device becomes healthy, the daemon brings the quorum device online and reports that action.

- `syncsa_serverd` (`svc:/system/cluster/sc_syncsa_server`): This daemon is the Security Association (SA) synchronization daemon. It is needed to support IPsec session failover (see "IPsec Security Association Failover for Scalable Services").

- `sc_zonesd` (`svc:/system/cluster/sc_zones`): This daemon reports events-based zone state changes.

The `rpc.metamhd` daemon (`svc:/network/rpc/metamh`) is the Solaris Volume Manager SCSI reservation daemon that is used only when the Solaris Cluster software is not present.

If you choose to harden your Oracle Solaris OS (see the section "Operating System Hardening" in Chapter 4, "Managing Your Oracle Solaris Cluster Environment"), you must not disable these daemons.

# 3

# Combining Virtualization Technologies with Oracle Solaris Cluster Software

Now that all the basic Oracle Solaris Cluster features have been covered, next comes how the software works with the various virtualization technologies. The factors that influence your selection of a virtualization technology include

- Electrical isolation
- Operating system fault isolation
- Support for different versions of operating systems
- Application fault isolation
- Security isolation
- Resource management

However, each virtualization technology possesses a different set of benefits, challenges, and constraints.

Before learning about the virtualization technologies that the Solaris Cluster software supports, you must clearly understand the concept of a Solaris Cluster node. The chapter continues by describing the two modes of control that the Solaris Cluster software offers the entities it manages, "black-box" and "fine-grained," and how these modes of control are relevant to virtualization technologies. The remainder of the chapter discusses each virtualization technology that the Solaris Cluster software supports.

# Defining a Cluster Node

In a cluster that runs any version of the Solaris operating system that was released before the Solaris 10 OS, a *cluster node* is a physical machine that contributes to cluster membership and is not a quorum device. In a cluster that runs the Solaris 10 OS, the concept of a cluster node changes. In this environment, a cluster node is a zone that is associated with a cluster. A zone is a virtualized operating system environment created within a single instance of the Oracle Solaris OS. In addition, a Solaris host, or simply a host, is one of the following hardware or software configurations that runs the Oracle Solaris OS and its own processes:

- A "bare metal" physical machine that is not configured with a virtual machine or as a dynamic system domain
- A Logical Domains guest domain (see "Oracle VM Server for SPARC")
- A Logical Domains I/O domain
- A Logical Domains control domain
- A dynamic system domain
- Oracle VM VirtualBox (formerly Sun VirtualBox) virtualization software (However, you would use such a configuration only for development or demonstration purposes, rather than as a production platform; see the section "Using Oracle VM VirtualBox Software to Test-Drive the Solaris 10 OS and the Solaris Cluster Software" in Chapter 8, "Example Oracle Solaris Cluster Implementations.")

Solaris hosts are generally attached to one or more multihost devices. Hosts that are not attached to multihost devices use the cluster file system to access the multihost devices. For example, a scalable services configuration can enable hosts to service requests without being directly attached to multihost devices.

All nodes in the cluster are grouped under a common name (the cluster name), which is used for accessing and managing the cluster. Public network adapters attach hosts to the public networks, providing client access to the cluster.

Cluster members communicate with the other hosts in the cluster through one or more physically independent networks. This set of physically independent networks is referred to as the private interconnect.

Every node in the cluster detects when another node joins or leaves the cluster. Additionally, every node in the cluster detects the resources that are running locally as well as the resources that are running on the other cluster nodes in the same cluster.

Hosts in the same cluster ideally have similar processing, memory, and I/O capability to enable failover to occur without significant degradation in performance. Because of the possibility of failover, every host must have sufficient excess capacity to support the workload of all hosts for which it is a backup or secondary host.

Each host boots its own individual root (/) file system.

## Defining a Cluster

The Solaris Cluster software extends the Oracle Solaris OS into a cluster operating system. A *cluster* is a collection of one or more nodes that belong exclusively to that collection. In the Solaris 10 OS, a *global cluster* and a *zone cluster* are the two types of clusters.

A *global-cluster voting node* is a *native*-brand global zone in a global cluster that contributes votes to the total number of quorum votes, that is, membership votes in the cluster. This total determines whether the cluster has sufficient votes to continue operating. A *global-cluster non-voting node* (see "Global-Cluster Non-Voting Node") is a native-brand non-global zone in a global cluster that does not contribute votes to the total number of quorum votes, that is, membership votes in the cluster.

> **Note**
>
> A global cluster can optionally also include *solaris8, solaris9, lx* (Linux), or native-brand non-global zones (see "Branded Zones (BrandZ)") that are not nodes but high-availability containers (see "HA Containers") as resources.

In the Solaris 10 OS, a zone cluster is a type of cluster that contains one or more cluster-brand voting nodes. A zone cluster depends on, and therefore requires, a global cluster. A global cluster does not contain a zone cluster. You cannot configure a zone cluster without a global cluster. A zone cluster has, at most, one zone-cluster node on a machine (see "Zone Clusters").

## Comparison of "Black-Box" and "Fine-Grained" Control of Virtualized Entities

A key distinction as to how the Solaris Cluster software interacts with the virtualization technologies is whether the Solaris Cluster software has a presence in the virtualized entity or controls the virtualized entity from the outside. Where the Solaris Cluster software has a presence in the virtualized entity, the term *fine-*

*grained* is chosen to describe the interaction. In contrast, when the Solaris Cluster software controls the virtualized entity without having any presence within the virtualized entity, the term *black-box* is used.

When the Solaris Cluster software has "black-box" control of a virtualized entity, it knows only how to start and stop the virtualized entity, and how to probe the "black-box" to ensure it is still running. Reducing the level of integration that the Solaris Cluster software has with the virtualized entity increases the scope of the types of virtualized entities that the Solaris Cluster software can control. For example, the Solaris Cluster software provides "black-box" control for the failover guest domain and highly available (HA) container resource types. In each instance, this approach allows the virtualized entity more scope with respect to the operating system it uses, but with the trade-off that the Solaris Cluster software is less able to control the services within the virtualized entity itself. In this instance, you could view the virtualized entity as the "application" that the Solaris Cluster software is controlling. Consequently, highly available containers that use non-native operating system brands, such as the Solaris 8, Solaris 9, or Linux brands, can still be controlled by the Solaris Cluster software.

In contrast, when the Solaris Cluster software has a presence in the virtualized entity (either because it is directly installed in that virtualized entity, or because of the relationship the virtualized entity has with its parent entity), the Solaris Cluster software can offer a greater level of application control. This increased level of control is why the term *fine-grained* control was chosen. Thus, in virtualized entities such as dynamic system domains, I/O and guest domain clusters, global-cluster non-voting nodes, and zone clusters, the Solaris Cluster software, or a subset of its functionality, is directly available within the virtualized entity. This allows the Solaris Cluster software to provide the full range of application control: starting, stopping, and monitoring the application. One consequence of this "fine-grained" control is that the operating system is, by the nature of the virtualization, homogeneous across the virtualized entity and its parent entity.

Finally, the two approaches result in different failover times for the services they contain. Because the "black-box" virtualization approach migrates an entire operating system between nodes, within the virtualized entity, the time required to reboot this operating environment must be added to the time required to restart the service. This is not the case for the "fine-grained" control approach because the target virtualized container is already booted.

## Dynamic System Domains

Dynamic system domains, often shortened to just domains, have been available for more than a decade. One of the first widely deployed systems to include this feature was the Sun Enterprise 10000 server [E10KDomains], introduced in 1997. Many of Oracle's current high-end systems use this capability to enable flexible and dynamic allocation of CPU/memory boards and I/O trays, connected to the centerplane, to one or more electrically isolated domains. Current Oracle servers with this capability include

- Sun Fire Enterprise 4900 and Enterprise 6900 servers
- Sun Fire Enterprise 20K and Enterprise 25K servers
- Sun SPARC Enterprise M4000, M5000, M8000, and M9000 servers

Domains are configured through a system controller. Because domains are electrically isolated from one another, each domain is protected from any failures that might occur in other domains within the same chassis. Furthermore, because the centerplanes of these systems are designed with a point-to-point topology, bandwidth between chassis slots (for CPU/memory cards and I/O trays) is not shared, providing some guarantee of performance. This approach offers lower complexity than, for example, a hypervisor-based system that is sharing the underlying hardware between multiple guest operating systems. In such a configuration, guest operating systems share the memory and I/O channels, making it more difficult to pinpoint performance problems.

Each domain within a chassis runs a completely separate instance of the Oracle Solaris operating system that is installed manually or through a provisioning system such as the following: Sun Ops Center, Sun N1 System Manager, Sun N1 Service Provisioning System (with the OS provisioning plug-in), Solaris JumpStart software, and JumpStart Enterprise Toolkit (JET). However, in all cases, the Oracle Solaris OS interacts directly with the underlying hardware, rather than with an intermediate hypervisor.

Where a domain-capable server platform supports the Solaris 9 OS, for example, the Sun Fire Enterprise Servers (E4900, E6900, and E25K), the server provides one of the only two available options to virtualize the Solaris 9 OS. The alternative approach is to use a `solaris9`-branded, highly available (HA) container on a cluster running the Solaris 10 OS (see "Branded Zones (BrandZ)" and "HA Containers").

Because each domain contains an independent instance of the Oracle Solaris OS, the Solaris Cluster software can be used to construct distinct clusters between any two or more domains, whether the domains are in the same chassis or in separate chassis, as shown in Figure 3.1. These clusters have their own Resource Group Manager daemon to control the services contained in the resource groups.

However, this approach means that each Solaris instance must be patched independently, unlike zones in the Solaris 10 OS (see "Solaris Zones").

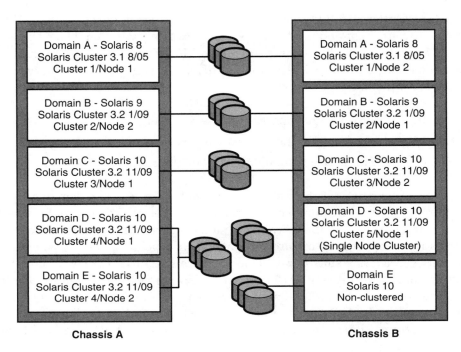

**Figure 3.1** Creating multiple distinct clusters between two chassis using dynamic system domains

If the cluster uses the Solaris 10 OS, then zones can be used to isolate services from a security, resource, and fault perspective. Additional hardware resources, such as CPU/memory boards and I/O trays, can be dynamically reconfigured into and out of the domains, with the exception of any CPU/memory boards that are holding portions of the kernel memory "cage."

## Oracle VM Server for SPARC

Sun Logical Domains or LDoms (now Oracle VM Server for SPARC) is a facility provided by Oracle's Sun servers that uses the Oracle Solaris CoolThreads technology, allowing one or more virtualized instances of the Solaris 10 OS (starting in the 11/06 release) to run on the same underlying hardware.

Oracle's Sun SPARC Enterprise and Sun Blade servers that support Logical Domains include

- Sun SPARC Enterprise T1000 and T2000 servers

- Sun SPARC Enterprise T5120 and T5220 servers
- Sun SPARC Enterprise T5140 and T5240 servers
- Sun SPARC Enterprise T5440 server
- Sun Blade T6300, T6320, and T6340 Server Modules

The Logical Domains technology differs from dynamic system domains insofar as it accesses the underlying hardware through a thin layer of software, held in firmware, known as a *hypervisor*. The physical hardware is presented to Logical Domains as a set of virtual resources. However, from a CPU and memory perspective, Logical Domains and dynamic system domains are very similar. The hypervisor serves as a software switch that controls a domain's access to the physical CPUs and memory. Additionally, the hypervisor provides the channel for the virtualized I/O between the virtual and physical devices.

With the Logical Domains version 1.2 release, virtual CPU resources and I/O can be dynamically added and removed from a domain running the Oracle Solaris OS. Memory can be reconfigured only at the next reboot of the domain. However, in contrast to a non-CPU-constrained zone, that is, one that does not have a CPU cap in place, Logical Domains can run on only the CPUs that are allocated to it.

The *Beginners Guide to LDoms: Understanding and Deploying Logical Domains* [BeginLDom] defines the different roles for domains. There are several different roles for domains, which are mainly defined by context; their usage defines them. A domain might have one or more of these roles, such as combining the functions of an I/O and a service domain.

- A *control domain* creates and manages other domains and services by communicating with the hypervisor. The control domain can also be considered as an I/O domain that runs the `ldm` daemon.
- A *service domain* provides services, such as a virtual network switch or a virtual disk service, to other domains.
- An *I/O domain* has direct ownership of and direct access to physical I/O devices, such as a PCI Express card or a network device. An I/O domain optionally shares those devices with other domains by providing services.
- A *guest domain* presents a virtual machine that subscribes to services provided by service domains. It is managed by the control domain.

The control domain runs the Logical Domain Manager software that creates and configures other domains on the system.

The Solaris Cluster software can be installed in either the I/O domains or directly into the guest domain, both of which provide "fine-grained" control of services.

Alternatively, the Solaris Cluster software can be installed in the control domain to support failover guest domains enabling a "black-box" approach to service control. Depending on the resources you have available, you can configure Logical Domains clusters with a single physical server or between multiple physical servers.

## I/O Domains

An I/O domain is a domain in which the devices on a PCI bus are directly under the control of the Solaris kernel. In an I/O domain, applications write to the underlying storage through the standard kernel sd disk device drivers, which is not the case for a guest domain.

Table 3.1 lists the architectural limit on the number of domains that can be used as a cluster node, per chassis. This limit applies even when you are considering the most minimal of cluster-node configurations, that is, using only two physical network interface cards (NICs), each of which has two tagged virtual local area networks (VLANs) configured (one for public and one for heartbeat), and one dual-port Fibre Channel host-bus adapter, which is used for both storage area network (SAN) booting and shared storage.

**Table 3.1** Maximum Number of I/O Domains That Can Be Used as Cluster Nodes per Chassis

| System | Maximum Number of I/O Domains | Number of I/O Domains for a Usable Solaris Cluster Configuration |
| --- | --- | --- |
| Sun SPARC Enterprise T1000 server | Two | One (because of limited PCI slots) |
| Sun SPARC Enterprise T2000 server | Two | Two |
| Sun SPARC Enterprise T5120 server | One | One |
| Sun SPARC Enterprise T5220 server | One | One |
| Sun SPARC Enterprise T5140 server | Two | Two |
| Sun SPARC Enterprise T5240 server | Two | Two |
| Sun SPARC Enterprise T5440 server | Four | Four |
| Sun Blade T6300 Server Module | Two | One |
| Sun Blade T6320 Server Module | One | One |
| Sun Blade T6340 Server Module | Two | Two |

As with dynamic system domains, this virtualization approach does not decrease the number of operating systems that must be managed. Each Oracle Solaris OS deployment must be provisioned and patched separately.

Although you can configure an I/O domain used as a cluster node to act as a service domain for other guest domains, it is important to recognize the unpredictable load that the guest can generate and the overall complexity involved. The latter is often a key cause of decreased availability. Furthermore, if the I/O domain fails, it not only shuts down the cluster node but also causes the dependent guest domains to appear to hang. This problem occurs because the guest domains lose access to the root (/) file system, unless you mirrored the root (/) file system through another I/O domain. The guest domain cannot become responsive again until the I/O domain becomes available.

## Guest Domains

You can create a guest domain by allocating CPUs and memory to it, and then assigning virtual I/O resources from one or more I/O domains. Because the Solaris Cluster 3.2 11/09 software does not currently support the I/O domain virtual disk failover capability, you must create your guest domain root (/) file system by mirroring virtual devices from more than one I/O domain, where possible. However, if the server has only one I/O domain, then you cannot create any resilience to I/O domain failure. If there are two I/O domains, then you can also allocate virtual NICs and LUNs for shared storage from both I/O domains. This approach enables you to create resilient IPMP groups and storage that can be mirrored to protect against an underlying path failure.

Unlike I/O domains, you can create as many guest domains as you have physical resources to support. The minimum recommended specification for a Solaris Cluster configuration (currently one CPU and 1 gigabyte of memory) places an upper limit on the number of guest domain clusters you can configure per chassis. When you configure the virtual switches to be used by the guest domains, you must ensure that the mode=sc option is used (see the following example). Setting the sc mode enables the expedited handling of cluster heartbeat packets. Apart from the mode=sc requirement, the installation of a guest domain cluster is almost identical to any standard cluster installation.

## Example 3.1  Setting sc Mode on the Logical Domains Private Switches

Use the ldm command to set the sc mode on the private switch definitions.

```
# ldm add-vswitch net-dev=nxge1 mode=sc private-vsw1 primary
# ldm add-vswitch net-dev=nxge2 mode=sc private-vsw2 primary
```

You can configure guest domain clusters both within a single CoolThreads server and between CoolThreads servers. Clearly, creating a guest domain cluster within a single CoolThreads server means that the server becomes a single point of failure for the entire cluster.

Figure 3.2 shows a two-node guest domain cluster within a single CoolThreads server.

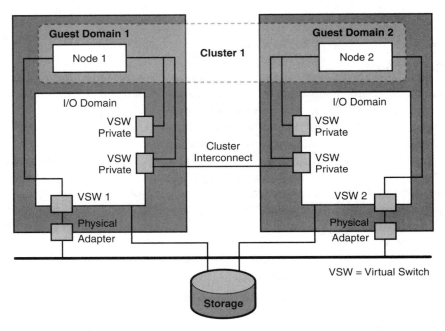

**Figure 3.2** Creating a two-node guest domain cluster within a single CoolThreads server

## Virtualized I/O

In contrast to I/O domains, the storage devices mapped into a guest domain are not always real disks. Indeed, they could be files allocated in a file system (UFS, ZFS, or VxFS) in a service domain. Thus, there is an intermediate layer of software that intercepts the guest domain's I/O requests to these virtual devices, which ultimately converts them into physical reads, writes, and `ioctl` system calls. The example in Figure 3.3 shows the path followed by an I/O from the domain through the service domain to the real underlying device.

Consequently, I/O to these devices carries additional overhead because of the virtualization, which might be in excess of 20 percent. Furthermore, the device drivers for storage must be capable of handling the SCSI reservations to the underlying mapped devices, which in turn must also be able to process the requests correctly. If they cannot do so, then you must use the software quorum feature (see the section "Software Quorum" in Chapter 2, "Oracle Solaris Cluster: Features and Architecture") and disable fencing (see the section "Storage Device Fencing Subsystem" in Chapter 2).

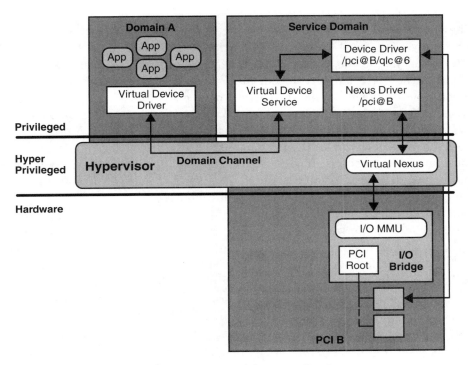

**Figure 3.3** Domain I/O virtualization

## Failover Guest Domains

As the name suggests, a *failover guest domain* is a domain that can be hosted on one of the nodes in a cluster at any one time. Therefore, the Solaris Cluster configuration that supports a failover guest domain must be constructed from clustered control domains. The devices used for the guest domain are mapped in from the appropriate I/O domains. The names used for these mappings must be the same on every node. In addition, the `failure-policy` for the guest domain must be set to `reset`.

## Example 3.2   Required Setting for the Guest Domain Failure Policy

Use the `ldm` command to set the guest domain failure policy to `reset`.

```
# ldm set-domain failure-policy=reset
```

The virtual devices mapped into the guest domains for use as their root (/) and other file systems must be placed on a global file system (see the section "The Cluster File System" in Chapter 2, "Oracle Solaris Cluster: Features and Architecture"), if warm migration is required. Otherwise, failover file systems can be used.

Where you use the global file system, you must also configure a `SUNW.HAStorage-Plus` (see the section "`SUNW.HAStoragePlus`" in Chapter 2, "Oracle Solaris Cluster: Features and Architecture") resource with the `Affinity_On` property set to `true` to ensure colocation of the primary I/O path of the global file system and the guest domain file systems. If you require the facility to migrate individual guest domains and maintain affinity with the primary I/O path, then you must configure separate global file systems for each guest domain.

The `SUNW.ldom` agent is an extension of the basic Generic Data Service (GDS) resource type (see the section "`SUNW.gds`" in Chapter 2, "Oracle Solaris Cluster: Features and Architecture"). The implementation treats the failover guest domain as a "black-box." No Solaris Cluster resource types are available within the guest domain. You must manage the control and probing of your applications manually or with your own custom scripts. If you provide your own probe scripts, you can arrange for the resource to call them through the `SUNW.ldom Plugin_probe` property. The benefit that the failover guest domain brings is protection against a hardware failure of the physical node and a software failure in the domain. Furthermore, if the guest domain fails, the fault probes for the failover guest domain resource type (`SUNW.ldom`) will attempt to either restart or fail over the guest domain for you.

As mentioned previously, you cannot combine any of the other data services with the `SUNW.ldom` agent because there is no way to specify the node construct for the resource group. Whereas for non-global zones or HA containers that you can declare a node list containing *physical_host:zone_name* entries, there is no equivalent construct for failover domains; that is, the Solaris Cluster framework does not support *physical_node:guest_domain* entries.

# Oracle Solaris Zones

The Oracle Solaris Zones (also called Oracle Solaris Containers) partitioning technology is a Solaris 10 OS virtualization feature. A Solaris 10 OS global zone is equivalent to a Solaris 9 OS instance. However, unlike the Solaris 9 OS, the Solaris 10 OS can present additional virtualized instances of Oracle Solaris OS. These are called non-global zones. Unlike other forms of virtualization, zones have very little overhead.

Zones are configured using the zonecfg command, which enables devices and file systems to be configured into a zone and establishes resource constraints, such as memory caps and processor pools. The latter is very valuable when hard CPU limits are enforced, as they might be required as part of the independent software vendor (ISV) software licensing term, that is, the maximum number of CPUs on which the software can be run. These constraints provide a mechanism by which you can configure the system so that you pay a license fee based on only the number of CPUs actually used instead of the total number of CPUs present. Furthermore, unlike dynamic system domains or Logical Domains, zones are available on any platform that runs the Solaris 10 OS.

When a system runs one or more zones (see Figure 3.4), only one Solaris kernel is active. This kernel controls the global zone. The additional virtual Solaris instances, called *non-global zones*, are represented by a set of extra Solaris processes running in the global zone, for example, zoneadmd. Thus, booting a zone is much faster than booting a full operating system, whether it is in a dynamic system domain, an I/O domain, or a guest domain. Figure 3.5 shows a two-node cluster that has an HA container configured and several non-global zones.

By default, a non-global zone has the same characteristics as the operating system in the global zone, which is running the Solaris 10 OS. These native non-global

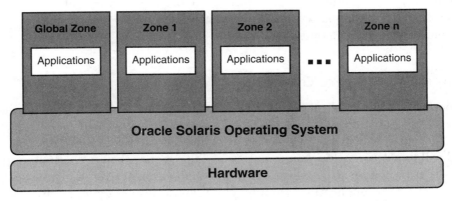

**Figure 3.4** Multiple zones running in a single Solaris instance

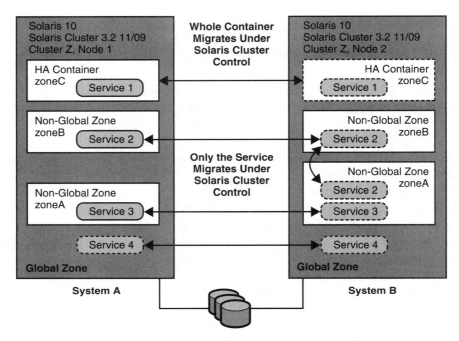

**Figure 3.5** Global-cluster non-voting nodes (zones) and HA containers participating in a Solaris cluster

zones and the global zone share their conformance to standards, runtime behavior, command sets, and performance characteristics.

The key point is that by deploying zones, you are reducing the number of Solaris instances that need to be managed. However, you do need to consider the ramifications for the patch process (see the section "Patching and Upgrading Your Cluster" in Chapter 4, "Managing Your Oracle Solaris Cluster Environment"). Another key reason to deploy zones is to provide better security and better resource management on the same OS instance.

## Minimal Performance Overhead

The performance of applications in a non-global zone is almost identical to the performance of applications in the global zone on a machine without non-global zones. This is because I/Os from processes running in a zone need to make only one additional call to a security function to authorize their request before continuing in their normal path. As a result, applications in non-global zones perform significantly better than the same applications running in an identically configured (with respect to CPU and memory resources) Logical Domain because of the additional virtual device drivers and hypervisor software layers that must be traversed in those configurations. The precise impact varies from service to service, so the only way to measure it is to conduct suitably constructed benchmarks before deployment. The same is also true of dynamic system domains when compared with guest domains.

## IP Exclusive and IP Shared Networking Options

Some services that run in a zone require exclusive access to the NIC. Dynamic Host Configuration Protocol (DHCP) is one such example. Usually, this need for exclusivity results in the parent node requiring a very large number of NICs, so the preferred zone configuration option is the IP shared networking option. With this option, you allow multiple zones to share the same NIC.

To dedicate an adapter using the exclusive IP option, the IP address is configured with the `ifconfig` command from within the zone itself, rather than using the net address properties in the `zonecfg` command (see the `zonecfg`(1M) man page) [HANet]. This option does not allow the use of a `SUNW.SharedAddress` resource because `SUNW.SharedAddress` resources run in the global zone, whereas the exclusive IP address is configured in the local zone itself. Furthermore, local zones that are configured to use exclusive IP addresses cannot access the `clprivnet0` virtual network interface (see the section "`clprivnet0` Virtual Network Interface" in Chapter 2, "Oracle Solaris Cluster: Features and Architecture"). However, you can configure `SUNW.LogicalHostname` resources in resource groups that have node lists containing zones using exclusive IP addresses.

## Oracle Solaris Zones Root Directory

The root directory of a non-global zone is a subdirectory of the global zone's root (/) file system, for example, `/zoneroot/ngz_zone_a/root`, which contains the `./usr`, `./etc`, and `./dev` subdirectories, as usual. Applications inside a zone are, in effect, running in an environment where the Solaris root (/) directory is altered to that location.

Two types of zones can be configured: sparse-root zones and whole-root zones. The difference between the two types is whether they share any of the global zone's directories. A *sparse-root zone* shares, among other things, a read-only copy of the global zone's `/usr` and `/lib` directories, whereas a *whole-root zone* contains a separate copy of all of the global zone's directories and, by implication, packages. The memory usage of the two approaches differs. Whereas the binaries in a sparse-root zone point to the same file as that in the global zone, the whole-root zone binaries do not. Consequently, the kernel cannot share the memory pages for those binaries in the latter instance. Thus, a whole-root zone has a larger memory footprint.

## Oracle Solaris Zones Patch Process

Although no difference exists between the patching mechanism of the sparse-root and whole-root zones, there is a constraint on how HA containers must be patched (see "HA Containers," and the section "Upgrading Nodes Using Oracle Solaris Zones" in Chapter 4, "Managing Your Oracle Solaris Cluster Environment"). An HA container can be treated as a resource where Solaris Cluster software does not run. As such, the Oracle Solaris OS version in that non-global zone does not have to match the Oracle Solaris OS version in the global zone. Any non-global zone containing Solaris Cluster software must have the same Oracle Solaris OS and Solaris Cluster version as the global zone. This is always true of zone clusters and non-global zones that do not fail over. Any requirement for the zone to be booted or shut down is documented in the patch README file. Patches can be applied during a rolling upgrade or a dual-partition upgrade. Zone characteristics can significantly affect these mechanisms. See the sections "Rolling Upgrade" and "Dual-Partition Upgrade" in Chapter 4, "Managing Your Oracle Solaris Cluster Environment," for more details.

## Services That Cannot Run in Oracle Solaris Zones

Zones can support most common applications, except those that require special hardware access or load kernel modules. NFS server software currently does not run in a zone. DHCP can run only in zones that use the exclusive IP networking option.

## Branded Zones (BrandZ)

It is also possible to run a different operating system inside a non-global zone. The branded zone (BrandZ) framework extends the Oracle Solaris Zones infrastructure to include the creation of brands, or alternative sets of runtime behaviors. The term *brand* can refer to a wide range of operating systems. For example, a non-global zone can emulate another version of the Oracle Solaris OS or an operating system such as Linux, or a non-global zone might augment the native-brand behaviors with additional characteristics or features. Every zone is configured with an associated brand.

Zones that provide an environment for Solaris 8 or Solaris 9 (SPARC only) or Linux (x86- or x64-based) applications can be made highly available through the Solaris Cluster HA for Solaris Containers (formerly known as Sun Cluster HA for Solaris Containers). Although neither the standard Solaris Cluster data service nor the Solaris Service Management Facility (SMF) is available within these zones, services can be made highly available using the sczsh script provided with the Solaris Cluster HA for Solaris Containers. This script allows developers to write start, stop, and probe scripts.

## HA Containers

The Sun Cluster 3.1 8/05 release was the first release of the product to ship with support for Solaris Zones. The Solaris Cluster HA for Solaris Containers treats a zone as a "black-box." The concept of a highly available (HA) container is identical to the more recent failover guest domain (see "Failover Guest Domains").

An HA container has an identical zone configured on multiple Solaris Cluster nodes, and the root (/) directory is stored on a failover file system. After the zone is installed, the failover file system can be switched between nodes under the control of the Solaris Cluster software. The start and stop methods boot and shut down the zone using the appropriate zoneadm boot and halt subcommands (see the zoneadm(1M) man page). The probe script for the agent checks that a zone is running the zsched process and that the zone reaches a suitable milestone boot point.

The Solaris Cluster HA for Solaris Containers uses a shell script (sczbt_register) and a configuration file to define and register a specific setup with the Solaris Cluster framework. When a zone fails over, the virtual instance of the Oracle Solaris OS is stopped on the first node and restarted on another. This process should not be confused with a live migration of a running operating system instance that might occur with VMware's VMotion technology. The services are unavailable during the time it takes to shut the services and the zone down, switch over the control of the required storage, and then restart the services and the zone. Depending on the nature of the services, this switchover can take from as little as a few seconds to several minutes for large databases.

The Sun Cluster 3.1 8/05 release of the Solaris Cluster software supported only standard Oracle Solaris Zones but allowed both failover and multi-master configurations. Although most of the standard Solaris Cluster data services in this release did not support zones, the Samba, WebSphere MQ, PostgreSQL, MySQL, and Tomcat agents were extended to use the sczsmf script supplied with the Solaris Containers' agent. The sczsmf script allowed these data services to integrate with the Solaris 10 Service Management Facility (SMF) inside the zone. This integration restarted the service when the zone was restarted or when it failed and checked the service's health through a probe script so that the service could be restarted if it was considered unhealthy.

Because an HA container is treated as a "black-box," you can also create the HA container with a non-native (non–Solaris 10) brand: Solaris 8 OS (solaris8), Solaris 9 OS (solaris9), or Linux (lx). Where you use a non-native brand, you forgo the standard Solaris Cluster agent services. However, doing so still leaves you free to construct your own SMF services or /etc/rc scripts to start or stop your services. Some of the Solaris Cluster agents, for example, Tomcat, MySQL, PostgreSQL, Service Provisioning System (SPS), Samba, and WebSphere MQ, already come with an SMF service that can be registered within the zone. These agents use the HA container SMF integration feature to enable some level of basic process-monitoring capabilities. Finally, the HA container agent allows HA containers to be configured to use the ip-type=exclusive option, as opposed to the ip-type=shared option. Note that the Solaris Cluster software does not monitor the state of IPMP groups configured within zones that have the ip-type=exclusive option set.

HA containers have some drawbacks with respect to availability during the patch process. When patches are applied to a system, all configured containers must be available on that node for patching. This requirement means that any HA containers must be failed over to the node to be patched, and the service must be shut down prior to beginning the patch process. Because the service is wholly contained within this single HA container, there is no other host for the service to run on. Thus, the service is unavailable for the entire duration of the patch process. Furthermore, the whole process must be repeated when the other node is patched. However, this service interruption can be mitigated to some extent by detaching the zone from the configuration by using the zoneadm -z zone-name detach command. For this reason, use the global-cluster non-voting node or zone-cluster approach, documented next, whenever possible. HA containers reside on shared storage. Thus, you cannot use the rolling upgrade or dual-partition upgrade to patch or update the software in an HA container.

## Global-Cluster Non-Voting Node

The Solaris Cluster software provides comprehensive support for zones, and most of the data services are container-aware, with the obvious exception of NFS. Zone names can appear in resource group node lists in a similar fashion to nodes themselves. Previously, where a service might have been defined with a node list equal to nodeA, nodeB, in the global cluster, the node list can now have a mix of full nodes and zones, for example, nodeA, nodeB:zoneA or nodeA:zoneA, nodeB:zoneA, and so on. Starting in the Solaris Cluster 3.2 release, it is possible to create a resource group that uses zones and to make a service highly available within the zones. The following example demonstrates how a failover Oracle service, as opposed to an Oracle Real Application Clusters (Oracle RAC) service, might be configured between two zones named zonex and zoney on physical cluster nodes nodea and nodeb, respectively, using the command-line interface (CLI). This configuration can also be performed using the Solaris Cluster Data Services Configuration wizard, which can guide you through the configuration of several data services, including Oracle, SAP, and NFS.

## Example 3.3  Configuring a Highly Available Oracle Service That Uses Global-Cluster Non-Voting Nodes

Register the resource types as needed.

```
# clresourcetype register -N SUNW.oracle_server
# clresourcetype register -N SUNW.oracle_listener
# clresourcetype register -N SUNW.HAStoragePlus
```

Create the resource group, such that the Oracle server runs in zonex of nodea or zoney of nodeb.

```
# clresourcegroup create -n nodea:zonex,nodeb:zoney oracle-rg
```

Add the logical hostname resource to the Oracle resource group.

```
# clreslogicalhostname create -g oracle-rg oracle-lh
```

Add a resource of type SUNW.HAStoragePlus to the resource group.

Here, the Oracle data is located under /failover/oracle.

```
# clresource create -g oracle-rg -t SUNW.HAStoragePlus \
      -p FileSystemMountPoints=/oracle:/failover/oracle \
      -p AffinityOn=TRUE oracle-data-store-rs
```

Add the Oracle server resource to the resource group.

```
# ORACLE_HOME=/oracle/oracle/product/10.2.0/db_1 export ORACLE_HOME
# clresource create -g oracle-rg -t SUNW.oracle_server \
      -p ORACLE_HOME=${ORACLE_HOME} \
      -p Alert_log_file=${ORACLE_HOME}/admin/acme/bdump/alert_acme.log \
      -p ORACLE_SID=acme -p Connect_string=hamon/H4M0nPwd \
      -p Resource_dependencies=oracle-data-store-rs oracle-svr-rs

# clresource create -g oracle-rg \
      -t SUNW.oracle_listener -p ORACLE_HOME=${ORACLE_HOME} \
      -p Resource_dependencies=oracle-data-store-rs \
      -p LISTENER_NAME=LISTENER_acme oracle-lsnr-rs
```

For comparison, an equivalent Oracle configuration in the global zone differs in only two of these steps, the resource group and the HAStoragePlus creation. These differences are shown in the following:

```
# clresourcegroup create -n nodea,nodeb oracle-rg
# clresource create -g oracle-rg -t SUNW.HAStoragePlus \
      -p FileSystemMountPoints=/failover/oracle \
      -p AffinityOn=TRUE oracle-data-store-rs
```

## Zone Clusters

Perhaps the most significant and valuable virtualization capability in the Solaris Cluster software is the zone clusters feature. A *zone cluster* is a virtual cluster in which a zone is configured as a virtual node. The zone cluster supports the consolidation of multiple applications from one or more physical clusters onto a single cluster. This section describes what a zone cluster is and how it differs from the global cluster that exists when you install and configure the Solaris Cluster software on a set of cluster nodes (see "Defining a Cluster Node").

A zone-cluster node requires that the global zone on the same Solaris host be booted in cluster mode in order for the zone-cluster node to be operational. All zone-cluster nodes must be on Solaris hosts belonging to the same global cluster. The zone-cluster nodes can be a subset of Solaris hosts for that same global cluster. Whereas a zone cluster depends on a global cluster, a global cluster does not depend on any zone cluster.

Figure 3.6 shows a four-node hardware configuration supported by the Solaris Cluster product, and Figure 3.7 shows multiple clusters running on that same four-node hardware configuration. An important point is that a cluster node is a

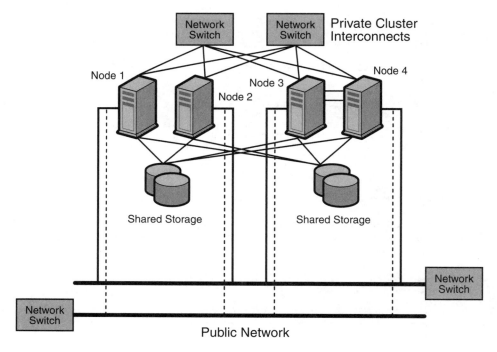

**Figure 3.6** A four-node cluster configuration

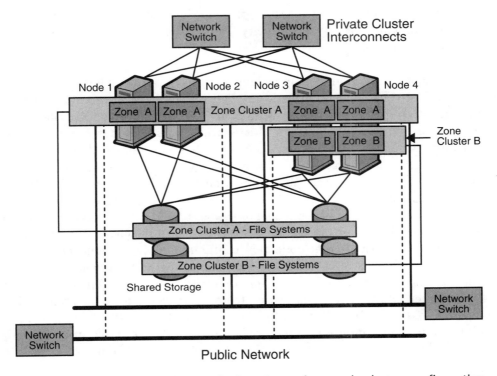

**Figure 3.7** Multiple zone clusters deployed on a four-node cluster configuration

Solaris Cluster software construct that does not necessarily have a one-to-one relationship to hardware. When the Solaris Cluster software runs the Solaris 9 OS, the Solaris host and the cluster node are the same thing. Also, except for hardware domains, the cluster node is also the physical machine. This traditional cluster is perhaps simpler to understand but is also less flexible.

A zone cluster can be viewed as a virtual cluster. The zone cluster appears to a cluster application as a traditional cluster with its own cluster membership.

## Security Isolation

A zone cluster is the security container for both failover and scalable applications. The zones in a zone cluster are ensured to have the same configuration information in two areas:

- Zones in the zone cluster provide the same kind of environment. The zone-cluster software enforces this consistency.

- Zones in the zone cluster must have the same security-related parameters in order to provide cluster-wide security. The zone-cluster software strictly enforces this consistency as well.

Thus, no instance of a failover or scalable application can run outside the encapsulating cluster-wide zone. In other words, all instances of a scalable application always run within a single cluster-wide zone, and a failover application cannot switch over or fail over outside of the cluster-wide zone. This is in contrast to scalable or failover applications that have a combination of cluster node names (in the global zone) and global-cluster non-voting node (zone) names in their resource group nodelist property. Here the application is clearly not confined to the global-cluster non-voting nodes.

A zone cluster follows the zone model of security. The only resources that can be viewed or affected from within a zone cluster are those resources that the system administrator from the global zone has configured into the zone cluster. It is impossible to add resources that have not been assigned to a zone cluster from within the zone cluster. Similarly, it is impossible to change zone-cluster configuration parameters from within the zone cluster. For example, it is impossible to change the share of CPUs allocated to a zone cluster from within the zone cluster. Similarly, you cannot create a SUNW.LogicalHostname resource in a zone cluster, unless the zone cluster has been assigned the required IP address.

## Application Fault Isolation

Operating systems provide some level of application fault isolation. For example, the panic of one application instance does not cause failures in all other applications. However, some actions that an application can take will cause failures of other applications. For example, an application such as Oracle RAC can order the node to reboot, which obviously affects all applications on that node.

The Oracle Solaris Zones feature set reduces the possibility that the misbehavior of one application will negatively affect other applications. Continuing with the same example, the system treats a reboot command issued within a zone as a zone reboot command, which ensures that the reboot command does not affect applications outside of that zone.

Oracle Solaris Zones disallows many operations that can negatively impact other applications outside of that zone. The zone cluster supports this principle.

## Resource Management

The Oracle Solaris OS has included a resource management subsystem for many years. The administrator can use the Solaris Resource Manager software to dedicate resources for some purpose or to assign a particular share of a resource type to a project or application. The Solaris Resource Manager software has more recently added a level of granularity for managing resources at the zone level. The system administrator from the global zone can manage the resource usage of the zone, and the operating system ensures that these controls cannot be changed from within the zone. This is particularly important for consolidating Solaris Cluster applications on a single system. The zone cluster uses this zone feature.

## Dedicated Cluster Model

A zone appears to a non-cluster application as a machine that is dedicated to the use of the application within that zone. The zone cluster appears to cluster applications as a cluster dedicated to the use of cluster applications within that zone cluster. Similarly, when a user logs in to the zone cluster, the user regards the zone cluster as a traditional cluster.

The zone cluster is a simplified cluster. Using a minimalist approach, only the components needed to directly support cluster applications are present, including the following:

- File systems
- Storage devices
- Networks
- Cluster membership

Cluster components that are not needed by cluster applications, such as quorum devices and heartbeats, are not present. Zone clusters do not mimic all aspects of the physical system. For example, zone clusters do not support zones nested within the zones of the zone cluster.

## Single Point of Administration

The administrator can administer a zone cluster from any machine in the cluster. The administrator creates the entire zone cluster with a single command, although multiple parameters are used, as with a single zone creation using the Solaris `zoneadm` command. This principle also applies to other administrative actions. The administrator can set the resource controls, such as the number of CPUs, on each node of the zone cluster with a single command. The administration of the zone cluster must be performed from the global zone. The administration of data services can be done from inside the zone cluster or from the global zone.

## Administrative Workload Reduction

Zone clusters are less complex than global clusters. A zone cluster has only cluster applications and the resources directly used by those cluster applications. For example, no quorum devices are required in a zone cluster (see "Zone-Cluster Membership"). Usually, the administrator configures the file system into the zone cluster, but not the underlying storage device.

A global cluster and all of the zone clusters within that Solaris Cluster share the same operating system. Operating system updates and patches need to be applied only once for both the global cluster and all of its zone clusters. When zone clusters can be substituted for global clusters, the result is a reduction in administrative work.

## Assigning Storage Resources

You can assign several different types of storage resources to a zone cluster. These storage resources include disk devices such as the following:

- Standard Solaris disk devices using controller, target, and disk-naming patterns, for example, `/dev/rdsk/c1t3d0s*`
- Solaris Cluster DID devices, for example, `/dev/did/rdsk/d5s*`
- Multi-owner Solaris Volume Manager devices, for example, `/dev/md/oraset/rdsk/d100`

However, you cannot assign non-multi-owner Solaris Volume Manager devices or global devices (see the section "Global Devices" in Chapter 2, "Oracle Solaris Cluster: Features and Architecture") to a zone cluster. The Device Configuration Service runs only in the global zone and not in the zone cluster.

You can also allocate file system resources, including the following:

- Shared QFS file systems
- Highly available local (failover) file systems based on UFS, VxFS, QFS, or ZFS (These file systems use a `SUNW.HAStoragePlus` resource to manage their switchover between global-cluster non-voting nodes; see the section "`SUNW.HAStoragePlus`" in Chapter 2, "Oracle Solaris Cluster: Features and Architecture.")

## Zone-Cluster Architecture

This section describes the zone-cluster architecture at a high level. Consult Chapter 2, "Oracle Solaris Cluster: Features and Architecture," for background information about the concepts described here.

## Virtual Node

A zone cluster consists of a set of zones in which each zone represents a virtual node. Each zone in a zone cluster is configured on a separate machine. As such, the maximum number of virtual nodes in a zone cluster is limited to the number of machines in the global cluster. The Oracle Solaris OS supports the modification and enhancement of a zone through use of the BrandZ framework. The zone-cluster design introduces a new brand of zone, called the *cluster brand*. The cluster brand is based on the original native brand type but adds enhancements for clustering. The BrandZ framework provides numerous hooks where other software can take action that is appropriate for each brand. For example, one hook is for software to be called during the zone boot, and zone clusters take advantage of this hook to notify the Solaris Cluster software about the boot of the virtual node.

> **Note**
>
> Because zone clusters use the BrandZ framework, at a minimum the Solaris 10 5/08 OS is required.

You do not need to be concerned about the brand type of zone. From your viewpoint and to the applications, the cluster brand zone appears and acts just like a native zone with cluster support enabled.

## Zone-Cluster Membership

Each zone cluster has its own membership. The membership format for a zone cluster is identical to that of a cluster running the Solaris 9 OS without zones. Applications running in a zone cluster receive the same kind of membership information as when they are running in the global zone. Thus, applications run identically in the zone cluster and global zone with respect to membership.

Naturally, a zone in a zone cluster can become operational only after the global zone on the hosting machine becomes operational. A zone in a zone cluster will not start clustering services when the global zone is not booted in cluster mode. A zone in a zone cluster can be configured to automatically boot after the machine boots, or the administrator can manually control when the zone boots. A zone in a zone cluster can fail, or an administrator can manually halt or reboot a zone. All of these events result in the zone cluster automatically updating its membership.

## Membership Monitoring

The Solaris 10 OS maintains membership information for zone clusters. Each machine hosts a component, called the Zone Cluster Membership Monitor

(ZCMM), that monitors the status of all cluster brand zones on that machine. The ZCMM knows which zones belong to which zone clusters.

Consider the instance where the global-cluster node membership changes because a node either joins or departs the cluster. The node reconfiguration process in the global zone determines the new cluster membership. After completing the machine reconfiguration process, the system selects a new ZCMM leader. If the previous ZCMM leader is still present, no change occurs. Otherwise, the system arbitrarily picks one ZCMM as the leader. The ZCMM leader collects zone-cluster virtual node information from the ZCMMs on each node, compiles the membership information, and then distributes it to all ZCMMs.

When a zone-cluster virtual node status changes, the ZCMM on that machine forwards that information to the ZCMM leader, which triggers a zone-cluster reconfiguration. The ZCMM leader then distributes the new membership information for that zone cluster to the ZCMM on each machine.

This membership-monitoring process quickly updates and delivers the zone-cluster membership information. In addition, zone-cluster membership changes do not trigger a global cluster reconfiguration. Those with cluster experience have probably noted that it takes time for global-cluster recovery to complete after a global-cluster reconfiguration. After a global-cluster node reconfiguration, the zone-cluster membership process begins and completes long before the global-cluster recovery process completes. This prevents significant delays in updating zone-cluster membership.

### Security

Zone-cluster security follows the security design used in the Oracle Solaris Zones feature. The zone is a security container. The operating system checks all requests to access resources, such as file systems, devices, and networks, to determine whether such access has been granted to that non-global zone. When permission has not been granted, the operating system denies access. Applications can send requests to software through a limited number of communication channels, such as system calls and doors. The operating system tags each communication with information identifying the zone from which the request originated. Software in the kernel or the global zone is considered to be trusted and is responsible for checking the access permissions based on the originating zone and denying any unauthorized access. Applications in a non-global zone cannot tamper with software in the kernel or in the global zone. The overall result is that the system restricts application access to authorized resources only.

Figure 3.8 shows the security architecture for zone clusters.

The zone components of a zone cluster are equivalent from a security perspective. For example, privilege-related properties such as `zonename` and `zonepath` are the same for all zone components in a zone cluster.

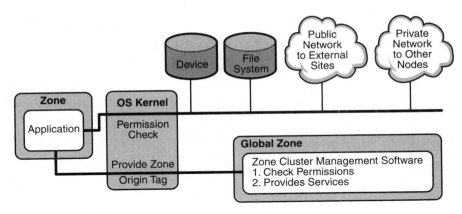

**Figure 3.8** Zone-cluster security architecture

## File Systems

Zone clusters support access to several types of file systems, including local, highly available, cluster, and NFS file systems. The subsequent subsections describe how these file systems are supported in zone clusters.

**Local File Systems**   A virtual node in a zone cluster can have access to a file system that is available only to that virtual node. Such a file system is called a *local file system*. The rules for zone-cluster support of local file systems are identical to those of a native zone. A zone cluster relies on the basic zone file system support for this feature. Local file system support for zone clusters includes ZFS, UFS, VxFS, and QFS.

**Highly Available File Systems**   A *highly available file system* is accessible to multiple virtual nodes but is mounted on only one virtual node at a time. The cluster will mount the highly available file system in another virtual node in response to a virtual node failure or to the manual switchover command from an administrator. Once mounted, a highly available file system works exactly like a local file system.

Zone clusters directly mount highly available file systems in a virtual node when the file system is mounted with read and write privileges. Only one zone cluster can access a particular highly available file system with read and write privileges at any given time. Zone clusters can mount highly available file systems for a virtual node using a loopback mount when it is mounted with read-only privileges. Multiple zone clusters can share a highly available file system with read-only privileges. Zone clusters support highly available file systems using the `SUNW.HAStoragePlus` subsystem.

Zone clusters record information about highly available file systems in the Cluster Configuration Repository (CCR). Zone clusters validate access permissions both when the administrator specifies an application dependency on a highly available file system and when the zone cluster actually mounts the file system.

Highly available file system support for zone clusters includes ZFS, UFS, VxFS, and QFS.

**Cluster File Systems**    A *cluster file system* can be mounted on all virtual nodes in a zone cluster at the same time. Cluster file systems are also sometimes called *global file systems*. Zone clusters directly mount cluster file systems on the virtual node. Only one zone cluster can access a particular cluster file system.

The zone cluster mounts the cluster file system at the same mount point for all virtual nodes in the zone cluster. Any mounted cluster file system is mounted on all virtual nodes in the zone cluster. The failure of one virtual node does not stop access to the cluster file system from other virtual nodes. The zone cluster ensures that any joining virtual node will automatically have the same cluster file systems mounted on the same mount points as the other virtual nodes in the zone cluster.

Zone clusters record information about cluster file systems in the CCR. Zone clusters validate access permissions both when the administrator specifies an application dependency on a cluster file system and when the zone cluster actually mounts the file system.

Zone clusters support a shared QFS file system as a cluster file system. The `SUNW.ScalMountPoint` resource type manages QFS shared file systems.

**NFS File Systems**    Each zone must directly mount the NFS file system within the zone. The zone cluster relies on the basic zone support for NFS file systems. As such, the support is identical. An NFS file system cannot be imported into one zone, such as the global zone, and then exported to another zone using loopback mounts.

## Storage Devices

Zone clusters support direct access to storage devices, including disks and RAID devices.

### Disks and RAID Devices

Zone clusters support direct access to both regular disks and RAID devices. Zone clusters also support access to volume manager devices as if they were a disk. Zone clusters allow only one zone cluster to have direct access to any particular disk or RAID device. When data on a disk or RAID device is accessed through a file system, the administrator should not grant direct access to the disk or RAID device.

When an application has direct access to a disk or RAID device, the application can issue `ioctl` system calls. A malicious application can issue a bad `ioctl` system call and cause a driver malfunction, which can cause operating system failure. Though a reliability concern, this possibility does not present a security risk. The use of file systems eliminates this reliability concern. However, some users require direct access and understand the risk. Therefore, zone clusters support this feature.

Zone clusters support the fencing of disks and RAID devices. The fencing feature ensures that a node that has left the cluster cannot continue to modify data on shared storage. This very important data integrity feature has been supported by the Solaris Cluster software for a long time. The zone-cluster feature supports the fencing of the nodes in the zone cluster and thus provides data integrity.

When a virtual node fails on a machine but the global zone remains operational, the operating system does not mark the zone as shut down until all I/O has terminated. Zone clusters do not mark a virtual node as shut down until the operating system has marked the zone as shut down. Thus, after the virtual node is shut down, the Solaris Cluster software can guarantee that no more I/O will come from the departed virtual node. In all instances, the Solaris Cluster software ensures that no I/O will come from a departed node.

The Solaris Cluster software supports the fencing of disks and RAID devices in all of the following instances:

- When access is directly to the device
- When access is through a volume manager
- When access is through a file system

Zone clusters also support access to volume manager devices. Zone clusters rely upon the basic zone support for volume manager devices. Both Solaris Volume Manager and Veritas Volume Manager administration must be performed from the global zone. Zone clusters support automatic volume manager reconfiguration from the global zone following zone-cluster membership changes.

> **Note**
>
> Solaris Volume Manager for Sun Cluster devices work in zone clusters, although other kinds of Solaris Volume Manager devices and Veritas Volume Manager devices do not. However, a file system mounted on a volume in the global zone can be configured to work in a zone cluster even when the volume cannot.

## Networks

Zone clusters support network communications over both public and private networks. *Public networks* refer to communications outside the cluster. *Private networks* refer to communications between cluster nodes.

### Private Interconnect

From the application perspective, private interconnect support in the zone cluster is identical to private interconnect support in the global zone. The system stripes traffic across all available paths using the `clprivnet` driver and guarantees data delivery without duplicates, as long as at least one path remains operational. The Solaris Cluster software supports up to six private interconnects on cluster configurations. The cluster transparently recovers from the failure of any of the private interconnects, until none are left.

Zone clusters automate the private interconnect setup. The zone cluster automatically selects a netmask and the IP addresses for the zone-cluster virtual nodes from a pool of private network netmasks and IP addresses that had been established when the global cluster was configured. The zone cluster automatically discovers the correct NICs based on the private interconnect configuration of the global cluster.

The zone cluster uses the same naming conventions that the global cluster uses. Each zone cluster has a separate namespace for cluster private network names. When a lookup occurs, the namespace for the zone cluster of the requester is used when the requester comes from a zone cluster. Otherwise, the namespace for the global zone is used. The zone cluster uses the same physical private interconnect as the global cluster. However, the zone cluster uses a unique netmask and unique IP addresses in order to separate the traffic on the zone cluster, thus providing security isolation.

### Public Network

The zone cluster, like an individual zone, communicates to public networks using an IP address across a NIC. The system administrator in the global zone grants privileges for that combination of IP address and NIC to that zone cluster through the `clzonecluster` command. The system administrator specifies only one NIC in an IP network multipathing (IPMP) group, and the system grants privileges for using that IP address with any NIC in that IPMP group. For security reasons, these networking privileges cannot be changed from within the zone cluster.

The `SUNW.LogicalHostname` resource is an IP address that is active on only one virtual node at a time. The administrator can switch over the `SUNW.LogicalHostname` resource from one virtual node to another virtual node. The system automatically configures the SUNW.LogicalHostname resource on the node where the application uses that resource. If a virtual node fails, the system automatically moves the SUNW.LogicalHostname resource along, with the dependent application, to a surviving node. The zone cluster validates the permissions of the SUNW.LogicalHostname resource when it is created and when activating a SUNW.LogicalHostname resource on a node. Any SUNW.LogicalHostname resource always operates within one zone cluster. The SUNW.SharedAddress resource is an IP address that appears to be active for the entire cluster. However, the IP address is actually hosted on only one machine, and the cluster distributes incoming traffic across the cluster based on the selected load-balancing policy. The system automatically changes the node hosting the IP address for the SUNW.SharedAddress resource if a node failure occurs. The zone cluster validates the permissions of the SUNW.SharedAddress resource when it is created and when activating a SUNW.SharedAddress resource on a node. A SUNW.SharedAddress resource operates strictly within one zone cluster.

Some cluster applications issue ifconfig commands to administer the IP addresses used by that cluster application. The zone cluster supports the following ifconfig commands:

- The ifconfig -a command lists logical interfaces that belong to the zone cluster, physical NICs that were explicitly configured to support an IP address authorized for the zone cluster, NICs that belong to an IPMP group with at least one NIC explicitly configured to support an authorized IP address, and clprivnet interfaces.

- The ifconfig addif command adds a logical interface where the IP address is authorized for the zone cluster, and the NIC has been explicitly configured to support this IP address or the NIC belongs to an IPMP group where the NIC has been explicitly configured to support this IP address.

- The ifconfig [up | down | plumb | removeif] commands perform the specified action on the logical interface. This logical interface must already belong to the zone cluster.

The ifconfig command has extensive subcommands and options. Zone clusters do not allow any other ifconfig subcommands and most ifconfig options. The goal was to enable commands needed by cluster applications, while at the same time disallowing commands that would permit someone in a zone environment to affect other zones.

Each zone cluster typically requires access to two NICs to form one IPMP group for public network communications and two NICs for the private interconnect. If each zone cluster required dedicated physical NICs for these connections, the number of physical NICs required would grow as fast as new zone clusters were deployed. However, because zone clusters use the IP shared networking option (`ip-type=shared`), physical NICs can be shared among zone clusters. This is done in a safe manner such that different zone clusters cannot view the traffic from other zone clusters. The other option for network access from a local zone is the IP exclusive option (`ip-type=exclusive`). This approach requires a dedicated NIC for each connection.

> **Note**
>
> Zone clusters do not support the IP exclusive option (`ip-type=exclusive`).

# 4

# Managing Your Oracle Solaris Cluster Environment

This chapter covers many important aspects of an Oracle Solaris Cluster system's lifecycle. It begins by outlining some of the planning you need to do prior to installing the Oracle Solaris operating system on a cluster node. Next comes information about how to secure your newly installed system against attack. The options for installing the Solaris Cluster software are then covered, followed by information about the day-to-day tasks involved in managing and monitoring the cluster. The chapter concludes by showing how to add support for new applications for which there is no third-party agent from Oracle or the application vendor.

## Installing the Oracle Solaris OS on a Cluster Node

You can install the Oracle Solaris OS in these ways:

- Interactively using the `installer` program
- With Solaris JumpStart to automate the process
- With public domain or third-party automation tools such as JumpStart Enterprise Toolkit [JetWiki]

If you choose an automated option, then you can perform the installation using collections of Solaris packages or a Solaris Flash archive file that is created using the `flarcreate` command from a previous template installation (see the `flarcreate`(1M) man page) [FlarInstall].

> **Note**
>
> Although it is technically feasible to install a cluster node from a Flash archive that already includes preconfigured Solaris Cluster software, Oracle does not support doing so. You can, however, use an archive with the unconfigured Solaris Cluster packages added.

If your root disk is not already protected by some form of hardware RAID, you should mirror it to protect your node against disk failure. You can protect your root disk using the bundled Solaris Volume Manager software or with the Oracle Solaris ZFS file system. ZFS is available only when you use the Solaris 10 OS. If you have a software license for Veritas Volume Manager, you can also use that to protect your root disk.

Solaris Live Upgrade eases the process of upgrading your systems. Solaris Live Upgrade is available in all Solaris releases beginning with the Solaris 8 OS. However, the combination of the Solaris 10 OS, ZFS, and Solaris Live Upgrade provides the simplest and most flexible upgrade option for your systems.

When choosing hostnames for your cluster nodes, you must ensure that they comply with RFC 1123 [RFC1123]. If you intend to install Solaris Cluster Geographic Edition, you must not use an "_" (underscore) in the hostnames. Other applications might place additional constraints on the hostnames. Changing a hostname after a cluster has been installed is a complex process and should be avoided, if possible.

Although these sections on installing the Solaris Cluster software cover many important points, they do not provide all the steps you need to follow. Therefore, you must consult the latest versions of the Oracle Solaris OS [S10InstallGuide] and the Solaris Cluster software [SCInstallGuide] installation guides.

## Root Disk Partition Requirement for the Solaris Cluster Software

You can use either UFS or ZFS as the root (/) file system for a Solaris Cluster node. The way you partition your root disks depends on which file system you choose and whether you also use Solaris Volume Manager.

After installation of the Solaris Cluster software, each node has a 512-megabyte `/global/.devices/node@X` file system that is mounted globally (the X represents the node number). To achieve this configuration, you can allow the `scinstall` program to create a `lofi`-based file system for you that works for both UFS and ZFS root (/) file systems. Alternatively, if you use UFS for the root (/) file system, you can create and mount a 512-megabyte file system on `/globaldevices` and allow the `scinstall` program to reuse it for the `/global/.devices/node@X` file system.

If you intend to use Solaris Volume Manager, then you must create the main state replica databases. These databases also require separate disk partitions, which should be 32 megabytes in size. This partition is usually placed on slice 7 of the root disk. This can pose a problem if you are using ZFS for the root disk because the standard Solaris installation uses the entire disk for the root zpool, unless you pre-partition your disk before the installation process begins. You can achieve a root disk layout where slice 7 is 32 megabytes in size, and use a ZFS root (/) file system, if you install your system using JumpStart Enterprise Toolkit (JET). However, you must not use ZFS volumes (zvols) to store the Solaris Volume Manager state replica databases, as this configuration is not supported.

Because Solaris Volume Manager relies on a state replica majority (see the section "Solaris Volume Manager's State Replica Majority" in Chapter 1, "Oracle Solaris Cluster: Overview") to maintain data integrity if a disk failure occurs, you should assign slices from three separate, nonshared disks. If you do not have three separate slices available, you can place all of the replicas on a single disk as shown in the following example.

### Example 4.1   Creating the Solaris Volume Manager Root State Replica Databases

Use the `metadb` command to create the Solaris Volume Manager root state replica databases.

```
# metadb -afc 3 c1t0d0s7
# metadb
        flags           first blk       block count
    a m  pc luo         16              8192            /dev/dsk/c1t0d0s7
    a    pc luo         8208            8192            /dev/dsk/c1t0d0s7
    a    pc luo         16400           8192            /dev/dsk/c1t0d0s7
```

If you use Veritas Volume Manager, you ideally use it only for shared disk management, and you use either Solaris Volume Manager or the Oracle Solaris ZFS file system to mirror your root disks.

## Planning for Upgrades

After you have installed your cluster, you must maintain it through its lifecycle. Doing so inevitably requires that you install both Solaris and cluster patches. You might also perform more major changes such as upgrading to a new Solaris Cluster release. To minimize any disruption, you must plan ahead.

"Patching and Upgrading Your Cluster" describes in more detail the options for ongoing cluster maintenance. If you choose ZFS for your root disk, then the upgrade procedure is fairly straightforward because Solaris Live Upgrade can create an alternate boot environment on the existing root zpool. However, if you choose UFS, then you must have the same number of slices available as your existing root disk has, which usually means using a separate disk. However, if you have only a root partition, you can plan for future upgrades by setting aside a separate partition of the same size on the root disk.

## Securing Your Solaris Operating System

The security of your Solaris Cluster system must be foremost in your mind. Without security measures in place, your system could be vulnerable to denial-of-service attacks or have its data stolen, compromised, or deleted. Any of these threats could lead to your service being unavailable. Therefore, you must put barriers in place to prevent such threats.

Although several methods for auditing security violations are available, this section focuses on how to reduce the number of targets that an unauthorized user can attack. Even when your cluster is in a physically secure location, you can still take the additional measures of operating system minimization and hardening.

> **Note**
>
> The Solaris Cluster software does not yet support Solaris 10 Trusted Extensions.

### Operating Environment Minimization

With operating system minimization, you install the fewest number of Solaris packages that are required to operate your cluster and the services it supports. The Solaris installation process allows you to choose which software groups you install. These groups are shown in Figure 4.1. Furthermore, you can customize the installation to the level of individual packages.

Clearly, choosing the software group at the center of the diagram means installing the fewest packages and thus presents the smallest "attack profile" to potential intruders. However, this installation is insufficient for the Solaris Cluster 3.2 1/09 software, which requires at least the End User Solaris Software Group (SUNWCuser) [SCInstallGuide].

One problem you face when trying to minimize your Oracle Solaris OS is that of ongoing maintenance, particularly with new or changing application require-

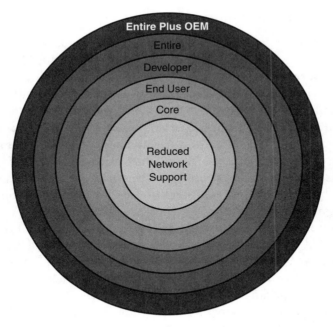

**Figure 4.1** Solaris software groups for installation

ments. Though your initial system might well be served by just the `SUNWCuser` package group, you could find that a new service requires some additional packages. Not only does this mean that you need to install the missing packages, but you might also have to reapply certain patches that would have been applied to these packages had they been installed in the first place. This also assumes that the Solaris packages on which your applications are dependent are clearly documented.

For these reasons, you must take a pragmatic approach to minimization. If your systems are unlikely to change over time, and testing has confirmed that the `SUNWCuser` group is sufficient for your needs, then installing that group should pose no problems. Conversely, if the services hosted on your cluster are likely to change, then installing the Entire package group will better serve your needs.

Regardless of your starting point, any subsequent change to the Solaris package installation list must be performed under a strong change management control process. Such a process would require thorough testing of your services in the new environment and verifying that they can still switch over successfully. Because such testing is disruptive, any preparatory work must be performed in a test environment before final testing during a planned maintenance period.

## Operating System Hardening

In contrast to operating system minimization, which reduces the number of packages installed on the system, operating system hardening disables or modifies the configuration of services that are installed on the system. An example is the disabling of the `rlogin`, `rsh`, and `rcp` commands in preference to their secure counterparts, `ssh` and `scp`.

As with Oracle Solaris OS minimization, there is clearly an almost unlimited scope for OS hardening. Unfortunately, not all changes are necessarily compatible with running the Solaris Cluster software. Furthermore, if you have made several custom changes to your system, it might prove tricky for Oracle's support services to determine whether any fault that might arise has a root cause in your hardening choices or in the Solaris Cluster software itself. Consequently, they might request that you reverse your hardening effort in order to facilitate their diagnosis. Doing so could be complicated if you do not have a well-documented change control process or an automated system for applying your hardening rules.

Fortunately, Sun has developed a supported system to help you harden your systems effectively. The package is known as the Solaris Security Toolkit (formally known as the JumpStart Architecture and Security Scripts, or JASS) [SSTAdmin-Guide]. This allows you to harden your Oracle Solaris OS in a supported and reversible manner, regardless of whether you are using the Solaris 9 OS or the Solaris 10 OS.

In addition, in the Solaris 10 OS 11/06 release comes the Secure by Default configuration [SBDBlog]. This configuration does not make the Solaris Security Toolkit obsolete, but it does subsume many of the settings that the toolkit previously changed as part of the hardening process. The latest version of the toolkit still provides fine-grained control of your hardening process and performs many other security-related tasks.

With Secure by Default configuration, you need to relax some of these settings in the Solaris 10 OS prior to installing the Solaris Cluster software. The commands you need to execute are provided in the following example [ThorstenBlog].

---

### Example 4.2  Reversing Some of the Solaris 10 Secure by Default Settings for a Solaris Cluster Installation

Ensure that the `local_only` property of `rpcbind` is set to `false`.

```
# svcprop network/rpc/bind:default | grep local_only
```

If `local_only` is not set to `false`, run

```
# svccfg
svc:> select network/rpc/bind
svc:/network/rpc/bind> setprop config/local_only=false
svc:/network/rpc/bind> quit
# svcadm refresh network/rpc/bind:default
```

This value is needed for cluster communication between nodes.

Ensure that the `tcp_listen` property of `webconsole` is set to `true`.

```
# svcprop /system/webconsole:console | grep tcp_listen
```

```
If tcp_listen is not true, run
```

```
# svccfg
svc:> select system/webconsole
svc:/system/webconsole> setprop options/tcp_listen=true
svc:/system/webconsole> quit
# svcadm refresh svc:/system/webconsole:console
# /usr/sbin/smcwebserver restart
```

This value is needed for Solaris Cluster Manager communication.

To verify that the port is listening to `*.6789`, run

```
# netstat -an | grep 6789
```

## Securing Network Communications

To secure your cluster on the network, start from the position of denying access to everything. Then proceed to allow access to ports that are specifically required by your applications and ports that are required by your management and administration procedures.

To secure network communications, you can use external firewalls. Alternatively, if you are using the Solaris 10 OS, you can use the built-in `ipfilter` capabilities. If you plan to use scalable services with shared IP addresses, you must use an external firewall. This is because the `ipfilter` software (see the `ipfilter`(5) man page) cannot detect the connection state after the shared address migrates from one cluster node to another cluster node.

In addition, if the applications on your cluster transmit sensitive data over the network to client systems, consider using the IP Security Architecture (IPsec) to protect the communication traffic (see the `IPsec`(7P) man page).

## Solaris Cluster Software Installation

After you have installed and secured the Oracle Solaris OS, you can install the Solaris Cluster software. If you use Solaris JumpStart, then you can set up the JumpStart server to install the Solaris Cluster software as part of the postinstallation scripts. This Solaris Cluster software installation process installs only the relevant packages for you and does not actually configure the software. To achieve this level of automation, you can add your own scripts to the JumpStart framework. Many installations performed by Sun Professional Services use the freely available JumpStart Enterprise Toolkit (JET). JET enables you to create individual modules to perform specific tasks such as installing or configuring software. One such module, available as part of certain Sun Professional Services engagements, can install and perform a basic configuration of the Solaris Cluster software.

The installation process has two parts: installing the software and configuring the software. The latter requires your nodes to be rebooted as part of that process. Software installation is performed through the `installer` program found on the installation media.

The `installer` program can be run in both character mode and as a full graphical user interface (GUI). To run the GUI `installer` program, ideally use `ssh` with X forwarding enabled. If you choose not to use `ssh`, you can use `telnet` or `rlogin` in combination with the `xhost` command to allow the cluster client node to display on the X server display you are using. If you use `telnet` or `rlogin`, you must set the `DISPLAY` environment variable to the workstation from which you are accessing the cluster.

When run from the command line, the `installer` program can be supplied with a text-based "response" file to allow automation of the Solaris Cluster software installation.

---

## Example 4.3  Starting the Solaris Cluster Software `installer` Program

Use the `-X` flag to `ssh` to forward the X11 protocol to your local display.

```
admin_console# ssh -X root@phys-earth1
Password:
Last login: Thu Nov 12 08:19:29 2009 from admin_console.
Sun Microsystems Inc.    SunOS 5.10     Generic January 2005
```

Check that `ssh` is configured to forward correctly.

```
cluster1# grep X11F /etc/ssh/sshd_config
X11Forwarding yes
```

Change to the Solaris Cluster media directory and run the installer.

```
cluster1# cd DVD-mount-point
cluster1# ls
Copyright      License         README         Solaris_sparc  Solaris_x86
```

```
cluster1# cd Solaris_sparc/
cluster1# ls -l
total 28
drwxr-xr-x   9 root      root          9 Aug  6 16:17 Product
-rwxr-xr-x   1 root      root      10892 Jan  8  2009 installer
-rw-r--r--   1 root      root         84 Jan  8  2009 release_info
cluster1# ./installer
```

Assuming you are installing from the installation media, after you have accepted the software license agreement, a wizard screen similar to Figure 4.2 is displayed.

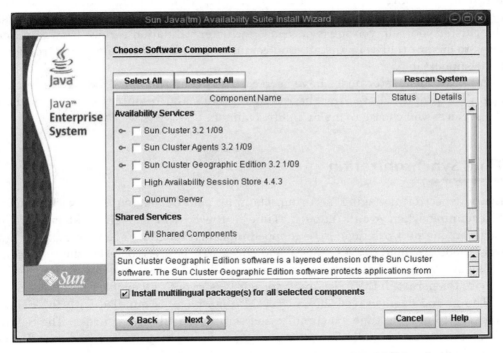

**Figure 4.2** Installation screen for the Solaris Cluster 3.2 01/09 software

In the wizard, select the check boxes for the software you have chosen to install. Note that the option to install the multilingual packages is checked by default, whereas with the text `installer` program, you must explicitly choose to install these packages. Follow the wizard instructions to complete the installation. You must perform this installation on all the nodes that will form your cluster.

After the packages have been installed on all the nodes, you can proceed with the configuration of the cluster itself by using the `scinstall` command. You have several configuration options to choose from. The simplest option configures the Solaris Cluster software on just one node. The most automated option automatically configures the Solaris Cluster software on all your cluster nodes from the single command.

As each node is configured, it is rebooted by the configuration process. Therefore, do not run this program unless your nodes can experience an outage at this time.

If the configuration is performed by a certified Solaris Cluster installer, he or she will follow Oracle System Installation standards methodology to complete the installation. Doing so mostly involves checking that certain settings have been made and that the appropriate patches have been installed. If you choose to install the cluster yourself, you must purchase a cluster validation service from Sun Services to ensure that your installation complies with the necessary standards for it to be supportable.

After all the cluster nodes have been correctly configured and validated, you can begin the process of creating the resource groups and resources that encapsulate the services you choose to make highly available.

## Time Synchronization

Every aspect of managing, securing, planning, and debugging a network involves determining when events happen. Time is the critical element that enables an event on one network node to be mapped to a corresponding event on another network node. In many cases, these challenges can be overcome by the enterprise deployment of the Network Time Protocol (NTP) service. You can configure this service to operate in the following modes: NTP server, NTP client, or NTP peer.

The `xntpd` daemon (see the `xntpd`(1M) man page) is bundled with the Solaris software to provide time synchronization services to all cluster nodes. The Solaris Cluster software installation creates a `/etc/inet/ntp.conf.cluster` file on each cluster node and a legacy `/etc/rc2.d/S74xntpd_cluster` script (or legacy Solaris Management Facility [SMF] service) to start `xntpd` with this file, instead of the default `/etc/inet/ntp.conf` file. The standard Solaris 10 SMF service, `/network/ntp:default`, is disabled.

The `ntp.conf.cluster` file, created by the Solaris Cluster configuration process, synchronizes the time across all cluster nodes by naming the cluster nodes as peers. You can also synchronize your cluster nodes to an external NTP server either by naming a specific NTP server or by broadcasting or multicasting for one. To do this, you can specify the appropriate directive in the `/etc/inet/ntp.conf.cluster` file on each cluster node. Because the `S74xntpd_cluster` script calls `ntpdate` (see the `ntpdate`(1M) man page), do not restart this service while the cluster is running. If the cluster nodes are not closely synchronized with the external source, restarting the service will result in a large and sudden change in the system clocks, either backward or forward. Under some circumstances, this change can result in a system panic. Instead, follow the recommended procedure, which involves rebooting the cluster. Clearly, you should schedule such a task for the next maintenance window.

> **Warning**
>
> When using NTP, do not attempt to adjust the cluster time while the cluster is running. Do not adjust the time by interactively using the `date`, `rdate`, `xntpd`, or `svcadm` command or within `cron` scripts.

## Cluster Management

For the most part, you can manage your cluster using either the command-line interface (CLI) or the Solaris Cluster Manager GUI. Although the capabilities provided by the GUI are a subset of what is available through the CLI, its graphical nature makes it less prone to user errors when creating or modifying complex objects. This is particularly true if a resource has many mandatory parameters or if a resource group requires several affinities to be configured.

### Command-Line Interface

The Solaris Cluster CLI commands are in the `/usr/cluster/bin` directory, and all begin with the `cl` prefix. Most of these commands have both a long form and a short form. The directory also contains the CLI commands used to manage systems installed with software releases prior to the Solaris Cluster 3.2 software, such as `scrgadm`, `scconf`, and `scswitch`.

All of the commands listed in Table 4.1, excluding `clsetup`, which is menu-driven, conform to this format: `command action argument ... operand`.

All the commands return an exit code of zero on success, allowing you to create scripts to automate procedures that you might perform regularly.

**Table 4.1** Solaris Cluster Commands

| CLI— Long Form | CLI— Short Form | Description |
|---|---|---|
| claccess | claccess | Manages the Solaris Cluster access policies for nodes |
| cldevice | cldev | Manages the Solaris Cluster devices |
| cldevicegroup | cldg | Manages the Solaris Cluster device groups |
| clinterconnect | clintr | Manages the Solaris Cluster private interconnects |
| clnasdevice | clnas | Manages access to NAS devices from the Solaris Cluster software |
| clnode | clnode | Manages the Solaris Cluster nodes |
| clquorum | clq | Manages the Solaris Cluster quorum devices and properties |
| clreslogicalhostname | clrslh | Manages resources for the Solaris Cluster logical hostnames |
| clresource | clrs | Manages resources for the Solaris Cluster data services |
| clresourcegroup | clrg | Manages resource groups for the Solaris Cluster data services |
| clresourcetype | clrt | Manages resource types for the Solaris Cluster data services |
| clressharedaddress | clrssa | Manages the Solaris Cluster resources for shared addresses |
| clsetup | clsetup | Menu-driven command used to configure the Solaris Cluster software interactively |
| clsnmphost | clsnmphost | Administers the list of Solaris Cluster Simple Network Management Protocol (SNMP) hosts |
| clsnmpmib | clsnmpmib | Administers the Solaris Cluster SNMP management information bases (MIBs) |
| clsnmpuser | clsnmpuser | Administers the Solaris Cluster SNMP users |
| cltelemetryattribute | clta | Configures system resource monitoring |
| cluster | cluster | Manages the global configuration and status of a cluster |
| clvxvm | clvxvm | Configures VxVM for the Solaris Cluster software |
| clzonecluster | clzc | Creates and manages zone clusters |

## The Solaris Cluster Manager Graphical User Interface

You can run the Solaris Cluster Manager GUI using a browser such as Mozilla Firefox or Microsoft Internet Explorer. Solaris Cluster Manager requires that you have already installed

- The common agent container (CAC) package (`SUNWcacaort`)
- The Solaris Cluster Manager packages (`SUNWscspmr`, `SUNWscspmu`)
- The Sun Java Web Console packages (`SUNWmcon`, `SUNWmconr`, `SUNWmctag`)

After the Sun Java Web Console is started, it listens for secure `https` connections on port 6789, if you have reversed the hardening performed by the standard Solaris installation process (see Example 4.2). In addition, at least version 2.2 of the CAC service must be running. CAC listens for Java Management Extensions (JMX) calls made by the Sun Java Web Console as a result of actions you perform through the Solaris Cluster Manager GUI.

### Example 4.4  Checking That the Required Components Are in Place to Run Solaris Cluster Manager

Check that the required packages are present.

```
# pkginfo SUNWcacaort
application SUNWcacaort Common Agent Container - Runtime

# pkginfo | grep SUNWscspm
application SUNWscspmr                          Sun Cluster Manager (root)
application SUNWscspmu                          Sun Cluster Manager (Usr)

# pkginfo SUNWmcon SUNWmconr SUNWmctag
application SUNWmcon  Sun Java(TM) Web Console 3.0.2 (Core)
system      SUNWmconr Sun Java(TM) Web Console 3.0.2 (Root)
application SUNWmctag Sun Java(TM) Web Console 3.0.2 (Tags & Components)
```

Check the CAC service version.

```
# cacaoadm -V
2.2.0.1
```

Check that CAC is online.

```
# svcs /application/management/common-agent-container-1
STATE          STIME    FMRI
online          7:58:28 svc:/application/management/common-agent-container-1:default
```

Check that the Java Web Console is online.

```
# svcs svc:/system/webconsole:console
STATE          STIME    FMRI
online         Jan_19   svc:/system/webconsole:console
```

Check that the Java Web Console is listening on all networks to port 6789.

```
# netstat -a | grep 6789
     *.6789                   *.*                   0      0 49152      0 LISTEN
```

Check the applications deployed to the Java Web Console.

```
# wcadmin list

Deployed web applications (application name, context name, status):

    SunClusterManager  SunClusterManager  [running]
    console            ROOT               [running]
    console            com_sun_web_ui     [running]
    console            console            [running]
    console            manager            [running]
    legacy             SunPlexManagerGeo  [running]
    zfs                zfs                [running]

Registered jar files (application name, identifier, path):

    SunClusterManager cacao_jars   /usr/lib/cacao/lib/*.jar
    SunClusterManager jdmk_jars    /opt/SUNWjdmk/5.1/lib/*.jar
    console           audit_jar    /usr/lib/audit/Audit.jar
    console           console_jars /usr/share/webconsole/lib/*.jar
    console           jato_jar     /usr/share/lib/jato/jato.jar
    console           javahelp_jar /usr/jdk/packages/javax.help-2.0/lib/*.jar
    console           shared_jars  /usr/share/webconsole/private/container/shared/
lib/*.jar

Registered login modules (application name, service name, identifier):

    console  ConsoleLogin  userlogin
    console  ConsoleLogin  rolelogin

Persistent Jvm options:

    -XX:ParallelGCThreads=4
    -server
    -Xmx256m
    -XX:+BackgroundCompilation
    -XX:+UseParallelGC

Shared service properties (name, value):

    ENABLE          yes
    java.options    -server -XX:+BackgroundCompilation -Xmx256m
```

After you have logged in to the Java Web Console and chosen the Solaris Cluster Manager option, a screen similar to Figure 4.3 is displayed. Using Solaris Cluster Manager, you can perform a wide range of tasks, including

- Creating, modifying, and deleting resource groups and resources
- Enabling and disabling resources
- Bringing resource groups online and offline
- Switching resource groups between nodes

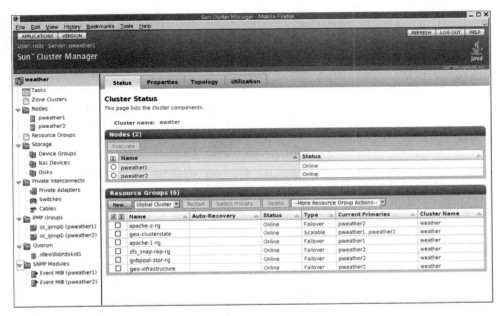

**Figure 4.3** Solaris Cluster Manager browser-based GUI

Solaris Cluster Manager also highlights faults in the system with a red marker over the components that have errors.

## Solaris Cluster Wizards

As with the `clsetup` menu-driven command, Solaris Cluster Manager has several wizards to help you set up some common highly available services, such as Network File System (NFS), Apache web server, and Oracle databases, as well as two more complex services: Oracle Real Application Clusters (Oracle RAC) and SAP web application server.

The wizards simplify your work by probing the system to discover the potential options that are available to you and then configuring the relevant resource groups and resources with the appropriate dependencies and affinities. A good example of this process is the Oracle RAC wizard. It can do the following:

- Create the RAC framework resource group and resources for you, depending on your answer regarding your volume management method (hardware RAID, Solaris Volume Manager for Sun Cluster, or the VxVM cluster feature), shared QFS file system, or another supported combination.
- Create the necessary scalable storage resource groups and resources.
- Create the RAC server proxy resource group and resource based on the Oracle RAC version, the ORACLE_HOME variable, and the ORACLE_SID variables you select. Again, most of these choices are discovered for you by the wizard.
- Create the Oracle Clusterware resources that integrate with the Solaris Cluster storage resources to give the Oracle RAC database instances visibility into the availability of their underlying storage.

The wizard completes the operations for you and displays the Solaris Cluster commands it used to achieve these steps. If anything goes wrong during the creation of these objects, then the wizard will undo the changes.

## Role-Based Access Control

By default, only the Solaris root user can manage the cluster. Non-root users cannot create, modify, or delete resource groups or resources, nor can they switch resource groups between the nodes. Non-root users can view the resource group and resource configuration because they are assigned the solaris.cluster.read rights profile as part of their standard authorizations. To delegate some of the management functions to specific system administrators who are not assigned full root access, you can use the role-based access control (RBAC) capabilities to assign them the necessary solaris.cluster.admin or solaris.cluster.modify Solaris Cluster management rights profile.

The following example shows you how to assign to the Solaris user myadmin all the Solaris Cluster management rights profiles, which include both solaris.cluster.admin and solaris.cluster.modify. Initially, without being assigned the solaris.cluster.modify rights profile, the user could not create the resource group foo-rg. After the user is assigned this rights profile, the user can create and delete the resource group. However, in order to manage or bring the resource group online, the user also needs to have the solaris.cluster.admin rights profile assigned. There is no simple way to assign roles such that individual users can control individual resource groups or resources.

## Example 4.5   Assigning a Solaris Cluster Management Rights Profile to a User

Use the `id` and `auths` commands to determine the current user ID and authorizations.

```
# id -a
uid=424242(myadmin) gid=424242(myadmin) groups=424242(myadmin)
# clresourcegroup list
apache-1-rg
geo-clusterstate
geo-infrastructure
apacheset-stor-rg
seasons_apache-rep-rg
apache-z-rg
# auths
    .
    .
    .
...solaris.cluster.read,solaris.cluster.device.read,solaris.cluster.network.read,
solaris.cluster.node.read,solaris.cluster.quorum.read,solaris.cluster.resource.read,
solaris.cluster.system.read,solaris.cluster.transport.read,solaris.cluster.gui,solaris
.cluster.geo.read
# clresourcegroup create foo-rg
clrg:  (C368238) You are not authorized to run this command with these options.
clrg:  (C666174) An RBAC authorization of "solaris.cluster.modify" is required.
clrg:  (C546315) Refer to the rbac(5) man page for more information about RBAC
authorizations.
```

Modify the `/etc/user_attr` file to include the required rights.

```
# grep myadmin /etc/user_attr
myadmin::::auths=solaris.cluster.*;
# id -a
uid=424242(myadmin) gid=424242(myadmin) groups=424242(myadmin)
# auths
solaris.cluster.*,
    .
    .
    .
solaris.cluster.read,solaris.cluster.device.read,solaris.cluster.network.read,solaris.
cluster.node.read,solaris.cluster.quorum.read,solaris.cluster.resource.read,solaris.
cluster.system.read,solaris.cluster.transport.read,solaris.cluster.gui,solaris.cluster
.geo.read
# clresourcegroup create foo-rg
# clresourcegroup list
apache-1-rg
geo-clusterstate
geo-infrastructure
apacheset-stor-rg
seasons_apache-rep-rg
apache-z-rg
foo-rg
# clresourcegroup delete foo-rg
```

Just as these rights profiles can be assigned to a particular user, they can also be assigned to roles, which a user can assume. In the following example, the role `clusadm` is created. Unless the user `myadmin` is assigned access to that role, the user is unable to assume it through the `su` command, even though he or she might have the right password. However, after being assigned the role, the user can perform the actions that the role is authorized to perform.

---

## Example 4.6   Using an RBAC Role to Allow a User to Perform Cluster Management Tasks

Display the `Cluster Management` entry in the profile description database.

```
# grep "Cluster Management" /etc/security/prof_attr | head -1
Cluster Management:::Sun Cluster
Management:auths=solaris.cluster.admin,solaris.cluster.modify,
         .
         .
         .
# roleadd  -P "Cluster Management"  clusadm
# tail -3 /etc/user_attr
root:::::auths=solaris.*,solaris.grant;profiles=Web Console Management,All;lock_after_
retries=no;min_label=admin_low;clearance=admin_high
zfssnap:::::type=role;auths=solaris.smf.manage.zfs-auto-snapshot;profiles=ZFS File
System Management
clusadm:::::type=role;profiles=Cluster Management
# passwd clusadm
New Password:
Re-enter new Password:
passwd: password successfully changed for clusadm
# su - myadmin
Sun Microsystems Inc.    SunOS 5.10       Generic January 2005
$ su clusadm
Password:
Roles can only be assumed by authorized users
su: Sorry
$ logout
# usermod -R clusadm myadmin
# tail -3 /etc/user_attr
zfssnap:::::type=role;auths=solaris.smf.manage.zfs-auto-snapshot;profiles=ZFS File
System Management
clusadm:::::type=role;profiles=Cluster Management
myadmin:::::type=normal;roles=clusadm
# su - myadmin
Sun Microsystems Inc.    SunOS 5.10       Generic January 2005
$ su clusadm
Password:
$ clresourcegroup create bar-rg
$ clresourcegroup delete bar-rg
```

---

## Cluster Monitoring

Most data centers use an enterprise management tool such as HP OpenView, BMC Patrol, or IBM Tivoli to monitor and manage their environment. If the data center has a large base of Sun servers, then the list might also include the Sun Management Center software. The Solaris Cluster software integrates with these tools using the Simple Network Management Protocol (SNMP), enabling administrators to monitor both the cluster nodes and the resource groups and resources they contain.

## Sun Management Center Integration

The Sun Management Center software enables you to manage and monitor all the Sun servers in your data center. The Sun Management Center software is implemented as a three-tier architecture: console, server, and agent. The agent is installed on the system you choose to monitor. It sends alerts to the server when certain events occur or when thresholds are exceeded. Each agent handles the monitoring of a specific function. For example, the Solaris Cluster agent monitors the cluster infrastructure and the resource groups and resources configured on your system. The Sun Management Center console aggregates the alarms and alerts pertaining to a specific node, marking the node with a symbol to denote the most serious condition that it is encountering. If there are no problems with the node, then no symbol is present. Figure 4.4 shows an example of a serious error with the cluster transports, but just a warning for the scalable resource group because it is offline.

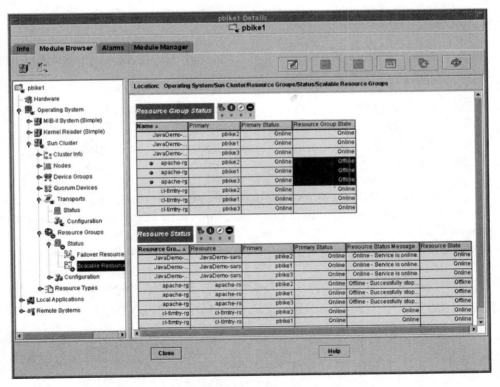

**Figure 4.4** Sun Management Center GUI

## Solaris Cluster SNMP Management Information Base

The Solaris Cluster software provides two Simple Network Management Protocol (SNMP) management information bases (MIBs): one for cluster events, the other for cluster objects and their status.

### SNMP MIB for Cluster Events

The Solaris Cluster SNMP event MIB can be enabled on any cluster node without relying on additional SNMP agent infrastructure. Because all cluster nodes receive the same cluster events, you need to enable the SNMP event MIB on only one cluster node.

The cluster events are graded in severity from low to high, as follows:

- INFO
- WARNING
- ERROR
- CRITICAL
- FATAL

When the SNMP event MIB is enabled on a node, the cluster event SNMP interface can do the following:

- Store up to 50 of the most recent WARNING or higher-severity cluster events in the MIB table.
- Send SNMP traps to one or more hosts when WARNING or higher-severity cluster events occur.

By default, the SNMP event module uses port number 11161, and traps use port number 11162. These port numbers can be changed by using the cacaoadm command, as shown in the following example.

The Solaris Cluster SNMP event MIB Object ID (OID) is 1.3.6.1.4.1.42.2.80.

### Example 4.7  Changing the SNMP Adapter Trap Port

Use the cacaoadm command to determine and change the SNMP adapter trap port.

```
phys-grass2# cacaoadm get-param snmp-adaptor-trap-port
snmp-adaptor-trap-port=11162
phys-grass2# cacaoadm stop
phys-grass2# cacaoadm set-param snmp-adaptor-trap-port=12345
phys-grass2# cacaoadm start
phys-grass2# cacaoadm get-param snmp-adaptor-trap-port
snmp-adaptor-trap-port=12345
```

## SNMP Interface for Cluster Objects

The SNMP interface for cluster objects such as nodes, resource groups, and quorum devices, along with their corresponding status, is provided through the Solaris Cluster software to the Sun Management Center integration module. The integration module is installed by default on all cluster nodes as part of the SUNWscsal and SUNWscsam packages.

To enable the integration module on a cluster node, the Sun Management Center agent infrastructure must be installed and running on that node. After the Sun Management Center agent starts on the node, the integration module can be loaded and enabled through the Sun Management Center console. The Sun Management Center server and console can be installed on one of the cluster nodes, but they are usually installed on another system.

Similar to the SNMP event MIB, the integration module needs to be enabled on only one cluster node to receive cluster SNMP MIB data and traps. The integration module MIB OID is 1.3.6.1.4.1.42.2.80.1.1.1.

The Sun Management Center agent running on a cluster node sends SNMP traps to the Sun Management Center server whenever the status of an object changes, such as a resource group going online or offline, or becoming managed or unmanaged. The SNMP traps also can be sent directly from the Sun Management Center agent to any other hosts by adding the secondary trap destination through the Sun Management Center es-trapdest command. The following example shows how to add myHost to the hosts that receive Sun Management Center SNMP traps from the agent on port 11162.

### Example 4.8   Adding a Secondary Trap Destination to the Sun Management Center Agent

Add myHost as a secondary trap destination using the es-trapdest command.

```
# /opt/SUNWsymon/sbin/es-trapdest -c agent -a myHost 11162
```

The agent has to be restarted for the setting to take effect.

## Service-Level Management and Telemetry

When you consolidate multiple services onto a Solaris Cluster installation, you must ensure that your service levels are met even when several services reside on the same cluster node. The Oracle Solaris OS has many features, such as resource controls and scheduler options, to help you achieve these goals. These resource allocations can be defined in the projects database stored locally in /etc/project or held in the name service maps.

The Solaris Cluster software can bind both resource groups and resources to projects using the RG_project_name and Resource_project_name properties, respectively. The following example shows how to create a processor pool (containing four CPUs) that uses the fair share scheduler (FSS). The processor pool is then associated with the user project that limits shared memory usage to 8 gigabytes. The FSS can be enabled by using the dispadmin -d FSS command.

## Example 4.9  Binding a Resource Group to a Project Associated with a Processor Pool

Determine the number of processors the system has using the psrinfo command.

Define a four-CPU-processor set called oracle_pset in a temporary file, and then use the file as input to the poolcfg command.

```
# psrinfo | wc -l
      24
# cat /tmp/create_oracle_pool.txt
create pset oracle_pset ( uint pset.min = 1 ; uint pset.max = 4)
create pool oracle_pool
associate pool oracle_pool ( pset oracle_pset )
modify pool oracle_pool ( string pool.scheduler = "FSS" )

# poolcfg -f /tmp/create_oracle_pool.txt
```

Instantiate the configuration using the pooladm command.

```
# pooladm -c
# pooladm

system default
        string  system.comment
        int     system.version 1
        boolean system.bind-default true
        string  system.poold.objectives wt-load

        pool pool_default
                int     pool.sys_id 0
                boolean pool.active true
                boolean pool.default true
                string  pool.scheduler FSS
                int     pool.importance 1
                string  pool.comment
                pset    pset_default

        pool oracle_pool
                int     pool.sys_id 2
                boolean pool.active true
                boolean pool.default false
                string  pool.scheduler FSS
                int     pool.importance 1
                string  pool.comment
                pset    oracle_pset
```

```
            pset oracle_pset
                    int       pset.sys_id 1
                    boolean pset.default false
                    uint      pset.min 1
                    uint      pset.max 4
                    string  pset.units population
                    uint      pset.load 17
                    uint      pset.size 4
                    string  pset.comment

                    cpu
                            int       cpu.sys_id 1
                            string  cpu.comment
                            string  cpu.status on-line

                    cpu
                            int       cpu.sys_id 0
                            string  cpu.comment
                            string  cpu.status on-line

                    cpu
                            int       cpu.sys_id 3
                            string  cpu.comment
                            string  cpu.status on-line

                    cpu
                            int       cpu.sys_id 2
                            string  cpu.comment
                            string  cpu.status on-line

            pset pset_default
                    int       pset.sys_id -1
                    boolean pset.default true
            .
            .
            .
```

Use the `projadd` command to make `oracle_pool` the project pool for user `oracle`.

```
# projadd -p 4242 -K "project.max-shm-memory=(privileged,8GB,deny)" \
>        -K project.pool=oracle_pool user.oracle
# su - oracle
Sun Microsystems Inc.    SunOS 5.10       Generic January 2005
$ id -p
uid=424242(oracle) gid=424242(oinstall) projid=4242(user.oracle)
$ exit
# clresourcegroup create -p RG_project_name=user.oracle oracle-rg
```

Similarly, using the `clzonecluster` command (see the `clzonecluster`(1M) man page), you can bind zone clusters to pools, dedicate or limit the number of CPUs allocated to them, and limit the physical, swap, or locked memory they can use.

## Gathering Telemetry from the Solaris Cluster Software

The Solaris Cluster service-level management feature enables you to configure the Solaris Cluster software to gather telemetry data from your cluster. Using this feature, you can collect statistics on CPU, memory, swap, and network utilization of the cluster node as well as on resource groups and system components such as disks and network adapters. By monitoring system resource usage through the Solaris Cluster software, you can collect data that reflects how a service using specific system resources is performing. You can also discover resource bottlenecks, overloads, and even underutilized hardware resources. Based on this data, you can assign applications to nodes that have the necessary resources and choose which node each application should fail over to.

This feature must be set up using the `clsetup` command. The telemetry data is stored in its own Java DB database held on a failover or global file system that you must provide for its use. After the setup is complete, you can enable the telemetry on the resource groups, choose the attributes to monitor, and set thresholds. Figure 4.5 and Figure 4.6 show the type of output you can receive from using this feature.

Figure 4.5 shows that an alarm has been generated because disk d4 has exceeded the threshold set for it.

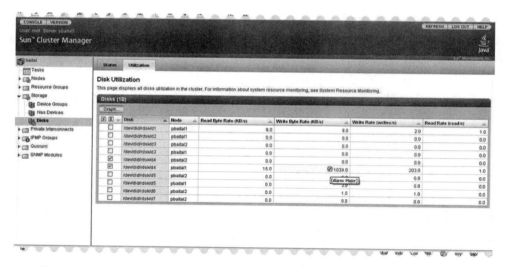

**Figure 4.5** Alarm showing that the write I/O rate to disk d4 has exceeded the threshold set

Figure 4.6 shows the utilization of the public network adapters bge0 and bge1 on cluster node pbaitall.

The telemetry uses the `RG_slm_type` resource group property, which can be set to one of two values: `automated` or `manual`. The default value for the `RG_slm_type` property is `manual`. Unless the `RG_slm_type` property value is explicitly set to

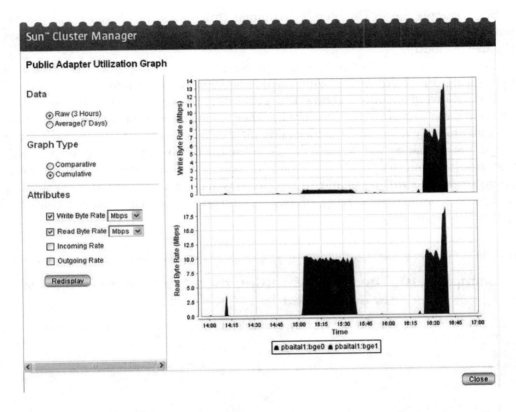

**Figure 4.6** Public network adapter utilization telemetry gathered using the service-level management feature

automated when a resource group is created, telemetry is not enabled for the resource group. If the resource group RG_slm_type property is changed, resource utilization monitoring begins only after the resource group is restarted.

When a resource group has the RG_slm_type property set to automated, the Resource Group Manager (RGM) internally generates a Solaris project to track the system resource utilization for all processes encapsulated by the resource of the resource group. This tracking happens regardless of whether the RG_project_ name and Resource_project_name properties are set. The telemetry can track only the system resource utilization: CPU usage, resident set size (RSS), and swap usage for resource groups that have the RG_slm_type property set to automated. Telemetry for other objects is gathered at the node, zone, disk, or network interface level, as appropriate.

See Example 8.9 in Chapter 8, "Example Oracle Solaris Cluster Implementations," for more information about how to set up, configure, and use the Solaris Cluster telemetry.

Using the Solaris Cluster Manager browser interface simplifies the process of configuring thresholds and viewing the telemetry monitoring data.

The following example shows the generated project name in the `RG_SLM_projectname` property. However, unlike other resource group properties, you cannot set this property manually. Furthermore, if `RG_slm_type` is set to `automated`, the `RG_project_name` and `Resource_project_name` properties will be ignored. Conversely, when `RG_slm_type` is set to `manual`, the processes of the resource group's resource will be bound to the projects named in the `RG_project_name` and `Resource_project_name` properties. However, the RGM will not track the system resources they use.

## Example 4.10  The Effect of Setting the `RG_slm_type` Property to `automated`

Use the `clresourcegroup` command to show the property settings for the `apache-1-rg` resource group.

```
# clresourcegroup show -v apache-1-rg

=== Resource Groups and Resources ===

Resource Group:                              apache-1-rg
  RG_description:                            <NULL>
  RG_mode:                                   Failover
  RG_state:                                  Managed
  RG_project_name:                           default
  RG_affinities:                             <NULL>
  RG_SLM_type:                               manual
  Auto_start_on_new_cluster:                 False
  Failback:                                  False
  Nodelist:                                  phys-winter1 phys-winter2
  Maximum_primaries:                         1
  Desired_primaries:                         1
  RG_dependencies:                           <NULL>
  Implicit_network_dependencies:             True
  Global_resources_used:                     <All>
  Pingpong_interval:                         3600
  Pathprefix:                                <NULL>
  RG_System:                                 False
  Suspend_automatic_recovery:                False

  --- Resources for Group apache-1-rg ---
      .
      .
      .
```

Use the `clresourcegroup` command to set the `RG_SLM_type` property to `automated`.

```
# clresourcegroup set -p RG_SLM_type=automated apache-1-rg
# clresourcegroup show -v apache-1-rg

=== Resource Groups and Resources ===

Resource Group:                           apache-1-rg
  RG_description:                           <NULL>
  RG_mode:                                  Failover
  RG_state:                                 Managed
  RG_project_name:                          default
  RG_affinities:                            <NULL>
  RG_SLM_type:                              automated
  RG_SLM_projectname:                       SCSLM_apache_1_rg
  RG_SLM_pset_type:                         default
  RG_SLM_CPU_SHARES:                        1
  RG_SLM_PSET_MIN:                          0
  Auto_start_on_new_cluster:                False
  Failback:                                 False
  Nodelist:                                 phys-winter1 phys-winter2
  Maximum_primaries:                        1
  Desired_primaries:                        1
  RG_dependencies:                          <NULL>
  Implicit_network_dependencies:            True
  Global_resources_used:                    <All>
  Pingpong_interval:                        3600
  Pathprefix:                               <NULL>
  RG_System:                                False
  Suspend_automatic_recovery:               False

--- Resources for Group apache-1-rg ---
  .
  .
  .
```

# Patching and Upgrading Your Cluster

The approach you take to patching and upgrading your cluster will vary depending on your data center standards. Some data centers apply only the bare minimum of changes, such as critical security patches, operating on the principle of "if it ain't broke, don't fix it." Clearly, if a system is stable, this is a reasonable approach, especially if availability is your highest priority. Other data centers schedule regular planned outages to perform patching, often choosing to lag a little behind the most recent patches to avoid encountering bad patches. Still others take the "latest and greatest" approach, given that the patches are meant to fix all the key, known issues. Whichever strategy you use, minimizing the overall outage will clearly be your main priority.

You can also upgrade the Solaris Cluster software by patching it with the patches that are built into a later release of the Solaris Cluster software. However, you must follow all the instructions in the README file contained within each patch.

## Upgrade Methods

Three main methods are available for patching or upgrading your operating system and Solaris Cluster software: standard upgrade, rolling upgrade, and dual-partition upgrade. Solaris Live Upgrade provides yet more options when used with these methods. Each method results in differing lengths of outage on your cluster, which further depends on the number and type of zones you have configured (see the section "Oracle Solaris Zones" in Chapter 3, "Combining Virtualization Technologies with Oracle Solaris Cluster Software"). The following sections describe these methods.

Before you begin making changes to the system, consider the following checklist:

- Has the upgrade procedure been tested on a test cluster before being implemented on the production system? If not, is management aware of the potential risk of untested procedures?

- Have you verified that the new configuration is supported by all your services? Some applications place greater restrictions on the operating system or other software versions they support.

- Have the proposed changes been agreed upon and recorded in your change control system?

- Do you have a full backup of the cluster prior to making any changes?

- Have you tested that you can switch over all services between cluster nodes prior to your changes? This testing isolates any post-upgrade problems to the upgrade and patches.

- Is there an agreed outage period of a set length?

- Is there a procedure to reverse any changes if the upgrade does not go according to plan? Have you determined when you will need to start backing out any changes if that happens?

- Have you tested that you can switch over all services between cluster nodes after the changes have been made? This testing ensures that if a failure occurs later, your system will continue to provide a set of highly available services.

### Standard Upgrade

With standard upgrade, you schedule a complete cluster outage to perform the patch or upgrade process. This method might be considered for applying patches, such as kernel patches, that need to be installed in single-user mode. Major operating system upgrades also fall into this category. You cannot run a Solaris Cluster configuration with nodes running different major versions of the Oracle Solaris OS, for example, Solaris 9 OS and Solaris 10 OS.

A standard upgrade is by far the simplest method but necessitates the longest cluster outage. During this period, your services are unavailable. Consequently, this method is the least desirable from an availability standpoint.

A standard upgrade can be combined with Solaris Live Upgrade. This approach significantly reduces the cluster outage by no longer requiring the entire cluster to be shut down while you are upgrading the software. You first create an alternative boot environment with the upgraded software on each machine (see "Solaris Live Upgrade" for details). When you are ready to activate the new software, halt the entire cluster, and then boot the entire cluster using the alternative boot environment with the new software on each machine.

## Rolling Upgrade

With rolling upgrade, the nodes in your cluster are upgraded one at a time. Any service hosted on a node to be upgraded is manually switched over to another cluster node prior to the target node being shut down for patching. After the target node has been patched, it is brought back into the cluster, and the process is repeated until all nodes have been upgraded. After all of the nodes have been upgraded, you execute the scversions -c command to commit the cluster to use the new software. The cluster software does not enable cluster-wide protocols until the commit happens. Prior to the commit, all nodes, including nodes with new software, continue to use the old cluster-wide protocols. There is no rolling downgrade after the commit happens. The outage incurred by a service is therefore just twice the time it takes to switch over from one cluster node to another. A switchover of a simple application can take about 30 seconds, though the time varies significantly depending on the application.

A rolling upgrade changes only the Solaris Cluster software or the Oracle Solaris OS. Rolling upgrades can be used as long as the major cluster release and major operating system remain the same, for example, the Solaris Cluster 3.2 software or the Solaris 10 OS. You cannot perform rolling upgrades between major cluster or major OS releases, for example, the Sun Cluster 3.1 software to the Solaris Cluster 3.2 software or the Solaris 9 OS to the Solaris 10 OS.

The rolling upgrade process updates the software on the local storage of a node when that node is not in cluster mode. The highly available (HA) container places the software on shared storage. Because the shared storage is never out of service, the rolling upgrade process has no opportunity to change the software residing on shared storage. Therefore, a rolling upgrade cannot be used to upgrade software on HA containers.

A rolling upgrade can also be combined with Solaris Live Upgrade. This combination does not reduce the service outage. A rolling upgrade without Solaris Live Upgrade reduces the service outage by performing software upgrades while the machines are not in the cluster. During this time period, the ability of the cluster to survive machine failures is reduced. The use of Solaris Live Upgrade can significantly reduce the time period of increased vulnerability. Solaris Live Upgrade also reduces the period of time in which nodes in the cluster have different software versions. You first create an alternative boot environment with the upgraded software on each machine (see "Solaris Live Upgrade"). You then serially halt each machine and boot that machine from the alternative boot environment with the upgraded software. After you have booted all nodes from the alternative boot environment with the upgraded software, you execute the `scversions -c` command to commit the cluster to use the new software.

### Dual-Partition Upgrade

A dual-partition upgrade offers the greatest flexibility in terms of what changes you can make to the system. The change can be a patch, an update release, or a major release. Changes in multiple areas can be applied simultaneously. A dual-partition upgrade can even be used when all the changes are in areas other than the Solaris Cluster software, including the following:

- The Oracle Solaris OS
- A Solaris Cluster software release
- Third-party volume managers and file systems
- Application software (as long as the applications are not installed on shared storage)

A dual-partition upgrade divides your cluster into two parts, each of which is updated separately and sequentially. To invoke a dual-partition upgrade, you must use the `scinstall` command from the target media of the release to which you are upgrading. This command then prompts you with the options shown in Example 4.11. Choose option 3 for a dual-partition upgrade. You must divide the cluster machines into two sets of nodes, which are called *partitions*. You must partition the cluster such that each partition has for each storage device at least one node that can access that storage device. During the upgrade process, each partition will host the cluster applications, and the cluster applications must be able to access storage. If you are unsure of how to partition the cluster, you can choose an option whereby the system presents you with the various ways to group your cluster nodes for the purposes of the upgrade. After you have chosen your partitioning, you next select the option to initiate the actual upgrade.

**Example 4.11   Main Menu of the `scinstall` Command
Located on the Solaris Cluster Release Media**

The main menu of the `scinstall` command provides you with the following options:

```
*** Main Menu ***

    Please select from one of the following (*) options:

        1) Create a new cluster or add a cluster node
        2) Configure a cluster to be JumpStarted from this install server
      * 3) Manage a dual-partition upgrade
      * 4) Upgrade this cluster node
      * 5) Print release information for this cluster node

      * ?) Help with menu options
      * q) Quit

    Option:  3
```

The system software makes changes to the quorum votes, migrates your services to the partition that is still running while the first partition is upgraded, and halts the nodes of the first partition. You boot the nodes of the first partition into non-cluster mode and upgrade the software. After you have completed the upgrade on the first partition, you choose to continue the dual-partition upgrade. The system software reboots the nodes of the first partition into cluster mode as a new cluster. Unlike what happens in an ordinary boot, the nodes of the first partition proceed through the boot process and stop just prior to the point where the cluster would activate resources used by applications (such as mounting file systems and plumbing IP addresses) and start applications. At this point, most of the boot process has completed. The system software halts the nodes of the second partition and waits for them to actually halt. Next, the system software imports volumes, mounts file systems, plumbs IP addresses, and starts applications. In effect, the system performs a switchover of all applications and their resources from the second partition to the new partition. Next, reboot each node of the second partition and upgrade the software. When done with that step, you choose to continue the upgrade. The system software reboots the nodes of the second partition into cluster mode. After all nodes are back in the cluster, the system software restores the quorum configuration and completes the dual-partition upgrade.

If the dual-partition upgrade fails, you boot all nodes in non-cluster mode and execute the `scinstall -u recover` command on each node to restore the initial copy of the Cluster Configuration Repository (CCR). The system is already completely shut down at this point, so a minimal downtime upgrade is not possible. You do not restart the dual-partition upgrade. Instead, you perform a standard upgrade.

The service outage when you perform a dual-partition upgrade on a system with failover application is approximately the same as for a rolling upgrade. Because a time comes when neither partition can host an instance of a scalable application, there is a service outage for the scalable application, and the service outage is approximately the same as that of a failover application. For the simplest scalable applications, the service outage can be about 30 seconds, though the time varies significantly based on the application.

You cannot upgrade any software or data on the shared storage because the services remain running throughout the upgrade process, except for the point when the services are switched over from the partition running the old software to the partition running the new software. Do not make any configuration changes during the dual-partition upgrade. Make configuration changes either before or after the dual-partition upgrade.

A dual-partition upgrade can also be combined with Solaris Live Upgrade. This combination does not reduce the service outage. A dual-partition upgrade without Solaris Live Upgrade reduces the service outage by performing software upgrades while the machines are not in the cluster. During this time period the ability of the cluster to survive machine failures is reduced. The use of Solaris Live Upgrade can significantly reduce the time period of increased vulnerability. You first create an alternative boot environment with the upgraded software on each machine (see "Solaris Live Upgrade"). You then initiate the actual dual-partition upgrade. The system software automatically manages all of the work of the dual-partition upgrade. There no longer is any need to boot into non-cluster mode, so the number of reboots is reduced by half. The net result is that the time required for upgrades is dramatically reduced.

## Choosing Which Upgrade Method to Use

The choice of an upgrade method is governed by three factors: the simplicity of the upgrade process, the compatibility of the current and target software environments, and the level of availability your services must achieve during the upgrade process. Thus, if you require simplicity above all else, then the standard upgrade is the best method. If your current and target software releases do not span a major release, and you want to maintain service availability even for scalable services, then you can use a rolling upgrade. Finally, if changes to your cluster environment involve software spanning major releases and you need to minimize your service outage, then you must choose a dual-partition upgrade.

## Solaris Live Upgrade

Solaris Live Upgrade is not a stand-alone technology for upgrading a Solaris Cluster system. Solaris Live Upgrade must be used as part of either a standard upgrade, a rolling upgrade, or a dual-partition upgrade. Solaris Live Upgrade makes it possible to create an alternate boot environment with the upgraded software while the machine continues to run unaffected using the current boot environment. See "Standard Upgrade," "Rolling Upgrade," or "Dual-Partition Upgrade" for details on when to bring the alternate boot environment with the updated software into operational status. The boot environment with the old software is not damaged when you boot the alternate boot environment with the new software. If you encounter a problem with the new software, you can recover by halting all nodes of the cluster and then booting the entire cluster from the boot environment with the old software and configuration information. Solaris Live Upgrade is available for all the operating system releases supported by the Solaris Cluster 3.2 software.

If you are using the Solaris 10 OS with a ZFS root (/) file system, then the effort involved in creating an alternate boot environment is virtually zero because the required new file systems can be created from the existing root zpool. However, if you are using a Solaris Volume Manager or a Veritas Volume Manager mirrored root disk, then the process is significantly more complicated because you must find additional partitions to match the existing root partition allocation. Consequently, using the Solaris 10 OS and ZFS for the root disk has significant advantages. However, do not upgrade the software version of the zpools in your cluster until you are satisfied that your new environment is working correctly. If you do upgrade the zpool version, you will not be able to fail back to your old boot environment, as the old environment might not be able to mount the zpools that already have a higher version number. Such zpools cannot be downgraded.

After you have updated the Oracle Solaris OS on your new boot environment, you can proceed with updating the Solaris Cluster software. When using Solaris Live Upgrade, you must follow the documentation on how to handle specific steps relating to the volume managers, Solaris Volume Manager and Veritas Volume Manager, and which version of the Java Runtime Environment (JRE) is required.

The process for updating the Solaris Cluster software on the alternate boot environment is outlined in the following steps:

1. Create an `installer` program state file to drive the upgrade of the shared components on the alternate boot environment, but without actually performing the actions.

2. Run the `installer` program again using this state file but targeted on the alternate boot environment.

3. Update the Solaris Cluster framework by running the `scinstall` command from the new Solaris Cluster media, again targeting the alternate boot environment.

4. Update the Solaris Cluster agents by running the `scinstall` command from the new Solaris Cluster media, again targeting the alternate boot environment.

## Upgrading Nodes Using Oracle Solaris Zones

When upgrading a cluster node that uses the Solaris 10 OS, you need to consider the impact the upgrade process has on any Oracle Solaris Zones (also known as Oracle Solaris Containers) that are configured on the system. These containers represent additional, virtual Solaris instances that must also be upgraded.

To maintain service availability during an upgrade, a resource group must have a node list that contains at least one physical cluster node that will still be available to host the resource group while the rolling upgrade or dual-partition upgrade is performed. This is feasible both for resource groups that use global-cluster non-voting nodes and for resource groups existing in zone clusters. However, HA containers are, by their very nature, the sole place in which the service resides. Therefore, taking the cluster node into single-user mode to patch it results in the HA container, and consequently the service, being unavailable for the duration of the update process [ZonePatch].

One way to minimize HA container service outage is to use Solaris Live Upgrade. The procedure is not particularly practical if you have tens or hundreds of HA containers because it involves many steps.

The following procedure is meant for environments where each HA container has its `zonepath`, on its own Oracle Solaris ZFS file system, in its own zpool, for example, `ora-pool/ora1` for `ora1`. Both `ora-pool` and `ora-pool/ora1` must have appropriate mount points set.

Solaris Live Upgrade requires full control over the zpools when the Oracle Solaris OS reboots in order to perform the necessary renaming of the ZFS file systems and the changes to the zones' configuration files. Therefore, the ZFS file systems must not be under Solaris Cluster software control during the shutdown and boot process. This can be achieved by creating an alternate boot environment where each zone and its associated `zonepath` are under cluster control. Then, prior to shutting down the system, you can offline and unmanage the resource groups controlling the HA containers and import each zpool that holds a `zonepath`. Finally, you can copy all the affected configuration files in the CCR and the `zpool.cache` file to the alternate boot environment.

In general, this procedure requires you to perform the following steps:

1. Alter the HA container's resource group node list to just the current node.
2. Perform a Solaris Live Upgrade on the node.
3. Disable the resources of the HA container's resource group, which takes the container offline and unmanages the resource groups.
4. Import the zpool holding the zone's `zonepath`.

5. Copy the `zpool.cache` file and corresponding CCR files for the resource group to the alternate boot environment.

6. Shut down and reboot the node.

7. After Solaris Live Upgrade has performed all of the necessary reconfigurations, manage and bring the resource group online.

8. Detach the HA container from its other nodes, and then use Solaris Live Upgrade and reboot the other nodes in turn.

9. Attach the `zonepath` of the HA container with the `-F` (force) option to bring the container's state back to `installed`.

10. Reset the HA container's resource group node list.

11. Check that switchover still works and finish by switching the HA container back to its primary machine.

Although this procedure requires a shorter outage, other factors might make it impractical. First, the HA container cannot be failed over while the upgrade is under way because the node list has been restricted to the single node. Additionally, the service-level agreements (SLAs) for other HA containers that are deployed on the system might limit when the outage can occur because any upgrade will affect them, too. If there isn't a single time period when groups of containers can be updated, then the restriction will prevent any of the changes from being made.

The final option for upgrading HA containers is to use the update on attach feature in the Solaris 10 10/08 release. This option can be used only to update the packages in a container and does not allow them to be downgraded. If you use this option, you must ensure that the process does not introduce any packages that are older than the current version the Solaris Cluster software requires. If it does, you must update them again using the `installer` program.

An outline of the steps for using the update on attach feature follows:

1. Evacuate (or switch over) all the containers that will not be patched from the target node (`nodeT`) using `clresourcegroup switch ...`, leaving just the containers to be patched.

2. On node `nodeT`, use `zoneadm -z ...` detach to detach each remaining container from `nodeT` so that the operating system will not attempt to patch them.

3. On node `nodeT`, patch `nodeT` and reboot back into the cluster.

4. Use `clresource disable ...` to disable the HA container resources that were switched over to the alternative node (`nodeA`), and switch their resource groups back to `nodeT`. This switches over the `zonepaths` to `nodeT`.

5. On node `nodeA`, detach the container from `nodeA` so that the operating system will not attempt to patch the container during the patch process or reboot the container after the upgrade.

6. On node `nodeT`, use `zoneadm -z ... attach -u` to reattach and patch the HA container on `nodeT`.

7. Test the containers by booting and halting them manually.

8. Place the containers back under cluster control by reenabling the HA container resource.

9. Repeat the upgrade process with `nodeA`.

Ensure that HA containers are prevented from failing between the nodes while this procedure is being followed.

## Backing Up Your Cluster

Although your data might be protected by hardware RAID or host-based mirroring software and even possibly replicated to another site for disaster recovery purposes, you must have a consistent, usable backup of the data on your cluster. The requirement is twofold, involving backup of the root disk and backup of the application data. Both have their own specific challenges.

### Root Disk Backup

Your root disk contains the Oracle Solaris OS with numerous configuration files that the system requires to perform its tasks. Not all of these files are static. Many of the log files you need to retain for auditing and debugging purposes are highly dynamic. Therefore, you must achieve a consistent backup of your system so that you can restore your system successfully, if the need arises.

When using UFS for the root disk, only two methods are available for achieving a guaranteed consistent backup of the root file system partitions:

- Boot the system into single-user mode.
- Use both `lockfs` and `fssnap` while the system is at its normal run level.

Obviously, booting a node into single-user mode requires that you switch over all the services hosted on this node. Not only does this result in service outages, but it also means that the application might have to share the resources on its new host node, which might degrade its performance somewhat. The `lockfs`/`fssnap` option seems better. However, they can result in the system pausing while the data is flushed from the buffer cache and a consistent view is reached. If this pause is too long, it might have an adverse effect on the cluster framework. Furthermore, any real-time process prevents `fssnap` from being able to lock the file system. Thus, with a Solaris Cluster installation, you must temporarily suspend the `xntpd` daemon. However, other processes, such as the Oracle 10*g* Real Application Clusters or Oracle 11*g* Real Application Clusters frameworks might make this approach unworkable.

After you have performed the backup, you can delete the snapshot and move on to the next partition on the root disk.

---

### Example 4.12  Using `lockfs` and `fssnap` to Create a Consistent Root (/) File System Snapshot

Stop the `xntpd` daemon before locking the root (/) file system with the `lockfs` command.

```
# /etc/rc2.d/S74xntpd.cluster stop
# lockfs -f
```

Take a snapshot of the root (/) file system using the `fssnap` command before restarting the `xntpd` daemon.

```
# time fssnap -o backing-store=/spare_disk /
/dev/fssnap/0

real    0m19.370s
user    0m0.003s
sys     0m0.454s
# /etc/rc2.d/S74xntpd.cluster start
Perform backup...
# fssnap -d /dev/fssnap/0
Deleted snapshot 0.
```

---

For an Oracle Solaris ZFS file system, the situation is much more straightforward. By issuing a `zfs snapshot` command, you can create a consistent view of a file system that you can back up and restore with confidence. Using the `-r` flag allows you to create these snapshots recursively for all file systems below a certain mount point, further simplifying the process.

## Backing Up Application Data on a Cluster

The first challenge with backing up application data when a service resides on a cluster is determining which cluster node the service is currently running on. If a failure has recently occurred, then the service might not be running on its primary node. If you are running Oracle RAC, the database is probably running on multiple nodes simultaneously. In addition, the data might be stored on raw disk or in Oracle's Automatic Storage Management (ASM), rather than in a file system. Consequently, any backup process must be capable of communicating with the node that currently hosts the application, rather than depending on the application being on a particular node, and potentially using application-specific backup procedures or software.

Although `fssnap` can be used in certain circumstances to achieve a consistent view of the root (/) file system partitions for backup, do not use it with failover UFS file systems. The pause in file system activity while the snapshot is being taken might result in the service fault probe detecting a fault and causing a service failover. Furthermore, `fssnap` cannot be used with global file systems (see the section "The Cluster File System" in Chapter 2, "Oracle Solaris Cluster: Features and Architecture") because `fssnap` must be run on the UFS mount point directly and works closely with the in-memory data structures of UFS. This means that the PxFS client and server (master) must interpret the `fssnap ioctl` system calls, but this capability is not currently present in PxFS.

Once more, the Oracle Solaris ZFS snapshot feature enables you to obtain a consistent view of the application data and so is a simpler option if there are no specific tools for consistently backing up the application data.

Many backup products are available from Oracle and from third-party sources. Many have application-specific integration features, for example, the ability to integrate with Oracle's RMAN backup function. Most products can back up data stored in any file system (UFS, ZFS, QFS, VxFS) that you might have configured in your cluster.

## Highly Available Backup Servers

It's obviously very important to perform regular, secure backups of your critical systems. This, in turn, means that the systems performing the backup must be sufficiently highly available. Otherwise, they might not be able to complete a backup within the time window available. Although there is little you can do to make an individual tape drive more available, you can have tape libraries housing multiple tape drives. Then the problem of availability rests with the system that controls the backups.

A backup (master) server contains the backup configuration information: catalogs of previous backups, schedules for subsequent backups, and target nodes to be backed up. Just like any other service, this collection of data files and the programs that access it can be made highly available. Thus, a highly available service can be achieved by placing the configuration files on a highly available file system, hosted by one or more Solaris Cluster nodes, and encapsulating the backup server program in a suitable resource in a resource group.

The most common data center backup configuration uses SAN-attached tape libraries with multiple tape drives. You configure the master server to manage the backup by communicating with the client software installed on each target cluster node to be backed up. Instead of defining an entire physical server as a target, you use the logical host of the individual services that require their data to be backed up. The master server then contacts the appropriate physical node when the time comes to back up the data. If you need to back up the individual nodes, then you define the backup so that it covers only the file systems that constitute the root (/) file system. When the time comes to perform the backup, the master server directs the client to stream the necessary dataset to one or more tapes in the library.

Solaris Cluster agents are available for both the StorageTek Enterprise Backup software and Veritas NetBackup. If a Solaris Cluster agent is not available for your backup software, you can easily create one, as described in the next section.

## Creating New Resource Types

As described in the section "Data Service and Application Agents" in Chapter 2, "Oracle Solaris Cluster: Features and Architecture," Oracle has a substantial list of supported agents that cover most of the applications in your data center. These application agents are maintained by Oracle and are extensively tested on each new release of both the Solaris Cluster software and the application itself. Even so, inevitably you will have an application that is not part of the existing agent portfolio.

### Application Suitability

Before creating a resource type for your application, you must determine whether the application meets the criteria for being made highly available. The following list highlights the main points you must consider. For a complete list see "Analyzing the Application for Suitability" in [SCDevGuide].

- Is your application crash-tolerant? This is important because in a highly available environment your application must be able to recover its data consistency without requiring manual intervention. If the application did require such intervention, then most of the benefits of a high-availability framework would be lost.
- Does your application rely on the physical node name of the machine, such as that resulting from calls to uname, gethostbyname, or equivalent interfaces?

If so, then when the application moves to another cluster node, the dependency on the physical hostname will probably cause the application to fail. There is a work-around to this problem, which is to interpose the `libschost.so.1` library. However, this work-around can sometimes raise support issues with application vendors.

- Can your application run on a multihomed system, that is, one with several public networks? Your application must be able to handle situations where IP addresses are configured and unconfigured from network adapters as services move around the cluster. This has consequences for the way your application binds to the network.

- Does your application use hard-coded path names for the location of its data? If so, then symbolic links might not be sufficient to ensure that the data is stored in a location that is compatible with using a failover or global file system. If the application renames a data file, it can break the symbolic links.

After you have determined that your application is suitable for being made highly available, you have several ways to achieve the necessary integration:

- You can use the Generic Data Service (GDS) directly and just supply the required parameters. Although you cannot define any new extension properties for the resource type you create, it is by far the simplest option.

- You can create a subclass of the GDS to create a completely new resource type. This option enables you to define one or more extension properties for your new resource type. This option is relatively simple and yet provides considerable flexibility.

- You can extend the GDS using the Advanced Agent Toolkit. Although this option does not create a new resource type, it does enable you to define one or more extension properties. This option is also relatively simple and provides considerable flexibility.

- You can use the GUI `scdsbuilder` tool and customize the resulting shell script or C source using the Resource Management API (RMAPI) and the Data Service Development Library (DSDL) APIs. If significant customization work is needed, this option might result in an increased maintenance burden.

- You can use the RMAPI or DSDL APIs directly to develop your resource type from scratch. This option trades the development and maintenance costs for ultimate flexibility and performance.

Each option is discussed in more detail in the following sections.

## Generic Data Service

The Generic Data Service (GDS) is provided with the Solaris Cluster software. The `SUNW.gds` agent is packaged in the `SUNWscgds` package, which is installed as standard by the Solaris Cluster software `installer` program. The `SUNW.gds` agent is considered the preferred way to create both failover and scalable resources. The GDS is supported by Oracle, but you must support the script that you provide for the `Start_command`, `Stop_command`, `Probe_command`, and `Validate_command` methods.

By default, the `SUNW.gds` resource type is not registered, so you must register it before attempting to create a resource of that type. The commands in the following example show how to determine if the resource type is registered and then how to register it, if it is not already present.

### Example 4.13  Registering the `SUNW.gds` Resource Type

Use the `clresourcetype` command to determine whether the `SUNW.gds` resource type needs to be registered.

```
# clresourcetype list | grep SUNW.gds
# clresourcetype register SUNW.gds
# clresourcetype list | grep SUNW.gds
SUNW.gds:6
```

In addition to the standard resource properties, the GDS agent has four properties to enable you to integrate your application: `Start_command`, `Stop_command`, `Probe_command`, and `Validate_command`. These properties are described in "Integrating Your Application-Specific Logic." By using the GDS as the basis for your application, you automatically benefit from all the patches and feature upgrades that the GDS receives.

Example 4.14 shows how you can use the GDS to make the X11 program `xeyes` highly available. You begin by creating a `Start_command` program. In this example, a script calls the full path name of the program with a parameter that is passed to the shell script. This script must exist on all the cluster nodes on which the application is intended to run.

Next, having checked that the `SUNW.gds` resource type is registered, you create the resource group. In this example, you allow the resource group's node list to default to all the cluster nodes.

Next, you create a resource to represent your program. In the example, the `Start_command` property is specified by the script you wrote (and which must exist on all nodes). The display parameter to use is also specified. Because this program does not listen on any network ports, you set the `network_aware` property to `false`. This means that the probe mechanism used will be the continued existence of the `xeyes` process that the `Start_command` program leaves running in the background. By default, any resource you create is enabled so that when the resource group is brought online, the resource is automatically started. To change the default, you can specify the `-d` argument to the `clresource create` command.

The last two steps instruct the RGM that it needs to control or manage the `xeyes-rg` resource group and then to bring that resource group online. The action of bringing the resource group online starts the resource because it was created in an enabled state.

Assuming you have allowed remote X11 clients to display on your X server using `xhost` and you have specified the correct X display to use (substitute a value suited to your environment for `myhost:1.0`), then the `xeyes` program will appear on your display. You can switch the resource group between nodes and the RGM will kill the `xeyes` process and restart it on the new node, `phys-summer2`, as the example shows.

## Example 4.14  Creating a Simple, Highly Available **xeyes** Service

List the script that will be used to start the `xeyes` command.

```
# cat /tmp/start_xeyes
#!/bin/ksh
/usr/openwin/demo/xeyes -display $1 &
exit 0
```

Check that the `SUNW.gds` resource type is registered, and then create the resource group and resource that will control the `xeyes` service.

```
# clresourcetype list | grep SUNW.gds
SUNW.gds:6
# clresourcegroup create xeyes-rg
# clresource create -t SUNW.gds \
> -p start_command="/tmp/start_xeyes myhost:1.0" \
> -p network_aware=false \
> -g xeyes-rg xeyes-rs
```

Use the `clresourcegroup` command to bring the `xeyes-rg` resource group online.

```
# clresourcegroup manage xeyes-rg
# clresourcegroup online xeyes-rg
# clresourcegroup status xeyes-rg

=== Cluster Resource Groups ===

Group Name      Node Name       Suspended    Status
----------      ---------       ---------    ------
xeyes-rg        phys-summer1    No           Online
                phys-summer2    No           Offline
```

```
# clresourcegroup switch -n phys-summer2 xeyes-rg
# clresourcegroup status xeyes-rg

=== Cluster Resource Groups ===

Group Name        Node Name        Suspended      Status
----------        ---------        ---------      ------
xeyes-rg          phys-summer1     No             Offline
                  phys-summer2     No             Online
```

To demonstrate how the GDS handles application failure, quit the xeyes program from your X display. You will notice that the RGM restarts the application almost instantaneously. The messages in /var/adm/messages (see Example 4.15) indicate that the RGM recognized the failure and restarted the service.

After the fault probe determines that the service is online, indicated by Service is online in /var/adm/messages, kill the process again. The resource has two properties that determine how many times it is restarted by the RGM within a certain time period. These properties are Retry_count and Retry_interval (see Example 4.16). After the specified number of failures, the built-in logic of the GDS determines that the current node is unhealthy and releases the service so that it can be started on another node. If the service also experiences problems on this node, then the RGM will not fail the service back to its original node unless the time period, in seconds, as defined by the resource group's Pingpong_interval property, has passed. Instead, the GDS attempts to keep the service running on the remaining node. This behavior is governed by another property called Failover_mode.

The purpose of the Pingpong_interval property is to prevent a service that fails to start from endlessly looping, resulting in the service migrating back and forth between cluster nodes. In a test environment, you might need to reset the value of Pingpong_interval to a lower value. Doing so enables you to restart your service once you have corrected any problems you encountered.

## Example 4.15  Sample RGM Messages

The /var/adm/messages file contains information on the state changes of the resource groups and resources in the cluster.

```
Nov 23 04:00:23 phys-summer2 Cluster.RGM.global.rgmd: [ID 529407 daemon.notice]
resource group xeyes-rg state on node phys-summer2 change to RG_ONLINE
Nov 23 04:01:23 phys-summer2 Cluster.RGM.global.rgmd: [ID 922363 daemon.notice]
resource xeyes-rs status msg on node phys-summer2 change to <Service is online.>
Nov 23 04:01:25 phys-summer2 Cluster.PMF.pmfd: [ID 887656 daemon.notice] Process:
tag="xeyes-rg,xeyes-rs,0.svc", cmd="/bin/sh -c /tmp/start_xeyes myhost:1.0", Failed
to stay up.
```

```
Nov 23 04:01:25 phys-summer2 Cluster.RGM.global.rgmd: [ID 784560 daemon.notice]
resource xeyes-rs status on node phys-summer2 change to R_FM_FAULTED
Nov 23 04:01:25 phys-summer2 Cluster.RGM.global.rgmd: [ID 922363 daemon.notice]
resource xeyes-rs status msg on node phys-summer2 change to <Service daemon not
running.>
Nov 23 04:01:25 phys-summer2 SC[,SUNW.gds:6,xeyes-rg,xeyes-rs,gds_probe]: [ID 423137
daemon.error] A resource restart attempt on resource xeyes-rs in resource group
xeyes-rg has been blocked because the number of restarts within the past Retry_
interval (370 seconds) would exceed Retry_count (2)
Nov 23 04:01:25 phys-summer2 SC[,SUNW.gds:6,xeyes-rg,xeyes-rs,gds_probe]: [ID 874133
daemon.notice] Issuing a failover request because the application exited.
Nov 23 04:01:25 phys-summer2 Cluster.RGM.global.rgmd: [ID 494478 daemon.notice]
resource xeyes-rs in resource group xeyes-rg has requested failover of the resource
group on phys-summer2.
Nov 23 04:01:25 phys-summer2 Cluster.RGM.global.rgmd: [ID 423291 daemon.error] RGM
isn't failing resource group <xeyes-rg> off of node <phys-summer2>, because there are
no other current or potential masters
Nov 23 04:01:25 phys-summer2 Cluster.RGM.global.rgmd: [ID 702911 daemon.error]
Resource <xeyes-rs> of Resource Group <xeyes-rg> failed pingpong check on node <phys-
summer1>.  The resource group will not be mastered by that node.
Nov 23 04:01:25 phys-summer2 SC[,SUNW.gds:6,xeyes-rg,xeyes-rs,gds_probe]: [ID 969827
daemon.error] Failover attempt has failed.
Nov 23 04:01:25 phys-summer2 SC[,SUNW.gds:6,xeyes-rg,xeyes-rs,gds_probe]: [ID 670283
daemon.notice] Issuing a resource restart request because the application exited.
```

## Example 4.16  Retry, Failover Mode, and Ping-pong Interval Properties

Use the `clresource` command to determine the property values of the `xeyes-rs` resource.

```
# clresource show \
>    -p retry_count,retry_interval,failover_mode xeyes-rs

=== Resources ===

Resource:                                  xeyes-rs

  --- Standard and extension properties ---

  Retry_interval:                          370
    Class:                                 standard
    Description:                           Time in which monitor attempts to
restart a failed resource Retry_count times.
    Type:                                  int

  Retry_count:                             2
    Class:                                 standard
    Description:                           Indicates the number of times a
monitor restarts the resource if it fails.
    Type:                                  int

  Failover_mode:                           SOFT
    Class:                                 standard
    Description:                           Modifies recovery actions taken
when the resource fails.
    Type:                                  enum
```

```
# clresourcegroup show -p pingpong_interval xeyes-rg

=== Resource Groups and Resources ===

Resource Group:                                    xeyes-rg
  Pingpong_interval:                                   3600
```

In the preceding example, the display variable property can be changed only by stopping the resource and modifying the `Start_command` property. Although of little importance here, because the `xeyes` program must be restarted to change the target X server on which it displays, it does make a difference in instances where a variable can be changed while a service is running. Examples include changing debugging levels to use and changing directories for log files.

To create a resource type that has new extension properties that can be changed when you need to change them, you need to either write your resource type from scratch or create a subclass of the GDS, as described in a later section.

## Supporting New Applications Using the Advanced Agent Toolkit

Many application agents in the current Solaris Cluster software release are derived from the Advanced Agent Toolkit methodology [AdvGDSTlkit]: HA-PostgreSQL, HA-MySQL, and HA containers, to name three. All three use the `SUNW.gds` agent as their basis. However, in its raw form, the `SUNW.gds` agent has some limitations.

The rationale behind the toolkit is that all new application agents have many common requirements:

- They might require one or more extension properties.
- They must provide debugging information.
- They might need to disable the process-monitoring facility (`pmfadm`) for applications that leave no obvious child processes to monitor.
- They must supply a `Start_command` script, as a minimum, and possibly `Stop_command`, `Probe_command`, and `Validate_command` scripts.

The toolkit also simplifies much of the work needed to handle Oracle Solaris Zones and SMF. Thus, providing this extended framework enables your developers to focus on the application-specific integration work rather than on debugging the framework itself. After the work is complete, the new resource type is registered using a registration script.

## Developing Resource Types by Creating a Subclass of the GDS

The advantage of creating a subclass of the GDS, rather than writing a new resource type from scratch, is that the new resource type inherits all the best practices that are already part of the standard GDS code. In addition, creating a subclass of the GDS enables you to create your own resource type extension properties while retaining the same level of flexibility as if you had started from scratch. Finally, your new resource type, which is a subclass of the GDS, has a distinct name, enabling you to easily distinguish resources of the new resource type. If you instead used the Advanced Agent Toolkit or the SUNW.gds agent, then you would have to determine what the resource is by examining the extension properties or reviewing the code. This step would be necessary because the resource type would be set to SUNW.gds, rather than MYCORP.appsvr, for example.

You create a subclass of the GDS by creating a resource type registration (RTR) file where the RT_basedir parameter is set to the directory containing binaries used by the standard GDS methods: Start, Stop, Validate, and so on. You then extend the RTR file by defining your own resource type extension properties. Finally, you set the method parameters in the RTR file to point to your scripts that override the standard GDS behavior.

Several existing Sun resource types are implemented this way, including the HA-Logical Domain agent (SUNW.ldom), which was covered in the section "Failover Guest Domains" in Chapter 3, "Combining Virtualization Technologies with Oracle Solaris Cluster Software."

The RTR file for the SUNW.ldom resource type is shown in Example 4.17. In this RTR file, the RT_basedir parameter is set to the standard directory for the GDS package, that is, /opt/SUNWscgds/bin. Of the standard methods, only Init, Boot, and Validate have been overridden using programs that are located in the ../../SUNWscxvm/bin directory. Unlike a standard GDS resource type, the Start_command, Stop_command, Probe_command, and Validate_command properties are assigned fixed values and cannot be changed. This is indicated by the Tunable = NONE settings. Furthermore, each command, apart from validate_command, is called with a consistent set of arguments, namely, -R %RS_NAME -T %RT_NAME -G %RG_NAME. The %variable construct is similar to the $variable syntax found in shell scripts. It means that when a resource of this type is instantiated, use the names you assigned it as arguments. For example, if you wrote a resource type called FOO.bar and then created a resource group called whizz-rg containing a resource called bang-rs of this type, the argument passed would be -R bang-rs -T FOO.bar -G whizz-rg. With these arguments, you can then make calls to the RMAPI or DSDL APIs to retrieve or set properties.

In contrast to the Start_command, Stop_command, and Probe_command properties, the Validate_command property does not use this construct. Instead, the

RGM passes the validate command all the properties listed for the resource type on the command line. Then the validate command parses this list and determines whether the configuration is valid.

## Example 4.17  RTR File for the SUNW.1dom Resource Type

The following text shows some of the key parts of the RTR file for the SUNW.1dom resource type:

```
      .
      .
      .
RESOURCE_TYPE = "ldom";
VENDOR_ID = SUNW;
RT_DESCRIPTION = "Sun Cluster HA for xVM Server SPARC Guest Domains";

RT_version ="1";
API_version = 10;

RT_basedir=/opt/SUNWscgds/bin;

Init                          =         ../../SUNWscxvm/bin/init_xvm;
Boot                          =         ../../SUNWscxvm/bin/boot_xvm;

Start                         =         gds_svc_start;
Stop                          =         gds_svc_stop;

Validate                      =         ../../SUNWscxvm/bin/validate_xvm;
Update                        =         gds_update;

Monitor_start                 =         gds_monitor_start;
Monitor_stop                  =         gds_monitor_stop;
Monitor_check                 =         gds_monitor_check;

Init_nodes = RG_PRIMARIES;
Failover = FALSE;

# The paramtable is a list of bracketed resource property declarations
# that come after the resource-type declarations
# The property-name declaration must be the first attribute
# after the open curly of a paramtable entry
#
# The following are the system defined properties. Each of the system defined
# properties have a default value set for each of the attributes. Look at
# man rt_reg(4) for a detailed explanation.
#
{
        PROPERTY = Start_timeout;
        MIN = 60;
        DEFAULT = 300;
}
{
        PROPERTY = Stop_timeout;
        MIN = 60;
        DEFAULT = 300;
}
      .
      .
      .
```

```
# This is an optional property. Any value provided will be used as
# the absolute path to a command to invoke to validate the application.
# If no value is provided, The validation will be skipped.
#
{
        PROPERTY = Validate_command;
        EXTENSION;
        STRING;
        DEFAULT = "";
        TUNABLE = NONE;
        DESCRIPTION = "Command to validate the  application";
}

# This property must be specified, since this is the only mechanism
# that indicates how to start the application.  Since a value must
# be provided, there is no default.  The value must be an absolute path.
{
        PROPERTY = Start_command;
        EXTENSION;
        STRINGARRAY;
        DEFAULT = "/opt/SUNWscxvm/bin/control_xvm start -R %RS_NAME -T %RT_NAME -G
           %RG_NAME";
        TUNABLE = NONE;
        DESCRIPTION = "Command to start application";
}

# This is an optional property.  Any value provided will be used as
# the absolute path to a command to invoke to stop the application.
# If no value is provided, signals will be used to stop the application.
#
# It is assumed that Stop_command will not return until the
# application has been stopped.
{
        PROPERTY = Stop_command;
        EXTENSION;
        STRING;
        DEFAULT = "/opt/SUNWscxvm/bin/control_xvm stop -R %RS_NAME -T %RT_NAME -G
           %RG_NAME";
        TUNABLE = NONE;
        DESCRIPTION = "Command to stop application";
}

# This is an optional property.  Any value provided will be used as
# the absolute path to a command to invoke to probe the application.
# If no value is provided, the "simple_probe" will be used to probe
# the application.
#
{
        PROPERTY = Probe_command;
        EXTENSION;
        STRING;
        DEFAULT = "/opt/SUNWscxvm/bin/control_xvm probe -R %RS_NAME -G %RG_NAME -T
           %RT_NAME";
        TUNABLE = NONE;
        DESCRIPTION = "Command to probe application";
}

# This is an optional property.  It determines whether the application
# uses network to communicate with its clients.
#
{
        PROPERTY = Network_aware;
        EXTENSION;
        BOOLEAN;
        DEFAULT = FALSE;
```

```
            TUNABLE = AT_CREATION;
            DESCRIPTION = "Determines whether the application uses network";
}

# This is an optional property, which determines the signal sent to the
# application for being stopped.
#
{
            PROPERTY = Stop_signal;
            EXTENSION;
            INT;
            MIN = 1;
            MAX = 37;
            DEFAULT = 15;
            TUNABLE = WHEN_DISABLED;
            DESCRIPTION = "The signal sent to the application for being stopped";
}

# This is an optional property, which determines whether to failover when
# retry_count is exceeded during retry_interval.
#
{
            PROPERTY = Failover_enabled;
            EXTENSION;
            BOOLEAN;
            DEFAULT = TRUE;
            TUNABLE = WHEN_DISABLED;
            DESCRIPTION = "Determines whether to failover when retry_count is exceeded
during retry_interval";
}

# This is an optional property that specifies the log level GDS events.
#
{
            PROPERTY = Log_level;
            EXTENSION;
            ENUM { NONE, INFO, ERR };
            DEFAULT = "INFO";
            TUNABLE = ANYTIME;
            DESCRIPTION = "Determines the log level for event based traces";
}

{
            Property = Debug_level;
            Extension;
            Per_node;
            Int;
            Min = 0;
            Max = 2;
            Default = 0;
            Tunable = ANYTIME;
            Description = "Debug level";
}

{
            Property = Domain_name;
            Extension;
            String;
            Minlength = 1;
            Tunable = WHEN_DISABLED;
            Description = "LDoms Guest Domain name";
}
```

```
{
        Property = Migration_type;
        Extension;
        Enum { NORMAL, MIGRATE };
        Default = "MIGRATE";
        Tunable = ANYTIME;
        Description = "Type of guest domain migration to be performed";
}

{
        PROPERTY = Plugin_probe;
        EXTENSION;
        STRING;
        DEFAULT = "";
        TUNABLE = ANYTIME;
        DESCRIPTION = "Script or command to check the guest domain";
}

{
        PROPERTY = Password_file;
        EXTENSION;
        STRING;
        DEFAULT = "";
        TUNABLE = WHEN_DISABLED;
        DESCRIPTION = "The complete path to the file containing the target host
password";
}
```

## scdsbuilder GUI

To customize an agent beyond what is permitted by the GDS, you can use the Agent Builder command, scdsbuilder (see the scdsbuilder(1HA) man page). This command has three code generation options, and the resulting files are wrapped in a Solaris package that you can install on your cluster nodes:

- DSDL code (see the section "Data Service Development Library").
- ksh code, including all the necessary scha_control commands (see the section "Resource Management API"). With the ksh code, you are creating your own resource type.
- A ksh registration script for a GDS agent. Here, the code generates the appropriate clresource create command.

You can customize the resulting code to your specific needs. However, with the ksh registration script for the GDS agent, the scope for modification is limited. The example in Figure 4.7 shows the use of the third option.

The scdsbuilder command starts the Solaris Cluster Agent Builder GUI, as shown in Figure 4.7. In this example, data has already been specified for each field available to the user. A short code of SUNW is specified for the vendor name, and tstgds is specified for the application name. This data is then used to generate

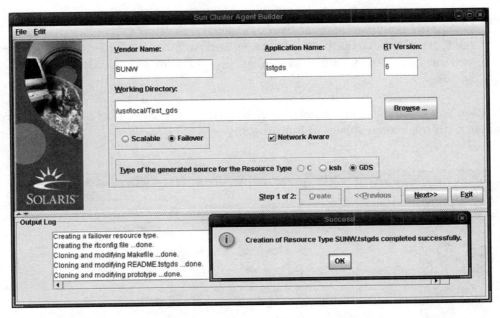

**Figure 4.7** Using the `scdsbuilder` GUI to create a new resource type

both the name of the package that Agent Builder creates for you and the name of the resource type that you will subsequently use.

The information you provide in the other fields is used as follows:

- The RT version enables you to specify a version number for this resource type. You can identify which version of the agent you are running when it is placed into production.

- The working directory is used by Agent Builder as a working area in which it can create your package and write other associated, intermediate files.

- Your target application determines whether you select the scalable or failover option. If a particular instance of an application can run on multiple nodes at once without corrupting any of its data files, then you can select the scalable option. A good example of such an application is a web server. For all other applications, such as databases and file services, select the failover option.

- The Network Aware check box is used to determine whether any resource created using this resource type needs to have the `port_list` property set. The `port_list` property is then used by the GDS service to provide a simple probe mechanism.

- The source type option determines whether the resulting code uses the C programming language, `ksh`, or the GDS (see the section "`SUNW.gds`" in Chapter 2, "Oracle Solaris Cluster: Features and Architecture") to create the data service. To use the C option, you must have a C compiler installed on your system.

After you have entered the data and clicked on the Next button, you are presented with the screen shown in Figure 4.8.

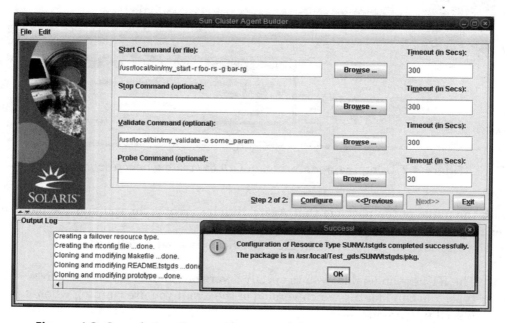

**Figure 4.8** Completing the resource type definition using `scdsbuilder`

## Integrating Your Application-Specific Logic

You use the fields in this second screen to provide the location of the programs (which can be compiled executables or scripts) and their associated arguments that will be used to start, stop, probe, and validate your data service when it is installed on the target cluster nodes. For each program, you can set a time limit on how long it can take for the program to complete. If the program does not complete within the allocated time period, then the resource is placed into a failed state, such as `STOP_FAILED`.

You are required to provide a value only for the start program. All the other programs are optional. Any programs specified must exit with a return code of zero only when they have successfully completed their work. If they fail to perform their allotted task, they must return a value greater than 100. Values below that are used by the Solaris Cluster commands and have specific meanings (see the intro(1CL) man page).

The programs you assign to the start and stop commands must return successfully only when your target application has actually completed the relevant operation. If the stop command leaves the application under its control running, or not completely stopped, but the stop command returns successfully, then the cluster framework erroneously determines that it is safe to start the resource group on another cluster node. In some instances, particularly when the application uses a global file system, this outcome could result in data corruption because the two instances of the application could write to their data files in an uncontrolled fashion.

If no stop command is provided, the process tree that results from the start command is terminated using the kill command.

The validate command enables you to check that your application is correctly configured on all the potential nodes on which it can run. Again, if the program determines that your application is misconfigured, the validate program must exit with a nonzero exit code.

The capability to incorporate a probe command is one of the key benefits of using the Solaris Cluster framework. A probe command enables you to write a program that determines the health of your application. As an example, if you are writing a probe for a database, you could test whether it can execute basic SQL statements, such as creating or deleting a table, or adding or deleting a record. If you do not provide a probe script, then default methods are used instead.

For non-network-aware applications, the process-monitoring command pmfadm (see the pmfadm(1M) man page) monitors the process tree spawned by your start command. Only if all the processes have failed will the cluster framework attempt to restart the service. Therefore, if your service consists of multiple processes and only one process fails, then pmfadm will not recognize this fault unless it causes all the other processes to fail as well. Consequently, if you need to monitor your application with a higher degree of granularity, you must provide a custom fault probe.

If the application is network-aware, then the default probe tries to open the port listed in the port_list property. Because this is a simple probe, it makes no attempt to retrieve any data. Even if the default probe successfully opens the ports, that does not necessarily indicate overall application health.

In the preceding example, you would install the package generated by scdsbuilder on all your cluster nodes. You would then register the new resource type so that you could create new resources of this type. When the RGM is requested to create a resource, it calls the validate command: /usr/local/bin/my_validate -o some_param. If that command succeeds and you enable the resource, the RGM calls the /usr/local/bin/my_start -r foo-rs -g bar-rg command. In both cases, the initial arguments are fixed, but you can modify them subsequently using the `clresource` command.

## Resource Type Registration File

If you decide to write an agent from scratch using either the RMAPI or DSDL APIs, you must first describe the properties of your proposed resource type in a file known as the resource type registration (RTR) file. This file provides the RGM with details on which programs to call and which variables are required to control the particular application.

Example 4.18 shows an extract from the `SUNW.LogicalHostname` RTR file. As the example shows, all the programs for this resource type are located in the directory defined by `RT_BASEDIR`. The RTR file also defines programs that will, among other tasks, start, stop, and probe (`Monitor_start`) the logical IP address that the resource plumbs. These addresses are, in turn, defined in the `HostnameList` property.

The extension properties you define are all application-specific. They could, for example, refer to the location of the software binaries, that is, the application home directory. If a property has a default value, then you can define it in the RTR file to save your system administrator from having to override it each time he or she creates a resource of this type. Furthermore, you can place limits on what values certain properties can take and when they can be changed.

---

### Example 4.18  Extract from the `SUNW.LogicalHostname` RTR File

The following text shows some of the key parts of the RTR file for the `SUNW.Logical-Hostname` resource type:

```
#
# Copyright 1998-2008 Sun Microsystems, Inc.  All rights reserved.
# Use is subject to license terms.
#

#ident "@(#)SUNW.LogicalHostname 1.20 08/05/20 SMI"

# Registration information and Paramtable for HA Failover IPaddress
#
# NOTE: Keywords are case insensitive, i.e. users may use any
# capitalization style they wish
#

RESOURCE_TYPE ="LogicalHostname";
VENDOR_ID = SUNW;
RT_DESCRIPTION = "Logical Hostname Resource Type";
```

```
SYSDEFINED_TYPE = LOGICAL_HOSTNAME;

RT_VERSION ="3";
API_VERSION = 2;

INIT_NODES = RG_PRIMARIES;

RT_BASEDIR=/usr/cluster/lib/rgm/rt/hafoip;

FAILOVER = TRUE;

# To enable Global_zone_override
GLOBAL_ZONE = TRUE;

START                           =       hafoip_start;
STOP                            =       hafoip_stop;

PRENET_START                    =       hafoip_prenet_start;

VALIDATE                        =       hafoip_validate;
UPDATE                          =       hafoip_update;

MONITOR_START                   =       hafoip_monitor_start;
MONITOR_STOP                    =       hafoip_monitor_stop;
MONITOR_CHECK                   =       hafoip_monitor_check;

PKGLIST = SUNWscu;


#
# Upgrade directives
#
#$upgrade
#$upgrade_from "1.0" anytime
#$upgrade_from "2" anytime

# The paramtable is a list of bracketed resource property declarations
# that come after the resource-type declarations
# The property-name declaration must be the first attribute
# after the open curly of a paramtable entry
#
# The Paramtable cannot contain TIMEOUT properties for methods
# that aren't in the RT
{
        PROPERTY = Start_timeout;
        MIN=360;
        DEFAULT=500;
}
      .
      .
      .

# HostnameList: List of hostnames managed by this resource. All must be
# on the same subnet. If need > 1 subnet with a RG, create as many
# resources as there are subnets.
{
        PROPERTY = HostnameList;
        EXTENSION;
        STRINGARRAY;
        TUNABLE = AT_CREATION;
        DESCRIPTION = "List of hostnames this resource manages";
}
      .
      .
      .
```

## Resource Management API

The Resource Management API (RMAPI) is a set of low-level functions contained in the `libscha.so` library with both C and shell interfaces. All the function names provided by this interface are prefixed with `scha_`. The shell interfaces are listed in section 1HA of the Solaris Cluster manual pages.

The `ksh` scripts generated by the Agent Builder are built using these commands, so you can insert additional lines in this code where the comments indicate. However, for greater control over the logic imposed on your application you must write your application agent from scratch.

## Data Service Development Library

The Data Service Development Library (DSDL) is a set of higher-level functions encapsulated in the `libdsdev.so` library that builds on the RMAPI functionality. This library can only be accessed using a C programming language interface. Consequently, it is potentially more time-consuming to write a complete application agent using this approach, although it does offer the greatest level of performance and flexibility.

If you used Agent Builder to create a resource type, you can customize it by inserting extra DSDL code where the comments indicate. Otherwise, you must write your agent from scratch.

All the function names provided by the library are prefixed with `scds_` and are documented in section 3HA of the Solaris Cluster manual pages. The NFS agent source code [NFSAgent] serves as a good example of how these APIs are used. Using the `nfs_svc_start.c` source as a specific example, the library is initialized with `scds_initialize()`. Resource and resource group names are then retrieved using `scds_get_resource_name()` and `scds_get_resource_group_name()` calls, respectively. Finally, the status of the resource is set by the RMAPI `scha_resource_setstatus()` call. Most of the coding effort involved with using these interfaces is consumed by the logic that describes how the agent should behave in various failure scenarios. For example, how many times should the agent attempt to restart the service before giving up and potentially failing over? What should the agent do in response to a network failure?

One advantage of using the GDS is that all the best practices for service behavior are already in the logic of the code that makes up the agent, saving you from re-creating that code.

## Useful Utilities for Building Custom Data Services

The Solaris Cluster software comes with two programs that you will find very useful if you create your resource type from scratch: `hatimerun` (see the `hatimerun`(1M) man page) and `pmfadm`.

### `hatimerun` Command

Throughout the `Start`, `Stop`, `Monitor_start`, and `Validate` methods of your resource type, you will need to run various programs to perform the required logic steps. Because your goal is high availability, you cannot wait for a program that might never respond or return, whether that program has gone into a loop or is unable to retrieve some important data from the network, disk, or other program. Consequently, you must place time constraints on the duration of the program's execution. This is the function of the `hatimerun` command. It enables you to execute a program under its control and set a limit on the time it can take to respond. If the program in question fails to respond in a timely fashion, it is terminated by default.

The `hatimerun` command also enables you to leave the program running asynchronously in the background, change the exit code returned after a timeout, or use a particular signal to terminate your program.

The most common usage of this command is in your probe commands or in the steps leading up to stopping or starting your application.

### `pmfadm` Command

If you write a custom probe for your service, you decide what constitutes a healthy service. The criteria might include application-specific checks to determine if the data it is delivering to potential clients is valid or timely. If the application consists of multiple processes, you might want to check that each process is running, using the `ps` command. All of these tests combine to give you the best assessment of your application's current health. However, your probe is scheduled to make its checks only at regular intervals. Even though you can tune these checks to occur at shorter intervals, doing so results in a greater load on your system. Consequently, you must wait, on average, half the probe period before your probe detects a situation where your application has completely failed, meaning that all the processes have exited. Once again, this does not help much toward your goal of high availability.

The solution is to use `pmfadm`, the process-monitoring facility command. When you start your application under `pmfadm`, it monitors all the processes your application spawns to a level that you determine. By default, it monitors all the application's child processes. If they all exit, `pmfadm` immediately restarts your application for you on the condition that it has not already exceeded a preset number of restarts within a certain time interval.

The most common usage of this command is in your start command to ensure that your key application processes are monitored and that complete failures are reacted to immediately.

### `libschost.so` Library

Some applications store or make use of configuration information about the physical hostname of the server on which the application is running. Such applications will most likely fail when the application is placed in a resource group and moved between the nodes of a cluster. This failure occurs because calls to `uname` or `gethostbyname` produce different responses on the global zone of each cluster node. Oracle Application Server and the Oracle E-Business Suite are two examples of programs that risk such failures [LibHost].

To overcome this limitation, you use the `LD_PRELOAD` feature to enable the runtime linker to interpose the `libschost.so.1` library in the dynamic linking process. The following example shows how this is done. You can use the same construct within your resource `Start` or `Monitor_start` (probe) methods, as required.

### Example 4.19  How to Use the `sclibhost.so.1` Library to Change the String Returned as the Hostname

Use the `uname` command to display the current hostname.

```
# uname -n
phys-winter1
```

Set the `LD_PRELOAD_32`, `LD_PRELOAD_64` and `SC_LHOSTNAME` environment variables, and then rerun the `uname` command.

```
# LD_PRELOAD_32=$LD_PRELOAD_32:/usr/cluster/lib/libschost.so.1
# LD_PRELOAD_64=$LD_PRELOAD_64:/usr/cluster/lib/64/libschost.so.1
# SC_LHOSTNAME=myhost
# export SC_LHOSTNAME LD_PRELOAD_32 LD_PRELOAD_64
# uname -n
myhost
```

## Tuning and Troubleshooting

If you are running your applications on a Solaris Cluster system, then service availability is one of your main concerns. The two major causes of service migration are cluster-node failures and the resource probes detecting that an application is unhealthy.

The Solaris Cluster framework is responsible for detecting and reacting quickly to node failures. When all the cluster private interconnects fail, the default heartbeat settings allow only 10 seconds to elapse before a cluster reconfiguration is triggered and any affected service is restarted on one of the remaining cluster nodes. The application fault probe is responsible for detecting and reacting to an application that is either unhealthy or has failed. Each fault probe can be tuned to take the appropriate action based on the number of failures within a given time interval. Similarly, the resource type `Start` and `Stop` methods for the application are responsible for ensuring that the application is successfully started and stopped. The `Start`, `Stop`, and `Monitor_start` (fault probe) methods have a tunable timeout interval, which is the maximum duration for each operation. The fault probe also has a probe interval, which determines how often the probe is run.

When tuning the probe interval and any associated timeout, you must trade off the impact of the probe on system load and application performance. If you set the values too low, you risk false failover. If you set them too high, you risk waiting longer than necessary to detect a critical problem. Because all applications and workloads are different, the only realistic way to achieve an optimal setting is by thorough testing. You start with high values and gradually reduce them until lower values result in misdiagnosed problems. You then increase the values again to give the fault probe some scope of variability. Of course, all your testing must be performed under realistic workload conditions.

For the start and stop timeouts, your task is slightly easier because the system logs (in `/var/adm/messages`) state how much of the available timeout was used by each method to complete the relevant action. Thus, you can tune your start and stop timeouts such that the application takes no more than, for example, 50 percent of this value under normal conditions.

If it is not obvious why a resource is not functioning correctly, then you can often obtain additional debugging information to help diagnose the problem. The `/var/adm/messages` file is your main source of help. All your resources will log messages here. You can increase the amount of debugging information logged by ensuring that your `syslog.conf` file directs `daemon.debug` output to a suitable file.

Some resource types use flags for specifying the amount of debugging output they produce. Others written in DSDL code (see the section "Data Service Development Library") rely on you specifying a log level from 1 to 9 (with 9 as the maximum) in a file named `/var/cluster/rgm/rt/`*resource-type-name*`/loglevel`.

# 5

# Oracle Solaris Cluster Geographic Edition: Overview

This chapter begins by explaining why a high-availability product, such as the Oracle Solaris Cluster software, might not be sufficient on its own to provide you with a complete disaster recovery solution. The chapter outlines the techniques you can use to implement such a solution before introducing the concepts of Recovery Point Objective (RPO) and Recovery Time Objective (RTO).

With this background established, the remainder of the chapter covers the value of Oracle Solaris Cluster Geographic Edition as a disaster recovery framework [SCGEOver]; the three broad categories of replication available; the topologies you can use to connect your data centers; what options you have to combine campus clusters and geographic solutions; and finally, how Solaris Cluster Geographic Edition can coexist with various virtualization technologies.

## Why Have a Disaster Recovery Solution?

A disaster is any event resulting in a large number of simultaneous failures, such that the protection offered by a cluster or local availability solution is unable to provide continuous service. The most common causes are fires and floods, but there can also be natural disasters, wars, and other such events. However, local disasters can have catastrophic consequences when data corruption or other faults prevent your systems from booting.

To protect against disasters, businesses need a business continuity plan that includes contingencies for staffing, telecommunications, buildings, and so on, as well as the critical systems that run the business. Any secondary site that houses alternative computing and data resources must be sufficiently far from the primary site to ensure it is not subject to the same event. This might mean that the secondary sites must be tens, hundreds, or even thousands of kilometers away. After this location is chosen, critical data must be replicated to the secondary site to enable the business to restart critical services if the need arises.

The pivotal IT concern when a disaster strikes is the state of the data and what hardware resources are available to host the critical service. If the data is inaccessible at the primary site, or becomes corrupted, then restarting these services on the secondary site is most likely to restore them in a timely fashion. However, this decision requires a human assessment of all factors, many of which are very difficult to measure or quantify by a computer. Therefore, moving services to a secondary site should be a manual process that involves a joint decision by the Incident (or Crisis) Management team, consisting of staff from all of the relevant business units and management teams.

## Choosing an Appropriate Disaster Recovery Solution

Mission-critical and some business-critical services must continue to meet their service-level agreements (SLAs), even in the face of a major disaster at the primary data center, for example, with stock market trading where downtime can cost millions of dollars per hour. To maintain these services if a disaster occurs, a secondary IT infrastructure must be available at a site sufficiently remote from the primary site that it is not affected by the same disaster. The time to recover and restart those services is then the sum of the time required to decide to enact the disaster recovery plan and switch to remote site operations, plus the time required for the services to be started on the systems at the secondary site.

For less critical services where data is not continuously replicated to the secondary site, the time required to start those services includes the additional time component of restoring data from tape or a point-in-time disk copy, if required.

You can protect your data against disaster in a number of ways. These include

- Backup and recovery from tape
- Regular transfer of data changes, for example, ZFS snapshots using send and receive features
- Host-based replication, for example, StorageTek Availability Suite (AVS)
- Storage-based replication, for example, EMC Symmetrix Remote Data Facility (SRDF) and Hitachi TrueCopy and Universal Replicator
- Application-based replication, for example, Oracle Data Guard and MySQL database replication

To determine your intended response to a disaster, you conduct a Business Impact Analysis (BIA). During this process you analyze what could go wrong, how likely it is that each specific event will occur, and what the impact of the failure would be on your business. From this analysis you determine the Maximum Tolerable Period of Disruption (MTPD) for the business. Your MTPD then enables you to calculate your RPO and RTO figures.

Your choice of technology to use and how to configure it will depend on your RPO and RTO. These figures determine at what point in time the data must be recovered and how quickly that must be achieved, respectively. Thus, if your business is engaged in large financial transactions, it is likely that you will set an RPO where no data is lost. However, this might well limit how far apart you can have your data centers and still maintain sufficient application performance. Similarly, to set your RTO such that you minimize your service outage, you might again have to compromise application performance.

Regardless of the technique used, it is important to monitor and address any changes to services and, in particular, to address any changes in data volume. If, for example, the primary site allocates more storage, but this change is not propagated to the data continuity solution on the secondary site, the mismatch can cause services to fail to start on the secondary site in a disaster situation.

## Benefits of a Third-Party Disaster Recovery Framework

Your data center very likely contains numerous applications, each with its own disaster recovery requirements and associated plans. Those that are business- or mission-critical probably use a continuous replication mechanism to ensure that their data is protected. These myriad protection technologies and the steps needed to recover these services drive the need for an automated disaster recovery framework.

The key advantage of a third-party framework is its automation of critical disaster recovery steps. A third-party framework can also provide a consistent user interface to different replication technologies. These two features reduce both the maintenance overhead as well as the number of manual steps required to perform a disaster recovery operation. This greatly simplifies the testing procedure, which is a primary requisite of any disaster recovery strategy. Consequently, if a disaster occurs, your staff members are well drilled on a considerably simpler procedure and can implement it with confidence.

Although nothing is inherently wrong with a manual recovery procedure, a real disaster situation is a time of considerable stress. If key staff members are unreachable, the process of transferring operations to the disaster recovery site might be considerably more risky and error-prone than if it were automated and controlled by a suitable disaster recovery framework.

# Solaris Cluster Geographic Edition Architecture

Solaris Cluster Geographic Edition is a layered extension to the Solaris Cluster software. The Geographic Edition software enables the controlled migration of production services from a primary cluster to one or more secondary clusters, either in the event of a disaster or as part of a planned procedure. Data is continuously replicated from the primary cluster to the secondary cluster, either synchronously or asynchronously (or a combination of both), depending on the RPOs of the application services supported by the clusters.

The Geographic Edition software supports a growing list of data replication technologies, including StorageTek Availability Suite (AVS) software, Hitachi TrueCopy and Universal Replicator, EMC Symmetrix Remote Data Facility (SRDF), Oracle Data Guard for Oracle Real Application Clusters (Oracle RAC), and MySQL database replication, all of which can be used to provide an integrated disaster recovery solution.

## Comparison of Automated and Automatic Service Migration

Solaris Cluster Geographic Edition provides an automated mechanism for migrating your services from a cluster at the primary site to a cluster at the secondary, or disaster recovery, site. Here, the term *automated* means that the whole process of coordinating the stopping and starting of the applications on each cluster, the direction of replication, and the sequence in which these should occur is managed for you. This capability is completely different from that provided by the Solaris Cluster software. In a clustered environment, high availability is the number-one goal. The Solaris Cluster software reacts automatically and as quickly as possible to node failures, or faults, detected by the application fault probes. As long as your resource type start and stop methods are robust, restarting a service on the same node, or a different one, has no detrimental effect on the application data.

However, migrating your services from a primary cluster to a disaster recovery site can have different consequences depending on the circumstances of the operation and the type of replication used. If the migration is a smooth transfer of control between sites when the sites are both operating normally, then there is no loss of replication consistency. The process can be reversed by repeating the operation in the opposite direction. In contrast, if the primary site has failed, as is usually the case in a disaster, then the disaster recovery site taking control of a service might result in the replication consistency between the two sites being lost. Losing replication consistency occurs most often when asynchronous replication is used and in circumstances where not all of the changed data has been transmitted to the disaster recovery site. If the missing data is very important, you might be prepared to reconstruct as much of it as possible from other sources before allowing users to access the services again. These sources might include logs held in other application tiers that were not subject to the failure, or even paper records, where such records are kept. Therefore, because the decision to perform a switchover or a takeover is administrator-initiated, the Geographic Edition software does not require a quorum device.

The nature of failure at the primary site determines your choices after you recover the systems. If the data is intact, you might decide to restart the services from the primary site and discard the changes made to the data at the disaster recovery site in the interim period. You might instead decide to continue using the disaster recovery site and bring the primary site back into synchronization before switching back the services during a convenient maintenance period. Finally, in extreme circumstances, you might be forced to resynchronize your entire dataset if the original data has been lost or compromised to the extent that it would be too risky to use. The capability of the replication products is also a factor in determining the options available.

Unlike local clusters, geographic installations are often separated by large distances, and infrastructure components are not under your control. Consequently, it is considerably more difficult to determine whether a site has actually experienced a disaster. Furthermore, it is almost impossible to determine with fault probes alone the potential duration of any ongoing outage at a site.

It is almost impossible for a disaster recovery framework to determine the trade-off between the time required to restore service, the time required to recover the primary site, and the impact that service restoration will have on the time required to restore data replication consistency. Consequently, the Solaris Cluster Geographic Edition software is an automated framework, not an automatic one. For this reason, it is best practice to *not* make the takeover process automatic.

## Protecting Your Data Using Replication

Widely separated host-based mirrors provide a single, logical copy of your data maintained synchronously by the server. In contrast, data replication offers both synchronous and asynchronous mechanisms for maintaining a separate physical copy of your data. When you implement a disaster recovery solution, three basic methods of data replication are available to you: storage-based replication, host-based replication, and application-based replication. The variety of synchronous and asynchronous replication capabilities they provide enable you to choose which option best meets each application's RPO and RTO requirements.

Regardless of whether you choose to implement storage-based or host-based replication with Solaris Cluster Geographic Edition, you must address the data consistency issue raised in the section "Data Protection Using Storage-Based Replication" in Chapter 1, "Oracle Solaris Cluster: Overview." Similarly, if you plan to replicate your data synchronously by any method, then you need to understand the performance limitations described in the section "Performance Impact of Separating Data Centers" in Chapter 1. These are product configuration factors or physical limitations that the Solaris Cluster Geographic Edition software cannot overcome.

## Storage-Based Replication: EMC Symmetrix Remote Data Facility and Hitachi Universal Replicator

Storage-based replication capabilities are often found only in enterprise-class storage arrays, such as EMC's Symmetrix range or the Hitachi Data Systems Universal Storage Platform range. The storage-based replication feature is built into the firmware of the array controller, enabling the storage arrays to selectively forward write requests to predefined sets of disks in a remote partner array.

Because these operations occur within the array itself, the feature has the advantage that it is both operating system and application neutral. This unified approach to data replication, coupled with the fact that the operations do not consume host CPU cycles, is often cited as the prime motivation for using this approach.

Although storage-based replication is beneficial because it enables you to run any class of application (failover, scalable, or even parallel), supporting any application does mean that the storage array is unable to recognize the significance of any data block it is transferring. Therefore, the storage array cannot optimize the way the data is transferred or subsequently handled. This contrasts with application-based replication, which, for databases specifically, can recognize transaction boundaries or choose to delay applying transaction logs for a set period of time.

Figure 5.1 shows a typical example of how storage-based replication is used in a two-data-center configuration. The separation of the sites determines whether synchronous or asynchronous replication is used for each application. The use of host-based mirrored or RAID-protected LUNs (from the storage array) allows parallel applications such as a shared QFS file system and Oracle RAC to operate, even though storage-based replication is being used between sites. This contrasts with the case where storage-based replication is used within an individual cluster, such as the configuration shown in Figure 5.6. The limitations on such systems are described in subsequent sections.

For more complex architectures, see "Three-Data-Center Architectures: Combining Campus and Geographic Options."

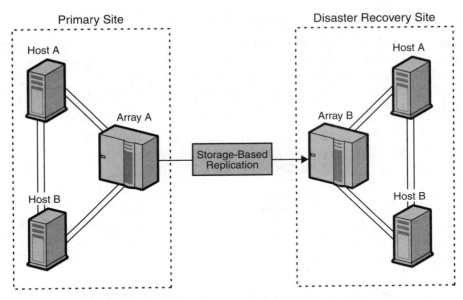

**Figure 5.1** Storage-based replication in a two-data-center configuration

## Using Storage-Based Replication with Volume Managers

When your storage administrator allocates your system administrator a logical LUN, it will consist of one or more physical disks housed in the storage array. Furthermore, the logical LUN will use RAID technology such as striping, mirroring, or RAID 5. This both balances the I/O to the back-end physical disks and provides protection against physical disk or controller failure. Your system administrator can then choose to further subdivide this logical LUN with a volume manager, creating metadevices that can be used by an application.

With storage-based replication, the entire logical LUN is replicated. Consequently, this form of replication synchronizes data from the entire source logical LUN with the target logical LUN at the remote site. If a volume manager is used, state replica databases, private regions, and other areas not directly visible to the user are also replicated.

This complete copy does not pose a problem for Veritas Volume Manager or its clustered version (used for Oracle RAC), but it does prevent both Solaris Volume Manager and its clustered version from working in a Solaris Cluster Geographic Edition cluster.

> **Note**
>
> The Solaris Cluster Geographic Edition software does not currently support the replication of data held on Solaris Volume Manager metadevices using storage-based replication products.

## Host-Based Replication: StorageTek Availability Suite

The StorageTek Availability Suite (AVS) software is a host-based replication product that runs on individual cluster nodes. Unlike storage-based replication, host-based replication intercepts the application writes in the Solaris kernel. Figure 5.2 contrasts how AVS and Hitachi Universal Replicator perform their data replication functions.

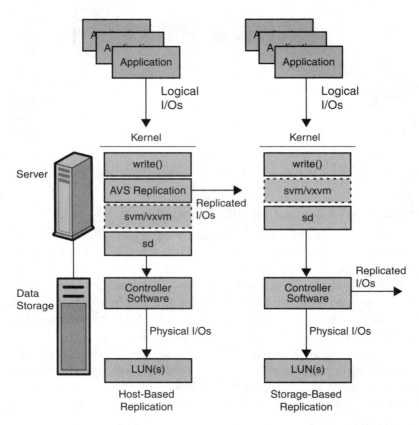

**Figure 5.2** Comparing host-based and storage-based data replication mechanisms

AVS can be configured to replicate individual datasets synchronously or asynchronously. If the network linking the sites fails for any reason, the software enters a logging mode to record which data blocks are changed in the intervening period. After the communication is reestablished, the changed blocks are sent to the remote site to synchronize the two copies of data. The time required to do so depends on the number of changes and the intersite bandwidth available.

Figure 5.3 shows a typical configuration that combines host-based mirroring with host-based replication. Although the example shows only a single replication between host A and host C, a configuration consisting of multiple applications might use several point-to-point, host-based replication streams. The exact number depends on how many applications use each replicated dataset. Each replication stream can have different source and target host combinations, each of which has the potential to change as the applications are switched between the nodes of the primary and disaster recovery sites.

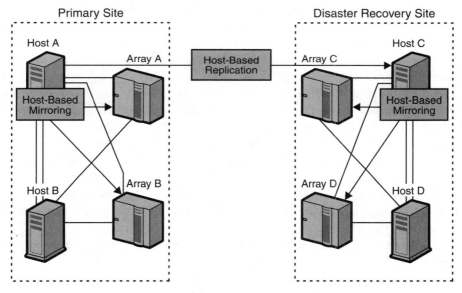

**Figure 5.3** Host-based mirroring combined with host-based replication in a two-data-center configuration

Because AVS intercepts application writes at the kernel level, it can handle writes coming from only one node at a time. This is sufficient to support failover, scalable, and multi-master services that use either a failover file system (see the section "Highly Available Local (Failover) File Systems" in Chapter 2, "Oracle Solaris Cluster: Features and Architecture") or a global file system (see the section "The Cluster File System" in Chapter 2). However, AVS cannot be used for Oracle RAC or for a shared QFS file system because these products can issue write I/Os simultaneously from multiple nodes to any single LUN.

## Application-Based Replication

Application-based replication can be achieved in a couple of ways. The first option is to use capabilities built into the application itself. Many databases, such as Oracle or MySQL, have this replication capability. The second option is to build this capability into any applications that you develop at the application logic layer. You can do so using an application server, such as Sun Java System Application Server or Oracle WebLogic Server, which would give you fine-grained control of the transactions you replicate to one or more sites.

Greater awareness of application logic and relationships between data gives application-based replication far more flexibility in terms of how the data is replicated, which hosts the data is sent to, and how and when application-based replication is applied on the remote sites. This is particularly true of database replication products. Because of their transactional nature, a clear boundary exists between one logical manipulation of the data and the next. This is not the case with host-based or storage-based products that replicate "anonymous" blocks of data that are written to disk. Indeed, storage-based replication products cannot directly detect the linkage between data blocks written to data files and those written to transaction logs. Consequently, it is necessary for your storage or system administrator to provide this information when setting up storage-based or host-based replication (see the section "Ensuring Data Consistency after a Rolling Failure" in Chapter 1, "Oracle Solaris Cluster: Overview"). With Hitachi Universal Replicator or AVS, this is done by placing all the datasets relating to a single database in the same consistency group.

Another advantage that application-based replication often has over host-based or storage-based replication is the capability to use the data on the standby site in a read-only fashion. For example, Oracle's Data Guard product allows its standby databases to be opened and used for reporting. This capability is not directly available in other forms of replication. For example, consider a file system replicated by AVS, Universal Replicator, or Symmetrix Remote Data Facility. The standby volume can be mounted read-only on the disaster recovery site. However, you access the data at your peril. As the data in the file system changes because of the replication, it becomes inconsistent with the view Solaris had when it mounted the system file because all the changes are happening without going through the local kernel. Consequently, any attempt to access the file system might lead to a kernel panic. Thus, the only safe way to access the data on the disaster recovery site is to take a snapshot and use that instead. Clearly, this involves greater overall complexity. The amount of additional storage required depends on whether the snapshot is a dependent or an independent one.

One final advantage that application-based replication has over host-based or storage-based replication is its flexibility with respect to virtualized environments.

Whereas host-based and storage-based replication occur at or below the level of the kernel, application-based replication is implemented by non-kernel processes. Consequently, application-based replication is independent of the type of environment it is running in.

For example, if you use the Oracle Solaris Zones technology (see the section "Oracle Solaris Zones" in Chapter 3, "Combining Virtualization Technologies with Oracle Solaris Cluster Software"), any AVS replication is performed at the global zone level. Similarly, any SRDF or Universal Replicator replication is performed in the attached arrays. Both options require administrative access to the global zone to manage and control them. In contrast, application-based replication can be managed and maintained from within the zone itself, without the need for access to the global zones.

Solaris Cluster Geographic Edition supports application-based replication for Oracle 10*g* and 11*g* Real Application Clusters databases using Oracle Data Guard and MySQL databases using MySQL's built-in replication features. You can add support for other replication technologies, including those based on application-based replication, using the Script-Based Plug-In (SBP) module supplied with the Solaris Cluster Geographic Edition software (see the section "Script-Based Plug-In Module" in Chapter 6, "Oracle Solaris Cluster Geographic Edition: Features and Architecture").

## Protecting File Systems with Host-Based and Storage-Based Replication

You have a choice of supported file systems when using the Solaris Cluster software. However, there are limitations on which replication technologies you can use with some file systems. Although UFS and VxFS can be replicated by both host-based and storage-based replication products, shared QFS and Oracle Solaris ZFS file systems are more restricted. The reasons for these limitations are described next.

### Shared QFS File System

Applications using a shared QFS file system can write to the underlying file system from multiple nodes simultaneously. This multiplicity of channels prevents host-based replication products, such as AVS, from being able to replicate the data. Although storage-based replication products, such as SRDF or Universal Replicator, do not experience this limitation, they do encounter an issue similar to the one raised in "Using Storage-Based Replication with Volume Managers." Information associated with the file system contains details about which node mounting the file system is the metadata master. The first data disk (whether or not it is of type mr/md/gx) holds details about physical nodes, at the primary site, in inode 4. This information is replicated, unchanged, to the secondary site. Because the nodes on the primary site are not part of the cluster on the secondary site, the cluster is unable to mount the shared QFS file system until the file system is manually updated using the `samsharefs` command (see the `samsharefs`(1M) man page and the following example). If you perform this step manually, also check the file system using the `samfsck` command (see the `samfsck`(1M) man page).

---

## Example 5.1  Manually Updating and Checking a Shared QFS File System

Use the `samsharefs` command to update the `my_sqfs_fs` file system, and then check the file system using the `samfsck` command.

```
# /opt/SUNWsamfs/sbin/samsharefs -R -u my_sqfs_fs
# /opt/SUNWsamfs/sbin/samfsck -F my_sqfs_fs
```

---

The current implementation of Solaris Cluster Geographic Edition does not have this capability built into either the SRDF or the TrueCopy/Universal Replicator module.

### Oracle Solaris ZFS File System

One of the biggest benefits of the Oracle Solaris ZFS file system is that it provides on-disk consistency [ZFS]. This capability removes the need to run a file system checker, such as `fsck`, which is required when the consistency of UFS or VxFS is in doubt. The ZFS file system achieves this using a copy-on-write (COW) mechanism, coupled with strong checksumming of all blocks written to disk. Instead of the superblocks used by UFS, the ZFS file system uses multiple copies of an *uberblock* distributed around the disks within the zpool. All the data blocks stored in the zpool are ultimately referenced from this block.

The benefits and integrity guarantees of the ZFS file system are undermined if you combine it with host-based or storage-based replication without understanding the ramifications of their various failure modes (see the section "Ensuring Data Consistency after a Rolling Failure" in Chapter 1, "Oracle Solaris Cluster: Overview"). How rolling failures are handled determines whether you can successfully import your zpool on the disaster recovery site. If the replication technology cannot guarantee that the order of writes to the zpool during a catch-up phase is identical to the order in which they were originally issued, then there is a risk that the zpool will have data corruption and inconsistencies. If ordering is not obeyed, then the write that changes the pointer from the newly copied data block can take place before the new data block is written. Fortunately, ZFS can correct most of these using the `scrub` option to the `zpool` command. However, you must be able to import the zpool to run this option. Thus, if the uberblocks have not been replicated consistently, it is likely that the zpool itself cannot be imported.

During an intersite communications failure, the AVS software enters a logging mode. After the link is restored, the AVS software attempts to transmit all the logged changes to the remote site to resynchronize the data. During this period, the original write ordering is not preserved, leaving applications exposed to potential data consistency issues. To minimize the potential ramifications of a rolling failure, the Solaris Cluster Geographic Edition AVS module can be configured to take an AVS point-in-time copy (snapshot) of the secondary dataset prior to the catch-up process being allowed to commence. If the catch-up process does not complete before a takeover command is issued, the zpool is rolled back to the consistent AVS snapshot rather than using the partially synchronized zpool. Here the ability to recover cleanly is traded off against the loss of data. In contrast, a switchover command is refused because the data is inconsistent. Only when the catch-up has completed will the switchover be permitted.

Only Hitachi's Universal Replicator guarantees to preserve the original write ordering during the catch-up phase following a communications failure. This is not the case with EMC's SRDF and Hitachi TrueCopy. Both lack the journaling capability (or equivalent) of the Universal Replicator product.

## Connection Topologies Supported by Solaris Cluster Geographic Edition

When you bring together two clusters to create a disaster recovery configuration using Solaris Cluster Geographic Edition, they form what is termed a *partnership*. To create a partnership, you must have, at a minimum, an IP network between the two sites. This IP network is used for host-based replication and intercluster heartbeats, unless you supply separate networks for these purposes. If you use storage-based replication, you might also need a storage network, based on Fibre Channel, Gigabit Ethernet, or ESCON, depending on the requirements of your storage array.

You can implement Solaris Cluster Geographic Edition using one of two physical topologies: N+1 or paired. These topologies are illustrated in Figure 5.4. The overriding rule is that a cluster cannot form more than one partnership with the same cluster. The term *cluster* refers to both single-node and multinode Solaris Cluster implementations. Using Solaris Cluster software even in a single-node implementation means that services benefit from the strong start and stop controls that the Resource Group Manager (RGM) provides.

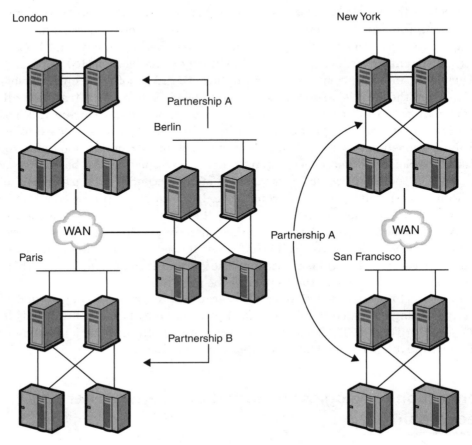

**Figure 5.4** Solaris Cluster Geographic Edition topologies: N+1 or pairs

Although in Figure 5.5 the data center on the right is labeled as a disaster recovery site, there is no reason why you cannot distribute active services between both sites. Indeed, doing so ensures that you minimize the cost of providing your disaster recovery solution. For example, using the Solaris Cluster resource group affinities, covered in the section "Resource Group Dependency and Affinity Options" in Chapter 2, "Oracle Solaris Cluster: Features and Architecture," you could shut down lower-priority workloads, such as development or user acceptance testing, if a production workload needed to be migrated to the site.

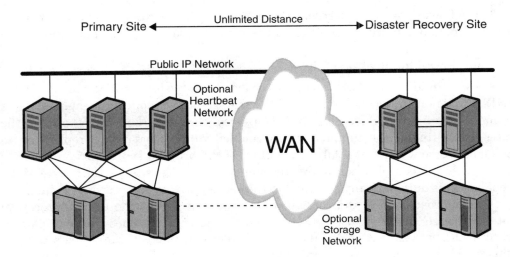

**Figure 5.5** Overview of the infrastructure needed for a Solaris Cluster Geographic Edition implementation

## Three-Data-Center Architectures: Combining Campus and Geographic Options

A three-data-center (often written as 3DC) configuration combines synchronous and asynchronous data replication with both high-availability (Solaris Cluster) and disaster recovery (Solaris Cluster Geographic Edition) software.

The high-availability component is often implemented as a campus cluster with the individual nodes separated by a distance of many kilometers. The separation must enable the applications to perform sufficiently well, even with the overhead that synchronous replication imposes, and provide protection against disasters that might affect the other site containing the other cluster nodes. Furthermore, because this component of the solution is a single cluster, the cluster must ensure that it can maintain quorum even if a site failure occurs. Placing a quorum server at the disaster recovery site enables this requirement to be met.

The Geographic Edition software then links this primary cluster with another backup cluster located a considerably greater distance away. Because of the distance involved, replication to this third site must be asynchronous.

There are potentially three ways of implementing such a solution: storage-based replication throughout (using SRDF or Universal Replicator), a combination of storage-based and host-based replication (AVS), or host-based mirroring (Solaris Volume Manager, Veritas Volume Manager, or ZFS) combined with host-based replication. Currently, not all of these options are supported by the Solaris Cluster Geographic Edition.

The following sections describe the options, indicate whether the options are supported, and list any restrictions that they might place on your applications.

### Storage-Based Replication Only

The EMC SRDF/Star [EMCStar] and Hitachi Data Systems Universal Replicator [HDSUniversal] products both have 3DC storage-based replication capabilities. A standard configuration (see Figure 5.6) uses synchronous replication between the sites, consisting of the campus cluster coupled with asynchronous replication to the more remote third site. After the failure of the primary source (primary site A) for asynchronous replication to the disaster recovery site (site C), the source of the replication is automatically switched to the second primary site (primary site B).

This approach limits the configurations you can use at the disaster recovery site. Although there are no restrictions on the number of nodes that can participate in the backup cluster, the disaster recovery cluster itself cannot be a campus cluster. There is no way to recombine the incoming asynchronous replication with ongoing synchronous replication at the disaster recovery site.

Because this configuration uses storage-based replication within the primary cluster, rather than host-based mirroring, the configuration cannot be used for either shared QFS file systems or Oracle RAC. These applications require direct access to the underlying LUNs at both sites simultaneously.

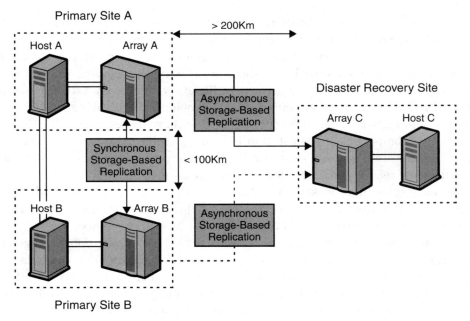

**Figure 5.6** Using storage-based replication in a 3DC environment

## Mixing Storage-Based and Host-Based Replication

You can combine storage-based and host-based replication to create a 3DC configuration. In theory, there are two possible ways to do so: intracluster host-based replication coupled with intercluster storage-based replication (see Figure 5.7), or intracluster storage-based replication coupled with intercluster host-based replication (see Figure 5.8). However, only the latter is actually technically feasible.

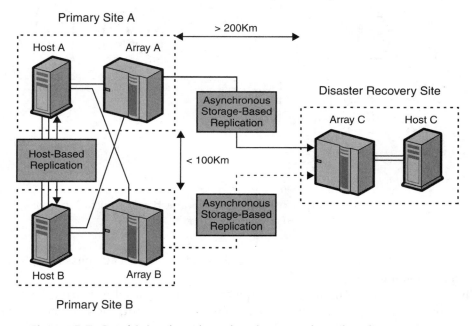

**Figure 5.7** Combining host-based and storage-based replication in an unworkable 3DC configuration

Combining host-based replication within a cluster and storage-based replication between sites is not a realistic option for the following two reasons. First, unlike SRDF, or TrueCopy and Universal Replicator, AVS has not been integrated into the Solaris Cluster software DID framework. Consequently, the DID devices for the underlying storage devices are different. Second, even if the integration existed, the state of the replication would be known only to AVS. From the perspective of the storage array software, the two storage arrays at the primary site have separate, unconnected relationships with the storage array on the disaster recovery site. Thus, when the replication is reversed within the primary cluster, there is no way to ensure a smooth handover of control and state between the two sources of asynchronous storage-based replication. Consequently, your remote dataset would need to be completely resynchronized after such an operation. This prevents the

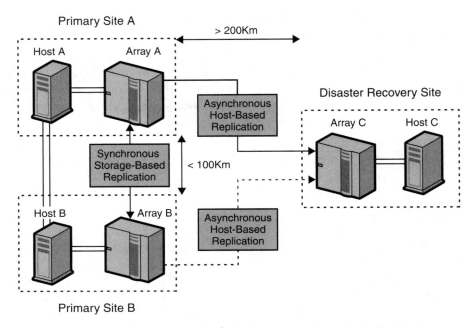

**Figure 5.8** Combining host-based and storage-based replication in a
3DC configuration

combination of host-based replication combined with storage-based replication from being a viable solution.

The same reasoning applies to a combination of host-based mirroring, instead of host-based replication, and storage-based replication. Again, the two primary storage arrays have separate relationships with the storage array on the disaster recovery site. The state of the primary/backup relationship cannot be passed between the two primary arrays if one of the primary arrays fails.

The converse configuration, using storage-based replication inside the primary cluster combined with host-based replication to the remote site, is a viable option.

For the configuration to behave correctly, you must ensure that the primary LUN for the storage-based replication is identical to the source for the AVS host-based replication to the disaster recovery site. This can be achieved by creating the appropriate affinities between the application resource group and the resource group containing the logical host for the AVS replication. Doing so means that when you switch your application between nodes on the primary cluster, the switchover takes with it not only the storage-based primary LUNs but also the source of the host-based replication.

Because the intersite replication occurs at the host level, there are no restrictions on the number of nodes or storage arrays you can have in the cluster at the disaster recovery site. Furthermore, because host-based replication is used between the sites, the host-based replication does not prevent a volume manager (Solaris Volume Manager or Veritas Volume Manager) from being used within the primary cluster. Thus, although the storage is being replicated between the nodes of the cluster, the information being replicated is already consistent between them.

This is the only 3DC configuration using storage-based replication that is currently feasible with Solaris Cluster Geographic Edition.

**Note**

Once again, the use of host-based replication precludes the use of either shared QFS file systems or Oracle RAC.

### Combining Host-Based Mirroring and Host-Based Replication

The final option for creating a 3DC configuration is to use host-based software products throughout the configuration.

Figure 5.9 shows a configuration that is equivalent to its two-data-center counterpart (see Figure 5.3) in most respects, except for the separation of the nodes

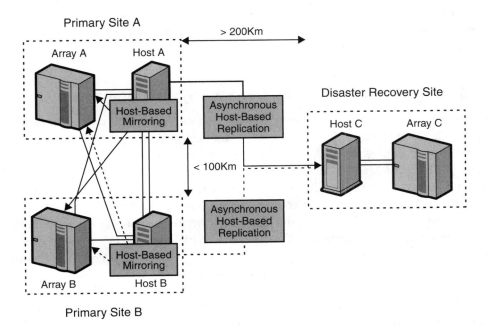

**Figure 5.9** Combining host-based mirroring and host-based replication in a 3DC configuration

that constitute the primary cluster. Indeed, there is no reason why the disaster recovery site cannot also consist of a multinode, multi-array cluster. The limiting factor on the separation of primary sites A and B is the additional I/O latency it imposes. Because the configuration uses host-based mirroring, mirroring is, by its very nature, a synchronous process, making it impossible to mask the extra write latency.

# Using Solaris Cluster Geographic Edition with Virtualization Technologies

Solaris Cluster Geographic Edition is not a stand-alone product. It relies directly on many features that the Solaris Cluster software provides in order to function. Consequently, Solaris Cluster Geographic Edition can operate only in a virtualized environment where you can directly install and run the Solaris Cluster software.

In most cases, this does not restrict your choice of high-availability and disaster recovery implementations. However, using Solaris Cluster Geographic Edition within zone clusters (see the section "Zone Clusters" in Chapter 3, "Combining Virtualization Technologies with Oracle Solaris Cluster Software") is currently not possible because the required Solaris (sysevent) interface is not available inside a zone cluster.

Despite this limitation, several virtualization combinations are fully supported and are covered in the following sections.

## Using Geographic Edition with Dynamic System Domains

Each dynamic system domain (see the section "Dynamic System Domains" in Chapter 3, "Combining Virtualization Technologies with Oracle Solaris Cluster Software") you configure within a domain-capable system, such as Oracle's Sun SPARC Enterprise M9000 server, runs a separate copy of the Oracle Solaris OS. Consequently, you must install the Solaris Cluster Geographic Edition software in each domain for which you require disaster recovery protection. You can view this requirement as both a benefit and a drawback because it enables you to delegate the management and administration of individual domains to separate business units. Conversely, it means you have multiple points of control if the system is managed centrally for a single line of business. However, you could create a single large domain and use Oracle Solaris Zones to provide your virtualization.

Because a dynamic system domain is, in effect, a physical virtualization of the system, it does not restrict your choice of host-based or storage-based replication.

## Using Geographic Edition with Oracle Solaris Zones

The section "Oracle Solaris Zones" in Chapter 3, "Combining Virtualization Technologies with Oracle Solaris Cluster Software," describes the three ways you can use zones to provide virtualization. Although you cannot yet combine Solaris Cluster Geographic Edition with zone clusters, you can use Geographic Edition with the other two virtualization options, which are described in more detail in the following sections.

### HA Containers

When you implement an HA container, you must place the container's root (/) file system on a failover file system. This gives the container, and the applications it encapsulates, its mobility. The Solaris Cluster software controls which node in the primary cluster hosts the container at any particular point. If possible, place your application data on a separate failover file system that is mounted into the HA container, then replicate only the data file system, rather than the container's root (/) file system, to avoid propagating errors that might result in the backup container becoming unusable.

Because an HA container is treated as a "black-box," you can also create it with a non-native (non–Solaris 10) brand: Solaris 8 OS, Solaris 9 OS, or Linux. Where you make this trade-off, you forgo the standard Solaris Cluster agent services. However, that still leaves you free to construct your own Service Management Framework (SMF) or /etc/rc scripts to start or stop your services. However, some of the Solaris Cluster agents, for example, Tomcat, MySQL, PostgreSQL, Sun N1 Service Provisioning System, Samba, and WebSphere MQ, include an SMF service that can be registered within the container. These agents use the HA container SMF integration feature to enable some level of basic process-monitoring capabilities.

To provide HA containers with disaster recovery protection using Solaris Cluster Geographic Edition, you need to replicate only the underlying failover file system. If you use host-based replication, then the Geographic Edition software creates the appropriate affinity between the resource group controlling the replication and the resource group controlling the HA container (see the section "Resource Group Dependency and Affinity Options" in Chapter 2, "Oracle Solaris Cluster: Features and Architecture"). For storage-based replication, no additional affinities are required because the replication occurs within the array. Consequently, the storage array does not need to be aware of which host is running the application.

> **Note**
>
> Running Oracle RAC, even as a single-instance database, in an HA container is not supported. Consequently, you cannot use Oracle Data Guard application-based replication.

### Global-Cluster Non-Voting Nodes

Global-cluster non-voting nodes have the storage resources for the applications they support mapped into them from the global zone. As with HA containers, global-cluster non-voting nodes require you to replicate only the storage resources using your chosen replication product. Indeed, do *not* replicate the storage that contains the zone's root directory hierarchy, because doing so risks data corruption or a file deletion, making the zone at the disaster recovery site also unusable.

If you run a highly available MySQL database within a set of global-cluster non-voting nodes, you can instead choose to replicate your database using the MySQL (application-based) replication module supplied with the Solaris Cluster Geographic Edition software. However, you must propagate any configuration files it might rely on separately because the MySQL database replication does not manage them.

Once again, the Geographic Edition software installs the correct affinities between the resource groups involved. In this case, the resource groups' `nodelist` properties list global-cluster non-voting nodes, of the form *host:zone*, rather than just plain physical hostnames.

If you use the Solaris Cluster Geographic Edition Script-Based Plug-In module (see the section "Script-Based Plug-In Module" in Chapter 6, "Oracle Solaris Cluster Geographic Edition: Features and Architecture") to add support for your own application-based replication, then you have control over whether it supports applications that are hosted in global-cluster non-voting nodes.

> **Note**
>
> You cannot run Oracle RAC in global-cluster non-voting nodes that are managed by the Solaris Cluster software. Consequently, you cannot construct an integrated disaster recovery solution for this combination using Solaris Cluster Geographic Edition.

## Using Geographic Edition with Logical Domains

If you want to use Solaris Cluster Geographic Edition to provide disaster recovery protection for applications virtualized on servers using Oracle Solaris Cool-Threads technology, you have three options: I/O domains, guest domains, or failover guest domains. Although the virtualization options discussed next are practically identical to the same Oracle Solaris OS running without the virtualization technology, many third-party vendors prefer to perform extensive testing before announcing support for the combination. Before deploying a particular virtualization option, you must confirm that any third-party storage or software vendor supports the combination of technologies you plan to use.

## I/O Domains

An I/O domain has direct control of one or more PCI buses within the physical system. Thus, from a Solaris perspective, an I/O domain is indistinguishable from a physical server that does not have Logical Domains capabilities because I/Os use the standard sd driver.

You can use AVS or MySQL database replication in this virtualization configuration.

## Guest Domains

A guest domain has CPU, memory, networks, and devices mapped into it by the control domain. Of the devices mapped in, some are used for the root disks and others for shared storage (see the section "Guest Domains" in Chapter 3, "Combining Virtualization Technologies with Oracle Solaris Cluster Software"). After Solaris has been installed, the Solaris Cluster and Geographic Edition software can also be added.

Because the Solaris installation is identical to that of a standard physical server, the AVS software can be installed, configured, and used in exactly the same way. This means that you can create Geographic Edition configurations inside guest domains that use AVS or MySQL database replication.

## Failover Guest Domains

If you create a Solaris Cluster configuration that spans a set of control domains, you can place a SUNW.ldom resource (see the section "Failover Guest Domains" in Chapter 3, "Combining Virtualization Technologies with Oracle Solaris Cluster Software") in a resource group to control failover guest domains. The capabilities of, and restrictions on, this configuration are similar to those of an HA container when used with Solaris Cluster Geographic Edition (see "HA Containers").

In this configuration, the Solaris Cluster software controls the failover of the guest domain between the local cluster nodes. The Solaris Cluster Geographic Edition software manages which site is considered the primary site and which is considered the disaster recovery site. When AVS (host-based) replication is used, the Geographic Edition software also establishes the affinity between the resource group containing the logical host resource for the AVS replication and the resource group containing the HA container resource. Once again, configurations using storage-based replication need no further affinities other than those created by the application group because the replication occurs within the storage array itself.

Because the failover guest domain contains a guest operating system, you can use any of the Solaris Cluster Geographic Edition host-based or storage-based replication modules to replicate the virtual device that underlies the guest domain. However, you cannot use any of the Solaris Cluster Geographic Edition application-based replication modules for applications inside this domain because the domain itself is treated as a "black-box."

# 6

# Oracle Solaris Cluster Geographic Edition: Features and Architecture

The Oracle Solaris Cluster Geographic Edition software is layered on top of the Oracle Solaris Cluster software. It provides a framework to enable the controlled migration of services between your primary and backup data centers. The chapter starts by covering the software components required to support the Geographic Edition software. It continues by introducing the key features of the Geographic Edition infrastructure:

- Partnerships
- Heartbeats
- Protection groups
- Replication components

The mechanism used to extend the supported replication technologies is discussed in the section on replication components. The chapter concludes by describing the four major state changes a protection group can undergo, namely

- Starting
- Stopping
- Being switched over
- Being taken over

# Software Infrastructure Required for the Geographic Edition Software

The Geographic Edition software orchestrates the controlled migration of Solaris Cluster software managed applications between data centers. Because the Solaris Cluster resource groups are the managed entities, the Solaris Cluster software is a prerequisite for the deployment of the Geographic Edition software.

## Solaris Cluster Resource Groups and Resources

Within a Solaris Cluster configuration (see Figure 6.1), services are encapsulated as resources in resource groups and manipulated by the Resource Group Manager (RGM). The Geographic Edition software builds on the same resource and resource group constructs to enable the controlled migration of a service, not only among nodes within an individual cluster, but also between the nodes of clusters partnering each other across data centers. It is the robustness of the Solaris Cluster

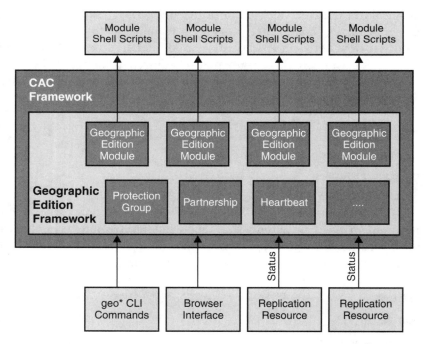

**Figure 6.1** Relationship between the components in a Solaris Cluster Geographic Edition system

agent's `Start` and `Stop` methods that enables this migration to happen safely, ensuring that services start only on the node or nodes on which they are supposed to.

## Geographic Edition Common Agent Container Modules

The core Geographic Edition software is implemented as a set of Common Agent Container (CAC) modules. These modules are installed on your cluster nodes as Java Archive (JAR) files in the `/usr/cluster/lib/cmass` directory with associated XML descriptor files in `/etc/cacao/instances/default/modules`. Consequently, you must have the CAC package (`SUNWcacaort`) installed and running in order to use the Geographic Edition software.

The following example shows you how to check the CAC software version. The example also shows you how to list the CAC modules that are loaded into the CAC framework by the Geographic Edition software.

---

### Example 6.1  Geographic Edition Common Agent Container Components

Use the `pkginfo` command to check that the `SUNWcacaort` package is installed.

```
# pkginfo SUNWcacaort
application SUNWcacaort Common Agent Container - Runtime
```

Use the `cacaoadm` command to check the version of the Common Agent Container, and then list the Geographic Edition modules that are loaded.

```
# cacaoadm -V
2.2.3.0
# cacaoadm list-modules | egrep "geo|notif"
com.sun.cluster.geocontrol 1.0
com.sun.cluster.geoutilities 1.0
com.sun.cluster.notifier 1.0
```

---

These CAC modules are controlled by two Solaris Cluster resource groups containing a total of four resources (see Figure 6.2 and Example 6.2). The more important of the two is the `geo-infrastructure` resource group, which contains the following resources:

- `geo-clustername` (a `SUNW.LogicalHostname`-type resource): represents the cluster as a whole
- `geo-failovercontrol` (a `SUNW.scmasa`-type resource): controls the locking and unlocking of the CAC `com.sun.cluster.geocontrol` module

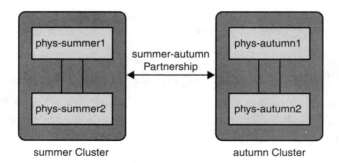

**Figure 6.2** Existing Geographic Edition partnership between `summer` and `autumn` clusters

## Example 6.2   Solaris Cluster Resource Groups and Resources Controlling the Geographic Edition Software

Use the `clresourcegroup` command to show the status of the `geo-clusterstate` and `geo-infrastructure` resource groups.

```
# clresourcegroup status geo-clusterstate geo-infrastructure

=== Cluster Resource Groups ===

Group Name              Node Name       Suspended     Status
----------              ---------       ---------     ------
geo-clusterstate        phys-summer1 No               Online
                        phys-summer2 No               Online

geo-infrastructure      phys-summer1 No               Online
                        phys-summer2 No               Offline

# clresource status -g geo-clusterstate

=== Cluster Resources ===

Resource Name           Node Name       State                       Status Message
-------------           ---------       -----                       --------------
geo-servicetag          phys-summer1    Online but not monitored    Online
                        phys-summer2    Online but not monitored    Online

# clresource status -g geo-infrastructure

=== Cluster Resources ===

Resource Name           Node Name       State           Status Message
-------------           ---------       -----           --------------
geo-clustername         phys-summer1    Online          Online - Logical
Hostname online.
                        phys-summer2    Offline         Offline

geo-hbmonitor           phys-summer1    Online          Online - Daemon OK
                        phys-summer2    Offline         Offline
```

```
geo-failovercontrol      phys-summer1      Online                  Online - Service
is online.
                         phys-summer2      Offline                 Offline

# clresource show -p type geo-failovercontrol

=== Resources ===

Resource:                                  geo-failovercontrol
  Type:                                    SUNW.scmasa

  --- Standard and extension properties ---
```

The following example shows the status output from the `cacaoadm` command on two different nodes in the same cluster: `phys-summer1` and `phys-summer2`. In this case, the `geo-infrastructure` resource group is online on node `phys-summer1`. Therefore, the administrative state of the `com.sun.cluster.geocontrol` CAC module is unlocked. In contrast, the module on the other node, `phys-summer2`, is locked. If you switch the `geo-infrastructure` resource group between nodes, the resource's `Stop` and `Start` methods toggle these values.

## Example 6.3 Difference in Administrative State of the `com.sun.cluster.geocontrol` CAC Module between Cluster Nodes

Use the `cacaoadm` command to display the status of the `com.sun.cluster.geocontrol` module on both nodes in the `summer` cluster.

```
phys-summer1# cacaoadm status com.sun.cluster.geocontrol
Operational State:ENABLED
Administrative State:UNLOCKED
Availability Status:[]
Module is in good health.
phys-summer2# cacaoadm status com.sun.cluster.geocontrol
Operational State:ENABLED
Administrative State:LOCKED
Availability Status:[]
Module is not in good health.
```

## Note

You must create hostnames in your name service that match the cluster names of each local cluster in your Geographic Edition configuration. You must then associate an IP address with each of these hostnames so that the clusters can communicate with each other.

## Event Propagation

A service under the control of the Geographic Edition software has the data replication on which it relies monitored by a Solaris Cluster resource. The resource itself is created by the specific Geographic Edition module for that data replication. As the state of the data replication changes, it is reflected in the status of the resource. These events, together with any change in the state of the application resource or resource group, are propagated to the Geographic Edition software so that the state change can be reflected in the status information produced by the GUI and CLI output.

The Geographic Edition `com.sun.cluster.notifier` CAC module controls how events are handled. Each component within the Geographic Edition framework has a notifier task queue. When notification of an event occurs, the component's notification handler determines whether the event is relevant. If it is, the handler places it on the queue of events to be processed. Much of the internal configuration propagation is also performed in this way.

The Solaris Cluster CAC event module (`com.sun.cluster.event`) serves as the interface between the underlying library /usr/cluster/lib/cmass/libcmas_agent_clusterevent.so and the `com.sun.cluster.notifier` module. The dependency between these two CAC modules is listed in the `com.sun.cluster.notifier.xml` file.

## CLI, GUI, and Module Implementation

The Geographic Edition command-line interface (CLI) is implemented in `perl`. The replication modules are written in `ksh`. The graphical user interface (GUI) uses the same framework as the Solaris Cluster Manager (see the section "The Solaris Cluster Manager Graphical User Interface" in Chapter 4, "Managing Your Oracle Solaris Cluster Environment"). The Java Server Page and HTML files for the Geographic Edition components are located in the /usr/cluster/lib/SunPlexManagerGeo directory.

## Storage of Geographic Edition Configuration Information

The Geographic Edition software uses the Solaris Cluster CCR (see the section "Cluster Configuration Repository" in Chapter 2, "Oracle Solaris Cluster: Features and Architecture") to store its configuration information. The use of this repository ensures that information is correctly propagated between nodes within a single cluster without requiring system administrator intervention.

The CCR files created by a Geographic Edition installation have the following name formats:

- `st_pg_`*`protection-group-name`*: contains information about the state of the protection group on the local cluster
- `pg_`*`protection-group-name`*: contains information about the protection group properties, including the resource groups and device groups it contains
- `pts_`*`partnership-name`*: contains information about the named partnership, including the heartbeats and cluster nodes it contains
- `gc_hb_`*`heartbeat-name`*: contains information about a specific heartbeat link

These files are readable only by the Solaris root user. Do not rely on the format of, or naming conventions used by, these files. If you need to query information held in them, you must use either the standard Geographic Edition commands (`geops`, `geopg`, or `geohb`) or the Geographic Edition API commands (`scgeo_protectiongroup_get`, `scgeo_devicegroup_get`, or `scgeo_partnership_get`). Currently, the latter three commands constitute an emerging API and might be subject to change.

## Creating Trust between Clusters

When your clusters participate in a Geographic Edition configuration, it is very likely that they are located in data centers separated by many hundreds of kilometers. In most cases, you do not own the communications infrastructure that links these sites. Consequently, you must establish secure communications between them.

The Geographic Edition software performs all of its intercluster communications using the CAC framework. Therefore, you must establish trust between the nodes of the participating clusters. Establishing trust is achieved through exchanging certificates. The following example shows you how to list the trusted certificates known to the CAC framework on each cluster. The example also shows you how to use the `geops` command to verify that the trust between clusters has been established.

### Example 6.4  Examining the Trust Established between Geographic Edition Clusters

Use the `cacaoadm` command to list the trusted certificates on both the `summer` and `autumn` clusters.

```
phys-summer1# cacaoadm list-trusted-certs
autumn.certificate1
cacao_ca
autumn.certificate0
```

```
phys-autumn1# cacaoadm list-trusted-certs
summer.certificate0
cacao_ca
summer.certificate1
phys-autumn1# cacaoadm show-trusted-cert summer.certificate0
-----BEGIN CERTIFICATE-----
MIIBoDCCAQmgAwIBAgIEPnntHTANBgkqhkiG...
                    .
                    .
                    .
-----END CERTIFICATE-----
phys-autumn1# geops verify-trust -c summer

Local cluster : autumn
Local node : phys-autumn1

Retrieving information from cluster summer ... Done

Verifying connections to nodes of cluster summer:
phys-autumn1 -> phys-summer2 / 10.11.58.182 ... OK
phys-autumn1 -> phys-summer1 / 10.11.58.181 ... OK

Operation completed successfully, able to establish secure connections from phys-
autumn1 to all nodes of cluster summer
```

You use the `geops` command to establish trust between two Solaris Cluster installations. The `add-trust` subcommand automates the process of exchanging the certificates between the two sites. After trust has been established, you can form partnerships between the trusted clusters.

Establishing trust between clusters does not mean that host-based or application-based data replication is encrypted, as this happens outside the CAC framework. To ensure that the replicated data is secure, you must set up and use IP Security Architecture (IPsec) on the network used for data replication. Similarly, to protect your Geographic Edition heartbeat networks, you must also configure IPsec for them. Configure IPsec on these networks before you attempt to establish trust between the clusters.

## Partnerships

The Geographic Edition software enables partnerships to be formed between clusters to provide mutual protection against disasters. The clusters in a partnership monitor each other by sending heartbeat messages to each other, similarly to how the nodes within a single cluster do. Unlike local clusters, the clusters in a partnership use the public network for these messages. Furthermore, failure of the heartbeat connections does not cause an automatic migration of services between the clusters. Instead, the failure is highlighted as an error condition in the CLI and GUI output. You can also configure the software to run a program or script if such a failure occurs.

In Figure 6.3 and Example 6.5, there are two clusters: `summer` (nodes `phys-summer1` and `phys-summer2`) and `winter` (nodes `phys-winter1` and `phys-winter2`). After having checked that both clusters can resolve each other's cluster logical hostname, you must establish trust between the clusters. After trust has been established on one node of each cluster, the partnership can be created. The `summer-winter` partnership is created from `phys-summer1`, and then `phys-winter1` joins the freshly created partnership.

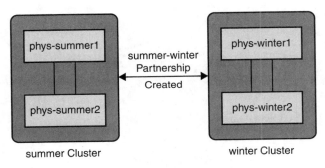

**Figure 6.3** Establishing Geographic Edition trust and partnership between `summer` and `winter` clusters

## Example 6.5  Configuring Trust and Creating a Partnership between Two Clusters

Use the `getent` command to determine whether IP addresses can be resolved for the hostnames `winter` and `summer`.

```
phys-summer1# getent hosts winter
10.17.252.49    winter
phys-winter1# getent hosts summer
10.11.58.198    summer
```

Use the `geops` command to allow the `summer` cluster to trust the `winter` cluster.

```
phys-summer1# geops add-trust -c winter

Local cluster : summer
Local node : phys-summer1

Cleaning up certificate files in /etc/cacao/instances/default/security/jsse on
phys-summer1

Retrieving certificates from winter ... Done

New Certificate:

Owner: CN=phys-winter2_agent
```

```
Issuer: CN=phys-winter2_ca
Serial number: 5b822a08
Valid from: Fri Mar 07 06:03:53 PST 2008 until: Tue Mar 07 06:03:53 PST 2028
Certificate fingerprints:
        MD5:  62:06:1E:0A:76:B4:7C:EA:71:91:1C:65:64:65:38:A5
        SHA1: BB:AD:38:C8:96:0B:97:47:C3:E6:9B:09:89:79:84:98:41:F5:8A:07

Do you trust this certificate? [y/n] y

Adding certificate to truststore on phys-summer1 ... Done

Adding certificate to truststore on phys-summer2 ... Done

New Certificate:

Owner: CN=phys-winter2_ca
Issuer: CN=phys-winter2_ca
Serial number: 23f03a0a
Valid from: Fri Mar 07 06:03:52 PST 2008 until: Tue Mar 07 06:03:52 PST 2028
Certificate fingerprints:
        MD5:  19:DE:88:FB:02:05:A3:EC:77:1C:E1:35:D4:ED:0A:4A
        SHA1: 13:12:5B:4E:1B:11:4D:AB:D5:DA:9E:FF:0B:F7:D4:54:B9:28:22:09

Do you trust this certificate? [y/n] y

Adding certificate to truststore on phys-summer1 ... Done

Adding certificate to truststore on phys-summer2 ... Done

Operation completed successfully. All certificates are added to truststore on nodes
of cluster summer
```

Use the `geops` command to allow the `winter` cluster to trust the `summer` cluster.

```
phys-winter1# geops add-trust -c summer

Local cluster : winter
Local node : phys-winter1

Cleaning up certificate files in /etc/cacao/instances/default/security/jsse on phys-
winter1

Retrieving certificates from summer ... Done

New Certificate:

Owner: CN=phys-summer1_agent
Issuer: CN=phys-summer1_ca
Serial number: 3e79ed1d
Valid from: Sat Jun 21 17:59:09 MET 1969 until: Fri Sep 21 18:59:09 MEST 2029
Certificate fingerprints:
        MD5:  A9:EC:DA:D7:DD:E2:AA:4C:A2:A0:00:4D:C5:BA:99:A3
        SHA1: 2A:B4:0A:58:43:CA:77:63:A4:FD:BD:ED:97:4A:49:65:25:26:DD:FA
        Signature algorithm name: SHA1withRSA
        Version: 3

Do you trust this certificate? [y/n] y

Adding certificate to truststore on phys-winter2 ... Done

Adding certificate to truststore on phys-winter1 ... Done

New Certificate:
```

```
Owner: CN=phys-summer1_ca
Issuer: CN=phys-summer1_ca
Serial number: 2036002
Valid from: Sat Jun 21 17:59:09 MET 1969 until: Fri Sep 21 18:59:09 MEST 2029
Certificate fingerprints:
      MD5:  4A:17:E2:6C:77:A9:62:32:DE:36:7F:B1:9B:12:41:B8
      SHA1: 85:89:B0:7E:CD:BF:F6:63:1C:82:61:52:EF:C7:34:84:D0:E4:7F:21
      Signature algorithm name: SHA1withRSA
      Version: 3

Do you trust this certificate? [y/n] y

Adding certificate to truststore on phys-winter2 ... Done

Adding certificate to truststore on phys-winter1 ... Done

Operation completed successfully. All certificates are added to truststore on nodes of
   cluster winter
```

On the `winter` cluster, use the `geops` command to define a partnership called `summer-winter`, and then join the partnership from the `summer` cluster.

```
phys-summer1# geops create -c winter summer-winter
Partnership between local cluster "summer" and remote cluster "winter" successfully
created.
phys-winter1# geops join-partnership summer summer-winter
Local cluster "winter" is now partner of cluster "summer".
phys-winter1# geops list summer-winter


     Partnership: summer-winter
          Description           :
          Local heartbeat       : hb_winter~summer
          Remote heartbeat      : hb_summer~winter
          Notification_ActionCmd :
          Notification_EmailAddrs :
```

# Geographic Edition Heartbeat Messages

The Geographic Edition software sends heartbeat messages to monitor the state between partner clusters. Heartbeat messages are sent over the public network to detect cluster failures at geographically separated sites. For example, heartbeat messages could be lost when a cluster loses access to the public network, and no communication occurs between the partner clusters. The same happens when all of the cluster nodes on a site are shut down.

Compared with the Solaris Cluster heartbeat messages, the Geographic Edition heartbeat messages are much less frequent. By default, they occur every 2 minutes. The following example shows a partnership named `rac-summer-autumn` that has been established between clusters called `summer` and `autumn`. The output from the `geohb` command shows the processes involved in the communication and the default port used, that is, 2084. This is important because you must ensure that your firewalls are configured to allow this traffic to pass through.

### Example 6.6   Obtaining Geographic Edition Heartbeat Information

Use the `geops` command to display information on the heartbeats configured between the `summer` and `autumn` clusters.

```
phys-summer1# geops list

Local cluster "summer" is in the following partnerships:

    Partnership: rac-summer-autumn
        Description           :
        Local heartbeat       : hb_summer~autumn
        Remote heartbeat      : hb_autumn~summer
        Notification_ActionCmd :
        Notification_EmailAddrs :
phys-summer1# geohb list hb_summer~autumn


Heartbeat name: hb_summer~autumn

    Source cluster    : summer
    Target cluster    : autumn
    Query_interval    : 120 seconds

    Following plug-ins are configured:

    Plug-in name: ping_plugin
        Type              : Backup
        Query_cmd         : /usr/cluster/lib/geo/lib/ping_plg_cmd
        Query_lib         :
        Requester_agent   :
        Responder_agent   :
        Plugin_properties : autumn

    Plug-in name: tcp_udp_plugin
        Type              : Primary
        Query_cmd         :
        Query_lib         : /usr/cluster/lib/geo/lib/libtcp_udp.so.1
        Requester_agent   : /usr/cluster/lib/geo/lib/tcp_udp_req
        Responder_agent   : /usr/cluster/lib/geo/lib/tcp_udp_resp
        Plugin_properties : autumn/UDP/2084,autumn/TCP/2084
```

## Heartbeat Module

Unlike the Solaris Cluster heartbeat module, the Geographic Edition heartbeat module is implemented as a number of normal Solaris processes because the scheduling constraints on them are far less severe. The responder daemon (`gchb_resd`) is started by the `/etc/rc3.d/S91initgchb_resd` script when the node boots in cluster mode. When you start the Geographic Edition software using the `geoadm` command, the requester daemon (`gchb_reqd`) is spawned. The requester daemon is started by the `Start` method of the `geo-hbmonitor` resource (a `SUNW.HBmonitor`-type resource) contained in the `geo-infrastructure` resource group.

Both the `gchb_resd` and `gchb_reqd` daemons register for cluster events of type `ESC_CLUSTER_CMD` and `ESC_CLUSTER_CONFIG_CHANGE`. These cluster events indicate CCR changes. When an event indicates that a partnership has been created, the heartbeat information is read, and the heartbeat requester and responder daemons are started. By default, `tcp_udp plugin` is used, resulting in the `tcp_udp_resp` and `tcp_udp_req` daemons being started. Each daemon handles all heartbeats of that type. As partnerships change, the heartbeat configuration is updated.

You can also define your own custom heartbeat mechanisms. They are started in a similar fashion by the `gchb_resd` or `gchb_reqd` daemons.

The Geographic Edition software also has a backup heartbeat mechanism that relies on `ICMP ECHO_REQUEST` messages, similar to those used by the Solaris `ping` command. Because the regular probe messages generated by `gchb_reqd` translate to invocations of the `ping` command, no `ping` requester process is required. Similarly, because the IP stack responds to ICMP echo messages in the kernel, no responder is required either.

All daemons run under process-monitoring-facility (`pmfadm`) control and are restarted on failure.

## Failure Notification

The Geographic Edition software uses the heartbeat status to notify administrators of failures. With the `geops` command, you can set two properties that can be used to highlight the loss of communication: `Notification_ActionCmd` and `Notification_EmailAddrs`. By default, the heartbeat query interval is 120 seconds and can be modified using the `geohb` command. The Geographic Edition software determines that the remote cluster has failed if five consecutive heartbeat messages are not received, that is, 10 minutes in total. The five messages include the initial and final lost messages, in addition to the number of retries missed (three, by default), defined by the `heartbeat.retries` property in the `com.sun.cluster.geocontrol.xml` file.

When the Geographic Edition software determines that the remote cluster has failed, because of a lack of heartbeat messages, an email is sent to the address defined by the `Notification_EmailAddrs` property. If you have defined a command in the `Notification_ActionCmd` property, then it will be run as well. The Geographic Edition software runs the command with the following arguments: `-c local-cluster-name -r remote-cluster-name -e 1 -n node-name -t time`. The `-e 1` parameter indicates that the heartbeats have been lost, and the time is given as the number of milliseconds since January 1, 1970, 00:00:00 GMT.

## Protection Groups

When you protect a service against disaster with the Geographic Edition software, you do so by placing it in a named *protection group*. A Geographic Edition configuration can contain many protection groups. Each protection group you create defines the type of replication it uses to protect the application data, for example, EMC Symmetrix Remote Data Facility, Hitachi Data Systems TrueCopy and Universal Replicator, StorageTek Availability Suite (AVS), Oracle Data Guard, and so on. Consequently, a Geographic Edition configuration can support multiple protection groups, each using different replication software. Furthermore, depending on the replication you use, there might be one or more replication-specific properties you can set.

Initially, the protection group exists only on the cluster on which you created it. To make it known to both clusters in the partnership, you must retrieve the configuration from the other cluster in the partnership using the `geopg` command, as shown in Example 6.7 (also see Figure 6.4). In this example, the protection group, `dummy-pg`, is created on the `winter` cluster and then retrieved by the `spring` cluster. After the configuration has been propagated, all subsequent changes, such as addition and removal of resource groups or property changes, are automatically propagated to the other cluster. However, when you delete a protection group, you must delete it from each cluster.

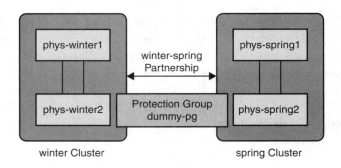

**Figure 6.4** Creating a dummy protection group on the `winter-spring` Geographic Edition partnership

Any resource group that you add to a protection group must have the `auto_start_on_new_cluster` property set to `false`. This value prevents the resource group from being started when the cluster is booted but still allows the Geographic Edition framework to manage the resource group being brought online and offline.

When you start a protection group using the `geopg` command, you can do so either locally or globally. If you start the protection group globally, the Geographic Edition software brings online the resource groups the protection group protects on the primary site and starts the data replication. On the disaster recovery site, the application resource groups are placed in the offline state. Usually, the local option is used when either the remote cluster is unavailable or you need to perform maintenance on the local cluster.

## Example 6.7  Creating and Starting a Protection Group with No Data Replication

On the `winter` cluster, use the `geopg` command to create the protection group called `dummy-pg`.

```
phys-winter1# geopg create --partnership winter-spring --role primary \
> --datarep-type none --property Description="Just a test" dummy-pg
Protection group "dummy-pg" successfully created.
```

On the `spring` cluster, retrieve the `dummy-pg` protection group configuration.

```
phys-spring1# geopg get --partnership winter-spring dummy-pg
Protection group "dummy-pg" successfully created.
```

On both clusters, create a resource group called `dummy-rg`.

```
phys-winter1# clresourcegroup create-p auto_start_on_new_cluster=false \
> dummy-rg

phys-spring1# clresourcegroup create \
> -p auto_start_on_new_cluster=false dummy-rg
```

Use the `geopg` command to add the `dummy-rg` resource group to the `dummy-pg` protection group and then start the protection group.

```
phys-winter1# geopg add-resource-group dummy-rg dummy-pg
Following resource groups successfully added:
      "dummy-rg".
phys-winter1# geopg start -e global dummy-pg
Processing operation... The timeout period for this operation on each cluster is 3600

seconds (3600000 milliseconds)...
Protection group "dummy-pg" successfully started.

phys-spring1# geopg list dummy-pg

Protection Group: dummy-pg

  Partnership name            : winter-spring

  Local Role                  : Secondary
  Deployed on clusters        : spring, winter
  Data Replication type       : NONE
  Configuration status        : OK
```

```
Synchronization status       : OK
Creation signature           : winter Dec 1, 2009 6:28:43 PM MET
Last update                  : Dec 2, 2009 12:49:51 PM MET

Local properties             : None

Global properties            :

     Description             : Just a test
     Timeout                 : 3600 seconds
     RoleChange_ActionCmd    :
     External_Dependency_Allowed : false
     RoleChange_ActionArgs   :

Protected resource groups:

     dummy-rg

*** No device groups defined in protection group "dummy-pg" ***
```

By associating a protection group with a Geographic Edition partnership, you constrain the primary cluster to be either one of the two clusters that constitute the partnership. After you have created the protection group, you add the specific replication components and resource groups that represent the replicated data and the applications that require protection.

See the following `geopg` output in Example 6.8. This example shows a basic Apache web service that is being protected by the Geographic Edition software. A protection group called `seasons_apache` has been created that uses AVS as the underlying data replication mechanism. The group is hosted on the `winter-spring` partnership, which contains the `winter` and `spring` clusters. The web server service is managed by a Solaris Cluster resource group called `apache-1-rg`, and its data is stored on a device group called `apacheset`. The `geopg` command output also indicates that the `spring` cluster is the disaster recovery site for this service.

## Example 6.8  A Protection Group Using AVS to Protect the Application Data

Use the `geopg` command to list the properties of the `seasons_apache` protection group.

```
# geopg list seasons_apache

Protection Group: seasons_apache

  Partnership name            : winter-spring

  Local Role                  : Primary
  Deployed on clusters        : winter, spring
```

```
        Data Replication type        : AVS
        Configuration status         : OK
        Synchronization status       : OK
        Creation signature           : winter Mar 16, 2009 6:06:41 PM MET
        Last update                  : Nov 20, 2009 3:03:13 PM MET

        Local properties             :

                nodelist                : phys-winter1,phys-winter2

        Global properties            :

                Description           : Apache test PG
                Timeout               : 3600 seconds
                RoleChange_ActionCmd       :
                External_Dependency_Allowed : false
                RoleChange_ActionArgs      :

        Protected resource groups:

                apache-1-rg

        AVS Device groups:

                apacheset

                apacheset_local_logical_host : avs-winter-1
                apacheset_enable_volume_set  : TRUE
                apacheset_remote_logical_host : avs-spring-1
```

If changes are made to a protection group on one cluster while the other cluster is shut down or unreachable, the configuration synchronization between the two clusters is broken. It can be reestablished after the other cluster is available using the `geopg update` subcommand.

## Replication Components

Protection groups that do not use the `none` replication type can contain one or more replication components. The replication components represent either host-based or storage-based replicated device groups or application-based replicated databases. Within any one protection group, all the replicated components use the same replication technology. Depending on the replication type, each replicated component might have one or more properties that can be set.

The Geographic Edition software supports the following replication mechanisms:

- StorageTek Availability Suite (AVS) software
- EMC Symmetrix Remote Data Facility (SRDF)
- Hitachi TrueCopy and Universal Replicator

- Oracle Data Guard (for Oracle 10*g* and 11*g* Real Application Clusters databases only)
- MySQL database replication

There is also the Script-Based Plug-In (SBP) module, which can be used to incorporate other replication products for which there is no Oracle-supported module available. Each replication product is described in the following sections.

When you add more than one replication component to a protection group (see Figure 6.5), the overall status given to the replication is that of the component in the least healthy state. Thus, only if all the replication components are healthy will the overall status of the protection group be considered OK.

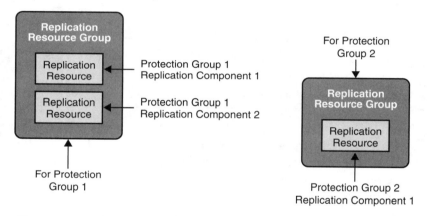

**Figure 6.5** Relationships between the protection group replication components and the replication resources

Figure 6.6 illustrates the concepts of partnerships, protection groups, replication components, and heartbeat message exchanges. The figure shows the relationships between three clusters called earth, mars, and venus that have two partnerships configured: earth-mars and earth-venus. Each partnership supports two protection groups. The protection groups are constrained to run only on the cluster contained within the partnership. Each protection group is configured with a single replication component, though several could be configured in each protection group. In the case of the srdf type of protection group, the replication components hr-dg and crm-dg represent device groups, and the protection groups with odg and sbp types both have replication components that represent database replications.

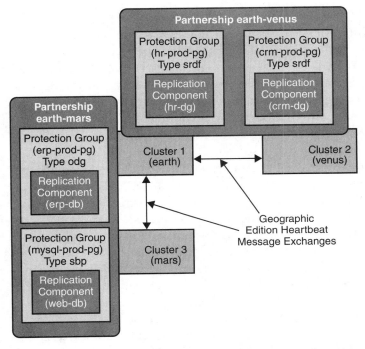

**Figure 6.6** Relationship between partnerships, protection groups, replication components, heartbeat message exchanges, and lusters in a Geographic Edition configuration

## StorageTek Availability Suite Software

The StorageTek Availability Suite (AVS) software includes a host-based replication mechanism that enables you to replicate disk volumes between geographically separated primary clusters and secondary clusters in real time. Data is replicated from a master volume of the primary cluster to a backup volume on the secondary cluster through a TCP/IP connection. You can configure multiple pairs of these volumes and replicate them synchronously or asynchronously on a per-pair basis. The volumes you replicate can be Solaris Volume Manager metadevices, Veritas Volume Manager disk volumes, or device groups that do not use a volume manager, that is, `rawdisk`-type devices. If you use a volume manager, either Solaris Volume Manager or Veritas Volume Manager, you must have identical metadevices set up on both the primary and disaster recovery clusters before configuring the replication.

## Initialization Files

The configuration for each device group used by the Geographic Edition software must be placed in a file called /var/cluster/geo/avs/*device-group-name-*volset.ini, where *device-group-name* is replaced by the actual name of the device group. Example 6.9 shows the initialization file for the Solaris Volume Manager diskset called apacheset on cluster winter. (The file for cluster spring is similar but uses different metadevice numbers.) The full syntax of the file is described in the rdc.cf(4) man page. However, some of the essential points relating to this example are discussed next.

The apacheset diskset exists on both clusters: winter and spring. Because the diskset can be owned by either node in each cluster, you cannot use the IP address of either cluster node as the source and target for the transfer of the replicated data. This means that you must create SUNW.LogicalHostname resources, held in a specifically named resource group, to provide IP addresses hosted on one node of each cluster. In this case, the two logical hostnames are avs-winter-1 and avs-spring-1. You must configure separate logical hostnames for each diskset to be replicated because each diskset can move between cluster nodes regardless of any other diskset's location.

The apacheset diskset itself has three (metadevice) data volumes that require replication. These data volumes can have different metadevice names at each site, as long as the devices are of the correct size. On the spring cluster the devices are d0, d26, and d36. On the winter cluster they are d0, d21, and d31. Each of the data volumes has an associated bitmap to record block changes in the data volumes if communication between the sites is lost. Again, these data volumes have different metadevice names at each site: d1, d27, and d37, and d1, d22, and d32, respectively.

All of the metadevices in this example are replicated asynchronously, as indicated by the async tag for each file entry. The three metadevices are also marked with the g field, indicating that they are part of a single I/O consistency group named apacheset. In asynchronous mode, write ordering must be preserved across all replicating volumes in a consistency group. If you choose to use consistency groups, all volumes must be in the same Solaris Cluster disk group. These volumes include volumes used for data, snapshots, and disk queues (disk queues store changes to be replicated on disk rather than in memory). Furthermore, all volume sets must share the same disk queue volume, if disk queues are configured.

In this example, the d0 metadevice has also been configured to use metadevice d72 as a disk queue on the winter cluster. The metadevice d71 performs the same role for data device d1 on cluster spring. The remaining devices use memory-based queues to hold the pending changes. You might use this approach if most of the changes requiring replication were to use metadevice d0 or d1 (depending on the direction of replication).

---

**Example 6.9   An AVS Initialization File for the `apacheset` Diskset**

Display the contents of the `apacheset-volset.ini` file.

```
phys-winter1# cat /var/cluster/geo/avs/apacheset-volset.ini
avs-spring-1 /dev/md/apacheset/rdsk/d0 /dev/md/apacheset/rdsk/d1 avs-winter-1 /dev/md/
apacheset/rdsk/d0 /dev/md/apacheset/rdsk/d1 ip async g apacheset q /dev/md/apacheset/
rdsk/d72 C apacheset
avs-spring-1 /dev/md/apacheset/rdsk/d26 /dev/md/apacheset/rdsk/d27 avs-winter-1 /dev/
md/apacheset/rdsk/d21 /dev/md/apacheset/rdsk/d22 ip async g apacheset C apacheset
avs-spring-1 /dev/md/apacheset/rdsk/d36 /dev/md/apacheset/rdsk/d37 avs-winter-1 /dev/
md/apacheset/rdsk/d31 /dev/md/apacheset/rdsk/d32 ip async g apacheset C apacheset
```

---

If communication is lost between the clusters, AVS is unable to transmit the replication data. Instead of returning an error to the application, AVS begins logging the changes that are made to the master volume with the intention of forwarding them when the link is reestablished. The changes are held in the bitmap volumes. When the communication problem has been resolved, the changes are sent in the order in which they appear in the bitmap volume. The transmission order does not usually match the order in which the I/Os were originally issued. If a second failure prevents all the changes from being transmitted, then the backup copy of the data is likely to be inconsistent (see the section "Ensuring Data Consistency after a Rolling Failure" in Chapter 1, "Oracle Solaris Cluster: Overview"). To avoid having a copy of data that is unusable, the Geographic Edition AVS module can be configured to take an automatic snapshot of a volume when it enters logging mode. If a subsequent failure occurs, the inconsistent data is replaced by the snapshot that provided the last point of consistency. The snapshot configuration is stored in a file called `/var/cluster/geo/avs/`*device-group-name*`-snapshot.ini`.

The following example shows that the `winter` cluster uses metadevices `d81`, `d23`, and `d33` as the snapshot shadow volumes for metadevices `d0`, `d21`, and `d31`, respectively. The differences between the master and shadow volumes are recorded in metadevices `d82`, `d24`, and `d34`. Entries in the *device-group-name*`-snapshot.ini` file must be placed on a single line and have three fields: the metadevice, the snapshot metadevice, and the differences metadevice.

---

**Example 6.10   An AVS Snapshot File for the `apacheset` Diskset**

Display the contents of the `apacheset-snapshot.ini` file.

```
phys-winter1# cat /var/cluster/geo/avs/apacheset-snapshot.ini
/dev/md/apacheset/rdsk/d0 /dev/md/apacheset/rdsk/d81 /dev/md/apacheset/rdsk/d82
/dev/md/apacheset/rdsk/d21 /dev/md/apacheset/rdsk/d23 /dev/md/apacheset/rdsk/d24
/dev/md/apacheset/rdsk/d31 /dev/md/apacheset/rdsk/d33 /dev/md/apacheset/rdsk/d34
```

## Resource Group Configuration

When you use AVS in a Solaris Cluster configuration, you must apply the following resource group and resource naming convention. The name of the resource group containing the logical hostname and `SUNW.HAStoragePlus` resource must be of the form *device-group-name-stor-rg*. This resource group must contain a `SUNW.HAStoragePlus` resource whose name is of the form *device-group-name-stor*. This is known as the lightweight AVS replication resource group.

The following example shows the configuration used for a device group called `apacheset`. A similar resource group must be configured on each cluster in the partnership hosting the protection group that contains this replication component. The logical host resource `apacheset-lh` on the `winter` cluster represents the logical hostname `avs-winter-1`. This logical hostname matches the hostname field in the `apacheset-volset.ini` file (see Example 6.9) and in the `local_logical_host` property in the `geopg` output in Example 6.8.

---

### Example 6.11  Required Solaris Cluster AVS Resource Group Configuration

Use the `clresourcegroup` command to display the properties of the `apacheset-stor-rg` resource group.

```
phys-winter1# clresourcegroup show apacheset-stor-rg

=== Resource Groups and Resources ===

Resource Group:                         apacheset-stor-rg
  RG_description:                         <NULL>
  RG_mode:                                Failover
  RG_state:                               Managed
  Failback:                               False
  Nodelist:                               phys-winter1 phys-winter2

  --- Resources for Group apacheset-stor-rg ---

  Resource:                             apacheset-lh
    Type:                                 SUNW.LogicalHostname:3
    Type_version:                         3
    Group:                                apacheset-stor-rg
    R_description:
    Resource_project_name:                default
    Enabled{phys-winter1}:                True
    Enabled{phys-winter2}:                True
    Monitored{phys-winter1}:              True
    Monitored{phys-winter2}:              True

  Resource:                             apacheset-stor
    Type:                                 SUNW.HAStoragePlus:6
    Type_version:                         6
    Group:                                apacheset-stor-rg
    R_description:
    Resource_project_name:                default
```

```
      Enabled{phys-winter1}:                    True
      Enabled{phys-winter2}:                    True
      Monitored{phys-winter1}:                  True
      Monitored{phys-winter2}:                  True
phys-winter1# clresource show -p HostnameList apacheset-lh

=== Resources ===

Resource:                                 apacheset-lh

  --- Standard and extension properties ---

  HostnameList:                           avs-winter-1
    Class:                                extension
    Description:                          List of hostnames this resource
manages
    Per-node:                             False
    Type:                                 stringarray
```

When you add an AVS replication component to a protection group, a replication resource group and a resource are created to monitor the state of the replication. The naming convention for the AVS Geographic Edition module results in a resource group called *protection-group-name*-rep-rg and a replication resource called *device-group-name*-rep-rs. The resource group is created with a strong positive affinity (+++) for the lightweight AVS replication resource group.

The following example shows the resource group and resource being created when you add device group `apacheset` to protection group `seasons_apache`. If the application uses a `SUNW.HAStoragePlus` resource in the application resource group and that resource has the `AffinityOn` property set to `true`, then the application resource group will also have a strong positive resource group affinity for the lightweight AVS resource group. If the `SUNW.HAStoragePlus` resource controls a zpool, it ignores the `AffinityOn` property and behaves as if it has the value `true`.

## Example 6.12  Replication Resource Groups and Resources Created When You Add an AVS Device Group to a Protection Group

On cluster `winter`, use the `geopg` command to create a protection group called `seasons_apache`. Commands are run on different hosts as noted in the prompts.

```
phys-winter1# geopg create --partnership winter-spring --role primary \
> --datarep-type avs --property Description="Apache test PG" \
> --property nodelist=phys-winter1,phys-winter2 \
> seasons_apache
Protection group "seasons_apache" successfully created.
```

On cluster `spring`, retrieve the `seasons_apache` protection group configuration using the `geopg` command.

```
phys-spring1# geopg get --partnership winter-spring seasons_apache
Protection group "seasons_apache" successfully created.
```

Use the `geopg` command to set the `nodelist` property.

```
phys-spring1# geopg set-prop \
> --property nodelist=phys-spring1,phys-spring2 seasons_apache
Protection group "seasons_apache" successfully modified.
```

Use the `geopg` command to add a replication component and then a resource group to the `seasons_apache` protection group.

```
phys-winter1# geopg add-replication-component \
> --property local_logical_host=avs-winter-1 \
> --property remote_logical_host=avs-spring-1 \
> --property enable_volume_set=TRUE \
> apacheset seasons_apache
Device group "apacheset" successfully added to the protection group "seasons_apache".
phys-winter1# geopg add-resource-group apache-1-rg seasons_apache
Following resource groups successfully added:
        "apache-1-rg".
```

Use the `geopg` command to start the `seasons_apache` protection group on both clusters.

```
phys-winter1# geopg start -e global seasons_apache
Processing operation... The timeout period for this operation on each cluster is 3600
seconds (3600000 milliseconds)...
Protection group "seasons_apache" successfully started.
phys-winter1# clresourcegroup show seasons_apache-rep-rg

=== Resource Groups and Resources ===

Resource Group:                             seasons_apache-rep-rg
  RG_description:                             <NULL>
  RG_mode:                                    Failover
  RG_state:                                   Managed
  Failback:                                   False
  Nodelist:                                   phys-winter1 phys-winter2

  --- Resources for Group seasons_apache-rep-rg ---

  Resource:                                 apacheset-rep-rs
    Type:                                     SUNW.GeoCtlAVS:1.2
    Type_version:                             1.2
    Group:                                    seasons_apache-rep-rg
    R_description:
    Resource_project_name:                    default
    Enabled{phys-winter1}:                    True
    Enabled{phys-winter2}:                    True
    Monitored{phys-winter1}:                  True
    Monitored{phys-winter2}:                  True

phys-winter1# clresourcegroup show -p RG_affinities seasons_apache-rep-rg

=== Resource Groups and Resources ===

Resource Group:                             seasons_apache-rep-rg
  RG_affinities:                              +++apacheset-stor-rg
```

The resulting configuration is shown in **Figure 6.7**. Note that there is no requirement for the logical hostname resources or the IP addresses they represent to be identical on both sites. Only the resource group name must be the same. Thus, you can have the service present different IP addresses depending on which site is the primary. However, if you do so, consider using the protection group `RoleChange_ActionCmd` property to specify a script that can automate the required hostname resolution changes (for example, in DNS).

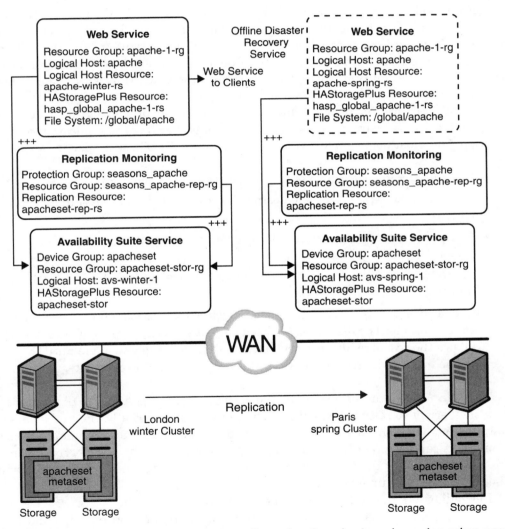

**Figure 6.7** A Geographic Edition AVS configuration for a basic web service using one Solaris Volume Manager device group

If more device groups are added to the protection group, then a replication resource is created in the replication resource group to represent each device group. Similarly, if more resource groups are placed under the control of the protection group, then the Geographic Edition software ensures that they have a strong positive resource group affinity for the lightweight AVS resource groups upon which their file systems (or raw-disk devices) depend.

## AVS Monitoring: The Replication Resource

When you add a device group to an AVS protection group, the Geographic Edition software creates a replication resource group, if required, and a replication resource. The replication resource is used to monitor the state of the replication. Changes in the state of this resource are propagated through the Cluster Management and Serviceability (CMAS) framework into the CAC framework, where they are used to calculate the overall health of the protection group.

The AVS replication resource has several extension properties that the Geographic Edition software uses to store information regarding the replication configuration. You must not attempt to modify these manually. These properties are

- `Device_group`: The name of the device group to be monitored.
- `Remote_logical_host`: The hostname for the target of the AVS data replication.
- `Role`: The current replication role. The value can be either `Primary` or `Secondary`.
- `Snapshot_volume`: The local AVS (Instant Image) snapshot volume set names.
- `Local_disk_queue`: The name of any disk queue associated with the replication volume. The disk queue is used only at the primary site. This property allows the resource at the secondary site to hold the queue name until the queue needs to be re-created when the site becomes a primary site.

The AVS replication resource calls the `/opt/SUNWscgrepavs/rt/bin/probe_avs` shell script to report the health of the replication. Internally, the probe parses output from a combination of the `sndradm`, `dscfg`, and `dsstat` commands. These commands can be run only on the nodes currently hosting the device group, hence the requirement for the "+++" affinity between the replication resource group and the lightweight resource group.

Depending on the output from the probe commands, the `scha_resource_setstatus` program is used to set the status of the replication resource and provide an associated resource status message.

## EMC Symmetrix Remote Data Facility

The EMC Symmetrix Remote Data Facility (SRDF) [EMCSRDF] provides storage-based replication for disaster recovery. SRDF groups define a relationship between local and remote EMC arrays through the intervening SRDF director ports and network. SRDF groups can be static groups created by EMC support personnel or dynamic groups created by your storage administrator [EMCGroups]. Within these groups, SRDF volumes are created that are either source (R1) volumes or target (R2) volumes.

With these R1 and R2 volumes, your storage administrator creates named RDF1 (source) or RDF2 (target) device groups. After device groups of the same name and size are configured at both sites, you can establish the replication between them. You can use synchronous or asynchronous replication on a per-device-group basis. However, at the time of this writing, the Geographic Edition software supports switchover of only synchronously replicated device groups.

Setting domino mode on either the primary volumes or the SRDF links can, under certain failure scenarios, block application writes to the primary volumes. If this happened, your service would suffer an outage at the primary site, which is an undesirable outcome for a highly available service. Consequently, do *not* set domino mode on any of the primary volumes or associated SRDF links.

The SRDF adaptive copy mode is primarily used for bulk data transfer. It does not preserve data write ordering, which makes it unsuitable for disaster recovery.

SRDF software supports composite groups to ensure that application data write consistency is maintained when data is replicated from multiple Symmetrix arrays. However, at the time of this writing, the Geographic Edition software supports only device groups and not composite groups. Consequently, data for a single application must not span Symmetrix arrays.

Data is replicated between Symmetrix arrays across Fibre Channel, ESCON, or Gigabit Ethernet links (depending on the SRDF director used), and the relationship between the pairs of device groups becomes operational as soon as these links are online. The volumes you replicate can be either Veritas Volume Manager or Veritas Volume Manager cluster feature disk groups or device groups that do not use a volume manager, that is, rawdisk-type devices.

### Note

At the time of this writing, you cannot use Solaris Volume Manager with the Symmetrix Remote Data Facility.

The array global memory stores information about the pair state, which can be queried using the Symmetrix command-line (SYMCLI) programs such as `symdev` and `symrdf`.

## Configuration

The two Symmetrix arrays that participate in an `srdf`-type protection group are identified by their storage unit identifier (SID). When creating a protection group, you must supply both the local and remote SID values. The array denoted by the `R1_SID` property contains the RDF1 device groups, whereas the array denoted by the `R2_SID` property contains the RDF2 device groups.

Information about your SRDF device groups is held in the SYMAPI configuration file called `symapi_db.bin`. This file is located in the `/var/symapi/db` directory. Because this is a binary file, you can use only SYMCLI commands to view or modify your configuration.

Group Name Services (GNS) is an EMC Symmetrix service that enables you to store device group configuration details centrally rather than on each host. If you do not use GNS, you must create and populate your device groups on all the primary cluster nodes. After you have completed this process, you must export the device group configuration to a file, which must then be copied to all of the nodes on the secondary cluster. To complete the creation of the device group, you must then import that configuration file on all the secondary cluster nodes unless, again, you have GNS running.

The following example shows a configuration with two clusters called `mars` and `saturn`. Each cluster consists of two Sun Fire V440 servers with 16 gigabytes of memory. Cluster `mars` consists of nodes `phys-mars1` and `phys-mars2`, and cluster `saturn` consists of nodes `phys-saturn3` and `phys-saturn4`. The example shows how to create and synchronize an EMC SRDF device group.

## Example 6.13  Creating and Synchronizing an EMC SRDF Device Group

Commands are run on different hosts as noted in the prompts.

First, list all dynamic, host-visible Symmetrix devices capable of being formed into RDF pairs.

```
phys-mars1# symdev list pd -dynamic

Symmetrix ID: 000187990182

           Device Name            Directors              Device
    ---------------------- ------------- ------------------------------------
                                                                        Cap
    Sym   Physical         SA :P DA :IT  Config       Attribute    Sts  (MB)
    ---------------------- ------------- ------------------------------------
```

```
         .
         .
         .
00DF  /dev/global/rdsk/d46s2  01D:0  16B:CE  RDF2+Mir   N/Grp'd   WD   4315
00E0  /dev/global/rdsk/d45s2  01D:0  01A:CE  RDF1+Mir   N/Grp'd   RW   4315

00E1  /dev/global/rdsk/d44s2  01D:0  15A:CE  2-Way Mir  N/Grp'd   RW   4315
         .
         .
         .
```

Create a Symmetrix device group called `mydevgroup` of type `rdf1`.

```
phys-mars1# symdg create mydevgroup -type rdf1
```

Add device `00E0` to device group `mydevgroup`.

```
phys-mars1# symld -g mydevgroup -sid 000187990182 add dev 00E0
```

Create the device group on the other node of the `mars` cluster.

```
phys-mars2# symdg create mydevgroup -type rdf1
```

Add device `00E0` to device group `mydevgroup`.

```
phys-mars2# symld -g mydevgroup -sid 000187990182 add dev 00E0
```

Now, both nodes on cluster `mars` have device group `mydevgroup` configured.

Export the configuration into a flat file that can be used to re-create the configuration on the other cluster.

```
phys-mars1# symdg export mydevgroup -f /tmp/mydevgroup.txt -rdf
```

View the contents of the file `/tmp/mydevgroup.txt`.

```
phys-mars1# cat /tmp/mydevgroup.txt
1 000187990182
S 0E0 DEV001
```

Copy the flat file to the nodes of cluster `saturn` and then import the file on both `saturn` cluster nodes using the `symdg` command.

```
phys-saturn3#  scp -q phys-mars1:/tmp/mydevgroup.txt /tmp
Password:
phys-saturn3# symdg import mydevgroup -f /tmp/mydevgroup.txt

Adding STD device 0E0 as DEV001...
phys-saturn3# symdev show 00E0 | grep "Device Physical Name"
    Device Physical Name    : /dev/global/rdsk/d45s2

phys-saturn4# scp phys-mars1:/tmp/mydevgroup.txt /tmp
Password:
phys-saturn4# symdg import mydevgroup -f /tmp/mydevgroup.txt

Adding STD device 0E0 as DEV001...
```

Establish the replication for device group `mydevgroup` using the `symrdf` command.

```
phys-mars1# symrdf -g mydevgroup -noprompt establish
```

```
An RDF 'Incremental Establish' operation execution is
in progress for device group 'mydevgroup'. Please wait...

     Suspend RDF link(s).......................................Done.
     Resume RDF link(s)........................................Started.
     Resume RDF link(s)........................................Done.

The RDF 'Incremental Establish' operation successfully initiated for
device group 'mydevgroup'.
```

Wait for a few minutes and then retrieve the status of the mydevgroup device group.

```
phys-mars1# symrdf -g mydevgroup query


Device Group (DG) Name              : mydevgroup
DG's Type                           : RDF1
DG's Symmetrix ID                   : 000187990182   (Microcode Version: 5671)
Remote Symmetrix ID                 : 000187900023   (Microcode Version: 5671)
RDF (RA) Group Number               : 11 (0A)

          Source (R1) View              Target (R2) View      MODES
-------------------------------   -------------------------  -----  ------------
              ST                  LI    ST
Standard       A                  N      A
Logical        T   R1 Inv  R2 Inv K      T   R1 Inv  R2 Inv          RDF Pair
Device  Dev    E   Tracks  Tracks S Dev  E   Tracks  Tracks  MDAE    STATE
-------------------------------   --  ----------------------  -----  ------------

DEV001  00E0 RW       0        0 RW 00E0 WD      0        0  S..-    Synchronized

Total        -------- --------       -------- --------
   Track(s)         0        0               0        0
   MB(s)          0.0      0.0             0.0      0.0

Legend for MODES:

M(ode of Operation)   : A = Async, S = Sync, E = Semi-sync, C = Adaptive Copy
D(omino)              : X = Enabled, . = Disabled
A(daptive Copy)       : D = Disk Mode, W = WP Mode, . = ACp off
(Consistency) E(xempt): X = Enabled, . = Disabled, M = Mixed, - = N/A
```

The SRDF device group can be used as either a rawdisk-type or Veritas Volume Manager device group. When propagating a Veritas Volume Manager device group, you must wait for the SRDF device group to synchronize the two sites. Doing so ensures that the information in the Veritas Volume Manager private regions of the LUNs participating in the device group have been copied over. After this synchronization has been completed, you can temporarily split the device group, import the Veritas Volume Manager device group on the disaster recovery site, and perform the necessary configuration work. After you have completed that work, you can bring offline the newly created Solaris Cluster device group (of type vxvm) and reestablish the synchronization, as shown in the following example.

## Example 6.14  Creating a Solaris Cluster `rawdisk`-Type Device Group to Match an SRDF Device Group

First, bring offline, disable, and then delete device group d45.

```
phys-mars1# cldevicegroup offline dsk/d45
phys-mars1# cldevicegroup disable dsk/d45
phys-mars1# cldevicegroup delete dsk/d45
```

Create a new `rawdisk`-type device group called mydevgroup using DID device d45.

```
phys-mars1# cldevicegroup create -n phys-mars1,phys-mars2 -t rawdisk \
> -d d45 mydevgroup
```

Bring the device group mydevgroup online and retrieve the status.

```
phys-mars1# cldevicegroup online mydevgroup
phys-mars1# cldevicegroup status mydevgroup

=== Cluster Device Groups ===

--- Device Group Status ---

Device Group Name      Primary      Secondary     Status
-----------------      -------      ---------     ------
mydevgroup             phys-mars1   phys-mars2    Online
```

Perform the same steps on cluster saturn from node phys-saturn3.

The step needs to be performed only once per cluster.

```
phys-saturn3# cldevicegroup offline dsk/d45
phys-saturn3# cldevicegroup disable dsk/d45
phys-saturn3# cldevicegroup delete dsk/d45
phys-saturn3# cldevicegroup create -n phys-saturn3,phys-saturn4 \
> -t rawdisk -d d45 mydevgroup
```

### Resource Group Configuration

After you have created your SRDF device group and your Solaris Cluster device group, you can create the Geographic Edition protection group. The following example shows how to place a basic resource group containing a logical host and a failover file system in a protection group. As shown in Figure 6.8, no affinities are created between the application resource group and the replication resource group. This is because, unlike AVS, the status of the SRDF replication can be queried from either node.

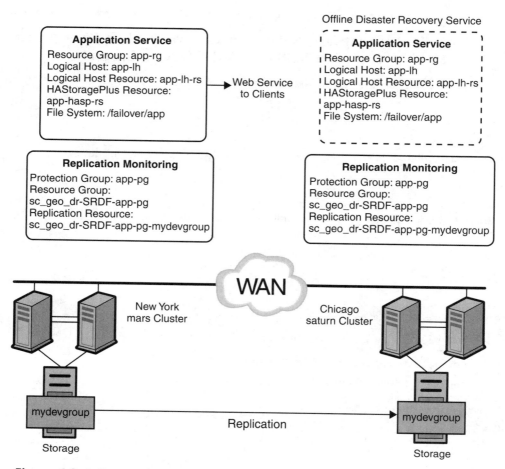

**Figure 6.8** A Geographic Edition SRDF configuration for a resource group using one device group

## Example 6.15  Creating a Resource Group and Placing It under Geographic Edition Control

Commands are run on different hosts as noted in the prompts.

On `phys-mars1`, check that file system `/failover/app` is defined in `/etc/vfstab`. You should also check this on `phys-mars2`.

```
phys-mars1# grep /failover/app /etc/vfstab
/dev/global/dsk/d45s2   /dev/global/rdsk/d45s2   /failover/app   ufs     -       no
  logging
```

Create a new resource group called `app-rg`.

```
phys-mars1# clresourcegroup create -p auto_start_on_new_cluster=false \
> app-rg
```

Add a logical hostname resource to resource group `app-rg`.

```
phys-mars1# clreslogicalhostname create -h app-lh \
> -g app-rg app-lh-rs
```

Create a `SUNW.HAStoragePlus` resource to control the file system `/failover/app`.

```
phys-mars1# clresource create -t SUNW.HAStoragePlus \
> -p FileSystemMountPoints=/failover/app \
> -p affinityon=true -g app-rg app-hasp-rs
```

Check that the file system entry is in `/etc/vfstab` on `phys-saturn3`. You should also check this on `phys-saturn4`.

```
phys-saturn3# grep /failover/app /etc/vfstab
/dev/global/dsk/d45s2   /dev/global/rdsk/d45s2   /failover/app   ufs   -   no
  logging
```

Create a new resource group called `app-rg` on cluster `saturn`, too.

```
phys-saturn3# clresourcegroup create \
> -p auto_start_on_new_cluster=false  app-rg
phys-saturn3# clreslogicalhostname create -h app-lh -g app-rg app-lh-rs
phys-saturn3# clresource create -t SUNW.HAStoragePlus \
> -p FileSystemMountPoints=/failover/app \
> -p affinityon=true -g app-rg app-hasp-rs
```

Create a protection group of type `SRDF` from node `phys-mars1` on cluster `mars`.

```
phys-mars1# geopg create --partnership mars-saturn --role primary \
> --datarep-type srdf \
> --property R1_SID=000187990182 \
> --property R2_SID=000187900023 \
> --property cluster_dgs=mydevgroup app-pg
Protection group "app-pg" successfully created.
```

Add device group `mydevgroup` to protection group `app-pg`.

```
phys-mars1# geopg add-replication-component mydevgroup app-pg
Device group "mydevgroup" successfully added to the protection group "app-pg".
```

Add resource group `app-rg` to protection group `app-pg`.

```
phys-mars1# geopg add-resource-group app-rg app-pg
Following resource groups successfully added:
       "app-rg".
```

From cluster node `phys-saturn3` on cluster `saturn`, bring over the newly created app-pg protection group.

```
phys-saturn3# geopg get --partnership mars-saturn app-pg
Protection group "app-pg" successfully created.
```

**Start the protection group on both clusters.**

```
phys-mars1# geopg start -e global app-pg
Processing operation... The timeout period for this operation on each cluster is 3600

seconds (3600000 milliseconds)...
Protection group "app-pg" successfully started.
```

The creation of the protection group and the addition of the device group result in the creation of a replication resource group and a resource. These entities are named using the form sc_geo_dr-SRDF-*protection-group-name* and sc_geo_dr-SRDF-*protection-group-name-device-group-name*, respectively. In this example, the two entities are called sc_geo_dr-SRDF-app-pg and sc_geo_dr-SRDF-app-pg-mydevgroup. If you add more device groups to the protection group, additional replication resources are created and placed in the replication resource group for the protection group you named in the geopg command.

When you switch over the control of the protection group between the two clusters, the SRDF Geographic Edition module coordinates the mounting and unmounting of any file systems, as well as the change in SRDF device group role. The SRDF module issues different sequences of symrdf commands depending on whether the role change is a controlled switchover or a forcible takeover.

## SRDF Monitoring: The Replication Resource

When you add a device group to an SRDF protection group, the Geographic Edition software creates a replication resource group, if required, and a replication resource, as shown in Example 6.16. The replication resource is used to monitor the state of the replication. Changes in the state of this resource are propagated through the CMAS framework into the CAC framework, where they are used to calculate the overall health of the protection group.

The SRDF replication resource has several extension properties that the Geographic Edition software uses to store information regarding the replication configuration. You must not attempt to modify these manually. These properties are

- SRDF_group: The name of the SRDF device group to be monitored.
- Replication_role: The current replication role. The value can be either Primary or Secondary.
- DG_or_CG: Determines whether the device group is a simple device group (DG) or composite device group (CG). Currently, this property must be set to DG.

- `R1_SID`: The system identifier of the Symmetrix array holding the R1 volumes.
- `R2_SID`: The system identifier of the Symmetrix array holding the R2 volumes.

The SRDF replication resource calls the `/opt/SUNWscgrepsrdf/rt/bin/GeoCtlSRDF_probe` shell script, which in turn calls `/opt/SUNWscgrepsrdf/lib/probe_SRDF` to report the health of the replication. Internally, the probe parses output from a combination of the `symdg` and `symrdf` commands. Depending on their output, the probe calls the `scha_resource_setstatus` command to set the status of the replication resource and provide an associated resource status message.

---

## Example 6.16  Replication Resource Group and Resource Created for Protection Group `app-pg`

The replication resource group for protection group `app-pg` is called `sc_geo_dr-SRDF-app-pg`. Use the `clrg` command to show the configuration of this resource group.

```
phys-mars1# clrg show sc_geo_dr-SRDF-app-pg

=== Resource Groups and Resources ===

Resource Group:                            sc_geo_dr-SRDF-app-pg
  RG_description:                            <NULL>
  RG_mode:                                   Failover
  RG_state:                                  Managed
  Failback:                                  False
  Nodelist:                                  phys-mars2 phys-mars1

  --- Resources for Group sc_geo_dr-SRDF-app-pg ---

  Resource:                                sc_geo_dr-SRDF-app-pg-mydevgroup
    Type:                                    SUNW.GeoCtlSRDF
    Type_version:                            1.0
    Group:                                   sc_geo_dr-SRDF-app-pg
    R_description:
    Resource_project_name:                   default
    Enabled{phys-mars2}:                     True
    Enabled{phys-mars1}:                     True
    Monitored{phys-mars2}:                   True
    Monitored{phys-mars1}:                   True
```

The replication resource for a device group called `mydevgroup` that is associated with the protection group `app-pg` is called `sc_geo_dr-SRDF-app-pg-mydevgroup`. Use the `clrs` command to show the status of this resource.

```
phys-mars1# clrs status sc_geo_dr-SRDF-app-pg-mydevgroup

=== Cluster Resources ===

Resource Name                     Node Name    State     Status Message
-------------                     ---------    -----     --------------
sc_geo_dr-SRDF-app-pg-mydevgroup  phys-mars2   Online    Online - Synchronized
                                  phys-mars1   Offline   Offline
```

## Hitachi Data Systems TrueCopy and Universal Replicator

The Hitachi Data Systems TrueCopy software is a storage-based replication mechanism that provides host-independent data replication. The latest version of the product is known as Universal Replicator. The software enables the primary volumes to be replicated to secondary volumes, either synchronously or asynchronously, while maintaining *data consistency*, that is, fidelity to the order of application writes.

Synchronous data replication seeks to ensure *mirror consistency*, that is, the data on the disaster recovery site matches the data on the primary site. The setting of a `fence_level` property then determines whether the array returns an I/O error to the application or continues to allow the application to write its data despite communications problems. The synchronous fence levels are defined as follows [URCCIGuide]:

- DATA: If a fault, such as a communications problem, results in mirror consistency being lost, a write error is returned to the application.

- STATUS: If a fault, such as a communications problem, results in mirror consistency being lost but the status on the remote volume can be set to indicate the error, then the application is allowed to continue writing. The application does not receive an I/O error.

- NEVER: The application is always allowed to continue writing to the primary volume and does not receive an error, even if the primary storage array cannot communicate with the storage array on the disaster recovery site.

> **Note**
>
> Both DATA and STATUS fence levels can return I/O errors to and block writes from your application, resulting in an outage in your highly available service. Consequently, do *not* use these fence levels with the Geographic Edition software.

When the Hitachi replication software is replicating data asynchronously, the ASYNC fence level is used. In this configuration, writes never return an I/O error to the application. However, mirror consistency is not guaranteed.

Your data replication configuration is described in terms of pairs of source and target LUNs or volumes. These volumes are grouped into what Universal Replicator calls device groups. Usually, data consistency is maintained only on a per-device-group basis. However, if your application spans multiple device groups, then you can use the *consistency group ID* (ctgid) property to indicate to the Hitachi replication software that data consistency must be maintained across all the nominated device groups.

The Universal Replicator software must be configured to use journal volumes. A minimum of two 12-gigabyte journal volumes is required per device group. This feature was not available in the TrueCopy product. These journal volumes are LUNs created in the primary and disaster recovery array and are used to store transactional information about the writes made to associated data volumes. A journal volume can be associated with a device group so that the Universal Replicator asynchronous replication software can guarantee data consistency even during a rolling disaster (see the section "Ensuring Data Consistency after a Rolling Failure" in Chapter 1, "Oracle Solaris Cluster: Overview").

### Configuration Files

To use the Universal Replicator software, you must configure and allocate one or more LUNs to your cluster nodes. These LUNs consist of the following:

- *Data volumes*: Used to store the data to be replicated. These LUNs are visible to the Oracle Solaris OS through the `format` command.

- *Journal volumes*: Used to store the metadata associated with the replicated data volume transactions. These LUNs are not visible to the Oracle Solaris OS. However, they can be referenced by various commands, such as `paircreate`.

- *Command devices*: Used by the HORC Manager daemon (`horcmd`) to interface the Solaris command-line requests you make to the storage array. These LUNs are visible to the Oracle Solaris OS `format` command. Command devices cannot be used to store user data or to act as a quorum device. You must allocate a separate command device to each cluster node.

The `horcmd` daemon process can be started automatically when the cluster node boots or manually by the system administrator. If the Geographic Edition software determines that the daemon is not running, it will attempt to start it. The `horcmd` daemon is part of the Hitachi Command Control Interface (CCI) package that you must install on all cluster nodes that connect to the storage array. Usually, each `horcmd` daemon communicates with its peer `horcmd` daemons on the other cluster nodes. Details of the IP address and port number for establishing communications with the remote `horcmd` daemon are provided in the `/etc/horcm.conf` file, specifically in the `HORCM_INST` section of the file.

The command device, along with your device group definitions, is stored in the `/etc/horcm.conf` file (see Example 6.17). The device group pairs can be specified using one of two formats:

- The `HORCM_DEV` format (device group, device name, port number, target ID, logical unit number, and mirror descriptor number)

- The HORCM_LDEV format (device group, device name, serial number, LDEV number, and mirror descriptor number)

**Note**

To use journal IDs, you must use the HORCM_LDEV format for the device groups that use journals.

## Example 6.17  A Sample /etc/horcm.conf File for Universal Replicator

Display the contents of the horcm.conf file.

```
# cat /etc/horcm.conf
#
#/******************** For HORCM_MON ***************************/
HORCM_MON
#ip_address            service         poll(10ms)      timeout(10ms)
10.11.197.184          horcm           1000            3000

#/******************** For HORCM_CMD ***************************/

HORCM_CMD
#dev_name                       dev_name                dev_name
/dev/rdsk/c4t50060E800000000000004E6000000007d0s2

#/******************** For HORCM_DEV ***************************/

HORCM_DEV
#dev_group       dev_name        port#           TargetID        LU#     MU#
VG02             pair2           CL2-C           0               24
VG02             pair3           CL2-C           0               22
VG03             pair4           CL2-C           0               25


HORCM_INST
#dev_group       ip_address      service
VG02             10.11.195.116   horcm
VG02             10.11.195.117   horcm
VG03             10.11.195.116   horcm
VG03             10.11.195.117   horcm
```

To create a protection group that uses the TrueCopy or Universal Replicator feature, you define its data replication type as truecopy and you specify any ctgid property value you want to use. After you have specified a value for the ctgid property, you cannot change it without re-creating the protection group.

## Example 6.18   Creating a TrueCopy Protection Group

Check the status of device group `VG02`.

```
phys-earth1# pairdisplay -g VG02 -CLI
Group    PairVol L/R   Port# TID  LU  Seq# LDEV# P/S Status Fence Seq# P-LDEV# M
VG02     pair2 L       CL1-A  0    5 61114     5 SMPL    -     -     -    - -
VG02     pair2 R       CL2-C  0   24 20064   613 SMPL    -     -     -    - -
VG02     pair3 L       CL1-A  0    3 61114     3 SMPL    -     -     -    - -
VG02     pair3 R       CL2-C  0   22 20064   611 SMPL    -     -     -    - -
```

Device group `VG02` is in the unpaired or simplex state.

You can also get this information using the `pairvolchk` command.

```
phys-earth1# pairvolchk -g VG02
pairvolchk : Volstat is SMPL.[status = SMPL]
```

On the primary cluster, create a protection group called `ur-test-pg` with a consistency group ID of `42` that is managed by the `earth-venus` partnership.

```
phys-earth1# geopg create --partnership earth-venus \
> --role primary --datarep-type truecopy --property ctgid=42 ur-test-pg
Protection group "ur-test-pg" successfully created.
```

Add the device group `VG02` to the protection group `ur-test-pg`. Set the device group to be replicated asynchronously.

```
phys-earth1# geopg add-replication-component --property \
> fence_level=async VG02 ur-test-pg
Device group "VG02" successfully added to the protection group "ur-test-pg".
```

Retrieve the `ur-test-pg` configuration from the disaster recovery cluster.

```
phys-venus1 # geopg get --partnership earth-venus ur-test-pg
Protection group "ur-test-pg" successfully created.
```

Start the protection group `ur-test-pg` on both clusters. This initializes and starts the replication.

```
phys-earth1# geopg start -e global ur-test-pg
Processing operation... The timeout period for this operation on each cluster is 3600

seconds (3600000 milliseconds)...
Protection group "ur-test-pg" successfully started.
```

List the protection groups configured.

```
phys-earth1# geopg list

Protection Group: ur-test-pg

  Partnership name             : earth-venus

  Local Role                   : Primary
  Deployed on clusters         : earth, venus
```

```
Data Replication type         : TRUECOPY
Configuration status          : OK
Synchronization status        : OK
Creation signature            : earth Dec 14, 2009 10:23:23 AM PST
Last update                   : Dec 14, 2009 10:29:10 AM PST

Local properties              :

    nodelist                      : phys-earth1,phys-earth2

Global properties             :

    cluster_dgs                   :
    Timeout                       : 3600 seconds
    Description                   :
    ctgid                         : 42
    RoleChange_ActionArgs         :
    External_Dependency_Allowed : false
    RoleChange_ActionCmd          :

*** No protected resource groups in protection group "ur-test-pg" ***

TRUECOPY Device groups:

    VG02

    VG02_fence_level              : async
```

Check the status of the VG02 device group again. Notice that the fence level is now ASYNC rather than SMPL and that the status is COPY.

```
phys-earth1# pairdisplay -g VG02 -CLI
Group   PairVol L/R    Port# TID  LU  Seq# LDEV# P/S Status Fence Seq# P-LDEV# M
VG02    pair2 L        CL1-A  0    5 61114     5 P-VOL COPY  ASYNC 20064   613 -
VG02    pair2 R        CL2-C  0   24 20064   613 S-VOL COPY  ASYNC     -     5 -
VG02    pair3 L        CL1-A  0    3 61114     3 P-VOL COPY  ASYNC 20064   611 -
VG02    pair3 R        CL2-C  0   22 20064   611 S-VOL COPY  ASYNC     -     3 -
```

Use the pairvolchk command to retrieve the overall device group status.

```
phys-earth1# pairvolchk -g VG02
pairvolchk : Volstat is P-VOL.[status = COPY fence = ASYNC CTGID = 42]
```

Wait while the device group synchronizes, and then stop the device group on both clusters.

```
phys-earth1# geopg stop -e global ur-test-pg
Processing operation... The timeout period for this operation on each cluster is 3600

seconds (3600000 milliseconds)...
Protection group "ur-test-pg" successfully stopped.
```

Use the pairdisplay command to show the status of the VG02 device group. Notice that the status is now PSUS, that is, suspended.

```
phys-earth1# pairdisplay -g VG02 -CLI
Group   PairVol L/R    Port# TID  LU  Seq# LDEV# P/S Status Fence Seq# P-LDEV# M
VG02    pair2 L        CL1-A  0    5 61114     5 P-VOL PSUS  ASYNC 20064   613 -
VG02    pair2 R        CL2-C  0   24 20064   613 S-VOL SSUS  ASYNC     -     5 -
VG02    pair3 L        CL1-A  0    3 61114     3 P-VOL PSUS  ASYNC 20064   611 -
VG02    pair3 R        CL2-C  0   22 20064   611 S-VOL SSUS  ASYNC     -     3 -
```

When you add the device group to the protection group, the Geographic Edition software determines if the device group is already initialized and if its consistency group ID matches the `ctgid` property of the protection group. If the device group is uninitialized, then when the protection group is started, the device group is created using the TrueCopy `paircreate` command (see Example 6.18).

The following example shows how to set up and protect a pair of failover file systems. For example, these file systems could be the directories that hold database binaries and their associated data file. Note that if you need to change the `cluster_dgs` property, you must first stop the protection group.

## Example 6.19  Adding a Resource Group to a TrueCopy Protection Group

Use the `raidscan` command to determine the mapping from the Solaris devices to the TrueCopy device group names.

```
phys-earth1# ls /dev/rdsk/* | raidscan -find verify | grep VG02
/dev/rdsk/c4t500060E8000000000000EEBA00000003d0s2  VG02    pair3     CL1-A    0
  3 -    61114      3
/dev/rdsk/c4t500060E8000000000000EEBA00000005d0s2  VG02    pair2     CL1-A    0
  5 -    61114      5
```

Use the `cldevice` command to determine the mapping from the Solaris device names to the Solaris Cluster device ID (DID) numbers.

```
phys-earth1# cldevice list c4t500060E8000000000000EEBA00000003d0 \
> c4t500060E8000000000000EEBA00000005d0
d4
d2
```

Use the `cldevicegroup` command to bring offline, disable, and then delete the `d2` and `d4` device groups.

```
phys-earth1# cldevicegroup offline dsk/d4 dsk/d2
phys-earth1# cldevicegroup disable dsk/d4 dsk/d2
phys-earth1# cldevicegroup delete dsk/d4 dsk/d2
```

Use the `cldevicegroup` command to create a new `rawdisk`-type device group called `mygroup` consisting of DID devices `d2` and `d4`.

```
phys-earth1# cldevicegroup create -n phys-earth1,phys-earth2 \
> -t rawdisk -d d2,d4 mygroup
```

Create mount points on both clusters for the file systems `/failover/fs1` and `/failover/fs2`.

```
phys-earth1# mkdir -p /failover/fs1 /failover/fs2
```

Add entries for these file systems to the /etc/vfstab file on all nodes of both clusters.

```
phys-earth1# grep failover /etc/vfstab
/dev/global/dsk/d2s2     /dev/global/rdsk/d2s2    /failover/fs1   ufs     -       no
logging
/dev/global/dsk/d4s2     /dev/global/rdsk/d4s2    /failover/fs2   ufs     -       no
logging
```

Use the clrg command to create a resource group called example-rg. Notice that the auto_start_on_new_cluster property is set to false.

```
phys-earth1# clrg create -p auto_start_on_new_cluster=false example-rg
```

Register the SUNW.HAStoragePlus resource type.

```
phys-earth1# clrt register SUNW.HAStoragePlus
```

Use the clrs command to create a resource called example-rs to control the failover file systems.

```
phys-earth1# clrs create -g example-rg -t SUNW.HAStoragePlus \
> -p FileSystemMountPoints=/failover/fs1,/failover/fs2 example-rs
```

Create the file systems using the newfs command.

```
phys-earth1# newfs /dev/global/rdsk/d2s2
newfs: construct a new file system /dev/global/rdsk/d2s2: (y/n)? y
Warning: 2784 sector(s) in last cylinder unallocated
/dev/global/rdsk/d2s2:  28450080 sectors in 4631 cylinders of 48 tracks, 128 sectors
        13891.6MB in 290 cyl groups (16 c/g, 48.00MB/g, 5824 i/g)
super-block backups (for fsck -F ufs -o b=#) at:
 32, 98464, 196896, 295328, 393760, 492192, 590624, 689056, 787488, 885920,
 27528224, 27626656, 27725088, 27823520, 27921952, 28020384, 28118816,
 28217248, 28315680, 28414112

phys-earth1# newfs /dev/global/rdsk/d4s2
newfs: construct a new file system /dev/global/rdsk/d4s2: (y/n)? y
Warning: 2784 sector(s) in last cylinder unallocated
/dev/global/rdsk/d4s2:  28450080 sectors in 4631 cylinders of 48 tracks, 128 sectors
        13891.6MB in 290 cyl groups (16 c/g, 48.00MB/g, 5824 i/g)
super-block backups (for fsck -F ufs -o b=#) at:
 32, 98464, 196896, 295328, 393760, 492192, 590624, 689056, 787488, 885920,
 27528224, 27626656, 27725088, 27823520, 27921952, 28020384, 28118816,
 28217248, 28315680, 28414112
```

Stop the protection group called ur-test-pg on both clusters.

```
phys-earth1# geopg stop -e global ur-test-pg
Processing operation... The timeout period for this operation on each cluster is 3600
seconds (3600000 milliseconds)...
Protection group "ur-test-pg" successfully stopped.
```

Set the cluster_dgs property of the ur-test-pg protection group to mygroup.

```
phys-earth1# geopg set-prop --property cluster_dgs=mygroup ur-test-pg
Protection group "ur-test-pg" successfully modified.
```

Add the `example-rg` resource group, which controls the failover file systems, to the protection group called `ur-test-pg`.

```
phys-earth1# geopg add-resource-group example-rg ur-test-pg
Following resource groups successfully added:
      "example-rg".
```

Start the protection group `ur-test-pg` on both clusters.

```
phys-earth1# geopg start -e global ur-test-pg
Processing operation... The timeout period for this operation on each cluster is 3600
seconds (3600000 milliseconds)...
Protection group "ur-test-pg" successfully started.
```

Notice that starting the protection group has resulted in the failover file systems being mounted on the local cluster.

```
phys-earth1# df -h /failover/fs1 /failover/fs2
Filesystem              size   used   avail capacity   Mounted on
/dev/global/dsk/d2s2    13G    14M    13G   1%         /failover/fs1
/dev/global/dsk/d4s2    13G    14M    13G   1%         /failover/fs2
```

## Resource Group Configuration

The creation of the protection group and the addition of the device group result in the creation of a replication resource group and a resource. These entities are named using the form `rg-tc-`*`protection-group-name`* and `r-tc-`*`protection-group-name-TC-device-group-name`*, respectively. In this example, the two entities are called `rg-tc-ur-test-pg` and `r-tc-ur-test-pg-VG02`. If you add more device groups to the protection group, additional replication resources are created and placed in the replication resource group for the protection group you named in the `geopg` command.

Neither the application resource group nor the replication resource group requires any additional resource group affinities to be set. Unlike with AVS, there is no lightweight resource group that the application resource group must have affinity with, so the setup for TrueCopy replication is similar to that of SRDF (see Figure 6.9).

## TrueCopy or Universal Replicator Monitoring: The Replication Resource

When you add a device group to a TrueCopy protection group, the Geographic Edition software creates a replication resource group, if required, and a replication resource. The replication resource is used to monitor the state of the replication. Changes in the state of this resource are propagated through the CMAS framework into the CAC framework, where they are used to calculate the overall health of the protection group.

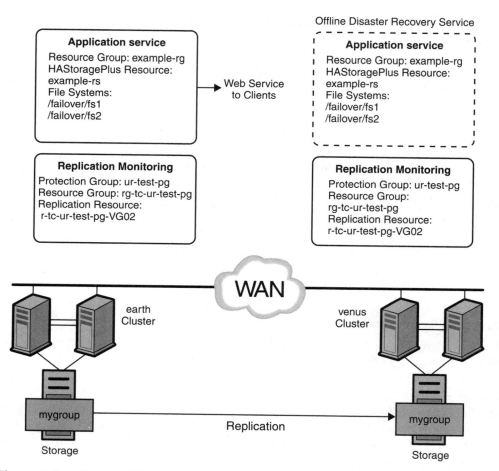

**Figure 6.9** A Geographic Edition TrueCopy configuration for a resource group using one device group

The TrueCopy replication resource has only two extension properties that the Geographic Edition software uses to store information regarding the replication configuration. You must not attempt to modify these manually. These properties are

- `dev_group`: The name of the TrueCopy or Universal Replicator device group to be monitored.

- `replication_role`: The current replication role. The value can be either `Primary` or `Secondary`.

The TrueCopy replication resource calls the `/opt/SUNWscgreptc/rt/bin/GeoCtlTC_probe` shell script, which in turn calls `/opt/SUNWscgreptc/rt/bin/probe_tc` to report the health of the replication.

The probe first determines if the local `horcmd` daemon is running. If it isn't, the probe sets an UNKNOWN status on the replication but makes no attempt to restart the `horcmd` daemon. The probe also determines if it can communicate with the command device, again setting an UNKNOWN status if it cannot do so. The probe then uses the output from a combination of the `pairvolchk` and `pairdisplay` commands to determine the health of the replication. Depending on the result, the probe calls the `scha_resource_setstatus` command to set the status of the replication resource and provide an associated resource status message.

## Oracle Data Guard for Oracle Real Application Clusters Databases

Relational database management systems (RDBMS) portfolios from IBM, Oracle, and Sybase include a wide range of tools to manage and administer data held in their respective databases: DB2, Oracle, and Sybase. The data replication tools include IBM DB2 DataPropagator, Oracle Data Guard, and Sybase Replication Server. These tools differ from products such as StorageTek Availability Suite (AVS) software and Hitachi TrueCopy and Universal Replicator software because the database tools work at the transactional level rather than at the disk-block level.

RDBMS software handles logical changes to the underlying data (for example, the insertion of a new row in a table or the decrement of all price fields by 5 percent) and has intimate knowledge of which low-level writes constitute a complete, atomic change. In contrast, a block-level replicator merely detects a stream of I/O requests, without recognizing where the transactions begin and end. As a result, database replication offers considerably greater flexibility and lower network traffic than a corresponding block-based replication solution (see Figure 6.10).

The Oracle Data Guard software uses the concept of primary and standby databases. A standby database can be either a physical or a logical copy of the primary database. A physical standby database has the same physical changes applied to it, whereas a logical standby database has the same SQL commands replayed to it, which might result in a different physical representation on the disk.

The production workload runs against the primary database, and you can configure one or more standby databases for disaster recovery purposes. However, unlike databases that are replicated using a host-based or storage-based replication mechanism, Oracle Data Guard–protected databases can be used for reporting purposes even while the replication process is running.

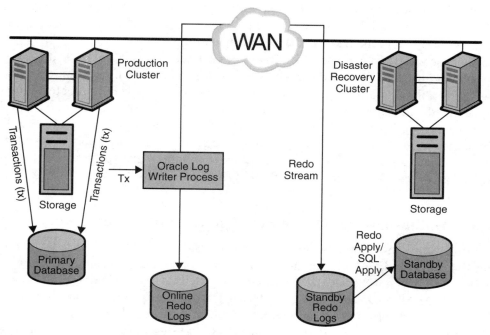

**Figure 6.10** Oracle Data Guard—redo stream transmission to a standby database

The Oracle Data Guard software supports three modes of replication:

- *Maximum protection mode*: In this mode, no data is lost because the redo information required to recover each transaction is written to the local log and one or more remote redo logs before the transaction is considered complete, or committed. Any fault prevents this write from occurring, causing the primary database to shut down.

- *Maximum availability mode*: If the consequences of maximum protection mode are too restrictive, then maximum availability mode offers an alternative option to deal with failures. Here, the primary database continues, but changes are stored until they can be passed on to the standby database. After connectivity is reestablished, the software reverts to continuous replication. In maximum availability mode, data is lost only when a prior failure prevents the resynchronization of the primary online redo log with the secondary standby redo log or logs.

- *Maximum performance mode*: In this mode, transactions are committed through the local primary redo log and are then asynchronously replicated to the secondary standby redo logs. When sufficient network bandwidth exists, this option approximates maximum availability. However, data is lost if a disaster occurs at the primary site before all of the outstanding transaction data is replicated.

The performance of Oracle Data Guard, as well as other RDBMS replication packages, is governed by the bandwidth and latency of the links between the primary and disaster recovery sites and is discussed in the section "Performance Impact of Separating Data Centers" in Chapter 1, "Oracle Solaris Cluster: Overview."

Because RDBMS software handles transactional changes to the underlying data, it is much simpler to revert to an earlier consistent state. As with other continuous replication technologies, the database replication software will also immediately propagate accidental data deletion or corruption. However, Oracle's Flashback technology enables these changes to be reversed relatively quickly, without requiring large bulk restores of data.

### Restriction of Use to Oracle 10g and 11g Real Application Clusters Databases

There are two command-line interfaces your Oracle database administrator can use to manage an Oracle Data Guard configuration: SQL*Plus or Data Guard Broker. The Data Guard Broker CLI is considerably simpler than the SQL*Plus CLI, requiring far fewer steps to perform, for example, a switchover. Data Guard Broker also has built-in health checks for the configuration as a whole. The only drawback was that, at the time the Geographic Edition module was written, the Data Guard Broker could not be used for non–Real Application Clusters database instances. Oracle Data Broker uses two configuration files, referenced by the SQL*Plus properties `dg_broker_config_file1` and `dg_broker_config_file2`, which have physical hostnames embedded in them. When an Oracle database failed over from one node to another node, for example, as part of a Solaris Cluster resource group, the hostname in the configuration file no longer matched the hostname in the configuration file. This caused the Oracle Data Guard Broker configuration to fail.

The Geographic Edition software uses Data Guard Broker CLI to control and monitor the Oracle Data Guard replication. Because of the hostname restrictions that were imposed by the Data Guard Broker configuration files, the Geographic Edition module currently supports only Oracle 10g and 11g Real Application Clusters databases. Consequently, both primary and standby databases must be configured as Oracle Real Application Clusters (Oracle RAC) databases, even if they are only single instances.

**Note**

You must use only Oracle 10g or 11g Oracle RAC databases in a Solaris Cluster Geographic Edition configuration that uses Oracle Data Guard replication.

## Configuration

The fundamental difference between an Oracle database protected by Oracle Data Guard and the same database protected by AVS, SRDF, or Hitachi Data Systems TrueCopy and Universal Replicator is that in the former case, the replication technology is part of the application itself. Thus, in an Oracle Data Guard configuration the database is open and the Oracle software is running at both the primary and disaster recovery sites. In contrast, an AVS-protected, single-instance Oracle database would be running at the primary site but would be offline on the disaster recovery site.

This difference has important ramifications for the way in which an Oracle Data Guard Geographic Edition protection group is set up. In any other protection group, your application resource group is placed under the control of the protection group. This then ensures that the resource group is brought online at the primary site but shut down and unmanaged at the disaster recovery site. However, this configuration is incompatible with the requirement for the database to be running at both sites. Consequently, you cannot place the RAC server proxy resource group that the Solaris Cluster wizard creates (see the section "Solaris Cluster Wizards" in Chapter 4, "Managing Your Oracle Solaris Cluster Environment") in the protection group. However, to maintain the consistency of having the protection group control the resource group, you can instead add the shadow RAC proxy server resource group that the Geographic Edition module creates (see Figure 6.11). The resource in this group then merely reflects the status of the local RAC proxy server resource, together with an indication of whether or not the site is an Oracle Data Guard primary site.

Before you create an Oracle Data Guard protection group, your database administrator must manually configure the Oracle Data Guard replication and place it in a named Data Guard Broker configuration. The name of this configuration is then used when you add it to the protection group. Although the Oracle Data Guard–type protection group has no additional properties, the replication component that represents the configuration requires quite a few properties to describe it. Table 6.1 describes these properties.

The `sysdba_password` property is required because, unlike the SQL*Plus command, which can authenticate the Solaris Oracle user with the `/ as sysdba` parameter, the `dgmgrl` command must also authenticate the user against the remote database. The password supplied is checked against the password stored in the Oracle password file shared among all the instances at the remote site.

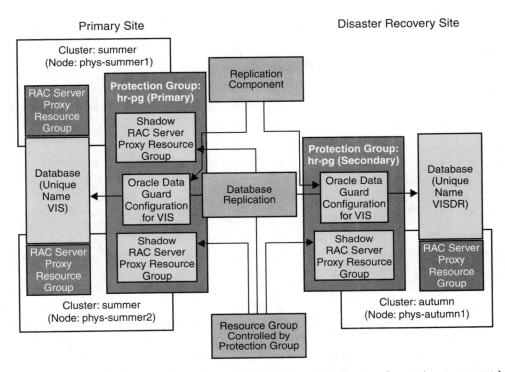

**Figure 6.11** Resource groups and Oracle Data Guard Broker configurations present in an `odg`-type protection group

**Table 6.1** Oracle Data Guard Replication Component Properties

| Property Name | Description |
| --- | --- |
| `local_rac_proxy_svr_rg_name` | The name of the local RAC proxy resource group created by the Solaris Cluster wizard. This property is used to gather information such as the node list, `ORACLE_HOME`, and `ORACLE_SID` information. |
| `remote_rac_proxy_svr_rg_name` | The name of the remote RAC proxy resource group created by the Solaris Cluster wizard. This property is used in the same way as the `local_rac_proxy_svr_rg_name` property. |
| `standby_type` | The type of Oracle Data Guard standby database (either logical or physical). |
| `local_database_name` | The unique name (`db_unique_name`) of the local database. |

*continues*

**Table 6.1**  Oracle Data Guard Replication Component Properties (*Continued*)

| Property Name | Description |
| --- | --- |
| remote_database_name | The unique name (db_unique_name) of the remote database. |
| local_db_service_name | The service name used to connect to the local database. |
| remote_db_service_name | The service name used to connect to the remote database. |
| replication_mode | The method used to replicate this database. The possible values are MaxPerformance, MaxAvailability, and MaxProtection. |
| sysdba_username | The name of a database user with sysdba privileges who can manage the configuration through the Oracle dgmgrl command. |
| sysdba_password | The password for the named sysdba privileged user. |

The Geographic Edition software prompts you for this password and does not echo the password you type. Furthermore, this password is only ever stored in root-readable files in cleartext format or in an obfuscated form in the root-readable CCR file for the protection group. Finally, it is never passed to programs on the command line. Thus, it cannot be intercepted by non-root-privileged users.

A completed configuration results in the output shown in Example 6.20. The Oracle 10*g* Real Application Clusters database called VIS is stored in the shared QFS file system /db_qfs/OraData. A resource group qfsmds-rac-rg and resource qfs-db_qfs-OraData-rs make the metadata server for the file system highly available. The scal-db_qfs-OraData-rs resource in the scalmnt-rg resource group mounts and monitors the /db_qfs/OraData file system. The Oracle RAC database instances represented by the rac_server_proxy-rs resource are contained in the rac_server_proxy-rg resource group. By declaring a Resource_dependencies_offline_restart dependency on the scal-db_qfs-OraData-rs resource, the Oracle instances can be quickly taken offline or restarted if the storage becomes unavailable.

In the following example, an Oracle Data Guard Broker configuration called VIS links the primary database VIS with the physical standby database called VISDR. The replication is being carried out in MaxPerformance mode, which is highlighted in the status of the vis-odg-rep-rs resource. Finally, the status of the vis-rac-proxy-svr-shadow-rs resource indicates that the local cluster is the primary site for the Oracle Data Guard replication.

# Example 6.20  Solaris Cluster Resource for an Oracle RAC Configuration

Display details of the shared QFS file system /db_qfs/OraData.

```
phys-summer1# df -h /db_qfs/OraData
Filesystem              size  used  avail capacity  Mounted on
OraData                 771G  750G   21G    98%     /db_qfs/OraData
```

Display the current status of the resource groups configured on the cluster.

```
phys-summer1# clresourcegroup status

=== Cluster Resource Groups ===

Group Name                 Node Name         Suspended   Status
----------                 ---------         ---------   ------
rac-framework-rg           phys-summer1      No          Online
                           phys-summer2      No          Online

qfsmds-rac-rg              phys-summer1      No          Offline
                           phys-summer2      No          Online

scalmnt-rg                 phys-summer1      No          Online
                           phys-summer2      No          Online

rac_server_proxy-rg        phys-summer1      No          Online
                           phys-summer2      No          Online

vis-pg-odg-rep-rg          phys-summer1      No          Online
                           phys-summer2      No          Offline

geo-clusterstate           phys-summer1      No          Online
                           phys-summer2      No          Online

geo-infrastructure         phys-summer1      No          Online
                           phys-summer2      No          Offline

vis-rac-proxy-svr-shadow-rg  phys-summer1    No          Online
                           phys-summer2      No          Online
```

Display the current status of the resources configured on the cluster.

```
phys-summer1# clresource status

=== Cluster Resources ===

Resource Name              Node Name         State       Status Message
-------------              ---------         -----       --------------
rac-framework-rs           phys-summer1      Online      Online
                           phys-summer2      Online      Online

rac-udlm-rs                phys-summer1      Online      Online
                           phys-summer2      Online      Online

crs_framework-rs           phys-summer1      Online      Online
                           phys-summer2      Online      Online

qfs-db_qfs-OraData-rs      phys-summer1      Offline     Offline
                           phys-summer2      Online      Online -
                                                         Service is online.
```

```
scal-db_qfs-OraData-rs          phys-summer1        Online                    Online
                                phys-summer2        Online                    Online

rac_server_proxy-rs             phys-summer1        Online                    Online -
Oracle instance UP
                                phys-summer2        Online                    Online -
Oracle instance UP

vis-odg-rep-rs                  phys-summer1        Online                    Online -
Replicating in MaxPerformance mode
                                phys-summer2        Offline                   Offline

geo-servicetag                  phys-summer1        Online but not monitored  Online
                                phys-summer2        Online but not monitored  Online

geo-clustername                 phys-summer1        Online                    Online –
LogicalHostname online.
                                phys-summer2        Offline                   Offline

geo-hbmonitor                   phys-summer1        Online                    Online –
Daemon OK
                                phys-summer2        Offline                   Offline

geo-failovercontrol             phys-summer1        Online                    Online –
Service is online.
                                phys-summer2        Offline                   Offline

vis-rac-proxy-svr-shadow-rs     phys-summer1        Online                    Online –
Oracle instance UP (Data Guard Primary)
                                phys-summer2        Online                    Online –
Oracle instance UP (Data Guard Primary)
```

## Become the `oracle` user.

```
# su - oracle
Sun Microsystems Inc.    SunOS 5.10      Generic January 2005
```

## Use Data Guard Broker CLI to show the `VIS` Data Guard Broker configuration.

```
$ dgmgrl sys/manager@VIS
DGMGRL for Solaris: Version 10.2.0.4.0 - 64bit Production

Copyright (c) 2000, 2005, Oracle. All rights reserved.

Welcome to DGMGRL, type "help" for information.
Connected.
DGMGRL> show configuration

Configuration
  Name:                vis
  Enabled:             YES
  Protection Mode:     MaxPerformance
  Fast-Start Failover: DISABLED
  Databases:
    visdr - Physical standby database
    vis   - Primary database

Current status for "vis":
SUCCESS

DGMGRL> exit
```

## Resource Group Configuration

When you add an Oracle Data Guard replication component to a protection group, the Geographic Edition software creates a replication resource group, if required, and a replication resource. These entities are named using the form *protection-group-name*-odg-rep-rg and *data-guard-broker-config-name*-odg-rep-rs, respectively. In addition, a shadow RAC server proxy resource group and resource are created. They can be placed under protection group control. Their names use the form *data-guard-broker-config-name*-rac-proxy-svr-shadow-rg and *data-guard-broker-config-name*-rac-proxy-svr-shadow-rs. Instances of the "." character in the Oracle Data Guard Broker configuration name are mapped to the "_" character to generate valid Solaris Cluster resource names.

Because the Oracle software might not be installed on all cluster nodes, the node list of the replication resource group is made to match that of the RAC server proxy resource group.

## Oracle Data Guard Monitoring: The Replication Resource

When you add a replication component, that is, an Oracle Data Guard configuration, to an Oracle Data Guard protection group, the Geographic Edition software creates a replication resource group, if required, and a replication resource. The replication resource is used to monitor the state of the replication. Changes in the state of this resource are propagated through the CMAS framework into the CAC framework, where they are used to calculate the overall health of the protection group.

The Oracle Data Guard replication resource uses the Solaris Cluster Generic Data Service (GDS) (see the section "SUNW.gds" in Chapter 2, "Oracle Solaris Cluster: Features and Architecture") as the base resource type. This means that only the Start_command, Stop_command, and Probe_command methods are supplied. Because the Start_command method does not result in any child processes, it uses the pmfadm command to stop any attempt to restart any processes listed under the tag associated with this GDS resource.

The probe command, /opt/SUNWscgrepodg/lib/odg_rep_rs_gds_probe, calls the Data Guard Broker command dgmgrl. Depending on the output from the show configuration request, the probe calls the scha_resource_setstatus command to set the status of the replication resource and provide an associated resource status message. If show configuration results in dgmgrl producing Oracle errors of the form ORA-*number message*, then these errors are reported in the status of the replication resource.

## MySQL Replication

Sun Microsystems announced plans to acquire MySQL AB in January 2008 [MySQLPress]. The MySQL database is the leading open-source database on the market with many large, high-profile users. The database has a built-in asynchronous replication capability that can be used to create one or more slave copies of the master (primary) database. These copies can be used for a range of purposes, including

- Allowing a single physical database to handle more queries by spreading the load across multiple servers while handling all the updates through the master server
- Enabling online and offline backups to be taken without impacting the primary copy
- Supporting both reporting and data-mining users
- Providing a disaster recovery solution

Clearly, the last purpose noted is the main point of interest. Unlike Oracle Data Guard Broker, the MySQL software has no built-in switchover capabilities. Instead, switchover operations must be performed manually by the database administrator or by an external program. The MySQL Geographic Edition software fulfills this requirement.

When replicating data between a master (primary) and a slave (backup) database, the MySQL database uses a "pull" model. This means that the slave database retrieves the updates from the master database rather than the master database actively transmitting them to the slave database. To successfully replicate the data, the master and slave database processes must be able to communicate across the network, regardless of which cluster node the respective databases are hosted on. To achieve this, logical hostnames (see the section "SUNW.LogicalHostname" in Chapter 2, "Oracle Solaris Cluster: Features and Architecture") are required for both the database services.

The MySQL master database is made highly available on a single cluster site using the HA-MySQL agent, which is contained in the SUNWscmys package. The agent itself uses the SUNW.gds resource type (see the section "SUNW.gds" in Chapter 2, "Oracle Solaris Cluster: Features and Architecture") as a foundation with several configuration files to define all the required properties.

The Geographic Edition MySQL module was written as a sample implementation for the Script-Based Plug-In (see "Script-Based Plug-In Module") and incorporates the necessary features within the HA-MySQL agent scripts.

## Configuration

The creation of a MySQL Geographic Edition configuration requires several text files that you must supply to the registration scripts. After you have built and started your MySQL database, you create a `mysql_config_file` file for both the primary and disaster recovery sites (see the following example). You can then use the `mysql_register` script to register your database and create the user account through which the database will be monitored.

### Example 6.21  A Sample `mysql_config_file` Configuration File

```
#####################################################################
# primary-mysql_config
#
# This file will be sourced in by mysql_register and the parameters
# listed below will be used.
#

# Where is mysql installed (BASEDIR)
MYSQL_BASE=/usr/local/mysql

# Mysql admin-user for localhost (Default is root)
MYSQL_USER=root

# Password for mysql admin user
MYSQL_PASSWD=root

# Configured logicalhost
MYSQL_HOST=nyc

# Specify a username for a faultmonitor user
FMUSER=fmuser

# Pick a password for that faultmonitor user
FMPASS=fmuser

# Socket name for mysqld ( Should be /tmp/logical-host.sock )
MYSQL_SOCK=/tmp/nyc.sock

# Specify the physical hostname for the physical NIC that this logicalhostname
# belongs to for every node in the cluster this Resource group can get located on.
# If you use the mysql_geocontrol features to implement the MySQL replication as
# the replication protocol in Sun Cluster geographic edition, specify all
# physical nodes of all clusters, specify at least all the nodes on both sites
# where the mysql databases can be hosted.
# IE: The logicalhost lh1 belongs to hme1 for physical-node phys-1 and
# hme3 for  physical-node phys-2. The hostname for hme1 is phys-1-hme0 and
# for hme3 on phys-2 it is phys-2-hme3.
# IE: MYSQL_NIC_HOSTNAME="phys-1-hme0 phys-2-hme3"
# IE: If two clusters are tied together by the mysql_geocontrol features, assuming the
# mysql database on cluster one belongs to cl1-phys1-hme0 and cl1-phys2-hme3, the
# mysql database on cluster two belongs to cl2-phys1-hme2 and cl2-phys2-hme4. Then the
# MYSQL_NIC_HOSTNAME variable needs to be set to:
# MYSQL_NIC_HOSTNAME="cl1-phys1-hme0 cl1-phys2-hme3 cl2-phys1-hme2 cl2-phys2-hme4"
```

```
MYSQL_NIC_HOSTNAME="zone1 zone2 zone3 zone4"

# where are your databases installed, (location of my.cnf)
MYSQL_DATADIR=/nyc/data
```

You must create an `ha_mysql_config` file that defines the MySQL application resource group and resources (see the following example). You then run the `ha_mysql_register` script to create the appropriate resource group and resources.

## Example 6.22   A Sample `ha_mysql_config` Configuration File

```
##################################################################
#primary-ha_mysql_config
##################################################################
# This file will be sourced in by ha_mysql_register and the parameters
# listed below will be used.
#
# These parameters can be customized in (key=value) form
#
#        RS - name of the resource for the application
#        RG - name of the resource group containing RS
#   PROJECT - A project in the zone, that will be used for this service
#             specify it if you have an su - in the start stop or probe,
#             or to define the smf credentials. If the variable is not
#             set,
#             it will be translated as :default for the sm and default
#             for the zsh component
#             Optional
#     ZUSER - A user in the zone which is used for the smf method
#             credentials. Your smf service will run under this user
#             Optional
#
#   BASEDIR - name of the Mysql bin directory
#   DATADIR - name of the Mysql Data directory
# MYSQLUSER - name of the user Mysql should be started of
#        LH - name of the LogicalHostname SC resource
# MYSQLHOST - name of the host in /etc/hosts
#     FMUSER - name of the Mysql fault monitor user
#     FMPASS - name of the Mysql fault monitor user password
#     LOGDIR - name of the directory mysqld should store it's logfile.
#      CHECK - should HA-MYSQL check MyISAM index files before start YES/NO.
#     HAS_RS - name of the MySQL HAStoragePlus SC resource

RS=nyc-mys-rs
RG=nyc-rg
PORT=22
LH=nyc
HAS_RS=nyc-hsp-rs

# local zone specific options

ZONE=
ZONE_BT=
ZUSER=
PROJECT=
```

```
# mysql specifications

BASEDIR=/usr/local/mysql
DATADIR=/nyc/data
MYSQLUSER=mysql
MYSQLHOST=nyc
FMUSER=fmuser
FMPASS=fmuser
LOGDIR=/nyc/data/logs
CHECK=YES
```

Finally, you must create a `mysql_geo_config` file (see the following example) to define the MySQL Geographic Edition protection group configuration, together with two Script-Based Plug-In configuration files (see Example 6.24). The latter must be deployed in a consistent location on every node of the clusters participating in the MySQL replication.

## Example 6.23   A Sample `mysql_geo_config` Configuration File

```
####################################################################
mysql_geo_config
####################################################################
# This file will be sourced in by mysql_geo_register and uses the
# parameters
# parameters listed below.
#
# These parameters can be customized in (key=value) form
#
#          PS - Name of the partnership
#          PG - Name of the protection group
#     REPCOMP - Name of the replicated component
#       REPRS - Name of the replication resource
#       REPRG - Name of the replication resource group
#        DESC - Description for the protection group
#  CONFIGFILE - Configuration file for the script based plug-in
#               evaluation rules.
#   REALMYSRG - List of resource group names containing the MySQL
#               database resource on the clusters. If the names differ
#               between the
#               clusters, provide a "," separated list.
#   REALMYSRS - List of resource names configured as the master and
#               slave MySQL
#               database resources. If the names differ between the
#               clusters,
#               provide a "," separated list.
#    READONLY - Switch for setting the read-only variable at the MySQL
#               slave.
#               If the read-only variable should not be set, leave this
#               value undefined.
#               Every entry here will trigger the read-only variable to
#               be set.
#       APPRG - Application resource group, which is unmanaged and
#               contains the logical host
#               at least.
```

```
#   SHORTPING - Timeout for short ping test, The default is 10 seconds
#               if unset.
#               The Short ping timeout is used whenever a connection
#               should succeed,
#               but does not have to.
#   LONGPING - Timeout for extensive ping test, The default is 60
#               seconds if unset.
#               This timeout is used at the check_takeover where we have
#               to guarantee,
#               that the remote site is unavailable.

PS=mysql-ps
PG=mysql-pg
REPCOMP=mysql.sbp
REPRS=mysql-rep-rs
REPRG=mysql-rep-rg
DESC="sbp realisation ror mysql replication"
CONFIGFILE=/geo-config/sbpconfig
REALMYSRG=nyc-rg,sfo-rg
REALMYSRS=nyc-mys-rs,sfo-mys-rs
READONLY=
APPRG=usa-rg
LONGPING=
SHORTPING=
```

The Script-Based Plug-In configuration file is used internally by the Geographic Edition framework to determine which cluster nodes are used by the service. This file also defines whether the MySQL control scripts should run on any or all of the cluster nodes. For MySQL configurations, this field should always be set to any.

## Example 6.24  A Sample Script-Based Plug-In Configuration File for the `mysql.sbp` Replication Component

The `mysql.sbp` replication component is defined to run on cluster node `phys-neptune1`.

```
# Fields are:
# Replication component name
# ANY or ALL - generally used for HA or scalable services, respectively.
# A comma-separated list of local cluster nodes on which the service
# runs.
mysql.sbp|ANY|phys-neptune1
```

Ideally, include an application resource group in your configuration that contains, at a minimum, a SUNW.LogicalHostname resource. This resource ensures that clients connect to the current primary MySQL database rather than the slave database. When you are ready, you can complete the final stage of registering the configuration using the `mysql_geo_register` command. The command must be run only on one node of the primary cluster.

The `mysql_geo_register` command creates your protection group for you and then adds the associated MySQL application resource group and any other application resource group that you have listed. Assuming no errors occur, this command results in a complete configuration (see the following example). The MySQL database resource group is not added to the protection group because this would result in the database being taken offline on the disaster recovery site, thus preventing the replication from working.

## Example 6.25  A Configured MySQL (SBP-Based) Protection Group

Use the `geopg` command to list the protection groups configured.

```
# geopg list

Protection Group: mysql-pg

  Partnership name             : mysql-ps

  Local Role                   : Secondary
  Deployed on clusters         : sfoclu, nycclu
  Data Replication type        : SBP
  Configuration status         : OK
  Synchronization status       : OK
  Creation signature           : nycclu Jun 10, 2009 9:28:36 AM CEST
  Last update                  : Sep 21, 2009 2:31:56 PM CEST

  Local properties             : None

  Global properties            :

      Timeout                  : 3600 seconds
      takeover_script          : /opt/SUNWscmys/geocontrol/bin/mysql_geo_control
      RoleChange_ActionArgs    :
      stop_replication_script  : /opt/SUNWscmys/geocontrol/bin/mysql_geo_control
      create_config_script     : /opt/SUNWscmys/geocontrol/bin/mysql_geo_control
      RoleChange_ActionCmd     :
      Description              : sbp for mysql replication
      start_replication_script : /opt/SUNWscmys/geocontrol/bin/mysql_geo_control
      add_app_rg_script        : /opt/SUNWscmys/geocontrol/bin/mysql_geo_control
      remove_app_rg_script     : /bin/true
      remove_app_rg_args       :
      configuration_file       : /geo-config/sbpconfig
      switchover_script        : /opt/SUNWscmys/geocontrol/bin/mysql_geo_control
      External_Dependency_Allowed : true
      add_app_rg_args          : -O mysql.sbp -r mysql-rep-rs -g mysql-rep-rg -R
nyc-mys-rs,sfo-mys-rs -G nyc-rg,sfo-rg -t 10 -T 60  -o
      remove_config_script     : /opt/SUNWscmys/geocontrol/bin/mysql_geo_control

  Protected resource groups:

      usa-rg
```

```
SBP Script-Based Plug-in configurations:

     mysql.sbp

        mysql_sbp_stop_replication_args : -O mysql.sbp -r mysql-rep-rs -g mysql-rep-rg
   -R nyc-mys-rs,sfo-mys-rs -G nyc-rg,sfo-rg -t 10 -T 60  -o
        mysql_sbp_create_config_args : -O mysql.sbp -r mysql-rep-rs -g mysql-rep-rg -R
   nyc-mys-rs,sfo-mys-rs -G nyc-rg,sfo-rg -t 10 -T 60  -o
        mysql_sbp_switchover_args : -O mysql.sbp -r mysql-rep-rs -g mysql-rep-rg -R
   nyc-mys-rs,sfo-mys-rs -G nyc-rg,sfo-rg -t 10 -T 60  -o
        mysql_sbp_local_service_password : ********
        mysql_sbp_takeover_args   : -O mysql.sbp -r mysql-rep-rs -g mysql-rep-rg -R
   nyc-mys-rs,sfo-mys-rs -G nyc-rg,sfo-rg -t 10 -T 60  -o
        mysql_sbp_remote_service_password : ********
        mysql_sbp_remove_config_args : -O mysql.sbp -r mysql-rep-rs -g mysql-rep-rg -R
   nyc-mys-rs,sfo-mys-rs -G nyc-rg,sfo-rg -t 10 -T 60  -o
        mysql_sbp_start_replication_args : -O mysql.sbp -r mysql-rep-rs -g mysql-rep-
   rg-R nyc-mys-rs,sfo-mys-rs -G nyc-rg,sfo-rg -t 10 -T 60  -o
```

## Resource Group Configuration

The registration process described in the preceding section creates the MySQL database resource group and resources as well as the MySQL replication resource group and resource. If you also listed an application resource group, then the scripts also create the appropriate affinities between it and the database resource group. The relationships between these resource groups are shown in Figure 6.12.

## MySQL Monitoring: The Replication Resource

The MySQL replication resource relies on the same monitoring functions used to probe the MySQL database when it is in a Solaris Cluster configuration. This task is performed by the /opt/SUNWscmys/bin/probe_mysql shell script, which calls the shell function in the agent's library to check the health of the database. The health probes use responses to various calls to the MySQL mysqladmin program to determine whether the replication is operating.

The results of the probe are reflected in the status of the replication resource. Changes in the status cause events that are detected by the Geographic Edition framework and used to calculate the overall health of the protection group.

## Script-Based Plug-In Module

The Geographic Edition software supports several replication technologies: Storage-Tek Availability Suite (AVS) software, Hitachi Data Systems TrueCopy and Universal Replicator, EMC Symmetrix Remote Data Replication Facility (SRDF), and Oracle Data Guard (for Oracle RAC databases). However, the creation of these modules requires detailed knowledge of both the replication software and the internals of the Geographic Edition product. The Geographic Edition software uses

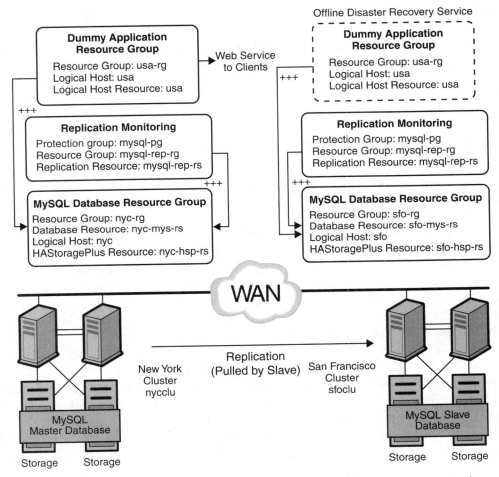

**Figure 6.12** A Geographic Edition resource group configuration for a single MySQL database

the Solaris common agent container (CAC) with a number of Java Management Extensions (JMX) MBeans that form the interface for the Geographic Edition monitoring and management infrastructure and the replication control software.

By providing a more generic interface module analogous to the Solaris Cluster Generic Data Service (GDS) (see the section "SUNW.gds" in Chapter 2, "Oracle Solaris Cluster: Features and Architecture"), the Geographic Edition Script-Based Plug-In (SBP) enables you to rapidly integrate additional replication technologies by supplying a few interface scripts to fulfill the necessary control functions. This capability frees you from needing to learn the internals of the Geographic Edition software or needing any knowledge of Java technology or MBeans. Instead, you can focus on the replication technology you require to protect your enterprise data.

The MySQL replication module described in "MySQL Replication" provides an example of how this feature is used. The development time for this module (approximately six weeks) was considerably shorter than the Oracle Data Guard equivalent because the module author did not need to understand the Geographic Edition internals.

### Limitations of a Script-Based Plug-In Approach

The limitations of an SBP approach stem from the generic nature of the plug-in that makes it so easy to use. By being generic, the plug-in lacks some of the tight integration that a custom Geographic Edition module can offer. For example, the arguments that you supply on the command line to an SBP configuration are at the script-argument level, rather than the highly specific replication-variable level. Thus, whereas the Solaris Cluster Geographic Edition Symmetrix Remote Data Facility module has specific arguments for the Symmetrix ID that are built in and that are prompted for separately in the Solaris Cluster Geographic Edition browser interface, an equivalent SBP version would pass such values only as one of a bundle of arguments to a script. It would be the script's task to determine which argument is which and whether each argument is valid.

Unlike other replication modules, the SBP is generic and capable of supporting a wide range of replication technologies. Consequently, the SBP does not contain a specific set of scripts to control a particular piece of replication software. Instead, it provides a framework for integrating a set of scripts or programs that you, as the developer, will write and that a system administrator will later use.

This flexibility means that the SBP cannot directly enforce the inclusion or exclusion of application resource groups in a protection group. Furthermore, the SBP cannot even restrict the node lists of these entities, or the relationship with the replication resource group that contains the replication resource required to supply the replication status, or indeed any other required resource group. Thus, the SBP calls the programs you list with the arguments you supply to perform specific tasks. After a protection group has been instantiated, the replication resource, representing a particular replicated object entity, reports its status to the module through the event framework.

Thus, the SBP developer is free to govern the relationships between any or all of these entities: application resource group, data replication resource group, and replication status resource group.

### Protection Group Properties

When you create an SBP-type protection group, you must supply a number of global properties, which are listed in Table 6.2. You can modify these properties only when your protection group is offline. The programs referenced by these properties are then used for all the replication components within that protection group. However, you can create other SBP-type protection groups that reference different programs, which gives you the freedom to use more than one SBP replication method.

**Table 6.2** The Script-Based Plug-In Global Protection Group Properties

| Property Name | Description | Type | Default Value |
|---|---|---|---|
| add_app_rg_args | Add Application Resource Group Script Arguments property: the arguments that are provided to the script add_app_rg_script | Global, optional | Not applicable |
| add_app_rg_script | Add Application Resource Group Script property: the script used to validate and perform tasks relevant for adding an application resource group to a protection group | Global, required | /bin/true |
| configuration_file | Configuration File property: the per-protection-group SBP configuration file containing details of the nodes pertinent to SBP replicated components held in the protection group | Global, required | /etc/opt/ SUNWscgrepsbp/ configuration |
| create_config_script | Create Configuration Script property: the script used to create, modify, and validate an SBP replicated component instance | Global, required | /bin/false |
| remove_app_rg_args | Remove Application Resource Group Script Arguments property: the arguments that are provided to the script remove_app_rg_script | Global, optional | Not applicable |

*continues*

**Table 6.2** The Script-Based Plug-In Global Protection Group Properties (*Continued*)

| Property Name | Description | Type | Default Value |
|---|---|---|---|
| remove_app_rg_script | Remove Application Resource Group Script property: the script used to validate and perform tasks relevant to removing an application resource group from a protection group | Global, required | /bin/true |
| remove_config_script | Remove Configuration Script property: the script used to remove an SBP replicated component instance | Global, required | /bin/true |
| start_replication_script | Start Replication Script property: the script used to start the data replication for an SBP replicated component instance | Global, required | /bin/true |
| stop_replication_script | Stop Replication Script property: the script used to stop the data replication for an SBP replicated component instance | Global, required | /bin/true |
| switchover_script | Switchover Replication Script property: the script used to switch over the data replication direction for an SBP replicated component instance | Global, required | /bin/true |
| takeover_script | Takeover Replication Script property: the script used to take over the data replication for an SBP replicated component instance | Global, required | /bin/true |

## Replication Component Properties

When you add a replication component to an SBP-type protection group, you must supply a number of global and local properties, which are listed in Table 6.3. Note that all of these properties are tunable when the protection group is offline.

**Table 6.3** The Script-Based Plug-In Replication Component Properties

| Property Name | Description | Type |
|---|---|---|
| create_config_args | Create Configuration Script Arguments property: the arguments passed to the script named by the create_config_script protection group property | Global, optional |
| remove_config_args | Remove Configuration Script Arguments property: the arguments passed to the script named by the remove_config_script protection group property | Global, optional |
| start_replication_args | Start Replication Script Arguments property: the arguments passed to the script named by the start_replication_script protection group property | Global, optional |
| stop_replication_args | Stop Replication Script Arguments: the arguments passed to the script named by the stop_replication_script protection group property | Global, optional |
| switchover_args | Switchover Replication Script Arguments property: the arguments passed to the script named by the switchover_script protection group property | Global, optional |
| takeover_args | Takeover Replication Script Arguments property: the arguments passed to the script named by the takeover_script protection group property | Global, optional |
| local_service_password | A password that might be needed by the scripts to perform some function on the local system that requires the entry of a password | Local, optional |
| remote_service_password | A password that might be needed by the scripts to perform some function on the remote system that requires the entry of a password | Local, optional |

These values are passed to the programs you listed in the protection-group-level properties together with information about what function the Geographic Edition software is calling, for example, create configuration, switch over, take over, and so on.

Unlike the GDS, which has only a few methods (`Start_command`, `Stop_command`, and `Probe_command`), all of which are called on a regular basis, the SBP has functions that are called fairly infrequently. For this reason, each program is required to provide its own validation function to verify that the arguments supplied through the `geopg` command are usable when the program is called at a later stage. This requirement helps to ensure that in a disaster, the `takeover` command does not fail because a critical argument was not specified as one of the command-line options to the takeover command.

### Replication Resource

Unlike with other Geographic Edition modules, the SBP developer can create a replication resource group and replication resource following his or her own chosen naming convention. To communicate the names of these objects to the Geographic Edition framework, the program named in the `create_config_script` protection group property must write the name of these entities to standard output prior to completing.

The `create_config_script` program can also name one or more resource groups that it considers internal to the SBP configuration it creates. These resource groups are ignored when checks are made for external resource group dependencies, that is, resource groups that are not currently in the protection group application list but are depended on by resource groups that are. For example, the AVS module implicitly ignores the AVS lightweight resource group.

# Null (none) Data Replication Type

The Geographic Edition software also supports the null (or none) data replication type signified by the use of the `--datarep-type none` argument to the `geopg` command. Although this data replication type might seem irrelevant for the Geographic Edition software, it does have its uses.

The most common reason to use the `none` data replication type is to provide a protection group for resource groups that encapsulate services that obtain their data from other sources. Good examples are application servers and web servers. Using this data replication type enables the resource groups to be stopped and started on the appropriate site through the same command interface.

Because this replication type has no data component, you cannot add replication components or device groups to a protection group of this type. Only the addition and removal of application resource groups are allowed. The Geographic Edition framework will still prevent you from adding resource groups with external dependencies, unless you set the `External_Dependency_Allowed` protection group property to `true`.

# Protecting Oracle RAC Databases with Storage-Based Replication Products

Although it is preferable to replicate Oracle RAC databases using the Oracle Data Guard software, Oracle RAC databases can instead be replicated using storage-based replication products. If you use this approach, you must adhere to several requirements:

- The storage for Oracle Clusterware's Oracle Cluster Registry (OCR) and voting disks must not be replicated because each Clusterware installation contains its own configuration details. Furthermore, Clusterware must be running at each site, which, consequently, requires read-write access to these devices.
- The Oracle data must be held in raw-disk devices. The Veritas Volume Manager cluster feature device group that presents these raw-disk devices must be controlled by a separate `SUNW.ScalDeviceGroup` resource. This enables the Geographic Edition software to bring this device group online or offline without affecting the device group that contains the OCR and voting disks.
- You must add the RAC server proxy resource group and scalable device group containing the data device groups to the protection group. However, you must not add the RAC framework resource group to the protection group. This requires that you set the `External_Dependency_Allowed` protection group property to `true`. This allows the Geographic Edition software to bring the protection group offline on the disaster recovery site without also bringing the RAC framework resource group offline.
- When you use a cluster file system to store Oracle RAC files and directories (such as for the flash recovery area, the alert log files, or trace log files), you must manually create on both clusters a separate resource group that uses the `SUNW.HAStoragePlus` resource to bring online these corresponding file systems. You must set a strong resource dependency from non-Clusterware `SUNW.ScalDeviceGroup` resources to this `SUNW.HAStoragePlus` resource, and then add this `SUNW.HAStoragePlus` resource group to the Oracle RAC protection group. This ensures that the cluster file system is controlled along with the database.

# Starting and Stopping Protection Groups

When you start and stop protection groups, you are controlling both the replication components and the resource groups contained within them. Therefore, to avoid affecting your service when you stop a protection group, you must remove the resource group from the protection group.

If your data replication is not active when you start your protection group, it is activated unless you specify the `--nodatarep` parameter. Similarly, when you stop your protection group, the data replication is stopped along with the application, unless you specify the `--only-datarep` parameter.

The following example builds on the configuration given in Example 6.15 and shows the effect of starting and stopping the protection group on the status of the data replication.

## Example 6.26   The Effect of Starting and Stopping a Protection Group on Data Replication

Display the current status of all the configured protection groups.

```
phys-saturn3# geoadm status

   Cluster:  saturn

   Partnership "mars-saturn"  : OK
        Partner clusters          : mars
        Synchronization           : OK
        ICRM Connection           : OK

        Heartbeat "hb_saturn~mars" monitoring "mars": OK
            Plug-in "ping_plugin"       : Inactive
            Plug-in "tcp_udp_plugin"    : OK

   Protection group "app-pg"   : OK
        Partnership               : mars-saturn
        Synchronization           : OK

        Cluster saturn            : OK
            Role                  : Primary
            Activation state      : Deactivated
            Configuration         : OK
            Data replication      : OK
            Resource groups       : OK

        Cluster mars              : OK
            Role                  : Secondary
            Activation state      : Deactivated
            Configuration         : OK
            Data replication      : OK
            Resource groups       : OK
```

Display the status of the EMC SRDF device group associated with protection group app-pg.

```
phys-saturn3# symrdf list pd | grep 0E0
00E0 00E0   R1:11   RW RW NR   S..1-      0       0 RW  RW   Split
```

Start protection group app-pg on both clusters.

```
phys-saturn3# geopg start -e global app-pg
Processing operation... The timeout period for this operation on each cluster is 3600
seconds (3600000 milliseconds)...
Protection group "app-pg" successfully started.
```

Again, display the status of the EMC SRDF device group associated with protection group app-pg. The device group is synchronized.

```
phys-saturn3# symrdf list pd | grep 0E0
00E0 00E0   R1:11   RW RW RW   S..1-       0          0 RW  WD   Synchronized
```

Stop protection group `app-pg` on both clusters.

```
phys-saturn3# geopg stop -e global app-pg
Processing operation... The timeout period for this operation on each cluster is 3600
seconds (3600000 milliseconds)...
Protection group "app-pg" successfully stopped.
```

Again, display the status of the EMC SRDF device group associated with protection group app-pg. The device group is `Split`.

```
phys-saturn3# symrdf list pd | grep 0E0
00E0 00E0   R1:11   RW RW NR   S..1-       0          0 RW  RW   Split
```

# Switchover and Takeover

The Geographic Edition software supports two types of migration of services: a switchover and a takeover. A *switchover* is a planned operation and requires that both clusters be operational during the process. In contrast, a *takeover* is usually performed only during a disaster and requires that only the backup cluster be available.

You can initiate the switchover of a service that is contained within a protection group from any of the nodes in the primary or the disaster recovery cluster. When the geopg command is issued, the Geographic Edition framework calls the appropriate replication module scripts to check if the replication is in a sufficiently healthy state to have its direction reversed cleanly. If the checks are successful, the orderly switchover process is started. This process involves first stopping the application resource groups that are contained in the protection group at the primary site and placing them in an unmanaged state. Next, any outstanding data replication is allowed to complete before the direction is reversed. Finally, the resource groups are brought online at the disaster recovery site. Example 6.27 shows how the protection group set up in Example 6.13 can be switched over. After a switchover is complete, the service can be migrated back to the primary site without copying the entire dataset back over. This is because the state of the replication is maintained during the process.

If you have multiple services in separate protection groups, then you must issue multiple geopg commands to switch over each one. If necessary, you can place these geopg commands in a script to perform all the actions in parallel or serially.

## Example 6.27  Performing a Switchover on a Protection Group

Display the status of all the configured protection groups.

```
phys-mars2# geoadm status

   Cluster:  mars

   Partnership "mars-saturn"  : OK
        Partner clusters        : saturn
        Synchronization         : OK
        ICRM Connection         : OK

        Heartbeat "hb_mars~saturn" monitoring "saturn": OK
             Plug-in "ping_plugin"       : Inactive
             Plug-in "tcp_udp_plugin"    : OK

   Protection group "app-pg"       : OK
        Partnership               : mars-saturn
        Synchronization           : OK

        Cluster mars              : OK
             Role                 : Primary
             Activation state     : Activated
             Configuration        : OK
             Data replication     : OK
             Resource groups      : OK

        Cluster saturn            : OK
             Role                 : Secondary
             Activation state     : Activated
             Configuration        : OK
             Data replication     : OK
             Resource groups      : OK
```

Confirm that /failover/app file system is mounted on one of the nodes in the local cluster.

```
phys-mars2# df -h /failover/app
Filesystem             size   used  avail capacity  Mounted on
/dev/global/dsk/d45s2
                       4.1G   4.2M   4.1G     1%    /failover/app
```

Switch over the protection group app-pg to cluster saturn.

```
phys-mars2# geopg switchover -m saturn app-pg
Are you sure you want to switchover protection group 'app-pg' to primary cluster
'saturn'? (yes|no) > yes
Processing operation... The timeout period for this operation on each cluster is 3600
seconds (3600000 milliseconds)...
"Switchover" operation succeeded for the protection group "app-pg".
```

Confirm that /failover/app file system is now mounted on one of the nodes in the remote cluster.

```
phys-saturn4# df -h /failover/app
Filesystem             size   used  avail capacity  Mounted on
/dev/global/dsk/d45s2
                       4.1G   4.2M   4.1G     1%    /failover/app
```

In contrast to a switchover, a takeover can be initiated only from the site to which you want the protection group to be migrated. A takeover is usually executed only in an emergency when the primary site is unavailable. However, if the primary site is available, the Geographic Edition software attempts to perform a more controlled takeover of the service. This process stops the application resource groups and allows the replication to complete before starting the service on the disaster recovery cluster. Unlike a switchover, the replication direction is not started in the reverse direction.

When the primary site is unavailable or cannot be reached, the Geographic Edition framework calls the appropriate replication module scripts to check if the replication is in a state where it can be taken over. Here, the guiding principle is that unless it is impossible to take control of the replication, the operation should be allowed to proceed. After this check is complete, the backup replication components are made active and the resource groups are brought online. No attempt is made to reverse or restart the data replication in the other direction after the takeover has completed.

Because the primary site is not reachable, it is likely that not all the changed data has been sent, so there is a high risk of data loss. If the primary site has been destroyed, then you must perform a complete resynchronization of the data between the two sites.

After the primary site is available again, you must propagate the configuration from the new primary cluster back to the old primary cluster, which will be in an error state and will require updating. This establishes the old primary as a secondary cluster (or backup), after which you can then restart the replication to synchronize the data.

## Example 6.28 Performing a Takeover on a Protection Group

Display the status of all the configured protection groups.

```
phys-saturn3# geoadm status

   Cluster:  saturn

   Partnership "mars-saturn"    : Error
        Partner clusters         : mars
        Synchronization          : Unknown
        ICRM Connection          : Error

        Heartbeat "hb_saturn~mars" monitoring "mars": OK
             Plug-in "ping_plugin"       : Inactive
             Plug-in "tcp_udp_plugin"    : OK

   Protection group "app-pg"     : Unknown
        Partnership               : mars-saturn
        Synchronization           : Unknown
```

```
      Cluster saturn            : OK
          Role                  : Secondary
          Activation state      : Activated
          Configuration         : OK
          Data replication      : OK
          Resource groups       : OK

      Cluster mars              : Unknown
          Role                  : Unknown
          Activation state      : Unknown
          Configuration         : Unknown
          Data replication      : Unknown
          Resource groups       : Unknown
```

This example simulates a disaster at the site containing cluster mars. Consequently, cluster mars is unreachable and showing an unknown state for the protection group app-pg.

Cluster saturn is Secondary for protection group app-pg, so issue a takeover command.

```
phys-saturn3# geopg takeover app-pg
WARNING: Unsynchronized data may be lost in takeover operation.
Are you sure you want to takeover protection group 'app-pg'? (yes|no) > yes
Processing operation... The timeout period for this operation on each cluster is 3600
seconds (3600000 milliseconds)...
"Takeover" operation succeeded for the protection group "app-pg".
```

Display the status of all the configured protection groups. Note that cluster saturn is now the Primary for protection group app-pg.

```
phys-saturn3# geoadm status

   Cluster:  saturn

   Partnership "mars-saturn"   : Error
       Partner clusters        : mars
       Synchronization         : Unknown
       ICRM Connection         : Error

       Heartbeat "hb_saturn~mars" monitoring "mars": OK
           Plug-in "ping_plugin"        : Inactive
           Plug-in "tcp_udp_plugin"     : OK

   Protection group "app-pg"   : Error
       Partnership             : mars-saturn
       Synchronization         : Unknown

       Cluster saturn          : Error
           Role                : Primary
           Activation state    : Activated
           Configuration       : OK
           Data replication    : Error
           Resource groups     : OK

       Cluster mars            : Unknown
           Role                : Unknown
           Activation state    : Unknown
           Configuration       : Unknown
           Data replication    : Unknown
           Resource groups     : Unknown
```

If you have multiple services in separate protection groups, then you must issue multiple `geopg` commands to take over control of each service. If necessary, you can place these `geopg` commands in a script to perform all the actions in parallel or serially.

# 7

# Managing Your Oracle Solaris Cluster Geographic Edition Systems

This chapter covers management topics specific to the Oracle Solaris Cluster Geographic Edition software. However, management of the replication technologies supported by the Geographic Edition software falls outside the scope of what can reasonably be covered by this book, so these areas are not discussed.

The chapter begins by describing the requirements for installing the Geographic Edition software. It then covers how to configure both the system and Common Agent Container (CAC) logging to aid in troubleshooting any issues that arise. The chapter concludes by explaining how to add support for a replication technology for which there is no existing Geographic Edition module.

## Installing and Removing the Geographic Edition Software

The Geographic Edition software is a layered product. You cannot install it on a Solaris system without first installing the Oracle Solaris Cluster software. Because the Geographic Edition software also uses the CAC framework, you must ensure that you have that framework enabled and not hardened out of your Solaris installation. Furthermore, you must ensure that you followed the rules for naming your cluster nodes, as explained in the section "Installing the Oracle Solaris OS on a Cluster Node" in Chapter 4, "Managing Your Oracle Solaris Cluster Environment." If you need to change a cluster hostname, you must first delete any partnership that references the host. Next, you must stop and then delete any protection group defined within the partnership. After changing the hostname, you re-create the partnerships and protection groups affected. The same procedure is necessary if you need to change the cluster names.

The software is installed in the same way as the Solaris Cluster software, namely, through the Solaris Cluster software `installer` program. After you've accepted the license agreement, you see a screen similar to Figure 7.1. The core component is mandatory, but the individual replication modules are optional. If you intend to use the Geographic Edition GUI manager, which uses the same interface as Solaris Cluster Manager (see the section "The Solaris Cluster Manager Graphical User Interface" in Chapter 4, "Managing Your Oracle Solaris Cluster Environment"), then you must also install the manager component.

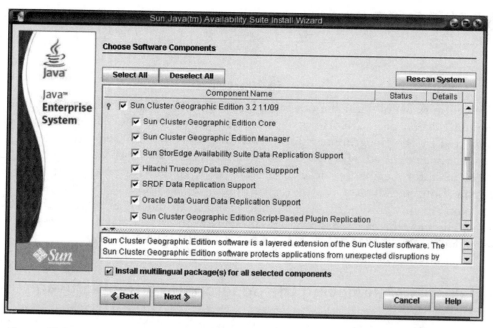

**Figure 7.1** Installation wizard for the Solaris Cluster Geographic Edition software

Whereas the Solaris Cluster software installation requires you to run the `scinstall` command, there is no equivalent for the Geographic Edition software. After the Geographic Edition software is installed, you create a logical IP address and hostname in your name service that matches your cluster name. This allows the Geographic Edition framework to start and create the necessary logical hostname resource through which partner clusters can communicate.

The following example shows how to start the Geographic Edition software. Initially, there are no partnerships in place, and none of your cluster services are protected. Your next steps are to establish trust between your clusters and to set up the partnerships you need, and then you can start creating protection groups to encapsulate your services and the data on which they rely.

## Example 7.1  Starting the Geographic Edition Software for the First Time

Determine the name of the local cluster.

```
phys-venus1# cluster list
venus
```

Confirm that the hostname venus can be resolved by the naming service.

```
phys-venus1# getent hosts venus
10.11.197.185    venus
```

Start the Geographic Edition framework.

```
phys-venus1# geoadm start
... checking for management agent ...
... management agent check done ....
... starting product infrastructure ... please wait ...
Registering resource type <SUNW.HBmonitor>...done.
Registering resource type <SUNW.SCGeoSvcTag>...done.
Resource type <SUNW.scmasa> has been registered already
Creating scalable resource group <geo-clusterstate>...done.
Creating service tag management resource <geo-servicetag>...
Service tag management resource created successfully ....
Creating failover resource group <geo-infrastructure>...done.
Creating logical host resource <geo-clustername>...
Logical host resource created successfully ....
Creating resource <geo-hbmonitor> ...done.
Creating resource <geo-failovercontrol> ...done.
Bringing resource group <geo-infrastructure> to managed state ...done.
Enabling resource <geo-clustername> ...done.
Enabling resource <geo-hbmonitor> ...done.
Enabling resource <geo-failovercontrol> ...done.
Node phys-venus1: Bringing resource group <geo-infrastructure> online ...done.
Bringing RG <geo-clusterstate> to managed state ...done.

Sun Cluster Geographic Edition infrastructure started successfully.
```

Display the status of the Geographic Edition framework.

```
phys-venus1# geoadm status

   Cluster: venus
*** No partnership defined on local cluster "venus" ***
```

If you need to uninstall the Geographic Edition software, you can do so without stopping the protected applications. You must first remove the applications from the protection groups, and then you can shut down all the protection groups and stop the Geographic Edition software. After the Geographic Edition software has been shut down, you can remove the software using the uninstall program that is located in the `/var/sadm/prod/SUNWentsys`*`version`* directory.

## Patching and Upgrading

Patching and upgrading the Geographic Edition software are relatively straightforward because the product is layered, rather than integrated directly with the Solaris kernel. To keep your services running during the patching or upgrade process, you must follow the documented procedure. The procedure requires you to remove the application group from the protection group prior to commencing the maintenance work. This prevents the application from being shut down when the protection group is stopped. Furthermore, to keep the data replication running during the upgrade process, you must restart it manually.

After you have shut down the Geographic Edition software, you can patch or upgrade the software as required. The Geographic Edition software allows you to run a mixed-version disaster recovery configuration in which the software releases differ by a single release, for example, 3.2 1/09 and 3.2 11/09. This allows you to perform a rolling upgrade with minimal impact.

Because the Geographic Edition configuration information is held in the Solaris Cluster software's cluster configuration repository (CCR), the information is not lost or overwritten during an upgrade, so when you restart the new or patched version of the software, the original configuration information is still intact.

After you have added the appropriate resource groups back to their respective protection groups, you can issue the `geopg` command to restart them.

## Cluster Management

For the most part, you can manage your cluster using either the command-line interface (CLI) or the Solaris Cluster Geographic Edition Manager graphical user interface (GUI). Although the functionality provided by the GUI is a subset of that available through the CLI, its graphical nature makes it less prone to errors when you create or modify complex objects. This is particularly true if, for example, a protection group or device group has many mandatory parameters.

## Command-Line Interface

The Geographic Edition CLI commands are in the /usr/cluster/bin directory. All begin with the geo prefix.

All of the commands listed in Table 7.1 conform to the format command *action argument ... operand.*

**Table 7.1** The Geographic Edition Command-Line Interface

| Command | Description |
| --- | --- |
| geoadm | Starts and stops the Geographic Edition software |
| geohb | Manages the Geographic Edition heartbeat configuration |
| geopg | Manages the Geographic Edition protection groups |
| geops | Manages the Geographic Edition partnerships |

All of the commands return an exit code of zero on success, enabling you to create scripts to automate procedures that you might perform regularly.

## Role-Based Access Control (RBAC)

By default, only the Solaris root user has the necessary privileges to manage the Geographic Edition configuration. A non-root user cannot create, modify, or delete protection groups, partnerships, or heartbeat configurations. Neither can a non-root user switch the protection groups between the clusters. However, non-root users can view or read the protection group, partnership, or heartbeat configurations because they are given the solaris.cluster.geo.read rights profile as part of their standard authorizations. To delegate some of the management functions to a specific system administrator who does not have full root access, you give him or her the necessary solaris.cluster.geo.admin or solaris.cluster.geo.modify Geographic Edition management rights profile.

## Monitoring

You can obtain an instantaneous snapshot of the state of the Geographic Edition protection groups using either the geoadm command or the GUI (see Figure 7.2).

Because most of the events of interest, such as resource groups switching nodes or going offline, form part of your Solaris Cluster monitoring task (see the section

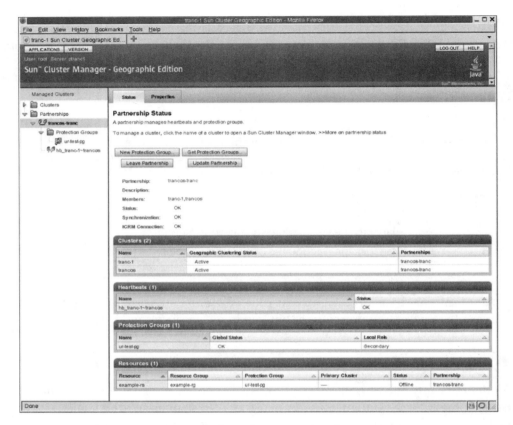

**Figure 7.2** Geographic Edition graphical user interface

"Cluster Monitoring" in Chapter 4, "Managing Your Oracle Solaris Cluster Environment"), few events are specific to the Geographic Edition software. One event that you might monitor for is the loss of heartbeat communication between the clusters in your partnerships. To be notified of a problem, you can set the `Notification_EmailAddrs` property for a particular partnership using the `geops` command. An email is then sent to the email address you supply when the framework has determined that communication has been lost.

You can also monitor changes in the heartbeat communication through the Solaris Cluster event framework. The Geographic Edition software generates `ESC_cluster_gchb_status_change` events when the heartbeat communication is lost or reestablished.

## Troubleshooting

If you need to troubleshoot problems with any of the Geographic Edition replication modules, then you must enable debugging. All the module shell scripts use the `scds_syslog` program (in the `/usr/cluster/lib/sc` directory) to log messages. To send all the messages up to a particular severity level to a separate file, you must add an entry to the `/etc/syslog.conf` file (see the `syslog.conf(4)` man page) and restart the system log service. You *must* use a tab character between the message list and the file name. The cluster framework uses `syslog` facility number 24. The following example shows how to send all the messages with a severity up to and including `debug` to a separate file.

### Example 7.2  Enabling Module Debugging Information to Be Sent to a File

Check that `syslog.conf` is configured to log `24.debug`-level messages to `/tmp/debug_log`.

```
phys-earth1# grep 24 /etc/syslog.conf
24.debug        /tmp/debug_log
```

Create an empty `/tmp/debug_log` file, and then restart the system logging service.

```
phys-earth1# touch /tmp/debug_log
phys-earth1# svcadm restart system-log
phys-earth1# tail -f /tmp/debug_log
Dec 16 07:02:48 phys-earth1 [SUNW.HBmonitor,geo-infrastructure,geo-hbmonitor]: [ID 727
651 daemon.info]  Probe for resource HBmonitor successful
Dec 16 07:03:17 phys-earth1 cacao:default[17335]: [ID 702911 daemon.info] com.sun.
cluster.agent.notifier.NotifierModule.isHealthy : SUCCESS: Health check passed for
Notifier module
```

To stop sending these messages to the file, remove the entry from the `syslog.conf` file and restart the system log service.

The CAC portion of each Geographic Edition module also generates debugging information. However, this information is significant only if you have access to the source code. Note that if you contact Oracle support services for assistance, you might be asked to supply this information.

CAC stores its log file in the `/var/cacao/instances/default/logs` directory by default. The log files are named `cacao.X` (where *X* is an integer) and are rotated after `cacao.0` reaches a specified size. The resource groups contained in the Geographic Edition protection groups can reside on any of the cluster nodes in their respective node lists. Consequently, some Geographic Edition operations must be performed on nodes other than the current primary node for the geo-infrastructure resource group. Thus, to achieve a full picture of the operations being performed, you must enable CAC debugging on all cluster nodes. Example 7.3 shows how to enable the highest level of debugging for the TrueCopy module for a single node. You must repeat this operation on all other cluster nodes.

The levels that the cacaoadm command allows for the logging filters are null, fine, finer, and finest.

## Example 7.3   Enabling CAC Debug Output for the TrueCopy Module

Use the cacaoadm command to list the debugging filters available.

```
phys-earth1# cacaoadm list-filters | grep geo | sort
com.sun.cluster.agent.geocontrol.cli.AdmEntryPoint=null
com.sun.cluster.agent.geocontrol.cli.CLIBackend=null
com.sun.cluster.agent.geocontrol.cli.HeartbeatAdministrator=null
com.sun.cluster.agent.geocontrol.cli.Monitor=null
com.sun.cluster.agent.geocontrol.cli.PartnershipAdministrator=null
com.sun.cluster.agent.geocontrol.cli.ProtectionGroupAdministrator=null
com.sun.cluster.agent.geocontrol.common.CommandInvoker=null
com.sun.cluster.agent.geocontrol.common.GCUtil=null
com.sun.cluster.agent.geocontrol.common.NotificationQueue=null
com.sun.cluster.agent.geocontrol.common.NotificationTask=null
com.sun.cluster.agent.geocontrol.common.icrmLock=null
com.sun.cluster.agent.geocontrol.datarep.DataReplicationRoleEnum=null
com.sun.cluster.agent.geocontrol.datarep.GeoDataReplication=null
com.sun.cluster.agent.geocontrol.datarep.truecopy=null
com.sun.cluster.agent.geocontrol.gctm.gctm=null
com.sun.cluster.agent.geocontrol.heartbeat.heartbeat=null
com.sun.cluster.agent.geocontrol.heartbeat.heartbeatmanager=null
com.sun.cluster.agent.geocontrol.heartbeat.plugin=null
com.sun.cluster.agent.geocontrol.i18n.I18n=null
com.sun.cluster.agent.geocontrol.icrm.guievent=null
com.sun.cluster.agent.geocontrol.icrm.partnership=null
com.sun.cluster.agent.geocontrol.icrm.partnershipmanager=null
com.sun.cluster.agent.geocontrol.icrm.partnershiptable=null
com.sun.cluster.agent.geocontrol.icrm.pgglobalstate=null
com.sun.cluster.agent.geocontrol.icrm.pglocalstate=null
com.sun.cluster.agent.geocontrol.icrm.pgtransaction=null
com.sun.cluster.agent.geocontrol.icrm.protectiongroup=null
com.sun.cluster.agent.geocontrol.icrm.protectiongroupmanager=null
com.sun.cluster.agent.geocontrol.icrm.protectiongrouptable=null
com.sun.cluster.agent.geocontrol=null
com.sun.cluster.agent.geoutilities.GeoUtil=null
com.sun.cluster.agent.geoutilities.datarep.DataReplicationCmdRouter=null
com.sun.cluster.agent.geoutilities=null
phys-earth1# cacaoadm set-filter \
> com.sun.cluster.agent.geocontrol.datarep.truecopy=FINEST
phys-earth1# tail -f cacao.0
   .
   .
   .
Dec 16, 2009 7:14:46 AM com.sun.cluster.agent.geocontrol.datarep.Truecopy
startReplication
```

```
INFO: thr#2431 TC-MBEAN-INFO: startReplication ur-test-pg : Method called
Dec 16, 2009 7:14:46 AM com.sun.cluster.agent.geocontrol.datarep.Truecopy
getCVMMaster
FINE: thr#2431 TC-MBEAN-FINE: getCVMMaster: tcNodelist=phys-earth1,phys-earth2
Dec 16, 2009 7:14:46 AM com.sun.cluster.agent.geocontrol.datarep.Truecopy
getCVMMaster
FINE: thr#2431 TC-MBEAN-FINE: getCVMMaster: Trying host phys-earth1
Dec 16, 2009 7:14:46 AM com.sun.cluster.agent.geocontrol.datarep.Truecopy control
Operation
INFO: thr#2431 TC-MBEAN-INFO: controlOperation ur-test-pg : Method called with command
= /opt/SUNWscgreptc/lib/tc_control_isCVMMaster nodename= phys-earth1 endMs=1260980086
240
        .
        .
        .
```

If you encounter problems with the Geographic Edition heartbeat communications, you can create the following *flag files*, which will cause the heartbeat daemon to log additional debugging messages to the system log after the `syslogd` daemon has been restarted:

- `/var/tmp/gc_debug_gchb_reqd`
- `/var/tmp/gc_debug_gchb_resd`
- `/var/tmp/gc_debug_tcp_udp_req`
- `/var/tmp/gc_debug_tcp_udp_resd`

## Creating Additional Data Replication Modules

The Geographic Edition software currently supports a fairly limited set of replication technologies. If you use a replication technology that is not in this list, you can add Geographic Edition support for it by writing a Script-Based Plug-In module. The capabilities of the module are then determined by your development team.

Support for the MySQL database replication was announced at the same time that the SBP module was released. The MySQL module, implemented as an SBP module, uses an enhanced version of the Solaris Cluster HA-MySQL agent to provide all the required back-end script calls.

You can take one of two broad approaches to developing your SBP module. You can either write separate programs for each required SBP script or create a single monolithic program and use the `function=Step-Name` portion of the standard command-line arguments to control the path through your code. The MySQL module uses a single monolithic script (`mysql_geo_control`) and a case statement to call the appropriate functions as shown in the following example. These functions are stored in the centralized function library.

## Example 7.4  How the MySQL Module Decides Which Function to Call

This code fragment from the MySQL SBP module shows how the shell script determines which function to call.

```
case ${function} in

      check_switchover)
              check_switchover >${LOGFILE}
              exit_value=${?};;

      perform_switchover)
              perform_switchover >${LOGFILE}
              exit_value=${?};;
      .
      .
      .
```

Your scripts must also be capable of correctly handling the validate step that the Geographic Edition calls when you add your replication component to your protection group and when the framework itself is started. This step ensures that the arguments your system administrator supplies when adding a replication component to a protection group are logically correct and sufficient for use in later operations.

The MySQL module uses a centralized validate_sbp() function to validate these arguments. If the arguments are valid, this function returns an exit code of zero.

# 8

# Example Oracle Solaris Cluster Implementations

This chapter contains step-by-step examples that show how to implement several of the most common highly available services in an Oracle Solaris Cluster configuration. Although the procedures are fairly detailed, they do not necessarily reflect the current Oracle System Installation standards, which must accommodate the latest patch levels and other settings appropriate to specific hardware and software configurations. Consequently, these example procedures sufficiently demonstrate product functionality, suitable for proof-of-concept work, but they do not provide production-ready configurations.

## Test-Driving Solaris 10 OS and Solaris Cluster Software Using Oracle VM VirtualBox Software

All the installation examples given in Chapters 8 and 9 require machines that have the Solaris 10 OS installed. This book assumes you have a working knowledge of this OS, so the Solaris 10 OS installation process is not covered in detail.

One of the best ways to become familiar with the Solaris 10 OS and the Solaris Cluster software, without having to dedicate an entire machine to the effort, is to use the Oracle VM VirtualBox software. If you have a Microsoft Windows platform with more than 2 gigabytes of memory and 20 gigabytes of available hard disk space, then you can create a single-node Solaris Cluster configuration.

To install the Solaris Cluster software you must have access to the Solaris 10 OS and Solaris Cluster software media, either as physical DVDs or as ISO-format files. Figure 8.1 shows VirtualBox configured with a number of similar machines, including one called `timsgarry`. When you start machine `timsgarry`, it boots from the Solaris 10 OS media file called `sol-10-u8-ga-x86-dvd.iso`.

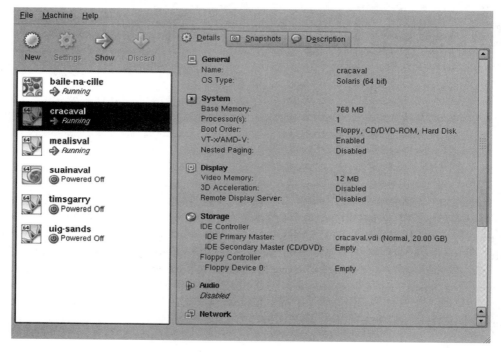

**Figure 8.1** VirtualBox configuration for a Solaris Cluster machine

After Solaris 10 OS boots, you are presented with the installation menu in Figure 8.2. To use a ZFS root file system, you must choose option 3 or 4. In this example, option 4 is chosen. After you have selected your language and keyboard layout, you are asked whether the machine is networked. Select "yes" and then define the particular network configuration for your machine (see Figure 8.3). You must have an Internet connection to register the installation and download patches over the Internet.

In this example, `timsgarry` is allocated a static IP address of `192.168.1.100` with a netmask of `255.255.255.0`. When asked whether you want to use UFS or ZFS for the root (`/`) file system, select ZFS.

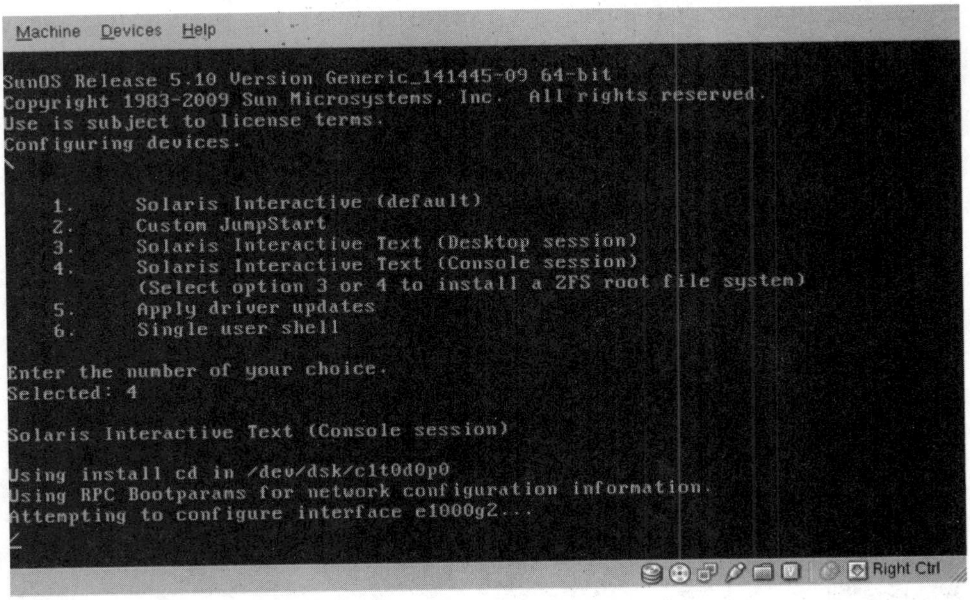

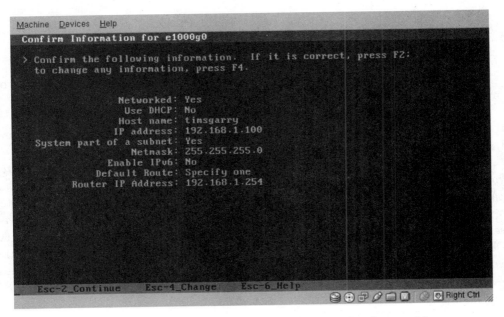

**Figure 8.2** Initial installation menu

**Figure 8.3** Defining the network configuration for the machine

To minimize the number of packages that are installed on your system, you can choose the End User System Support option, as shown in Figure 8.4.

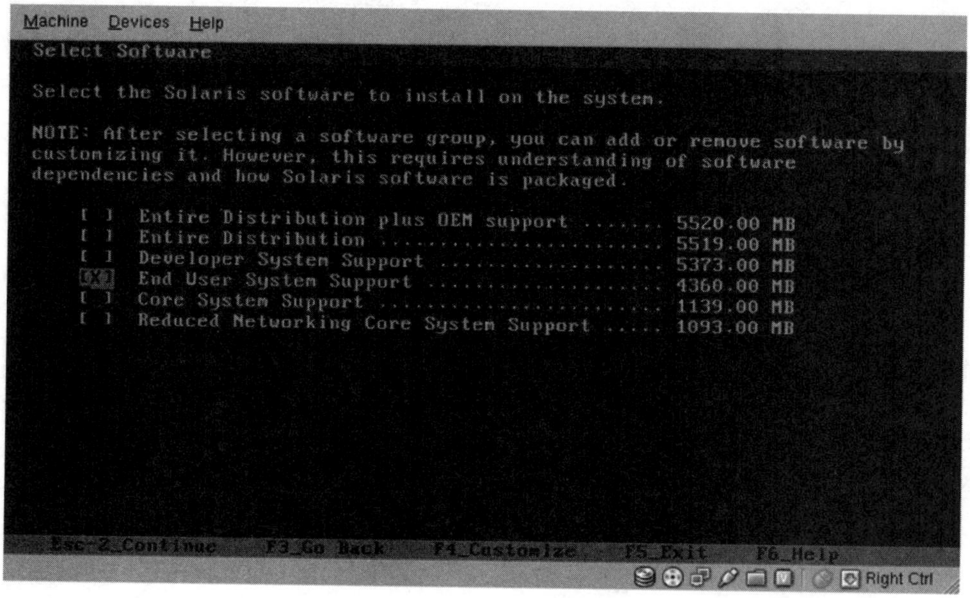

**Figure 8.4** Choosing which Solaris software group to install

After you have chosen your root disk, you can begin the installation process by pressing Esc-2, as shown in Figure 8.5.

After the installation process is complete, you must detach the DVD image from the VirtualBox machine configuration to prevent the machine from rebooting from the DVD image.

After your machine has booted the Solaris 10 OS, you are prompted to register your installation. If you have a service contract, then you should register and patch your system. Finally, you must follow the steps in Example 4.2 (in Chapter 4, "Managing Your Oracle Solaris Cluster Environment") to enable the required remote services. When you have completed these steps, you can install the Solaris Cluster software (see Figure 8.6 through Figure 8.12). Before you configure the Solaris Cluster software, run `updatemanager` to apply all the latest patches. Finally, you can configure your machine to be a single-node cluster (see the following example).

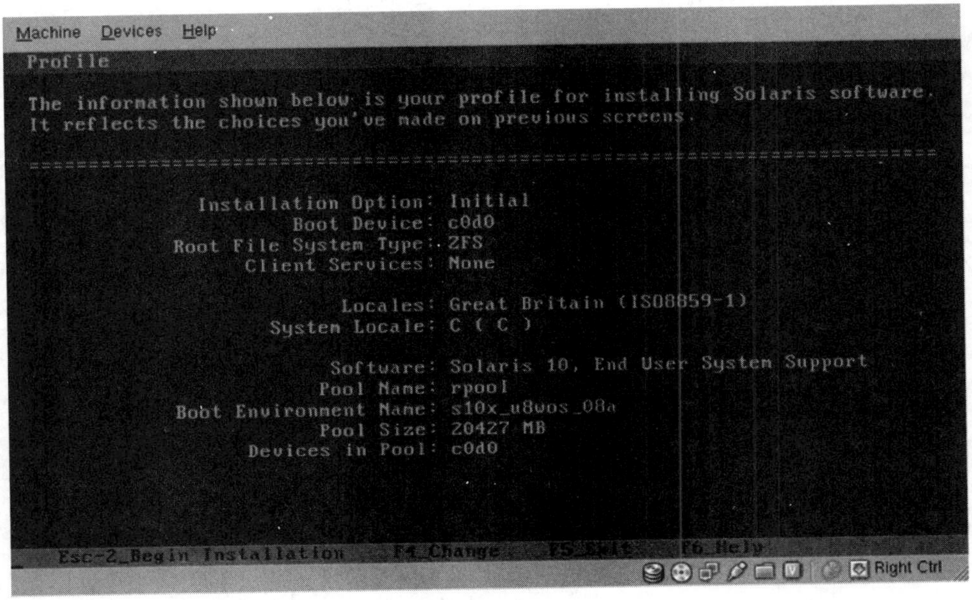

**Figure 8.5** Installation summary screen

---

## Example 8.1  Creating a Single-Node Solaris Cluster System

Set the PATH environment variable to include the /usr/cluster/bin directory, and then run the scinstall command.

```
# PATH=$PATH:/usr/cluster/bin: export PATH
# scinstall
```

---

```
*** Main Menu ***

    Please select from one of the following (*) options:

      * 1) Create a new cluster or add a cluster node
        2) Configure a cluster to be JumpStarted from this install server
        3) Manage a dual-partition upgrade
        4) Upgrade this cluster node
      * 5) Print release information for this cluster node

      * ?) Help with menu options
      * q) Quit

    Option:  1
```

```
*** New Cluster and Cluster Node Menu ***

    Please select from any one of the following options:

        1) Create a new cluster
        2) Create just the first node of a new cluster on this machine
        3) Add this machine as a node in an existing cluster

        ?) Help with menu options
        q) Return to the Main Menu

    Option:  1
```

```
*** Create a New Cluster ***


    This option creates and configures a new cluster.

    You must use the Java Enterprise System (JES) installer to install the
    Sun Cluster framework software on each machine in the new cluster
    before you select this option.

    If the "remote configuration" option is unselected from the JES
    installer when you install the Sun Cluster framework on any of the new
    nodes, then you must configure either the remote shell (see rsh(1)) or
    the secure shell (see ssh(1)) before you select this option. If rsh or
    ssh is used, you must enable root access to all of the new member
    nodes from this node.

    Press Control-d at any time to return to the Main Menu.


    Do you want to continue (yes/no) [yes]? yes
```

```
>>> Typical or Custom Mode <<<

    This tool supports two modes of operation, Typical mode and Custom.
    For most clusters, you can use Typical mode. However, you might need
    to select the Custom mode option if not all of the Typical defaults
    can be applied to your cluster.

    For more information about the differences between Typical and Custom
    modes, select the Help option from the menu.

    Please select from one of the following options:

        1) Typical
        2) Custom

        ?) Help
        q) Return to the Main Menu

    Option [1]:  1
```

```
>>> Cluster Name <<<

    Each cluster has a name assigned to it. The name can be made up of any
    characters other than whitespace. Each cluster name should be unique
    within the namespace of your enterprise.

    What is the name of the cluster you want to establish?  lewis


  >>> Cluster Nodes <<<

    This Sun Cluster release supports a total of up to 16 nodes.

    Please list the names of the other nodes planned for the initial
    cluster configuration. List one node name per line. When finished,
    type Control-D:

    Node name (Control-D to finish):  ^D


    This is the complete list of nodes:

        timsgarry

    This is a single-node cluster.
    Is that correct (yes/no) [yes]? yes


    Testing for "/globaldevices" on "timsgarry" ... failed

/globaldevices is not a directory or file system mount point.
Cannot use "/globaldevices" on "timsgarry".

    Do you want to use a lofi device instead and continue the installation (yes/no)
[yes]? yes

>>> Automatic Reboot <<<

    Once scinstall has successfully initialized the Solaris Cluster software
    for this machine, the machine must be rebooted. After the reboot, this
    machine will be established as the first node in the new cluster.

    Do you want scinstall to reboot for you (yes/no) [yes]?  no

    You will need to manually reboot this node in "cluster mode" after
    scinstall successfully completes.


Press Enter to continue:


>>> Confirmation <<<

    Your responses indicate the following options to scinstall:

      scinstall -i \
           -C lewis \
           -F \
```

```
            -o \
            -G lofi \
            -P task=quorum,state=INIT

    Are these the options you want to use (yes/no) [yes]? yes

    Do you want to continue with this configuration step (yes/no) [yes] yes
```

```
>>> Check <<<

    This step allows you to run cluster check to verify that certain basic
    hardware and software pre-configuration requirements have been met. If
    cluster check detects potential problems with configuring this machine
    as a cluster node, a report of violated checks is prepared and
    available for display on the screen.

    Do you want to run cluster check (yes/no) [yes]?  no


Initializing cluster name to "lewis" ... done
Initializing authentication options ... done


Setting the node ID for "timsgarry" ... done (id=1)


Updating nsswitch.conf ... done

Adding cluster node entries to /etc/inet/hosts ... done


Configuring IP multipathing groups ...done

mv: cannot access /usr/lib/brand/cluster/config.xml.orig

Verifying that power management is NOT configured ... done
Unconfiguring power management ... done
/etc/power.conf has been renamed to /etc/power.conf.011110122037
Power management is incompatible with the HA goals of the cluster.
Please do not attempt to re-configure power management.

Ensure network routing is disabled ... done
Network routing has been disabled on this node by creating /etc/notrouter.
Having a cluster node act as a router is not supported by Sun Cluster.
Please do not re-enable network routing.

Press Enter to continue:
```

```
*** New Cluster and Cluster Node Menu ***

    Please select from any one of the following options:

        1) Create a new cluster
        2) Create just the first node of a new cluster on this machine
        3) Add this machine as a node in an existing cluster
```

```
        ?) Help with menu options
        q) Return to the Main Menu

   Option:  q


_____


*** Main Menu ***

   Please select from one of the following (*) options:

      1) Create a new cluster or add a cluster node
      2) Configure a cluster to be JumpStarted from this install server
    * 3) Manage a dual-partition upgrade
    * 4) Upgrade this cluster node
    * 5) Print release information for this cluster node

    * ?) Help with menu options
    * q) Quit

   Option:  q



 Log file - /var/cluster/logs/install/scinstall.log.1129
 # shutdown -g0 -y -i6
```

After the VirtualBox software has rebooted your single-node cluster, you can experiment with the Solaris Cluster software CLI and GUI.

## Installing the Solaris Cluster Software to Create a Two-Node Cluster

After you have completed the Oracle Solaris OS installation and applied the latest patches, you can install the Solaris Cluster software. The Solaris Cluster software must be installed using the `installer` command. Depending on the system you are using, this command is located in either the `Solaris_sparc` or the `Solaris_x86` subdirectory of your installation media. See Example 4.3 in Chapter 4, "Managing Your Oracle Solaris Cluster Environment," for details on how to run this command. You must accept the license agreement before you are presented with a list of software you can install (see Figure 8.6). The examples in Chapters 8 and 9 assume you have chosen to install all the Solaris Cluster and Geographic Edition components. As you gain experience, you can limit your choices to just the components you require.

The installation program then guides you through a series of additional screens (see Figure 8.7 through Figure 8.12).

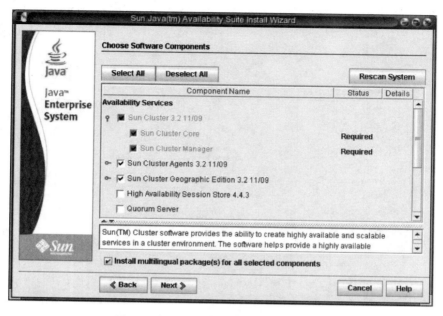

**Figure 8.6** Initial installation screen

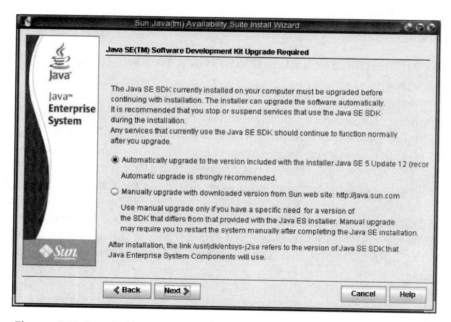

**Figure 8.7** Required Java SE Software Development Kit upgrade for the Solaris Cluster software

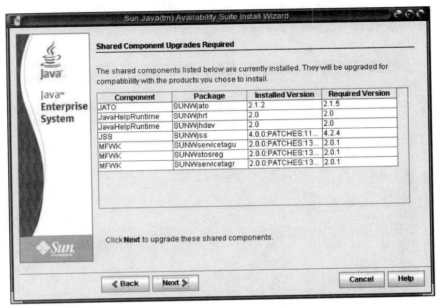

**Figure 8.8** Required shared component upgrades for the Solaris Cluster software

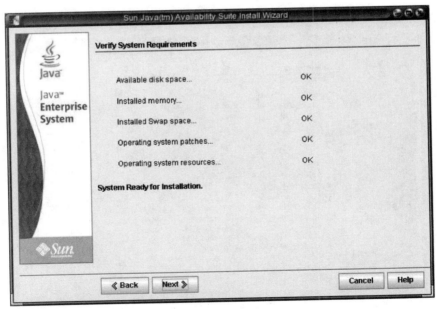

**Figure 8.9** Verification of the system requirements for the Solaris Cluster software

Because the Solaris Cluster software must always be configured after the software has been installed, you can select either option in Figure 8.10.

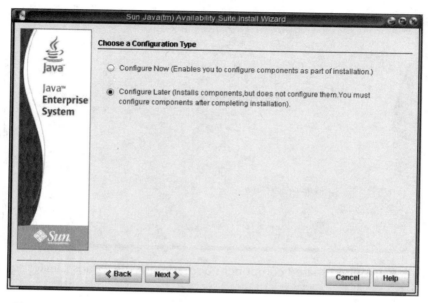

**Figure 8.10** Choosing to configure the Solaris Cluster software later

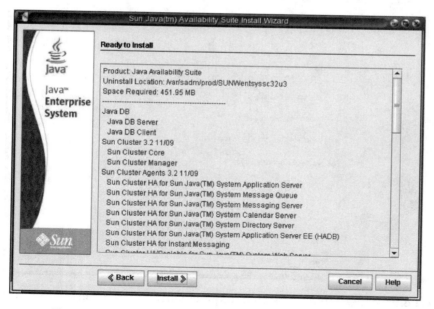

**Figure 8.11** Ready to install the Solaris Cluster software

After the software has been installed, you must apply all the mandatory updates that are listed in the software release notes. The best method for doing so is the `updatemanager` program. The Solaris Cluster core patch cannot be applied directly through `updatemanager`, but it can be applied after it has been downloaded using the commands in Example 8.2.

> **Note**
>
> Always read the patch README file before applying the patch to ensure that you are following the correct procedure.

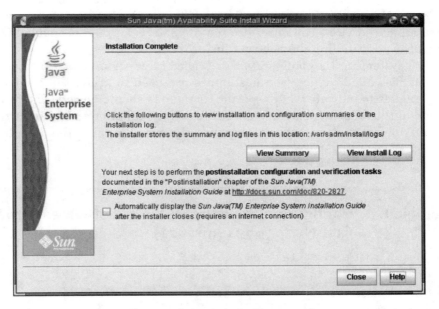

**Figure 8.12** Installation of the Solaris Cluster software completed

## Example 8.2  Applying the Solaris Cluster Software Core Patch Using `smpatch`

Use the `smpatch` command to install the Solaris Cluster software core patch.

```
# smpatch add -i 126106-39
add patch 126106-39
Transition old-style patching.
Patch 126106-39 has been successfully installed.
```

After you have completed the patching process, you can start configuring your cluster. The configuration steps documented in Example 8.3 and Example 8.4 use two Sun Fire V240 servers. Each server has 8 gigabytes of RAM, two internal 72-gigabyte disks, and one PCI four-port Gigabit Ethernet card (ports bge0 to bge3) installed. The servers share access to ten 20-gigabyte LUNs provided by Oracle's StorageTek 3511 storage array.

Both servers have the Solaris 10 10/09 OS installed and patched to the latest patches available. The two internal disks provide the mirrored zpool for the root (/) file system. Note that there are no internal disk slices available for Solaris Volume Manager state replica databases. Consequently, the following example uses the ZFS file system rather than UFS with Solaris Volume Manager. Example 8.3 and Example 8.4 also assume that you have performed the steps in Example 4.2 in Chapter 4, "Managing Your Oracle Solaris Cluster Environment," to enable the required remote services. You must also run stmsboot -D fp -e to enable I/O multi-pathing *prior* to installing the Solaris Cluster software.

The two systems in the configuration are called phys-grass1 and phys-grass2. The cluster is called grass. The hostnames are used to prefix the commands in these examples to indicate where specific commands should be run. The procedure described in the following example uses a custom installation to highlight the configuration options that are offered. However, the example takes the default option in most cases.

## Example 8.3  Configuring the Solaris Cluster Software on the First Node (phys-grass1)

First, create a suitable .profile file on both nodes.

```
phys-grass1 # cat /.profile
PATH=$PATH:/usr/cluster/bin: export PATH
MANPATH=/usr/share/man:/usr/cluster/man: export MANPATH
```

Check that each node has the other node's IP address in the /etc/inet/hosts file.

```
phys-grass1 # cat /etc/inet/hosts | grep grass
10.11.112.21     phys-grass1        loghost
10.11.112.22     phys-grass2

phys-grass2 # cat /etc/inet/hosts | grep grass
10.11.112.21     phys-grass1
10.11.112.22     phys-grass2        loghost
```

Next, run the scinstall program on phys-grass1.

```
phys-grass1 # scinstall
```

```
*** Main Menu ***

  Please select from one of the following (*) options:

     * 1) Create a new cluster or add a cluster node
       2) Configure a cluster to be JumpStarted from this install server
       3) Manage a dual-partition upgrade
       4) Upgrade this cluster node
     * 5) Print release information for this cluster node

     * ?) Help with menu options
     * q) Quit

  Option:  1
```

```
*** New Cluster and Cluster Node Menu ***

  Please select from any one of the following options:

     1) Create a new cluster
     2) Create just the first node of a new cluster on this machine
     3) Add this machine as a node in an existing cluster

     ?) Help with menu options
     q) Return to the Main Menu

  Option:  2
```

```
*** Establish Just the First Node of a New Cluster ***


  This option is used to establish a new cluster using this machine as
  the first node in that cluster.

  Before you select this option, the Sun Cluster framework software must
  already be installed. Use the Java Enterprise System (JES) installer
  to install Solaris Cluster software.

  Press Control-d at any time to return to the Main Menu.


  Do you want to continue (yes/no) [yes]? yes
```

```
>>> Typical or Custom Mode <<<

  This tool supports two modes of operation, Typical mode and Custom.
  For most clusters, you can use Typical mode. However, you might need
  to select the Custom mode option if not all of the Typical defaults
  can be applied to your cluster.

  For more information about the differences between Typical and Custom
  modes, select the Help option from the menu.

  Please select from one of the following options:

     1) Typical
     2) Custom
```

```
        ?) Help
        q) Return to the Main Menu

    Option [1]:  2




>>> Cluster Name <<<

    Each cluster has a name assigned to it. The name can be made up of any
    characters other than whitespace. Each cluster name should be unique
    within the namespace of your enterprise.

    What is the name of the cluster you want to establish?  grass



>>> Check <<<

    This step allows you to run cluster check to verify that certain basic
    hardware and software pre-configuration requirements have been met. If
    cluster check detects potential problems with configuring this machine
    as a cluster node, a report of violated checks is prepared and
    available for display on the screen.

    Do you want to run cluster check (yes/no) [yes]? yes


    Running cluster check ...

  initializing...
  initializing xml output...
  loading auxiliary data...
  filtering out checks not marked with one of keywords: installtime
  starting check run...
        phys-grass1:   S6708638.... starting:  Node has insufficient physical memory.
        phys-grass1:   S6708638      passed
        phys-grass1:   S6708496.... starting:  Cluster node (3.1 or later) OpenBoot Prom
(O...
        phys-grass1:   S6708496      passed
        phys-grass1:   S6708605.... starting:  The /dev/rmt directory is missing.
        phys-grass1:   S6708605      passed
        phys-grass1:   S6708606.... starting:  Multiple network interfaces on a single
subn...
        phys-grass1:   S6708606        not applicable
        phys-grass1:   S6708642.... starting:  /proc fails to mount periodically during
reb...
          searching /var/adm/messages
          searching /var/adm/messages.0
          searching /var/adm/messages.1
        phys-grass1:   S6708642        passed
  finished check run
  finishing xml output...
  Maximum severity of all violations: No Violations
  Reports in: /var/cluster/logs/install/cluster_check/
  cleaning up...



Press Enter to continue:
```

```
>>> Cluster Nodes <<<

    This Sun Cluster release supports a total of up to 16 nodes.

    Please list the names of the other nodes planned for the initial
    cluster configuration. List one node name per line. When finished,
    type Control-D:

    Node name (Control-D to finish):  phys-grass2
    Node name (Control-D to finish):


    This is the complete list of nodes:

        phys-grass1
        phys-grass2

    Is it correct (yes/no) [yes]? yes
```

```
>>> Authenticating Requests to Add Nodes <<<

    Once the first node establishes itself as a single node cluster, other
    nodes attempting to add themselves to the cluster configuration must
    be found on the list of nodes you just provided. You can modify this
    list by using claccess(1CL) or other tools once the cluster has been
    established.

    By default, nodes are not securely authenticated as they attempt to
    add themselves to the cluster configuration. This is generally
    considered adequate, since nodes which are not physically connected to
    the private cluster interconnect will never be able to actually join
    the cluster. However, DES authentication is available. If DES
    authentication is selected, you must configure all necessary
    encryption keys before any node will be allowed to join the cluster
    (see keyserv(1M), publickey(4)).

    Do you need to use DES authentication (yes/no) [no]? no
```

```
>>> Minimum Number of Private Networks <<<

    Each cluster is typically configured with at least two private
    networks. Configuring a cluster with just one private interconnect
    provides less availability and will require the cluster to spend more
    time in automatic recovery if that private interconnect fails.

    Should this cluster use at least two private networks (yes/no) [yes]? yes
```

```
>>> Point-to-Point Cables <<<

    The two nodes of a two-node cluster may use a directly-connected
    interconnect. That is, no cluster switches are configured. However,
    when there are greater than two nodes, this interactive form of
    scinstall assumes that there will be exactly one switch for each
    private network.
```

```
     Does this two-node cluster use switches (yes/no) [yes]? yes
```

```
>>> Cluster Switches <<<

     All cluster transport adapters in this cluster must be cabled to a
     "switch". And, each adapter on a given node must be cabled to a
     different switch. Interactive scinstall requires that you identify one
     switch for each private network in the cluster.

     What is the name of the first switch in the cluster [switch1]? switch1

     What is the name of the second switch in the cluster [switch2]? switch2
```

```
>>> Cluster Transport Adapters and Cables <<<

     You must configure the cluster transport adapters for each node in the
     cluster. These are the adapters which attach to the private cluster
interconnect.

     Select the first cluster transport adapter:

         1) bge1
         2) bge2
         3) bge3
         4) ce0
         5) ce1
         6) ce2
         7) ce3
         8) Other

     Option:  1

     Will this be a dedicated cluster transport adapter (yes/no) [yes]? yes

     Adapter "bge1" is an Ethernet adapter.

     Searching for any unexpected network traffic on "bge1" ... done
     Verification completed. No traffic was detected over a 10 second
     sample period.

     The "dlpi" transport type will be set for this cluster.

     Name of the switch to which "bge1" is connected [switch1]? switch1

     Each adapter is cabled to a particular port on a switch. And, each
     port is assigned a name. You can explicitly assign a name to each
     port. Or, for Ethernet and Infiniband switches, you can choose to
     allow scinstall to assign a default name for you. The default port
     name assignment sets the name to the node number of the node hosting
     the transport adapter at the other end of the cable.

     Use the default port name for the "bge1" connection (yes/no) [yes]? yes

     Select the second cluster transport adapter:

         1) bge1
         2) bge2
         3) bge3
         4) ce0
```

```
        5) ce1
        6) ce2
        7) ce3
        8) Other

    Option:  5

    Will this be a dedicated cluster transport adapter (yes/no) [yes]? yes

    Adapter "ce1" is an Ethernet adapter.

    Searching for any unexpected network traffic on "ce1" ... done
    Verification completed. No traffic was detected over a 10 second
    sample period.

    Name of the switch to which "ce1" is connected [switch2]? switch2

    Use the default port name for the "ce1" connection (yes/no) [yes]? yes
```

---

```
>>> Network Address for the Cluster Transport <<<

    The cluster transport uses a default network address of 172.16.0.0. If
    this IP address is already in use elsewhere within your enterprise,
    specify another address from the range of recommended private
    addresses (see RFC 1918 for details).

    The default netmask is 255.255.240.0. You can select another netmask,
    as long as it minimally masks all bits that are given in the network
    address.

    The default private netmask and network address result in an IP
    address range that supports a cluster with a maximum of 64 nodes, 10
    private networks and 0 virtual clusters.

    Is it okay to accept the default network address (yes/no) [yes]? yes

    Is it okay to accept the default netmask (yes/no) [yes]? yes

    Plumbing network address 172.16.0.0 on adapter bge1 >> NOT DUPLICATE ... done
Plumbing network address 172.16.0.0 on adapter ce1 >> NOT DUPLICATE ... done
```

---

```
>>> Global Devices File System <<<

    Each node in the cluster must have a local file system mounted on
    /global/.devices/node@<nodeID> before it can successfully participate
    as a cluster member. Since the "nodeID" is not assigned until
    scinstall is run, scinstall will set this up for you.

    You must supply the name of either an already-mounted file system or a
    raw disk partition which scinstall can use to create the global
    devices file system. This file system or partition should be at least
    512 MB in size.

    Alternatively, you can use a loopback file (lofi), with a new file
    system, and mount it on /global/.devices/node@<nodeid>.

    If an already-mounted file system is used, the file system must be
    empty. If a raw disk partition is used, a new file system will be
    created for you.
```

If the lofi method is used, scinstall creates a new 100 MB file system
from a lofi device by using the file /.globaldevices. The lofi method
is typically preferred, since it does not require the allocation of a
dedicated disk slice.

The default is to use /globaldevices.

Is it okay to use this default (yes/no) [yes]? yes

/globaldevices is not a directory or file system mount point.
Cannot use "/globaldevices".

Is it okay to use the lofi method (yes/no) [yes]? yes

---

>>> Set Global Fencing <<<

Fencing is a mechanism that a cluster uses to protect data integrity
when the cluster interconnect between nodes is lost. By default,
fencing is turned on for global fencing, and each disk uses the global
fencing setting. This screen allows you to turn off the global
fencing.

Most of the time, leave fencing turned on. However, turn off fencing
when at least one of the following conditions is true: 1) Your shared
storage devices, such as Serial Advanced Technology Attachment (SATA)
disks, do not support SCSI; 2) You want to allow systems outside your
cluster to access storage devices attached to your cluster; 3) Sun
Microsystems has not qualified the SCSI persistent group reservation
(PGR) support for your shared storage devices.

If you choose to turn off global fencing now, after your cluster
starts you can still use the cluster(1CL) command to turn on global
fencing.

Do you want to turn off global fencing (yes/no) [no]? no

---

>>> Quorum Configuration <<<

Every two-node cluster requires at least one quorum device. By
default, scinstall selects and configures a shared disk quorum device
for you.

This screen allows you to disable the automatic selection and
configuration of a quorum device.

You have chosen to turn on the global fencing. If your shared storage
devices do not support SCSI, such as Serial Advanced Technology
Attachment (SATA) disks, or if your shared disks do not support
SCSI-2, you must disable this feature.

If you disable automatic quorum device selection now, or if you intend
to use a quorum device that is not a shared disk, you must instead use
clsetup(1M) to manually configure quorum once both nodes have joined
the cluster for the first time.

Do you want to disable automatic quorum device selection (yes/no) [no]? no

```
>>> Automatic Reboot <<<

    Once scinstall has successfully initialized the Solaris Cluster software
    for this machine, the machine must be rebooted. After the reboot, this
    machine will be established as the first node in the new cluster.

    Do you want scinstall to reboot for you (yes/no) [yes]? yes

  >>> Confirmation <<<

    Your responses indicate the following options to scinstall:

        scinstall -i \
            -C grass \
            -F \
            -G lofi \
            -T node=phys-grass1,node=phys-grass2,authtype=sys \
            -w netaddr=172.16.0.0,netmask=255.255.240.0,maxnodes=64,maxprivatenets=10,
numvirtualclusters=12 \
            -A trtype=dlpi,name=bge1 -A trtype=dlpi,name=ce1 \
            -B type=switch,name=switch1 -B type=switch,name=switch2 \
            -m endpoint=:bge1,endpoint=switch1 \
            -m endpoint=:ce1,endpoint=switch2 \
            -P task=quorum,state=INIT

    Are these the options you want to use (yes/no) [yes]? yes

    Do you want to continue with this configuration step (yes/no) [yes]? yes


Initializing cluster name to "grass" ... done
Initializing authentication options ... done
Initializing configuration for adapter "bge1" ... done
Initializing configuration for adapter "ce1" ... done
Initializing configuration for switch "switch1" ... done
Initializing configuration for switch "switch2" ... done
Initializing configuration for cable ... done
Initializing configuration for cable ... done
Initializing private network address options ... done


Setting the node ID for "phys-grass1" ... done (id=1)


Verifying that NTP is configured ... done
Initializing NTP configuration ... done

Updating nsswitch.conf ... done

Adding cluster node entries to /etc/inet/hosts ... done


Configuring IP multipathing groups ...done

mv: cannot access /usr/lib/brand/cluster/config.xml.orig

Verifying that power management is NOT configured ... done
Unconfiguring power management ... done
/etc/power.conf has been renamed to /etc/power.conf.010710080441
Power management is incompatible with the HA goals of the cluster.
Please do not attempt to re-configure power management.
```

```
Ensure that the EEPROM parameter "local-mac-address?" is set to "true" ... done

Ensure network routing is disabled ... done
Network routing has been disabled on this node by creating /etc/notrouter.
Having a cluster node act as a router is not supported by Sun Cluster.
Please do not re-enable network routing.

Log file - /var/cluster/logs/install/scinstall.log.12257


Rebooting ...

updating /platform/sun4u/boot_archive
15+0 records in
15+0 records out
```

After the first cluster node finishes rebooting, log in and check that it has started all the cluster services. You can then configure the second cluster node (see the following example).

## Example 8.4  Configuring the Solaris Cluster Software on the Second Node (`phys-grass2`)

Check that the `phys-grass1` node has booted correctly and that no cluster services other than the `scsymon-srv` service have failed to start.

```
phys-grass1 # svcs -x
svc:/application/print/server:default (LP print server)
 State: disabled since Thu Jan 07 08:06:30 2010
Reason: Disabled by an administrator.
   See: http://sun.com/msg/SMF-8000-05
   See: lpsched(1M)
Impact: 1 dependent service is not running.  (Use -v for list.)

svc:/system/cluster/scsymon-srv:default (Sun Cluster SyMON Server Daemon)
 State: offline since Thu Jan 07 08:07:08 2010
Reason: Dependency svc:/application/management/sunmcagent:default is absent.
   See: http://sun.com/msg/SMF-8000-E2
Impact: This service is not running.
```

Next, configure `phys-grass2`.

```
phys-grass2 # scinstall


  *** Main Menu ***

   Please select from one of the following (*) options:

     * 1) Create a new cluster or add a cluster node
       2) Configure a cluster to be JumpStarted from this install server
       3) Manage a dual-partition upgrade
       4) Upgrade this cluster node
     * 5) Print release information for this cluster node
```

```
     * ?) Help with menu options
     * q) Quit

   Option:  1
```

```
*** New Cluster and Cluster Node Menu ***

   Please select from any one of the following options:

      1) Create a new cluster
      2) Create just the first node of a new cluster on this machine
      3) Add this machine as a node in an existing cluster

      ?) Help with menu options
      q) Return to the Main Menu

   Option:  3
```

```
*** Add a Node to an Existing Cluster ***


   This option is used to add this machine as a node in an already
   established cluster. If this is a new cluster, there may only be a
   single node which has established itself in the new cluster.

   Before you select this option, the Sun Cluster framework software must
   already be installed. Use the Java Enterprise System (JES) installer
   to install Solaris Cluster software.

   Press Control-d at any time to return to the Main Menu.


   Do you want to continue (yes/no) [yes]? yes
```

```
>>> Typical or Custom Mode <<<

   This tool supports two modes of operation, Typical mode and Custom.
   For most clusters, you can use Typical mode. However, you might need
   to select the Custom mode option if not all of the Typical defaults
   can be applied to your cluster.

   For more information about the differences between Typical and Custom
   modes, select the Help option from the menu.

   Please select from one of the following options:

      1) Typical
      2) Custom

      ?) Help
      q) Return to the Main Menu

   Option [1]:  2
```

```
>>> Sponsoring Node <<<

    For any machine to join a cluster, it must identify a node in that
    cluster willing to "sponsor" its membership in the cluster. When
    configuring a new cluster, this "sponsor" node is typically the first
    node used to build the new cluster. However, if the cluster is already
    established, the "sponsoring" node can be any node in that cluster.

    Already established clusters can keep a list of hosts which are able
    to configure themselves as new cluster members. This machine should be
    in the join list of any cluster which it tries to join. If the list
    does not include this machine, you may need to add it by using
    claccess(1CL) or other tools.

    And, if the target cluster uses DES to authenticate new machines
    attempting to configure themselves as new cluster members, the
    necessary encryption keys must be configured before any attempt to
    join.

    What is the name of the sponsoring node?  phys-grass1
```

```
>>> Cluster Name <<<

    Each cluster has a name assigned to it. When adding a node to the
    cluster, you must identify the name of the cluster you are attempting
    to join. A sanity check is performed to verify that the "sponsoring"
    node is a member of that cluster.

    What is the name of the cluster you want to join?  grass

    Attempting to contact "phys-grass1" ... done

    Cluster name "grass" is correct.

Press Enter to continue:
```

```
>>> Check <<<

    This step allows you to run cluster check to verify that certain basic
    hardware and software pre-configuration requirements have been met. If
    cluster check detects potential problems with configuring this machine
    as a cluster node, a report of violated checks is prepared and
    available for display on the screen.

    Do you want to run cluster check (yes/no) [yes]?  no
```

```
>>> Autodiscovery of Cluster Transport <<<

    If you are using Ethernet or Infiniband adapters as the cluster
    transport adapters, autodiscovery is the best method for configuring
    the cluster transport.

    Do you want to use autodiscovery (yes/no) [yes]? yes


    Probing ............
```

```
The following connections were discovered:

    phys-grass1:bge1   switch1   phys-grass2:bge1
    phys-grass1:ce1    switch2   phys-grass2:ce1

Is it okay to configure these connections (yes/no) [yes]? yes
```

```
>>> Global Devices File System <<<

    Each node in the cluster must have a local file system mounted on
    /global/.devices/node@<nodeID> before it can successfully participate
    as a cluster member. Since the "nodeID" is not assigned until
    scinstall is run, scinstall will set this up for you.

    You must supply the name of either an already-mounted file system or a
    raw disk partition which scinstall can use to create the global
    devices file system. This file system or partition should be at least
    512 MB in size.

    Alternatively, you can use a loopback file (lofi), with a new file
    system, and mount it on /global/.devices/node@<nodeid>.

    If an already-mounted file system is used, the file system must be
    empty. If a raw disk partition is used, a new file system will be
    created for you.

    If the lofi method is used, scinstall creates a new 100 MB file system
    from a lofi device by using the file /.globaldevices. The lofi method
    is typically preferred, since it does not require the allocation of a
    dedicated disk slice.

    The default is to use /globaldevices.

    Is it okay to use this default (yes/no) [yes]? yes

/globaldevices is not a directory or file system mount point.
Cannot use "/globaldevices".

    Is it okay to use the lofi method (yes/no) [yes]? yes
```

```
>>> Automatic Reboot <<<

    Once scinstall has successfully initialized the Solaris Cluster software
    for this machine, the machine must be rebooted. The reboot will cause
    this machine to join the cluster for the first time.

    Do you want scinstall to reboot for you (yes/no) [yes]? yes

  >>> Confirmation <<<

    Your responses indicate the following options to scinstall:

       scinstall -i \
            -C grass \
            -N phys-grass1 \
            -G lofi \
            -A trtype=dlpi,name=bge1 -A trtype=dlpi,name=ce1 \
            -m endpoint=:bge1,endpoint=switch1 \
            -m endpoint=:ce1,endpoint=switch2
```

```
    Are these the options you want to use (yes/no) [yes]? yes

    Do you want to continue with this configuration step (yes/no) [yes]? yes


Adding node "phys-grass2" to the cluster configuration ... done
Adding adapter "bge1" to the cluster configuration ... done
Adding adapter "ce1" to the cluster configuration ... done
Adding cable to the cluster configuration ... done
Adding cable to the cluster configuration ... done

Copying the config from "phys-grass1" ... done

Copying the postconfig file from "phys-grass1" if it exists ... done


Setting the node ID for "phys-grass2" ... done (id=2)

Verifying the major number for the "did" driver with "phys-grass1" ... done


Verifying that NTP is configured ... done
Initializing NTP configuration ... done

Updating nsswitch.conf ... done

Adding cluster node entries to /etc/inet/hosts ... done


Configuring IP multipathing groups ...done

mv: cannot access /usr/lib/brand/cluster/config.xml.orig

Verifying that power management is NOT configured ... done
Unconfiguring power management ... done
/etc/power.conf has been renamed to /etc/power.conf.010710083056
Power management is incompatible with the HA goals of the cluster.
Please do not attempt to re-configure power management.

Ensure that the EEPROM parameter "local-mac-address?" is set to "true" ... done

Ensure network routing is disabled ... done
Network routing has been disabled on this node by creating /etc/notrouter.
Having a cluster node act as a router is not supported by Sun Cluster.
Please do not re-enable network routing.

Updating file ("ntp.conf.cluster") on node phys-grass1 ... done
Updating file ("hosts") on node phys-grass1 ... done

Log file - /var/cluster/logs/install/scinstall.log.11405


Rebooting ...

updating /platform/sun4u/boot_archive
15+0 records in
15+0 records out
```

After `phys-grass2` finishes rebooting, the `grass` cluster is considered installed. Next, resource groups can be created. The following example shows that both nodes are running and that LUN `d1` has been chosen as the quorum device. The output from the `cldev` command indicates which LUNs are dual-hosted by having two entries for each of these LUNs.

## Example 8.5  Checking the Status of the `grass` Cluster

Use the `clnode` command to check the status of the cluster nodes.

```
phys-grass2 # clnode status

=== Cluster Nodes ===

--- Node Status ---

Node Name                              Status
---------                              ------
phys-grass1                            Online
phys-grass2                            Online
```

Use the `clquorum` command to display quorum information.

```
phys-grass2 # clquorum show

=== Cluster Nodes ===

Node Name:                             phys-grass1
   Node ID:                            1
   Quorum Vote Count:                  1
   Reservation Key:                    0x4B4605F900000001

Node Name:                             phys-grass2
   Node ID:                            2
   Quorum Vote Count:                  1
   Reservation Key:                    0x4B4605F900000002


=== Quorum Devices ===

Quorum Device Name:                    d1
   Enabled:                            yes
   Votes:                              1
   Global Name:                        /dev/did/rdsk/d1s2
   Type:                               shared_disk
   Access Mode:                        scsi2
   Hosts (enabled):                    phys-grass1, phys-grass2
```

Use the `cldev` command to list the DID devices configured on the cluster.

```
phys-grass2 # cldev list -v
DID Device        Full Device Path
----------        ----------------
d1                phys-grass1:/dev/rdsk/c4t600C0FF0000000000921C20AC2C56F02d0
d1                phys-grass2:/dev/rdsk/c4t600C0FF0000000000921C20AC2C56F02d0
d2                phys-grass1:/dev/rdsk/c4t600C0FF0000000000921C20AC2C56F08d0
d2                phys-grass2:/dev/rdsk/c4t600C0FF0000000000921C20AC2C56F08d0
d3                phys-grass1:/dev/rdsk/c4t600C0FF0000000000921C20AC2C56F09d0
d3                phys-grass2:/dev/rdsk/c4t600C0FF0000000000921C20AC2C56F09d0
d4                phys-grass1:/dev/rdsk/c4t600C0FF0000000000921C20AC2C56F03d0
d4                phys-grass2:/dev/rdsk/c4t600C0FF0000000000921C20AC2C56F03d0
d5                phys-grass1:/dev/rdsk/c4t600C0FF0000000000921C20AC2C56F01d0
```

```
d5      phys-grass2:/dev/rdsk/c4t600C0FF0000000000921C20AC2C56F01d0
d6      phys-grass1:/dev/rdsk/c4t600C0FF0000000000921C20AC2C56F00d0
d6      phys-grass2:/dev/rdsk/c4t600C0FF0000000000921C20AC2C56F00d0
d7      phys-grass1:/dev/rdsk/c4t600C0FF0000000000921C20AC2C56F04d0
d7      phys-grass2:/dev/rdsk/c4t600C0FF0000000000921C20AC2C56F04d0
d8      phys-grass1:/dev/rdsk/c1t1d0
d9      phys-grass1:/dev/rdsk/c4t600C0FF0000000000921C20AC2C56F05d0
d9      phys-grass2:/dev/rdsk/c4t600C0FF0000000000921C20AC2C56F05d0
d10     phys-grass1:/dev/rdsk/c4t600C0FF0000000000921C20AC2C56F07d0
d10     phys-grass2:/dev/rdsk/c4t600C0FF0000000000921C20AC2C56F07d0
d11     phys-grass1:/dev/rdsk/c1t0d0
d12     phys-grass1:/dev/rdsk/c4t600C0FF0000000000921C20AC2C56F06d0
d12     phys-grass2:/dev/rdsk/c4t600C0FF0000000000921C20AC2C56F06d0
d13     phys-grass2:/dev/rdsk/c1t0d0
d14     phys-grass2:/dev/rdsk/c1t1d0
```

## Creating a Highly Available Oracle 11*g* Release 1 Database

This example uses the cluster shown in Example 8.5 to create a highly available Oracle 11*g* Release 1 database. The Oracle 11*g* Release 1 database is a single-instance database that can be started on one of the cluster nodes at any time. As such, this database is not an Oracle 11*g* Release 1 Real Application Clusters (RAC) database.

The Oracle 11*g* Release 1 software requires the SUNWsprot package to be installed, so if you installed only the Solaris 10 End User software group, you must install the SUNWsprot package from the Solaris 10 media.

Example 8.6 and Figure 8.13 through Figure 8.16 show how to set up and install the Oracle 11*g* software on both nodes. Installing the Oracle software on both cluster nodes, rather than a central shared location, enables you to perform software maintenance with minimal service outages. Service outages are minimized because the Oracle database can be switched over to the node where you are not performing maintenance while you upgrade the software on the other node.

The example also shows how to use a SUNW.gds service to start and stop the Oracle Enterprise Manager database control service.

### Example 8.6   Creating the Oracle User Environment

First, install the additional SUNWsprot package on both nodes.

```
phys-grass1# cd Solaris-10-release_media-directory
phys-grass1# cd Solaris_10/Product
phys-grass1# pkgadd -d . SUNWsprot
        .
        .
        .
```

Create the required Oracle groups on both nodes.

```
phys-grass1# groupadd oinstall
phys-grass1# groupadd dba
phys-grass1# tail -2 /etc/group
oinstall::98194051:
dba::98194052:
```

Check that they are identical on both nodes.

```
phys-grass2# tail -2 /etc/group
oinstall::98194051:
dba::98194052:
```

Create the `oracle` user and set a password on both nodes.

```
phys-grass1# useradd -g oinstall -G dba -m -d /export/home/oracle \
> -s /bin/bash -c "Oracle DBA" oracle
phys-grass1# tail -1 /etc/passwd
oracle:x:238532:98194051:Oracle DBA:/export/home/oracle:/bin/bash
phys-grass1# passwd oracle
New Password:
Re-enter new Password:
passwd: password successfully changed for oracle
```

Create an Oracle base directory on both nodes.

```
phys-grass1# zfs create -o mountpoint=/oracle rpool/oracle
phys-grass1# chown oracle:oinstall /oracle
```

Add more swap space on both nodes, if necessary. For a server with 8 gigabytes of memory, Oracle 11*g* expects 8 gigabytes of swap space.

```
phys-grass1# swap -s
total: 699032k bytes allocated + 229720k reserved = 928752k used, 6824336k available
phys-grass1# zfs create -V 7G rpool/swap1
phys-grass1# swap -a /dev/zvol/dsk/rpool/swap1
```

Add entries to `/etc/vfstab`.

```
phys-grass1# grep swap1 /etc/vfstab
/dev/zvol/dsk/rpool/swap1       -       -       swap    -       no      -
```

You can now log in as the `oracle` user and install the Oracle software only from the Oracle 11*g* Release 1 database release media. You must perform the same steps on both nodes.

```
phys-grass1$ cd Oracle-11g-R1-Database-Media-Directory
phys-grass1$ ./runInstaller
```

See Figure 8.13 through Figure 8.16.

After the software installation is complete, you must run two scripts as the `root` user.

```
phys-grass1# /oracle/app/oraInventory/orainstRoot.sh
Changing permissions of /oracle/app/oraInventory to 770.
Changing groupname of /oracle/app/oraInventory to oinstall.
The execution of the script is complete
```

```
phys-grass1# mkdir -p /usr/local/bin
phys-grass1# /oracle/app/oracle/product/11.1.0/db_1/root.sh
Running Oracle 11g root.sh script...

The following environment variables are set as:
    ORACLE_OWNER= oracle
    ORACLE_HOME=  /oracle/app/oracle/product/11.1.0/db_1

Enter the full pathname of the local bin directory: [/usr/local/bin]:
    Copying dbhome to /usr/local/bin ...
    Copying oraenv to /usr/local/bin ...
    Copying coraenv to /usr/local/bin ...


Creating /var/opt/oracle/oratab file...
Entries will be added to the /var/opt/oracle/oratab file as needed by
Database Configuration Assistant when a database is created
Finished running generic part of root.sh script.
Now product-specific root actions will be performed.
Finished product-specific root actions.
```

Next, you can create the database (see Example 8.7).

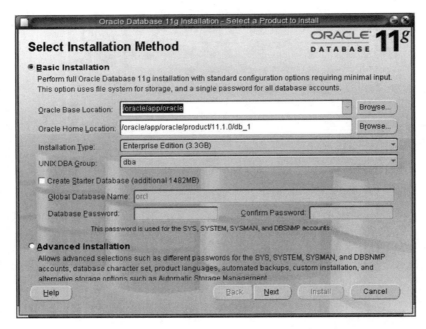

**Figure 8.13** Oracle 11*g* software installation: initial screen

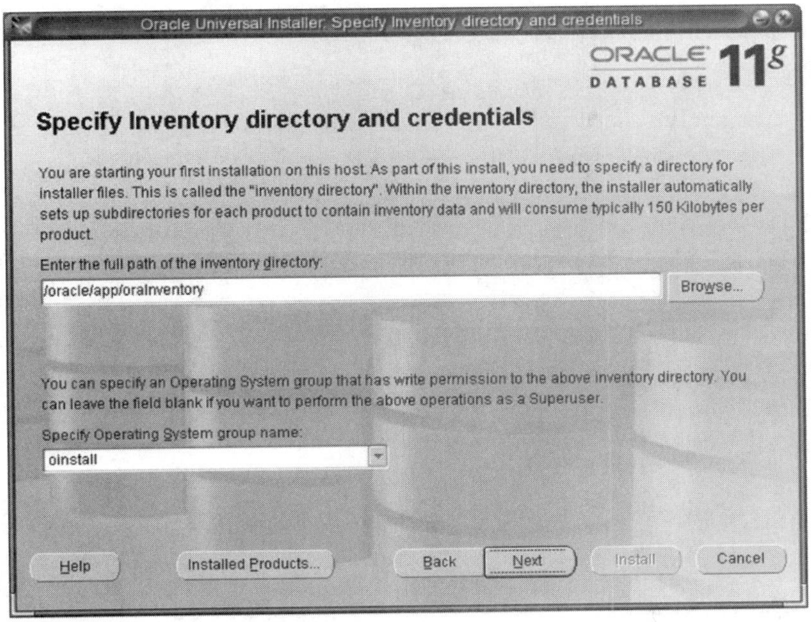

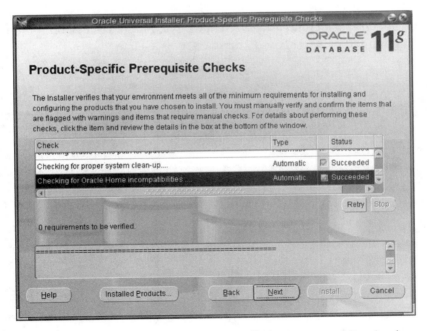

**Figure 8.14** Oracle 11*g* software installation: specifying the inventory location

**Figure 8.15** Oracle 11*g* software installation: prerequisite checks

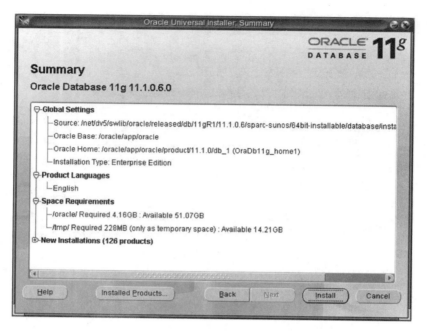

**Figure 8.16** Oracle 11*g* software installation: ready to install the software

The Oracle database created in the following example resides on a failover ZFS file system mounted on `/failover/oracle`.

## Example 8.7  Preparing for the Oracle Database Creation

First, create the zpool that will be used for the failover file system.

These commands need to be run only on one node.

```
phys-grass1# prtvtoc /dev/did/rdsk/d2s2
* /dev/did/rdsk/d2s2 partition map
*
* Dimensions:
*     512 bytes/sector
*      32 sectors/track
*      64 tracks/cylinder
*    2048 sectors/cylinder
*   20480 cylinders
*   20478 accessible cylinders
*
* Flags:
*   1: unmountable
*  10: read-only
*
```

```
*  Unallocated space:
*      First     Sector     Last
*      Sector     Count     Sector
*          0   41938944   41938943
*
*
*                          First     Sector     Last
*  Partition  Tag  Flags   Sector     Count     Sector  Mount Directory
         2      5    00         0   41938944   41938943
phys-grass1# zpool create failover_oracle_zpool /dev/did/dsk/d2s2
phys-grass1# zfs set mountpoint=/failover/oracle failover_oracle_zpool
phys-grass1# df -h /failover/oracle
Filesystem              size   used  avail capacity  Mounted on
failover_oracle_zpool
                         20G    21K   20G     1%     /failover/oracle

phys-grass1# chown oracle:oinstall /failover/oracle
```

Next, create the Oracle resource group.

```
phys-grass1# clresourcegroup create oracle-rg
phys-grass1# clrt list
SUNW.LogicalHostname:3
SUNW.SharedAddress:2
phys-grass1# clresourcetype register SUNW.HAStoragePlus
phys-grass1# clresourcetype register SUNW.oracle_server
phys-grass1# clresourcetype register SUNW.oracle_listener
```

Next, add a logical hostname and IP address to the /etc/inet/hosts file on *both* nodes.

```
phys-grass1# grep oracle-lh /etc/inet/hosts
10.11.112.25    oracle-lh

phys-grass2 # grep oracle-lh /etc/inet/hosts
10.11.112.25    oracle-lh
```

Next, create the Oracle SUNW.LogicalHostname resource. You run this command only on one node.

```
phys-grass1# clreslogicalhostname create -h oracle-lh -g oracle-rg \
> oracle-rs
```

Next, create the Oracle SUNW.HAStoragePlus resource. You run this command only on one node.

```
phys-grass1# clresource create -t SUNW.HAStoragePlus \
> -p zpools=failover_oracle_zpool -g oracle-rg oracle-hasp-rs
```

Next, bring the resource group into the managed and online state.

```
phys-grass1# clresourcegroup online -eM oracle-rg
phys-grass1# ping oracle-lh
oracle-lh is alive
phys-grass1# clresourcegroup status oracle-rg

=== Cluster Resource Groups ===

Group Name      Node Name       Suspended     Status
----------      ---------       ---------     ------
oracle-rg       phys-grass1     No            Online
                phys-grass2     No            Offline
```

As the `oracle` user, create the `listener.ora` and `sqlnet.ora` files on both nodes.
You can create them using the `netca` command. Each `listener.ora` file will initially
contain its own hostname or IP address.

```
phys-grass1$ cat listener.ora
LISTENER_DEMO =
  (DESCRIPTION_LIST =
    (DESCRIPTION =
      (ADDRESS = (PROTOCOL = TCP)(HOST = phys-grass1)(PORT = 1521))
      (ADDRESS = (PROTOCOL = IPC)(KEY = EXTPROC1521))
    )
  )

phys-grass1$ cat sqlnet.ora
NAMES.DIRECTORY_PATH= (TNSNAMES)
```

### Check that the listener is running.

```
phys-grass1$ lsnrctl status LISTENER_DEMO

LSNRCTL for Solaris: Version 11.1.0.6.0 - Production on 14-JAN-2010 01:42:52

Copyright (c) 1991, 2007, Oracle.  All rights reserved.

Connecting to (DESCRIPTION=(ADDRESS=(PROTOCOL=TCP)(HOST=phys-grass1)(PORT=1521)))
STATUS of the LISTENER
------------------------
Alias                     LISTENER_DEMO
Version                   TNSLSNR for Solaris: Version 11.1.0.6.0 - Production
Start Date                14-JAN-2010 01:42:32
Uptime                    0 days 0 hr. 0 min. 20 sec
Trace Level               off
Security                  ON: Local OS Authentication
SNMP                      OFF
Listener Parameter File   /oracle/app/oracle/product/11.1.0/db_1/network/admin/
listener.ora
Listener Log File         /oracle/app/oracle/product/11.1.0/db_1/log/diag/tnslsnr/
phys
-grass1/listener_demo/alert/log.xml
Listening Endpoints Summary...
  (DESCRIPTION=(ADDRESS=(PROTOCOL=tcp)(HOST=phys-grass1)(PORT=1521)))
  (DESCRIPTION=(ADDRESS=(PROTOCOL=ipc)(KEY=EXTPROC1521)))
The listener supports no services
The command completed successfully
```

As the `oracle` user, create the database using the Database Configuration Assistant (`dbca`).
```
phys-grass1$ dbca
```

You can create your database using your preferred method: `dbca`, `sqlplus`, or
through scripts. In this example, the database has an `ORACLE_SID` of `demo`. Figure 8.17 through Figure 8.20 show the key configuration information supplied during the configuration process using the `dbca` program. The other data supplied during the `dbca` configuration process are just the default options.

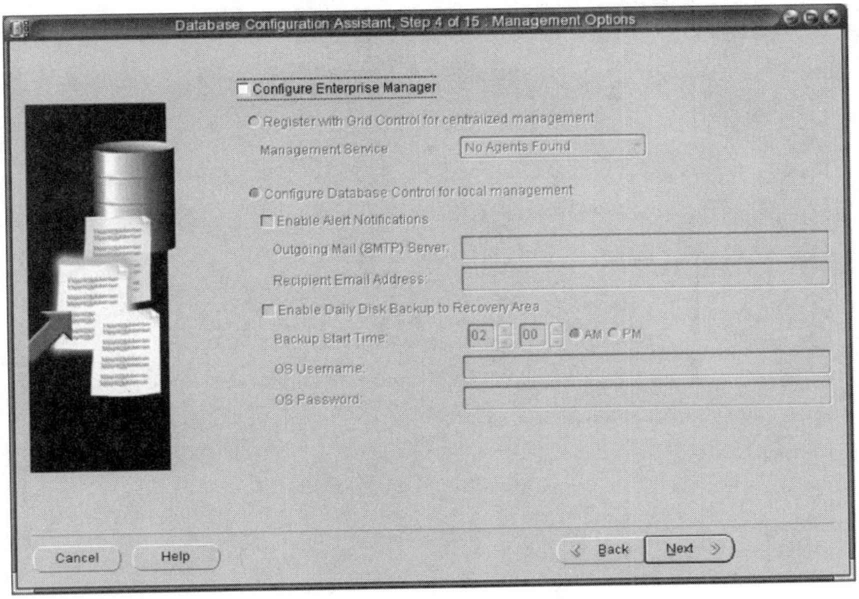

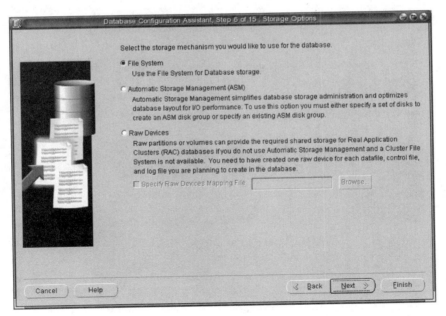

**Figure 8.17** Choosing not to configure Enterprise Manager during the database creation process

**Figure 8.18** Choosing the storage mechanism for the Oracle database

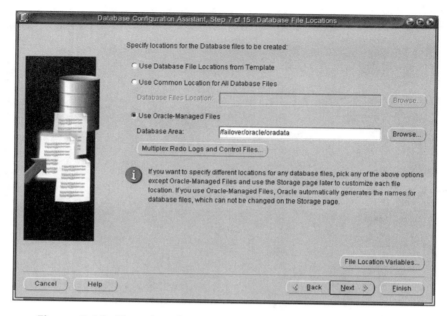

**Figure 8.19** Choosing the location for the Oracle database files

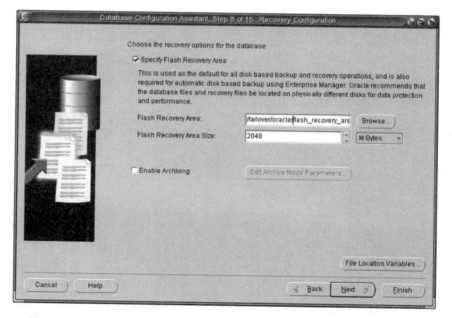

**Figure 8.20** Choosing the recovery option for the Oracle database

When `dbca` has finished, the database is left running. The final steps create the Enterprise Manager database control service, place the Oracle database and listener under the control of the Solaris Cluster software, and create a basic `SUNW.gds` service for the Enterprise Manager database control service.

## Example 8.8  Completing the HA-Oracle Setup

As the `oracle` user on the first node, edit the `tnsnames.ora` file to reference the logical hostname and to add an entry for `LISTENER_DEMO`.

```
phys-grass1$ cd $ORACLE_HOME/network/admin
phys-grass1$ cat tnsnames.ora
DEMO =
  (DESCRIPTION =
    (ADDRESS = (PROTOCOL = TCP)(HOST = oracle-lh)(PORT = 1521))
    (CONNECT_DATA =
      (SERVER = DEDICATED)
      (SERVICE_NAME = demo)
    )
  )

LISTENER_DEMO =
  (DESCRIPTION =
    (ADDRESS = (PROTOCOL = TCP)(HOST = oracle-lh)(PORT = 1521))
  )
```

As the `oracle` user on the second node, copy over the server initialization file, password file, `tnsnames.ora` file, and the `diag` and `admin` directory structure for the "demo" SID.

```
phys-grass2$ cd $ORACLE_HOME/dbs
phys-grass2$ scp -q oracle@phys-grass1:`pwd`/spfiledemo.ora .
Password:
phys-grass2$ scp -q oracle@phys-grass1:`pwd`/orapwdemo .
Password:
phys-grass2$ cd $ORACLE_HOME/network/admin
phys-grass2$ scp -q oracle@phys-grass1:`pwd`/tnsnames.ora .
Password:
phys-grass2$ cd /oracle/app/oracle/diag/rdbms
phys-grass2$ scp -q -r oracle@phys-grass1:/oracle/app/oracle/diag/rdbms/demo .
Password:
phys-grass2$ cd /oracle/app/oracle
phys-grass2$ scp -r -q oracle@phys-grass1:`pwd`/admin .
Password:
```

As the `oracle` user on the second node, add an entry for the database to the `oratab` file.

```
phys-grass2$ grep demo /var/opt/oracle/oratab
demo:/oracle/app/oracle/product/11.1.0/db_1:N
```

As the `oracle` user on the first node, create the database-monitoring user, `hamon`, and set the `local_listener` property to `LISTENER_DEMO`.

```
phys-grass1$ sqlplus '/ as sysdba'

SQL*Plus: Release 11.1.0.6.0 - Production on Wed Jan 13 06:05:03 2010

Copyright (c) 1982, 2007, Oracle.  All rights reserved.


Connected to:
Oracle Database 11g Enterprise Edition Release 11.1.0.6.0 - 64bit Production
With the Partitioning, OLAP, Data Mining and Real Application Testing options

SQL> create user hamon identified by HaMon2010;

User created.

SQL> alter user hamon default tablespace system quota 1m on system;

User altered.

SQL> grant select on v_$sysstat to hamon;

Grant succeeded.

SQL> grant select on v_$archive_dest to hamon;

Grant succeeded.

SQL> grant select on v_$database to hamon;

Grant succeeded.

SQL> grant create session to hamon;

Grant succeeded.

SQL> grant create table to hamon;

Grant succeeded.

SQL> alter system set local_listener=LISTENER_DEMO;

System altered.

SQL> quit
Disconnected from Oracle Database 11g Enterprise Edition Release 11.1.0.6.0 - 64bit
Production
With the Partitioning, OLAP, Data Mining and Real Application Testing options
```

As the `oracle` user on the first node, re-create the Oracle Enterprise Manager database control service using the logical hostname.

```
phys-grass1$ ORACLE_SID=demo export ORACLE_SID
phys-grass1$ ORACLE_HOSTNAME=oracle-lh export ORACLE_HOSTNAME
phys-grass1$ emca -config dbcontrol db -repos recreate

STARTED EMCA at Jan 14, 2010 4:43:02 AM
EM Configuration Assistant, Version 11.1.0.5.0 Production
Copyright (c) 2003, 2005, Oracle.  All rights reserved.

Enter the following information:
Database SID: demo
Listener port number: 1521
```

```
Password for SYS user:
Password for DBSNMP user:
Password for SYSMAN user:
Email address for notifications (optional):
Outgoing Mail (SMTP) server for notifications (optional):
------------------------------------------------------------------
Do you wish to continue? [yes(Y)/no(N)]: Y
Jan 14, 2010 5:43:51 AM oracle.sysman.emcp.EMConfig perform
INFO: This operation is being logged at /oracle/app/oracle/cfgtoollogs/emca/demo/
emca_
2010_01_14_05_43_28.log.
Jan 14, 2010 5:43:54 AM oracle.sysman.emcp.EMReposConfig invoke
INFO: Dropping the EM repository (this may take a while) ...
Jan 14, 2010 5:47:46 AM oracle.sysman.emcp.EMReposConfig invoke
INFO: Repository successfully dropped
Jan 14, 2010 5:47:46 AM oracle.sysman.emcp.EMReposConfig createRepository
INFO: Creating the EM repository (this may take a while) ...
Jan 14, 2010 6:01:16 AM oracle.sysman.emcp.EMReposConfig invoke
INFO: Repository successfully created
Jan 14, 2010 6:01:23 AM oracle.sysman.emcp.EMReposConfig uploadConfigDataToRepository
INFO: Uploading configuration data to EM repository (this may take a while) ...
Jan 14, 2010 6:03:22 AM oracle.sysman.emcp.EMReposConfig invoke
INFO: Uploaded configuration data successfully
Jan 14, 2010 6:03:24 AM oracle.sysman.emcp.util.DBControlUtil configureSoftwareLib
INFO: Software library configured successfully.
Jan 14, 2010 6:03:24 AM oracle.sysman.emcp.EMDBPostConfig configureSoftwareLibrary
INFO: Deploying Provisioning archives ...
Jan 14, 2010 6:03:39 AM oracle.sysman.emcp.EMDBPostConfig configureSoftwareLibrary
INFO: Provisioning archives deployed successfully.
Jan 14, 2010 6:03:39 AM oracle.sysman.emcp.util.DBControlUtil secureDBConsole
INFO: Securing Database Control (this may take a while) ...
Jan 14, 2010 6:03:55 AM oracle.sysman.emcp.util.DBControlUtil secureDBConsole
INFO: Database Control secured successfully.
Jan 14, 2010 6:03:55 AM oracle.sysman.emcp.util.DBControlUtil startOMS
INFO: Starting Database Control (this may take a while) ...
Jan 14, 2010 6:05:15 AM oracle.sysman.emcp.EMDBPostConfig performConfiguration
INFO: Database Control started successfully
Jan 14, 2010 6:05:16 AM oracle.sysman.emcp.EMDBPostConfig performConfiguration
INFO: >>>>>>>>>> The Database Control URL is https://oracle-lh:1158/em <<<<<<<<<<
Jan 14, 2010 6:05:25 AM oracle.sysman.emcp.EMDBPostConfig invoke
WARNING:
************************  WARNING  ************************

Management Repository has been placed in secure mode wherein Enterprise Manager data
will be encrypted.  The encryption key has been placed in the file: /oracle/app/oracle
/product/11.1.0/db_1/oracle-lh_demo/sysman/config/emkey.ora.   Please ensure this file
is backed up as the encrypted data will become unusable if this file is lost.


*************************************************************
Enterprise Manager configuration completed successfully
FINISHED EMCA at Jan 14, 2010 6:05:25 AM
```

As the `oracle` user, stop the Enterprise Manager database control service on the first node.

```
phys-grass1$ ORACLE_SID=demo export ORACLE_SID
phys-grass1$ emctl stop dbconsole
Oracle Enterprise Manager 11g Database Control Release 11.1.0.6.0
Copyright (c) 1996, 2007 Oracle Corporation.  All rights reserved.
https://phys-grass1:1158/em/console/aboutApplication
Stopping Oracle Enterprise Manager 11g Database Control ...
 ... Stopped.
```

As the `oracle` user on both nodes, change the `listener.ora` file to add the logical hostname to the addresses on which the listener listens.

```
phys-grass2$ cat $ORACLE_HOME/network/admin/listener.ora
# listener.ora Network Configuration File: /oracle/app/oracle/product/11.1.0/db_1/
network/admin/listener.ora
# Generated by Oracle configuration tools.

LISTENER_DEMO =
  (DESCRIPTION_LIST =
    (DESCRIPTION =
      (ADDRESS = (PROTOCOL = TCP)(HOST = phys-grass2)(PORT = 1521))
      (ADDRESS = (PROTOCOL = TCP)(HOST = oracle-lh)(PORT = 1521))
      (ADDRESS = (PROTOCOL = IPC)(KEY = EXTPROC1521))
    )
  )
```

On one node, as the `root` user, create the Solaris Cluster resource for the listener and the database.

```
phys-grass1# clresource create -t SUNW.oracle_listener -g oracle-rg \
> -p ORACLE_HOME=/oracle/app/oracle/product/11.1.0/db_1 \
> -p LISTENER_NAME=LISTENER_DEMO \
> -p resource_dependencies=oracle-hasp-rs oracle-lsnr-rs

phys-grass1# clresource create -t SUNW.oracle_server -g oracle-rg \
> -p ORACLE_HOME=/oracle/app/oracle/product/11.1.0/db_1 \
> -p ORACLE_SID=demo \
> -p Alert_log_file=/oracle/app/oracle/diag/rdbms/demo/demo/trace/alert_demo.log \
> -p resource_dependencies=oracle-hasp-rs \
> -p connect_string=hamon/HaMon2010 oracle-svr-rs
```

As the `root` user on both nodes, create the script that will be used to start and stop the Enterprise Manager database control service.

```
phys-grass1# cat /usr/local/bin/em_gds.ksh
#!/bin/ksh
/bin/su oracle -c "ORACLE_SID=demo export ORACLE_SID; \
    ORACLE_HOME=/oracle/app/oracle/product/11.1.0/db_1 \
    export ORACLE_HOME; PATH=\$PATH:\$ORACLE_HOME/bin: \
    export PATH; ORACLE_HOSTNAME=oracle-lh \
    export ORACLE_HOSTNAME; emctl $1 dbconsole"
phys-grass1# chmod +x /usr/local/bin/em_gds.ksh
```

As the `root` user on either node, register the `SUNW.gds` resource type and create a resource (initially disabled) to stop and start the Enterprise Manager database control service, and then switch the resource group to the second node.

```
phys-grass1# clresourcetype register SUNW.gds
phys-grass1# clresource create -d -t SUNW.gds -g oracle-rg
> -p resource_dependencies=oracle-svr-rs -p Network_aware=false \
> -p Start_command="/usr/local/bin/em_gds.ksh start" \
> -p Stop_command="/usr/local/bin/em_gds.ksh stop" oracle-dbcon-rs

phys-grass2# clresourcegroup switch -n phys-grass2 oracle-rg
phys-grass2# clresource status
```

```
=== Cluster Resources ===

Resource Name         Node Name      State      Status Message
-------------         ---------      -----      --------------
oracle-rs             phys-grass1    Offline    Offline - LogicalHostname offline.
                      phys-grass2    Online     Online - LogicalHostname online.
oracle-hasp-rs        phys-grass1    Offline    Offline
                      phys-grass2    Online     Online

oracle-lsnr-rs        phys-grass1    Offline    Offline
                      phys-grass2    Online     Online

oracle-svr-rs         phys-grass1    Offline    Offline
                      phys-grass2    Online     Online

oracle-dbcon-rs       phys-grass1    Offline    Offline
                      phys-grass2    Offline    Offline
```

As the `oracle` user on the second node, re-create the Enterprise Manager database control service, again using the logical hostname. When complete, stop the database control service.

```
phys-grass2$ ORACLE_SID=demo export ORACLE_SID
phys-grass2$ ORACLE_HOSTNAME=oracle-lh export ORACLE_HOSTNAME
phys-grass2$ emca -config dbcontrol db -repos recreate
STARTED EMCA at Jan 14, 2010 7:52:11 AM
EM Configuration Assistant, Version 11.1.0.5.0 Production
Copyright (c) 2003, 2005, Oracle.  All rights reserved.

Enter the following information:
Database SID: demo
Listener port number: 1521
Password for SYS user:
Password for DBSNMP user:
Password for SYSMAN user:
Email address for notifications (optional):
Outgoing Mail (SMTP) server for notifications (optional):
----------------------------------------------------------------
Do you wish to continue? [yes(Y)/no(N)]: Y
      .
      .
      .
Jan 14, 2010 8:14:49 AM oracle.sysman.emcp.EMDBPostConfig invoke
WARNING:
************************  WARNING  ************************

Management Repository has been placed in secure mode wherein Enterprise Manager data
will be encrypted.  The encryption key has been placed in the file: /oracle/app/oracle
/product/11.1.0/db_1/oracle-lh_demo/sysman/config/emkey.ora.   Please ensure this file
 is backed up as the encrypted data will become unusable if this file is lost.

**********************************************************
Enterprise Manager configuration completed successfully
FINISHED EMCA at Jan 14, 2010 8:14:49 AM

phys-grass2$ emctl stop dbconsole
Oracle Enterprise Manager 11g Database Control Release 11.1.0.6.0
Copyright (c) 1996, 2007 Oracle Corporation.  All rights reserved.
https://oracle-lh:1158/em/console/aboutApplication
Stopping Oracle Enterprise Manager 11g Database Control ...
 ... Stopped.
```

As the `oracle` user on the first node, copy the re-created `emkey.ora` file from the second node.

```
phys-grass1$ cd $ORACLE_HOME/oracle-1h_demo/sysman/config
phys-grass1$ scp -q oracle@phys-grass2:`pwd`/emkey.ora .
```

As the `root` user on either node, enable the Enterprise Manager database control resource, and then switch the resource group to the other node.

```
phys-grass2# clresource enable oracle-dbcon-rs
phys-grass2# clresourcegroup switch -n phys-grass1 oracle-rg
```

If you install the Oracle software binaries in a single, central location, then fewer steps are required to synchronize some of the additional configuration files. Furthermore, if you enable redo log archiving, you must choose a location on the failover file system you created.

## Setting Up Solaris Cluster Telemetry

This example uses the Oracle database resource group created in Example 8.8. The example shows how telemetry can be set up on a Solaris Cluster system and then used to capture telemetry data for CPU and memory usage for a specific resource group, in this case the Oracle resource group. The example also demonstrates how thresholds can be set up.

### Example 8.9  Setting Up Telemetry on a Solaris Cluster System

First, check the layout of the chosen disk. Because a non–Solaris Volume Manager device will be used, the `/dev/global` device must be used instead of the `/dev/did` device.

```
phys-grass1# prtvtoc /dev/global/rdsk/d3s2
* /dev/global/rdsk/d3s2 partition map
*
* Dimensions:
*     512 bytes/sector
*      32 sectors/track
*      64 tracks/cylinder
*    2048 sectors/cylinder
*   20480 cylinders
*   20478 accessible cylinders
*
* Flags:
*   1: unmountable
*   10: read-only
*
```

```
* Unallocated space:
*       First    Sector    Last
*       Sector   Count     Sector
*          0    41938944  41938943
*
*                          First     Sector    Last
* Partition  Tag  Flags    Sector    Count     Sector   Mount Directory
      2       5    00          0    41938944  41938943
```

Next, create a UFS file system.

```
phys-grass1# newfs /dev/global/rdsk/d3s2
newfs: construct a new file system /dev/global/rdsk/d3s2: (y/n)? y
/dev/global/rdsk/d3s2:  41938944 sectors in 6826 cylinders of 48 tracks, 128 sectors
        20478.0MB in 427 cyl groups (16 c/g, 48.00MB/g, 5824 i/g)
super-block backups (for fsck -F ufs -o b=#) at:
 32, 98464, 196896, 295328, 393760, 492192, 590624, 689056, 787488, 885920,
Initializing cylinder groups:
.......
super-block backups for last 10 cylinder groups at:
 40997024, 41095456, 41193888, 41292320, 41390752, 41489184, 41587616,
 41686048, 41784480, 41882912
```

Create the mount point on both nodes.

```
phys-grass1# mkdir /telemetry
phys-grass2# mkdir /telemetry
```

Add the mount entries to the `/etc/vfstab` file on both nodes. Check that they are consistent.

```
phys-grass1# grep /telemetry /etc/vfstab
/dev/global/dsk/d3s2    /dev/global/rdsk/d3s2   /telemetry      ufs     -       no
  logging
phys-grass2# grep /telemetry /etc/vfstab
/dev/global/dsk/d3s2    /dev/global/rdsk/d3s2   /telemetry      ufs     -       no
  logging
```

Create the resource group that will hold the telemetry storage resource.

```
phys-grass1# clresourcegroup create telemetry-rg
```

Create the telemetry storage resource.

```
phys-grass1# clresource create -t SUNW.HAStoragePlus \
> -p FileSystemMountPoints=/telemetry -g telemetry-rg telemetry-hasp-rs
```

Bring the resource group online.

```
phys-grass1# clresourcegroup online -eM telemetry-rg
```

Run `clsetup` to set up Solaris Cluster telemetry.

```
phys-grass1# clsetup

  *** Main Menu ***
```

```
        Please select from one of the following options:

            1) Quorum
            2) Resource groups
            3) Data Services
            4) Cluster interconnect
            5) Device groups and volumes
            6) Private hostnames
            7) New nodes
            8) Other cluster tasks

            ?) Help with menu options
            q) Quit
         Option:  8
```

```
*** Other Cluster Tasks Menu ***

        Please select from one of the following options:

            1) Change the name of the cluster
            2) Configure Telemetry

            ?) Help
            q) Return to the Main Menu

         Option:  2
```

```
>>> Configure Cluster Telemetry <<<

        This wizard creates resources and resource groups required for cluster
        telemetry. In addition, a database used to store telemetry data is
        installed in the location you specify.

        In order to successfully configure telemetry for this cluster, you
        must have already done the following:

         * Configured a file system for the database.
         * Created an HA Storage Plus resource for that file system.

        Is it okay to continue (yes/no) [yes]? yes

        Which HA Storage Plus resource would you like to use?
            1) telemetry-hasp-rs
            2) oracle-hasp-rs
         Option: 1

        The following mount points are accessible from the HA Storage Plus resource.
    Select the one you want to use for the database :

            1) /telemetry

         Option:  1
```

```
*** Summary ***

        The following Sun Cluster configuration will now be created. If you
```

```
     want to modify the configuration to be created, select the property
     you want to change.

         1) HA Storage Plus resource              telemetry-hasp-rs
         X) HA Storage Plus resource group        telemetry-rg
         2) Mount point                           /telemetry
         3) Telemetry database resource group     cl-db-rg
         4) Telemetry database resource           cl-db-rs
         5) Telemetry resource group              cl-tlmtry-rg
         6) Telemetry resource                    cl-tlmtry-rs
         c) Configure with current values
         q) Return to the Other Cluster Tasks Menu
      Option:  c

      Is it okay to proceed with the update (yes/no) [yes]? yes

/usr/cluster/lib/rgm/rt/sctelemetry/sctelemetry -i -o hasp_mnt_pt=/telemetry,hasp_rg=
telemetry-rg,hasp_rs=telemetry-hasp-rs,db_rg=cl-db-rg,db_rs=cl-db-rs,telemetry_rg=cl-
tlmtry-rg,telemetry_rs=cl-tlmtry-rs

      Command completed successfully.


Press Enter to continue:
```

Quit from `clsetup`.

List the telemetry attributes available.

```
phys-grass1# cltelemetryattribute list -v
Telemetry Attribute   Object Type
-------------------   -----------
rbyte.rate            disk
wbyte.rate            disk
write.rate            disk
read.rate             disk
mem.used              resourcegroup
swap.used             resourcegroup
cpu.used              resourcegroup
cpu.idle              node
cpu.iowait            node
cpu.used              node
cpu.loadavg.1mn       node
cpu.loadavg.5mn       node
cpu.loadavg.15mn      node
mem.used              node
mem.free              node
swap.used             node
swap.free             node
wbyte.rate            netif
rbyte.rate            netif
ipacket.rate          netif
opacket.rate          netif
cpu.idle              zone
```

Next, bring offline the Oracle resource group created in Example 8.8.

```
phys-grass1# clresourcegroup offline oracle-rg
```

Check the `RG_slm_type` property value.

```
phys-grass1# clresourcegroup show -p RG_slm_type oracle-rg
```

```
=== Resource Groups and Resources ===

Resource Group:                         oracle-rg
  RG_SLM_type:                          manual
```

Set the `RG_slm_type` property value to `automated`.

```
phys-grass1# clresourcegroup set \
>    -p RG_slm_type=automated oracle-rg
```

Enable telemetry collection on CPU and memory usage.

```
phys-grass1# cltelemetryattribute enable \
> -t resourcegroup cpu.used mem.used
```

Bring the Oracle resource group online.

```
phys-grass1# clresourcegroup online oracle-rg
```

Print the collected telemetry information for the Oracle resource group only.

```
phys-grass1# cltelemetryattribute  -d  2010-01-15T05:34+ -b oracle-rg
```

| Date | Instance | Type | Attribute | Node | Value |
|------|----------|------|-----------|------|-------|
| Fri Jan 15 05:34:47 PST 2010 0641.218750 MBytes | oracle-rg | resourcegroup | mem.used | phys-grass1 | 3 |
| Fri Jan 15 05:35:47 PST 2010 0637.757812 MBytes | oracle-rg | resourcegroup | mem.used | phys-grass1 | 3 |
| Fri Jan 15 05:36:47 PST 2010 0638.476562 MBytes | oracle-rg | resourcegroup | mem.used | phys-grass1 | 3 |
| Fri Jan 15 05:37:47 PST 2010 0637.648438 MBytes | oracle-rg | resourcegroup | mem.used | phys-grass1 | 3 |
| Fri Jan 15 05:34:47 PST 2010 .020000 CPUs | oracle-rg | resourcegroup | cpu.used | phys-grass1 | 0 |
| Fri Jan 15 05:35:47 PST 2010 .030000 CPUs | oracle-rg | resourcegroup | cpu.used | phys-grass1 | 0 |
| Fri Jan 15 05:36:47 PST 2010 .010000 CPUs | oracle-rg | resourcegroup | cpu.used | phys-grass1 | 0 |
| Fri Jan 15 05:37:47 PST 2010 .010000 CPUs | oracle-rg | resourcegroup | cpu.used | phys-grass1 | 0 |

Set a threshold on the CPU usage of the Oracle resource group.

```
phys-grass1# cltelemetryattribute set-threshold -t resourcegroup \
> -b oracle-rg -p severity=warning,direction=rising,value=0.2 cpu.used
```

Check the status of the Oracle resource group.

```
phys-grass1# cltelemetryattribute status -b oracle-rg
```

| Instance | Type | Attribute | Node | Value | Status |
|----------|------|-----------|------|-------|--------|
| oracle-rg | resourcegroup | cpu.used | phys-grass1 | 0.020000 CPUs | ok |

Perform some database work.

```
phys-grass2# su - oracle
Sun Microsystems Inc.   SunOS 5.10      Generic January 2005
phys-grass2$ sqlplus sys/oracle@demo as sysdba

SQL*Plus: Release 11.1.0.6.0 - Production on Fri Jan 15 05:47:43 2010

Copyright (c) 1982, 2007, Oracle.  All rights reserved.


Connected to:
Oracle Database 11g Enterprise Edition Release 11.1.0.6.0 - 64bit Production
With the Partitioning, OLAP, Data Mining and Real Application Testing options

SQL> create table foo ( bar char(20) );

Table created.

SQL> insert into foo values ( 'hello world' );

1 row created.

SQL> insert into foo select * from foo;

1 row created.

SQL> /
(repeat as necessary)

SQL> quit
Disconnected from Oracle Database 11g Enterprise Edition Release 11.1.0.6.0 - 64bit
Production
With the Partitioning, OLAP, Data Mining and Real Application Testing options


phys-grass1# cltelemetryattribute status -b oracle-rg

Instance    Type         Attribute    Node          Value          Status
--------    ----         ---------    ----          -----          ------
oracle-rg   resourcegroup cpu.used    phys-grass1   0.530000 CPUs  warning
```

The CPU load generated at the end of the example can be graphed using Solaris Cluster Manager, as shown in Figure 8.21.

# Creating a Scalable Web Service Using Global-Cluster Non-Voting Nodes

The following example creates a scalable Sun Java System Web Server service that runs in non-global zones. One non-global zone is configured on each of the cluster nodes. Non-global zone lzgrass1a is configured on phys-grass1, and lzgrass2a is configured on phys-grass2.

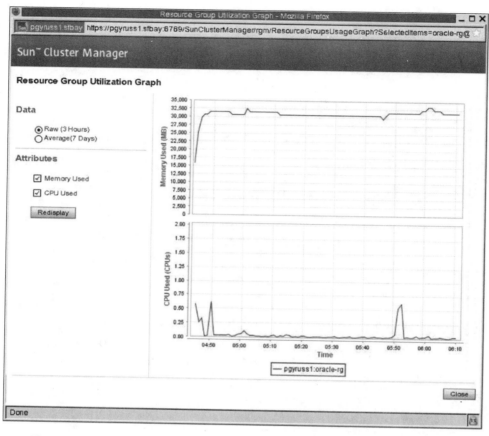

**Figure 8.21** Displaying the telemetry data collected for the `oracle-rg` resource group

## Example 8.10  Creating Zones for the Web Servers

First, add the zone IP addresses to the `/etc/inet/hosts` file on all cluster nodes.

```
phys-grass1# grep grass /etc/hosts
10.11.112.44     lzgrass1a     # hostname for NGZ phys-grass1
10.11.112.38     lzgrass2a     # hostname for NGZ phys-grass2
```

Next, create a separate ZFS file system for the zones.

```
phys-grass1# zfs create -o mountpoint=/zones rpool/zones
```

As the `root` user, create the `lzgrass1a` non-global zone on `phys-grass1` and the `lzgrass2a` non-global zone on `phys-grass2`.

```
phys-grass1# zonecfg -z lzgrass1a
lzgrass1a: No such zone configured
Use 'create' to begin configuring a new zone.
zonecfg:lzgrass1a> create
zonecfg:lzgrass1a> set zonepath=/zones/lzgrass1a
zonecfg:lzgrass1a> add net
zonecfg:lzgrass1a:net> set address=lzgrass1a/24
zonecfg:lzgrass1a:net> set physical=bge0
zonecfg:lzgrass1a:net> set defrouter=10.11.112.1
zonecfg:lzgrass1a:net> end
zonecfg:lzgrass1a> set autoboot=true
zonecfg:lzgrass1a> commit
zonecfg:lzgrass1a> exit
phys-grass1# zoneadm -z lzgrass1a install
A ZFS file system has been created for this zone.
Preparing to install zone <lzgrass1a>.
Creating list of files to copy from the global zone.
Copying <10196> files to the zone.
Initializing zone product registry.
Determining zone package initialization order.
Preparing to initialize <958> packages on the zone.
Initialized <958> packages on zone.
Zone <lzgrass1a> is initialized.
Installation of <1> packages was skipped.
The file </zones/lzgrass1a/root/var/sadm/system/logs/install_log> contains a log of
the zone installation.

phys-grass2# zonecfg -z lzgrass2a
lzgrass2a: No such zone configured
Use 'create' to begin configuring a new zone.
zonecfg:lzgrass2a> create
zonecfg:lzgrass2a> set zonepath=/zones/lzgrass2a
zonecfg:lzgrass2a> add net
zonecfg:lzgrass2a:net> set address=lzgrass2a/24
zonecfg:lzgrass2a:net> set physical=bge0
zonecfg:lzgrass2a:net> set defrouter=10.11.112.1
zonecfg:lzgrass2a:net> end
zonecfg:lzgrass2a> set autoboot=true
zonecfg:lzgrass2a> commit
zonecfg:lzgrass2a> exit
phys-grass2# zoneadm -z lzgrass2a install
A ZFS file system has been created for this zone.
Preparing to install zone <lzgrass2a>.
Creating list of files to copy from the global zone.
Copying <10196> files to the zone.
Initializing zone product registry.
Determining zone package initialization order.
Preparing to initialize <958> packages on the zone.
Initialized <958> packages on zone.
Zone <lzgrass2a> is initialized.
Installation of <1> packages was skipped.
The file </zones/lzgrass2a/root/var/sadm/system/logs/install_log> contains a log of
the zone installation.
```

Boot both zones.

```
phys-grass1# zoneadm -z lzgrass1a boot

phys-grass2# zoneadm -z lzgrass2a boot
```

Use zlogin to log in to and configure the zones.

```
phys-grass1# zlogin -C lzgrass1a
         .
         .
         .
rebooting system due to change(s) in /etc/default/init

[NOTICE: Zone rebooting]

phys-grass2# zlogin -C lzgrass2a
         .
         .
         .
rebooting system due to change(s) in /etc/default/init

[NOTICE: Zone rebooting]
```

Create the resource group to hold the shared address.

```
phys-grass1# clrg create \
> -n phys-grass1:lzgrass1a,phys-grass2:lzgrass2a web-svr-sa-rg
```

Create the shared address resource using the hostname `tgrass1-0a`.

```
phys-grass1# clrssa create -g web-svr-sa-rg \
>    -h tgrass1-0a web-svr-sa-rs
```

Bring the shared address resource group into the online and managed state.

```
phys-grass1# clrg online -eM web-svr-sa-rg
```

Create a file system that will be mounted globally to hold the web server binaries and data.

```
phys-grass1# newfs /dev/global/rdsk/d4s2
newfs: construct a new file system /dev/global/rdsk/d4s2: (y/n)? y
/dev/global/rdsk/d4s2:  41938944 sectors in 6826 cylinders of 48 tracks, 128 sectors
        20478.0MB in 427 cyl groups (16 c/g, 48.00MB/g, 5824 i/g)
super-block backups (for fsck -F ufs -o b=#) at:
 32, 98464, 196896, 295328, 393760, 492192, 590624, 689056, 787488, 885920,
Initializing cylinder groups:
........
super-block backups for last 10 cylinder groups at:
 40997024, 41095456, 41193888, 41292320, 41390752, 41489184, 41587616,
 41686048, 41784480, 41882912
```

Add entries to the global zone `/etc/vfstab` files on both nodes.

```
phys-grass1# grep /global/websvr /etc/vfstab
/dev/global/dsk/d4s2    /dev/global/rdsk/d4s2   /global/websvr ufs    -      no
  global,logging
```

Create the mount points for `/global/websvr` in the global zone on both nodes.

```
phys-grass1# mkdir -p /global/websvr
```

Create the mount points for `/global/websvr` in the non-global zone on both nodes.

```
lzgrass1a # mkdir -p /global/websvr
```

Create a scalable resource group to hold the file system and web server resources.

```
phys-grass1# clrg create \
> -n phys-grass1:lzgrass1a,phys-grass2:lzgrass2a \
> -p maximum_primaries=2 -p desired_primaries=2 web-svr-rg
```

Create the SUNW.HAStoragePlus resource that performs the loopback mount of the global file system in the non-global zones. In this case, the loopback mount mounts the file system at the same location in the zone.

```
phys-grass1# clrs create -g web-svr-rg -t SUNW.HAStoragePlus \
> -p FileSystemMountPoints=/global/websvr:/global/websvr \
> web-svr-hasp-rs
```

Bring the resource group into the online and managed state.

```
phys-grass1# clrg online -eM web-svr-rg
```

Check the status of the web-svr-sa-rg and web-svr-rg resource groups.

```
phys-grass1# clrg status web-svr-sa-rg web-svr-rg

=== Cluster Resource Groups ===

Group Name      Node Name             Suspended    Status
----------      ---------             ---------    ------
web-svr-sa-rg   phys-grass1:lzgrass1a    No        Online
                phys-grass2:lzgrass2a    No        Offline

web-svr-rg      phys-grass1:lzgrass1a    No        Online
                phys-grass2:lzgrass2a    No        Online
```

Check that the file system is mounted in each zone.

```
lzgrass1a# df -h /global/websvr
Filesystem              size   used   avail capacity  Mounted on
/global/websvr          20G    20M    19G     1%      /global/websvr
```

Create a document root (docroot) for the web server.

```
lzgrass1a# mkdir -p /global/websvr/docroot
```

Create a cgi-bin directory.

```
lzgrass1a# mkdir -p /global/websvr/cgi-bin
```

Create a shell script called host.sh in the /global/websvr/cgi-bin directory, and then make the script executable.

```
lzgrass1a# cat /global/websvr/cgi-bin/host.sh
#!/bin/ksh
/bin/cat << EOF
Content-type: text/html

<html>
        <body>The server host was $( /bin/uname -n ).</body>
</html>
EOF
lzgrass1a# chmod +x /global/websvr/cgi-bin/host.sh
```

In both zones, create a directory to store the web server `logs` and `error` files, and then change the owner and group of the directory to user `nobody`.

```
lzgrass1a # mkdir -p /var/sjsws/tgrass1-0a/logs
lzgrass1a # chown nobody:nobody /var/sjsws/tgrass1-0a/logs
```

In both zones, create the access log file and set the permissions on the file.

```
lzgrass1a# touch /var/sjsws/tgrass1-0a/logs/access
lzgrass1a# chown webservd:webservd /var/sjsws/tgrass1-0a/logs/access
```

Next, you can install the Sun Java System Web Server software from one of the non-global zones. Figure 8.22 through Figure 8.26 show the key choices to make during the installation process.

The software is installed in a directory (`/global/websvr/webserver7`) in the global file system.

To enable greater flexibility with your installation options, choose to perform a custom installation. When you are prompted for the administration options (see Figure 8.24), choose to create an administration server and a web server instance.

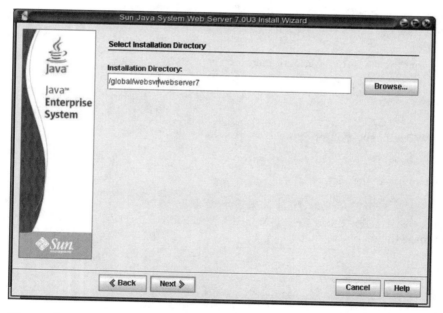

**Figure 8.22** Choosing the installation directory for the Sun Java System Web Server software

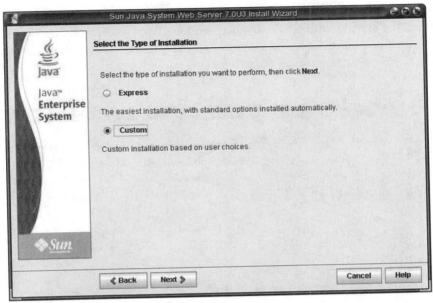

**Figure 8.23** Choosing to perform a custom Sun Java System Web Server installation

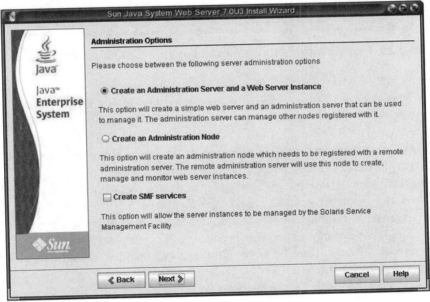

**Figure 8.24** Creating a Sun Java System Administration Server and Web Server instance

When you supply the hostname for the administration server and the web server, use the shared address that you specified when creating the `web-svr-sa-rg` resource group. In this case, the hostname you provide should be fully qualified, that is, `tgrass1-0a.example.com`.

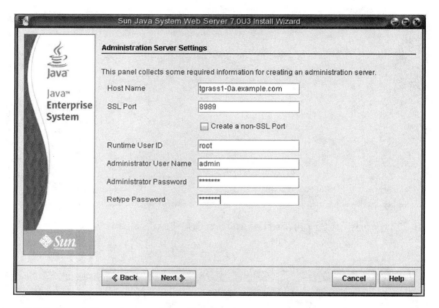

**Figure 8.25** Providing the settings for the Sun Java System Administration Server

When you provide the `docroot` property for the web server, ensure that the directory given is on the global file system. In this example, `/global/websvr/docroot` is used.

After the software is installed, connect to the Sun Java System Web Server administration console using the URL https://tgrass1-0a:8989.

Figure 8.27 shows the changes required to direct the web server log and access log files to the local directories created in Example 8.10. Figure 8.28 shows the changes required to enable the web server to access the shell script in the `/global/websvr/cgi-bin` directory that was created in Example 8.10.

Both sets of changes must be saved and deployed before you can create the web server resource in Example 8.11.

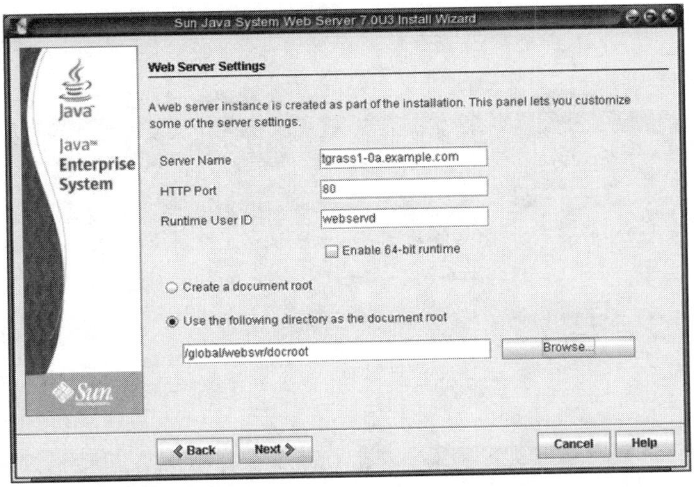

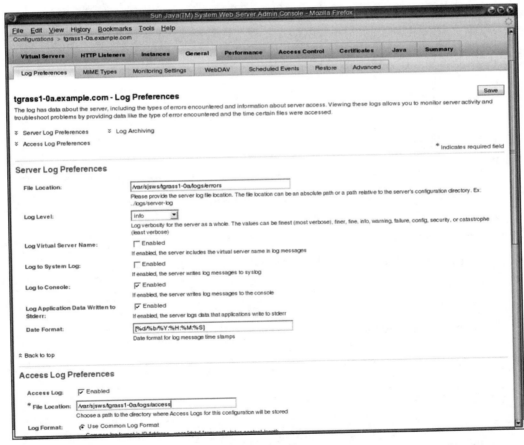

**Figure 8.26** Providing the settings for the Sun Java System Web Server instance

**Figure 8.27** Configuring the server log and access log file locations for the Sun Java System Web Server

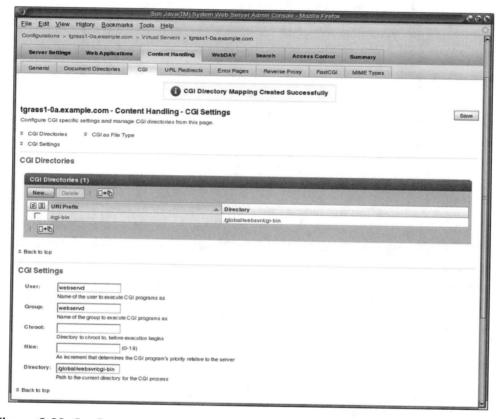

**Figure 8.28** Configuring the Sun Java System Web Server `cgi-bin` directory settings

## Example 8.11   Completing the Web Server Configuration

Register the `SUNW.iws` resource type.

```
phys-grass1# clrt register SUNW.iws
```

Create the Sun Java System Web Server resource.

```
phys-grass1# clrs create -g web-svr-rg -t SUNW.iws \
> -p confdir_list=/global/websvr/webserver7/https-tgrass1-0a.example.com \
> -p scalable=true \
> -p resource_dependencies=web-svr-hasp-rs,web-svr-sa-rs \
> -p port_list=80/tcp \
> web-svr-rs
```

Because the `web-svr-rg` resource group is already online, the web servers are started immediately.

Obtain the status for the resources in both the `web-svr-sa-rg` and `web-svr-rg` resource groups.

```
phys-grass1# clrs status -g web-svr-sa-rg,web-svr-rg

=== Cluster Resources ===

Resource Name       Node Name            State     Status Message
-------------       ---------            -----     --------------
web-svr-sa-rs       phys-grass1:lzgrass1a Online   Online - SharedAddress online.
                    phys-grass2:lzgrass2a Offline  Offline

web-svr-hasp-rs     phys-grass1:lzgrass1a Online   Online
                    phys-grass2:lzgrass2a Online   Online

web-svr-rs          phys-grass1:lzgrass1a Online   Online - Service is online.
                    phys-grass2:lzgrass2a Online   Online - Service is online.
```

From a non-cluster node, check your web server load balancing using the `wget` command.

```
client-ws # /usr/sfw/bin/wget -q -O - \
> http://tgrass1-0a.example.com/cgi-bin/host.sh
<html>
        <body>The server host was lzgrass1a.</body>
</html>
client-ws # /usr/sfw/bin/wget -q -O - \
> http://tgrass1-0a.example.com/cgi-bin/host.sh
<html>
        <body>The server host was lzgrass2a.</body>
</html>
```

Disable the web server on one node, and try the command again.

```
phys-grass1# clrs disable -n phys-grass1:lzgrass1a web-svr-rs
```

This results in the same response each time.

```
client-ws # /usr/sfw/bin/wget -q -O - \
> http://tgrass1-0a.example.com/cgi-bin/host.sh
<html>
        <body>The server host was lzgrass2a.</body>
</html>
client-ws # /usr/sfw/bin/wget -q -O - \
> http://tgrass1-0a.example.com/cgi-bin/host.sh
<html>
        <body>The server host was lzgrass2a.</body>
</html>
```

# Creating an HA-Oracle Database Instance in a Zone Cluster

In this example, a highly available Oracle database instance is created. The Oracle database data and binaries are stored on a highly available zpool, rather than on the individual zone-cluster nodes.

## Example 8.12  Creating a Zone Cluster

From the global zone of either cluster node, create the zone cluster using the `clzc` command. When supplying the `root_password` property, you must provide a pre-encrypted entry. For example, you could take this entry from a user in an existing `/etc/shadow` file.

```
phys-grass1# clzc configure oracle-zc
oracle-zc: No such zone cluster configured
Use 'create' to begin configuring a new zone cluster.
clzc:oracle-zc> create
clzc:oracle-zc> set zonepath=/zones/oracle-zc
clzc:oracle-zc> set autoboot=true
clzc:oracle-zc> add node
clzc:oracle-zc:node> set physical-host=phys-grass1
clzc:oracle-zc:node> set hostname=lzgrass1b
clzc:oracle-zc:node> add net
clzc:oracle-zc:node:net> set address=lzgrass1b/24
clzc:oracle-zc:node:net> set physical=bge0
clzc:oracle-zc:node:net> end
clzc:oracle-zc:node> end
clzc:oracle-zc> add node
clzc:oracle-zc:node> set physical-host=phys-grass2
clzc:oracle-zc:node> set hostname=lzgrass2b
clzc:oracle-zc:node> add net
clzc:oracle-zc:node:net> set address=lzgrass2b/24
clzc:oracle-zc:node:net> set physical=bge0
clzc:oracle-zc:node:net> end
clzc:oracle-zc:node> end
clzc:oracle-zc> add sysid
clzc:oracle-zc:sysid> set system_locale=C
clzc:oracle-zc:sysid> set terminal=dtterm
clzc:oracle-zc:sysid> set security_policy=NONE
clzc:oracle-zc:sysid> set name_service="NIS{domain_name=dev.example.com name_server=ni
ssvr(10.11.112.4)}"
clzc:oracle-zc:sysid> set root_password=*********
clzc:oracle-zc:sysid> set timezone=US/Pacific
clzc:oracle-zc:sysid> set nfs4_domain=dynamic
clzc:oracle-zc:sysid> end
clzc:oracle-zc> set limitpriv=default,proc_priocntl
clzc:oracle-zc> set max-shm-memory=4294967296
clzc:oracle-zc> add capped-cpu
clzc:oracle-zc:capped-cpu> set ncpus=1
clzc:oracle-zc:capped-cpu> end
clzc:oracle-zc> commit
clzc:oracle-zc> exit

phys-grass1# clzc install oracle-zc
Waiting for zone install commands to complete on all the nodes of the zone cluster
"oracle-zc"...
A ZFS file system has been created for this zone.
Preparing to install zone <oracle-zc>.
Creating list of files to copy from the global zone.
Copying <10196> files to the zone.
Initializing zone product registry.
Determining zone package initialization order.
Preparing to initialize <958> packages on the zone.
Initialized <958> packages on zone.
Zone <oracle-zc> is initialized.
Installation of <1> packages was skipped.
The file </zones/oracle-zc/root/var/sadm/system/logs/install_log> contains a log of
the zone installation.
```

From the global zone of one cluster node, create a zpool to hold the Oracle binaries.

```
phys-grass1# zpool create oracle-zc_zpool \
> mirror /dev/did/dsk/d5s2 /dev/did/dsk/d6s2 \
> mirror /dev/did/dsk/d7s2 /dev/did/dsk/d9s2
```

Configure the zone cluster to enable use of the logical host and zpool that will be used by the HA-Oracle database.

```
phys-grass1# clzc configure oracle-zc
clzc:oracle-zc> add net
clzc:oracle-zc:net> set address=tgrass1-0b
clzc:oracle-zc:net> end
clzc:oracle-zc> add dataset
clzc:oracle-zc:dataset> set name=oracle-zc_zpool
clzc:oracle-zc:dataset> end
clzc:oracle-zc> commit
clzc:oracle-zc> exit
```

From one cluster node, boot the `oracle-zc` zone cluster.

```
phys-grass1# clzc boot oracle-zc
Waiting for zone boot commands to complete on all the nodes of the zone cluster
"oracle-zc"...
```

On all cluster nodes, ensure that `tgrass1-0b` is in the `/etc/inet/hosts` file.

```
phys-grass1# grep tgrass1-0b /etc/inet/hosts
10.11.112.30    tgrass1-0b
```

On one cluster node, log in to the zone-cluster node and create the Oracle resource group.

```
phys-grass1# zlogin -C oracle-zc
[Connected to zone 'oracle-zc' console]

lzgrass1b console login: root
Password:
Feb  9 06:56:38 lzgrass1b login: ROOT LOGIN /dev/console
Last login: Tue Feb  9 05:15:14 on console
Sun Microsystems Inc.   SunOS 5.10      Generic January 2005
# exec bash
lzgrass1b# PATH=$PATH:/usr/cluster/bin export PATH
```

Create a resource group called `oracle-zc-rg`.

```
lzgrass1b# clrg create oracle-zc-rg
```

Determine if the `SUNW.HAStoragePlus` resource type is registered.

```
lzgrass1b# clrt list
SUNW.LogicalHostname:3
SUNW.SharedAddress:2
```

If the `SUNW.HAStoragePlus` resource type is not registered, register it.

```
lzgrass1b# clrt register SUNW.HAStoragePlus
```

Create a resource of type `SUNW.HAStoragePlus` to mount the `zpool` for the Oracle binaries.

```
lzgrass1b# clrs create -g oracle-zc-rg -t SUNW.HAStoragePlus \
> -p zpools=oracle-zc_zpool oracle-zc-hasp-rs
```

Create a logical hostname resource that will be used by the Oracle listener.

```
lzgrass1b# clrslh create -g oracle-zc-rg \
>     -h tgrass1-0b oracle-zc-lh-rs
```

Bring the resource group online.

```
lzgrass1b# clrg online -eM oracle-zc-rg
```

On all zone-cluster nodes, create identical `oracle` user and group IDs following the steps in Example 8.6.

Change the ownership of the Oracle zpool that will be used for the Oracle software.

```
lzgrass1b# chown oracle:oinstall /oracle-zc_zpool
```

Log in as the oracle user on the zone-cluster node with the `/oracle-zc_zpool` mounted, and install the Oracle software following Example 8.6. This time, set `ORACLE_BASE` to `/oracle-zc_zpool/app/oracle`.

If you installed sparse-root zones, you must choose an alternative to the `/usr/local/bin` directory. This is because the `/usr/local/bin` directory will be inherited read-only from the global zone.

After the Oracle software installation process is complete, you must switch over the `oracle-zc-rg` resource group and run the `root.sh` script on the alternate zone-cluster node.

```
lzgrass1b# clrg switch -n lzgrass2b oracle-zc-rg
```

As the `oracle` user on the zone-cluster node that has the `/oracle-zc_zpool` file system mounted, create the listener and the database. You must have set up your Oracle environment variables and `PATH` correctly.

```
lzgrass2b$ echo $ORACLE_HOME
/oracle-zc_zpool/app/oracle/product/11.1.0/db_1
lzgrass2b$ echo $PATH
/usr/bin::/usr/sbin:/oracle-zc_zpool/app/oracle/product/11.1.0/db_1/bin
```

As the `oracle` user, run `netca`.

```
lzgrass2b$ netca
```

```
The default choices produce the following a listener.ora file.
lzgrass2b$ cat $ORACLE_HOME/network/admin/listener.ora
# listener.ora Network Configuration File: /oracle-zc_zpool/app/oracle/product/
11.1.0/db_1/network/admin/listener.ora
# Generated by Oracle configuration tools.
```

```
LISTENER =
  (DESCRIPTION_LIST =
    (DESCRIPTION =
      (ADDRESS = (PROTOCOL = TCP)(HOST = lzgrass2b)(PORT = 1521))
      (ADDRESS = (PROTOCOL = IPC)(KEY = EXTPROC1521))
    )
  )

lzgrass2b$ dbca
```

Choose the Oracle Managed File option and install the database data files in directory ${ORACLE_BASE}/oradata and the flash archive recovery files in ${ORACLE_BASE}/flash_recovery_area.

In this example, the database is created with the ORACLE_SID of zcdemo.

After dbca has created the database, stop the listener and modify both the listener.ora and tnsnames.ora files, and then restart the listener.

```
lzgrass2b$ lsnrctl stop
lzgrass2b$ cat listener.ora
# listener.ora Network Configuration File: /oracle-zc_zpool/app/oracle/product/
11.1.0/
db_1/network/admin/listener.ora
# Generated by Oracle configuration tools.

LISTENER =
  (DESCRIPTION_LIST =
    (DESCRIPTION =
      (ADDRESS = (PROTOCOL = TCP)(HOST = tgrass1-0b)(PORT = 1521))
      (ADDRESS = (PROTOCOL = IPC)(KEY = EXTPROC1521))
    )
  )

lzgrass2b$ cat tnsnames.ora
# tnsnames.ora Network Configuration File: /oracle-zc_zpool/app/oracle/product/
11.1.0/
db_1/network/admin/tnsnames.ora
# Generated by Oracle configuration tools.

ZCDEMO =
  (DESCRIPTION =
    (ADDRESS = (PROTOCOL = TCP)(HOST = tgrass1-0b)(PORT = 1521))
    (CONNECT_DATA =
      (SERVER = DEDICATED)
      (SERVICE_NAME = zcdemo)
    )
  )

LISTENER =
  (DESCRIPTION =
    (ADDRESS = (PROTOCOL = TCP)(HOST = tgrass1-0b)(PORT = 1521))
  )

lzgrass2b$ lsnrctl start
    .
    .
    .
```

As the oracle user on the first cluster node, create the database-monitoring user, hamon, and set the local_listener property to LISTENER.

```
lzgrass2b$ sqlplus '/ as sysdba'

SQL*Plus: Release 11.1.0.6.0 - Production on Wed Jan 13 06:05:03 2010

Copyright (c) 1982, 2007, Oracle.  All rights reserved.


Connected to:
Oracle Database 11g Enterprise Edition Release 11.1.0.6.0 - 64bit Production
With the Partitioning, OLAP, Data Mining and Real Application Testing options

SQL> create user hamon identified by HaMon2010;

User created.

SQL> alter user hamon default tablespace system quota 1m on system;

User altered.

SQL> grant select on v_$sysstat to hamon;

Grant succeeded.

SQL> grant select on v_$archive_dest to hamon;

Grant succeeded.

SQL> grant select on v_$database to hamon;

Grant succeeded.

SQL> grant create session to hamon;

Grant succeeded.

SQL> grant create table to hamon;

Grant succeeded.

SQL> alter system set local_listener=LISTENER;

System altered.

SQL> quit
Disconnected from Oracle Database 11g Enterprise Edition Release 11.1.0.6.0 - 64bit
Production
With the Partitioning, OLAP, Data Mining and Real Application Testing options
```

On one non-global zone, as the `root` user, register the `SUNW.oracle_listener` and `SUNW.oracle_server` resource types, and then create the Solaris Cluster resource for the listener and the database.

```
lzgrass2b# clrt register SUNW.oracle_listener

lzgrass2b# clrt register SUNW.oracle_server

lzgrass2b# clresource create -t SUNW.oracle_listener -g oracle-zc-rg \
> -p ORACLE_HOME=/oracle-zc_zpool/app/oracle/product/11.1.0/db_1 \
> -p LISTENER_NAME=LISTENER \
> -p resource_dependencies=oracle-zc-hasp-rs oracle-zc-lsnr-rs
```

```
lzgrass2b# clresource create -t SUNW.oracle_server -g oracle-zc-rg \
> -p ORACLE_HOME=/oracle-zc_zpool/app/oracle/product/11.1.0/db_1 \
> -p ORACLE_SID=zcdemo \
> -p Alert_log_file=/oracle-zc_zpool/app/oracle/diag/rdbms/zcdemo/zcdemo/trace/alert_
zcdemo.log \
> -p resource_dependencies=oracle-zc-hasp-rs \
> -p connect_string=hamon/HaMon2010 oracle-zc-svr-rs
```

Check the status of the resource group, and then switch it back to the other global-cluster non-voting node.

```
lzgrass2b# clrg status

=== Cluster Resource Groups ===

Group Name      Node Name       Suspended       Status
----------      ---------       ---------       ------
oracle-zc-rg    lzgrass1b       No              Offline
                lzgrass2b       No              Online

lzgrass2b# clrg switch -n lzgrass1b oracle-zc-rg
lzgrass2b# clrg status

=== Cluster Resource Groups ===

Group Name      Node Name       Suspended       Status
----------      ---------       ---------       ------
oracle-zc-rg    lzgrass1b       No              Online
                lzgrass2b       No              Offline
```

# 9

# Example Oracle Solaris Cluster Geographic Edition Implementations

This chapter builds on the examples in the previous chapter. In particular, it assumes that you have two identically built clusters named `grass` and `papyrus`. The `papyrus` cluster consists of nodes `phys-papyrus1` and `phys-papyrus2`.

## Configuring Oracle Solaris Cluster Geographic Edition

If you did not install the Oracle Solaris Cluster Geographic Edition packages during the original Oracle Solaris Cluster software installation, then you must install the additional packages now (refer to Figure 7.1). You can install these packages without interrupting existing cluster services.

After the Geographic Edition software is installed, you must start it and then configure trust and partnerships. For each cluster, you must have a spare IP address to allocate to a hostname that matches the name of the cluster that participates in the Geographic Edition configuration. The configuration steps are shown in the following example.

## Example 9.1   Starting the Geographic Edition Framework and Configuring a Partnership

Note: Commands are executed on different clusters. The shell prompts indicate which cluster the node belongs to, either `grass` or `papyrus`.

First, check that both clusters can resolve unused hostnames that will match their respective cluster names.

```
phys-grass1# getent hosts grass
10.11.112.32    grass tgrass2-0b
phys-grass1# ping grass 2
no answer from grass
phys-grass1# getent hosts papyrus
10.11.112.36    papyrus tpapyrus2-0b
phys-grass1# ping papyrus 2
no answer from papyrus
```

As the `root` user, on one node of each cluster, start the Geographic Edition software.

```
phys-grass1# geoadm start
... checking for management agent ...
... management agent check done ....
... starting product infrastructure ... please wait ...
Registering resource type <SUNW.HBmonitor>...done.
Registering resource type <SUNW.SCGeoSvcTag>...done.
Registering resource type <SUNW.scmasa>...done.
Creating scalable resource group <geo-clusterstate>...done.
Creating service tag management resource <geo-servicetag>...
Service tag management resource created successfully ....
Creating failover resource group <geo-infrastructure>...done.
Creating logical host resource <geo-clustername>...
Logical host resource created successfully ....
Creating resource <geo-hbmonitor> ...done.
Creating resource <geo-failovercontrol> ...done.
Bringing resource group <geo-infrastructure> to managed state ...done.
Enabling resource <geo-clustername> ...done.
Enabling resource <geo-hbmonitor> ...done.
Enabling resource <geo-failovercontrol> ...done.
Node phys-grass1: Bringing resource group <geo-infrastructure> online ...done.
Bringing RG <geo-clusterstate> to managed state ...done.

Sun Cluster Geographic Edition infrastructure started successfully.

phys-papyrus1# geoadm start
... checking for management agent ...
... management agent check done ....
... starting product infrastructure ... please wait ...
Registering resource type <SUNW.HBmonitor>...done.
Registering resource type <SUNW.SCGeoSvcTag>...done.
Resource type <SUNW.scmasa> has been registered already
Creating scalable resource group <geo-clusterstate>...done.
Creating service tag management resource <geo-servicetag>...
Service tag management resource created successfully ....
Creating failover resource group <geo-infrastructure>...done.
Creating logical host resource <geo-clustername>...
Logical host resource created successfully ....
Creating resource <geo-hbmonitor> ...done.
Creating resource <geo-failovercontrol> ...done.
Bringing resource group <geo-infrastructure> to managed state ...done.
```

```
Enabling resource <geo-clustername> ...done.
Enabling resource <geo-hbmonitor> ...done.
Enabling resource <geo-failovercontrol> ...done.
Node phys-papyrus1: Bringing resource group <geo-infrastructure> online ...done.
Bringing RG <geo-clusterstate> to managed state ...done.

Sun Cluster Geographic Edition infrastructure started successfully.
```

## As the root user, on one node of each cluster, create trust between the clusters.

```
phys-grass1# geops add-trust --cluster papyrus

Local cluster : grass
Local node : phys-grass1

Cleaning up certificate files in /etc/cacao/instances/default/security/jsse on
phys-grass1

Retrieving certificates from papyrus ... Done

New Certificate:

Owner: CN=phys-papyrus1_agent
Issuer: CN=phys-papyrus1_ca
Serial number: 5c7b865
Valid from: Wed Jun 11 05:42:57 PDT 1969 until: Mon Feb 11 04:42:57 PST 2030
Certificate fingerprints:
        MD5:   D4:90:10:EE:CB:C1:90:98:80:CA:07:E4:A6:CF:8D:7C
        SHA1: 94:96:77:AA:FB:A7:8B:26:2A:1B:CD:F4:61:2D:46:2F:1D:53:9B:22

Do you trust this certificate? [y/n] y

Adding certificate to truststore on phys-grass1 ... Done

Adding certificate to truststore on phys-grass2 ... Done

New Certificate:

Owner: CN=phys-papyrus1_ca
Issuer: CN=phys-papyrus1_ca
Serial number: 363055ba
Valid from: Wed Jun 11 05:42:55 PDT 1969 until: Mon Feb 11 04:42:55 PST 2030
Certificate fingerprints:
        MD5:   5F:B2:DE:22:25:B0:DE:7F:6C:3B:10:8B:75:58:35:4A
        SHA1: 28:CD:ED:FC:21:14:F5:9B:2C:FA:E1:BD:DA:EA:93:87:AD:1F:A9:85

Do you trust this certificate? [y/n] y

Adding certificate to truststore on phys-grass1 ... Done

Adding certificate to truststore on phys-grass2 ... Done

Operation completed successfully. All certificates are added to truststore on nodes of
 cluster grass

phys-papyrus1# geops add-trust --cluster grass

Local cluster : papyrus
Local node : phys-papyrus1

Cleaning up certificate files in /etc/cacao/instances/default/security/jsse on phys
-papyrus1

Retrieving certificates from grass ... Done
```

```
New Certificate:

Owner: CN=phys-grass1_agent
Issuer: CN=phys-grass1_ca
Serial number: 59d57800
Valid from: Fri Jun 06 07:33:40 PDT 1969 until: Sun Jan 06 06:33:40 PST 2030
Certificate fingerprints:
      MD5:  8E:0E:4B:C4:72:BC:6A:84:C7:D6:50:44:2E:62:AE:9A
      SHA1: 0C:42:02:7C:B1:2D:65:C9:7C:58:87:3A:1F:2F:60:F5:A0:6A:6A:4C

Do you trust this certificate? [y/n] y

Adding certificate to truststore on phys-papyrus1 ... Done

Adding certificate to truststore on phys-papyrus2 ... Done

New Certificate:

Owner: CN=phys-grass1_ca
Issuer: CN=phys-grass1_ca
Serial number: 78c56a80
Valid from: Fri Jun 06 07:33:38 PDT 1969 until: Sun Jan 06 06:33:38 PST 2030
Certificate fingerprints:
      MD5:  47:FB:53:7F:5F:D8:4A:A4:38:42:D9:76:C0:3F:C5:25
      SHA1: 17:8C:AE:72:58:56:41:86:7B:A9:26:29:01:58:63:80:B7:48:14:1C

Do you trust this certificate? [y/n] y

Adding certificate to truststore on phys-papyrus1 ... Done

Adding certificate to truststore on phys-papyrus2 ... Done

Operation completed successfully. All certificates are added to truststore on nodes
of cluster papyrus
```

As the `root` user, on one node of the `grass` cluster, create a partnership between the clusters.

```
phys-grass1# geops create --cluster papyrus grass-papyrus
Partnership between local cluster "grass" and remote cluster "papyrus" successfully
created.
```

As the `root` user, on one node of the `papyrus` cluster, join the partnership created between the clusters.

```
phys-papyrus1# geops join-partnership grass grass-papyrus
Local cluster "papyrus" is now partner of cluster "grass".
```

# Protecting a Scalable Web Service Using StorageTek Availability Suite

This example uses the scalable web server that runs in global-cluster non-voting nodes (see Example 8.10 in Chapter 8, "Example Oracle Solaris Cluster Implementations") as the service that will be protected. The global file system will be replicated using the StorageTek Availability Suite (AVS) software. The AVS software must be installed on all cluster nodes.

## Example 9.2   Installing the StorageTek Availability Suite Software

Choose a shared disk slice that is 6 megabytes in size to hold the AVS configuration information. In this example, `/dev/did/rdsk/d10s0` is used.

As the `root` user on one node of each cluster, change directories to the AVS software distribution and run the installation script.

```
phys-papyrus1# ./install.sh -a

Display software license agreement [y,n,?] n



Do you agree to the terms and conditions stated in software license
agreement [y,n,?] y

Checking CORE package status..

Processing package instance <SUNWscmr> from </net/myhost/rpool/software/AVS_v4.0/sparc
/CORE>

        .
        .
        .

Installation of Availability Suite 4.0 is complete.


Configuring  Availability Suite 4.0 for first time use.
Could not find a valid local configuration database.
Initializing local configuration database...
Successfully initialized local configuration database


----------ENTER DATABASE CONFIGURATION LOCATION----------------
Note:    Please ensure this location meets all requirements specified
in the Availability Suite Installation Guide.

Enter location: [?] /dev/did/rdsk/d10s0
Initializing cluster configuration database...
Successfully initialized cluster configuration database

If you would like to start using the Availability Suite immediately, you may
start the SMF services now.  You may also choose to start the services later
using the dscfgadm -e command.

Would you like to start the services now?  [y,n,?] y
```

As the `root` user on the other node in the cluster, change directories to the AVS software distribution and run the installation script. When asked whether you want to preserve the existing configuration, choose `yes`.

```
phys-papyrus2# ./install.sh -a

Display software license agreement [y,n,?] n

        .
        .
        .
```

```
----------ENTER DATABASE CONFIGURATION LOCATION----------------
Note:    Please ensure this location meets all requirements specified
in the Availability Suite Installation Guide.

Enter location: [?] /dev/did/rdsk/d10s0

It appears a valid database configuration exists here already.

Would you like to preserve this information and continue?
        y - preserve current configuration
        n - overwrite with new configuration
        maybe - view contents of current configuration

Enter appropriate value [y,n,maybe,?] y

If you would like to start using the Availability Suite immediately, you may
start the SMF services now.  You may also choose to start the services later
using the dscfgadm -e command.

Would you like to start the services now?  [y,n,?] y
```

As the `root` user on each cluster node, check that the software is correctly configured.

```
phys-grass1# dscfgadm -i
SERVICE         STATE           ENABLED
nws_scm         online          true
nws_sv          online          true
nws_ii          online          true
nws_rdc         online          true
nws_rdcsyncd    online          true

Availability Suite Configuration:
Local configuration database: valid
cluster configuration database: valid
cluster configuration location: /dev/did/rdsk/d10s0
```

If the services are not enabled, then run the `dscfgadm` command to enable them.

```
phys-grass1# dscfgadm -e
```

To replicate the scalable web service, two equivalent zones must be built on the `papyrus` cluster (see Example 8.10 in Chapter 8, "Example Oracle Solaris Cluster Implementations"). The zones on the `papyrus` cluster are called `lzpapyrus1a` and `lzpapyrus2a`.

After the zones are built and booted, you can configure the AVS replication. The original file system on `/dev/global/rdsk/d4s2` requires an equivalent target device on the secondary cluster. Additionally, both clusters require bitmap devices to accompany the data disks. The bitmap disk slices need to be 161 blocks in size. This space is allocated on disk slice `d10s1`.

## Example 9.3   Configuring the AVS Replication

Check the size required for the bitmap for slice d4s2.

```
phys-grass1# dsbitmap -r /dev/global/rdsk/d4s2
Remote Mirror bitmap sizing

Data volume (/dev/global/rdsk/d4s2) size: 41938944 blocks
Required bitmap volume size:
  Sync replication: 161 blocks
  Async replication with memory queue: 161 blocks
  Async replication with disk queue: 1441 blocks
  Async replication with disk queue and 32 bit refcount: 5281 blocks
```

Check that the space allocated to the bitmap in d10s1 is sufficient. In this case, slice 1 is 2048 sectors/blocks.

```
phys-grass1# prtvtoc /dev/global/rdsk/d10s2
* /dev/global/rdsk/d10s2 partition map
*
* Dimensions:
*     512 bytes/sector
*      32 sectors/track
*      64 tracks/cylinder
*    2048 sectors/cylinder
*   20480 cylinders
*   20478 accessible cylinders
*
* Flags:
*   1: unmountable
*  10: read-only
*
* Unallocated space:
*        First     Sector     Last
*       Sector     Count     Sector
*           0      2048      2047
*       16384   41922560   41938943
*
*                  First    Sector   Last
* Partition  Tag  Flags   Sector    Count    Sector  Mount Directory
        0     0    00      2048     12288    14335
        1     0    00     14336      2048    16383
        2     5    00         0  41938944  41938943
```

As the root user on the grass cluster, alter the properties of the web-svr-sa-rg and web-svr-rg resource groups so that they are not brought online automatically when the cluster starts.

```
phys-grass1# clrg set -p auto_start_on_new_cluster=false web-svr-sa-rg
phys-grass1# clrg set -p auto_start_on_new_cluster=false web-svr-rg
```

As the root user on both nodes of the papyrus cluster, create the mount point for the file system that will be replicated.

```
phys-papyrus1# mkdir -p /global/websvr
```

As the `root` user on the `lzpapyrus1a` and `lzpapyrus2a` zones of the `papyrus` cluster, create the mount point for the file system that will be replicated and the log directory for the web server, and then create the access log file that the web server will use and set its ownership.

```
lzpapyrus1a# mkdir -p /global/websvr
lzpapyrus1a# mkdir -p /var/sjsws/tgrass1-0a/logs
lzpapyrus1a# touch /var/sjsws/tgrass1-0a/logs/access
lzpapyrus1a# chown webservd:webservd /var/sjsws/tgrass1-0a/logs/access
```

As the `root` user on both nodes of the `papyrus` cluster, ensure that the entry for the `/global/websvr` file system is in `/etc/vfstab`.

```
phys-papyrus1# grep /global/websvr /etc/vfstab
/dev/global/dsk/d4s2    /dev/global/rdsk/d4s2   /global/websvr ufs    - no    global,
logging
```

As the `root` user on one node of the `papyrus` cluster, create the shared address resource group and the shared address resource.

```
phys-papyrus1#  clrg create \
> -n phys-papyrus1:lzpapyrus1a,phys-papyrus2:lzpapyrus2a \
> -p auto_start_on_new_cluster=false web-svr-sa-rg
```

Ensure that the same logical hostname is used.

```
phys-papyrus1# clrssa create -g web-svr-sa-rg -h tgrass1-0a \
> web-svr-sa-rs
```

As the `root` user on one node of the `papyrus` cluster, create the web server resource group and the `SUNW.HAStoragePlus` resource.

```
phys-papyrus1# clrg create \
> -n phys-papyrus1:lzpapyrus1a,phys-papyrus2:lzpapyrus2a \
> -p maximum_primaries=2 -p desired_primaries=2 \
> -p auto_start_on_new_cluster=false web-svr-rg

phys-papyrus1# clrs create -g web-svr-rg -t SUNW.HAStoragePlus \
> -p FileSystemMountPoints=/global/websvr:/global/websvr \
> web-svr-hasp-rs
```

As the `root` user on one node of the `papyrus` cluster, register the `SUNW.iws` resource type if it is not already registered.

```
phys-papyrus1# clrt register SUNW.iws
```

As the `root` user on both nodes of the `grass` and `papyrus` clusters, create the `webset-volset.ini` configuration file that defines the replication.

```
phys-grass1# cat /var/cluster/geo/avs/webset-volset.ini
tgrass2-0a /dev/global/rdsk/d4s2 /dev/global/rdsk/d10s1 tpapyrus2-0a /dev/global/
rdsk/d4s2 /dev/global/rdsk/d10s1 ip async g webset C webset
```

As the `root` user on one node of the `grass` cluster, create the `webset` device group from DID devices `d4` (for the data) and `d10` (for the bitmap).

```
phys-grass1# clrg offline web-svr-rg
phys-grass1# umount /global/websvr
phys-grass1# cldg offline dsk/d4
phys-grass1# cldg disable dsk/d4
phys-grass1# cldg delete dsk/d4
phys-grass1# cldg offline dsk/d10
phys-grass1# cldg disable dsk/d10
phys-grass1# cldg delete dsk/d10
phys-grass1# cldg create -n phys-grass1,phys-grass2 -t rawdisk \
> -d d4,d10 webset
phys-grass1# clrg online web-svr-rg
```

As the `root` user on one node of the `papyrus` cluster, create the `webset` device group from DID devices `d4` (for the data) and `d10` (for the bitmap).

```
phys-papyrus1# cldg offline dsk/d4
phys-papyrus1# cldg disable dsk/d4
phys-papyrus1# cldg delete dsk/d4
phys-papyrus1# cldg offline dsk/d10
phys-papyrus1# cldg disable dsk/d10
phys-papyrus1# cldg delete dsk/d10
phys-papyrus1# cldg create -n phys-papyrus1,phys-papyrus2 -t rawdisk \
> -d d4,d10 webset
```

As the `root` user on both nodes of the `grass` and `papyrus` clusters, check that the source and target hostnames used for the AVS replication are in the `/etc/inet/hosts` file.

```
phys-grass1# grep tgrass2-0a /etc/inet/hosts
10.11.112.31    tgrass2-0a
phys-grass1# grep tpapyrus2-0a /etc/inet/hosts
10.11.112.35    tpapyrus2-0a
```

As the `root` user on one node of the `grass` cluster, create the AVS protection group.

```
phys-grass1# geopg create --partnership grass-papyrus --role primary \
> --datarep-type avs web-svr-pg
Protection group "web-svr-pg" successfully created.
```

As the `root` user on one node of the `papyrus` cluster, retrieve the protection group configuration from the `grass` cluster.

```
phys-papyrus1# geopg get --partnership grass-papyrus web-svr-pg
Protection group "web-svr-pg" successfully created.
```

As the `root` user on one node of the `grass` cluster, add the `webset` device group to the protection group.

```
phys-grass1# geopg add-device-group \
> --property local_logical_host=tgrass2-0a \
> --property remote_logical_host=tpapyrus2-0a \
> --property enable_volume_set=true webset web-svr-pg
Device group "webset" successfully added to the protection group "web-svr-pg".
```

As the `root` user on one node of the `grass` cluster, start the protection group.

```
phys-grass1# geopg start -e global web-svr-pg
Processing operation... The timeout period for this operation on each cluster is 3600
seconds (3600000 milliseconds)...
Protection group "web-svr-pg" successfully started.
```

Wait for the data to be replicated to the remote cluster.

```
phys-grass1# dsstat
name            t  s    pct role   ckps   dkps   tps  svt
lobal/rdsk/d4s2 P  R   0.00 net     -       0      0    0
obal/rdsk/d10s1           bmp      0       0      0    0
phys-grass1# clrs status webset-rep-rs

=== Cluster Resources ===

Resource Name        Node Name       State        Status Message
-------------        ---------       -----        --------------
webset-rep-rs        phys-grass1     Online       Online - Replicating; Autosync ON
                     phys-grass2     Offline      Offline
```

As the `root` user on one node of the `grass` cluster, stop the `web-svr-sa-rg` and `web-svr-rg` resource groups, disable the resources, and place the resource groups into an unmanaged state.

```
phys-grass1# clrg offline web-svr-sa-rg web-svr-rg
phys-grass1# clrs disable web-svr-sa-rs web-svr-hasp-rs web-svr-rs
phys-grass1# clrg unmanage web-svr-sa-rg web-svr-rg
```

As the `root` user on one node of the `grass` cluster, switch the protection group over to the `papyrus` cluster.

```
phys-grass1# geopg switchover -m papyrus web-svr-pg
Are you sure you want to switchover protection group 'web-svr-pg' to primary cluster
'papyrus'? (yes|no) > yes
Processing operation... The timeout period for this operation on each cluster is 3600
seconds (3600000 milliseconds)...
"Switchover" operation succeeded for the protection group "web-svr-pg".
```

As the `root` user on one node of the `papyrus` cluster, bring the `web-svr-sa-rg` and `web-svr-rg` resource groups online and then add the `web-svr-rs` resource.

```
phys-papyrus1# clrg online -eM web-svr-sa-rg
phys-papyrus1# clrg online -eM web-svr-rg
```

With the replicated data now available on the local cluster, the validate step for the resource creation succeeds.

```
phys-papyrus1# clrs create -d -g web-svr-rg -t SUNW.iws \
> -p confdir_list=/global/websvr/webserver7/https-tgrass1-0a.example.com \
> -p scalable=true \
> -p resource_dependencies=web-svr-hasp-rs,web-svr-sa-rs \
> -p port_list=80/tcp web-svr-rs
```

As the `root` user on one node of the `papyrus` cluster, add the `web-svr-sa-rg` and `web-svr-rg` resource groups to the `web-svr-pg` protection group.

```
phys-papyrus1# geopg add-resource-group web-svr-sa-rg,web-svr-rg \
> web-svr-pg
Following resource groups successfully added:
        "web-svr-sa-rg,web-svr-rg".
```

As the `root` user on one node of the `papyrus` cluster, switch over the `web-svr-pg` protection group to the `grass` cluster.

```
phys-papyrus1# geopg switchover -m grass web-svr-pg
Are you sure you want to switchover protection group 'web-svr-pg' to primary cluster
'grass'? (yes|no) > yes
Processing operation... The timeout period for this operation on each cluster is 3600
seconds (3600000 milliseconds)...
"Switchover" operation succeeded for the protection group "web-svr-pg".
```

As the `root` user on one node of the `grass` cluster, obtain the status of the Geographic Edition system.

```
phys-grass1# geoadm status

    Cluster:  grass

    Partnership "grass-papyrus"  : OK
        Partner clusters         : papyrus
        Synchronization          : OK
        ICRM Connection          : OK

        Heartbeat "hb_grass~papyrus" monitoring "papyrus": OK
            Plug-in "ping_plugin"        : Inactive
            Plug-in "tcp_udp_plugin"     : OK

    Protection group "web-svr-pg"        : OK
        Partnership              : grass-papyrus
        Synchronization          : OK

        Cluster grass            : OK
            Role                 : Primary
            Activation state     : Activated
            Configuration        : OK
            Data replication     : OK
            Resource groups      : OK

        Cluster papyrus          : OK
            Role                 : Secondary
            Activation state     : Activated
            Configuration        : OK
            Data replication     : OK
            Resource groups      : OK
```

# Bibliography

## References

[11gRefArch] "Sun Reference Architecture for Oracle 11g Grid," https://www.sun.com/offers/docs/Oracle11g_arch.pdf.

[AdvGDSTlkit] Ulherr, Detlef, and Thorsten Früauf. "Sun Cluster Agent Development—Advanced GDS Methodology," http://hub.opensolaris.org/bin/download/Community+Group+ha-clusters/GDS-template/SCAgentDevelopment-AdvancedGDSMethodology.pdf, March 2007.

[BeginLDom] Shoumack, Tony. "Beginners Guide to LDoms: Understanding and Deploying Logical Domains for Logical Domains 1.0 Release," http://www.sun.com/blueprints/0207/820-0832.html, 2007.

[DepRes] Rattner, Martin. "Disabling a Depended-on Resource in Sun Cluster 3.2," http://blogs.sun.com/SC/entry/disabling_a_depended_on_resource, July 2007.

[Design] Elling, Richard, and Tim Read. *Designing Enterprise Solutions with Sun Cluster 3.0.* Upper Saddle River, NJ: Prentice Hall, 2002.

[E10KDomains] "Sun Enterprise 10000 Server: Dynamic System Domains," http://www.sun.com/servers/white-papers/domains.html, 2005.

[EMCGroups] "An Overview of Groups in EMC Symmetrix and Solutions Enabler Environments—A Detailed Review," http://uk.emc.com/collateral/hardware/white-papers/h2313-overview-grps-symmetrix-sol-enblr-env.pdf, April 2009.

[EMCSRDF] *EMC® Symmetrix® Remote Data Facility (SRDF®) Product Guide*, P/N 300-00-165, REV A09, EMC Corporation.

[EMCStar] "EMC SRDF Family of Software Data Sheet," http://www.emc.com/collateral/software/data-sheet/1523-emc-srdf.pdf.

[FlarInstall] Madhan Kumar Balasubramanian, "What Is Flash Archive Installation?" http://blogs.sun.com/SC/entry/what_is_flash_archive_installation%3F, 2006.

[HANet] Victor, Jeff. "High-Availability Networking for Solaris Containers," http://blogs.sun.com/JeffV/entry/high_availability_networking_for_solaris, March 2008.

[HDSUniversal] Bertrand, Christophe, Bill Martin, Roselinda Schulman, and Claus Mikkelsen. "Hitachi Universal Replicator Software Architecture Overview," http://www.hds.com/assets/pdf/universal-replicator-software-architecture-overview-wp.pdf, November 2008.

[IPMP] Schleich, Juergen, Stephan Befort, Axel Klatt, Mike Reinicke, and Klaus-Peter Muhl. "Summary of Typical IPMP Configurations," http://sunsolve.sun.com/search/document.do?assetkey=1-61-214668, SunSpectrum Document #214668 (available only to SunSpectrum customers).

[iSCSI-RFC] Satran J., et al. "RFC-3720 Internet Small Computer Systems Interface (iSCSI)," http://tools.ietf.org/html/rfc3720, April 2004.

[JetWiki] Ramchand, Mike. "Jumpstart Enterprise Toolkit," http://wikis.sun.com/display/JET/Home, 2009.

[JMRM] Mauro, Jim, and Richard McDougall. *Solaris Internals Core Kernel Architecture*. Upper Saddle River, NJ: Prentice Hall, 2000.

[Lamport] Lamport, Leslie. "A New Solution of Dijkstra's Concurrent Programming Problem." *Communications of the ACM* 17, no. 8 (August 1974): 453–55.

[LibHost] Früauf, Thorsten. "Tricking Applications Which Bind to Nodename Only with libschost.so.1," http://blogs.sun.com/TF/entry/fooling_applications_which_bind_to, July 2007.

[MySQLPress] "Sun to Acquire MySQL," http://www.mysql.com/news-and-events/sun-to-acquire-mysql.html, January 16, 2008.

[NFSAgent] Open HA Cluster source code for the NFS agent, http://src.opensolaris.org/source/xref/ohac/ohacds/usr/src/cmd/ha-services/nfs/.

[QFSDoc] "Sun StorageTek QFS File System Configuration and Administration Guide," http://dlc.sun.com/pdf/819-7935-10/819-7935-10.pdf.

[RFC1123] Braden, R. "Requirements for Internet Hosts—Application and Support," http://tools.ietf.org/html/rfc1123, October 1989.

[RFC768] RFC 768, http://tools.ietf.org/html/rfc.

[RFC793] RFC 768, http://tools.ietf.org/html/rfc.

[S10InstallGuide] "Solaris 10 10/09 Installation Guide: Basic Installations," http://docs.sun.com/app/docs/doc/821-0440?l=en, 2009.

[SBDBlog] Brunette, Glen. "New Solaris Secure by Default Presentation," http://blogs.sun.com/gbrunett/entry/new_solaris_secure_by_default, 2006.

[SCDevGuide] "Sun Cluster Data Services Developer's Guide for Solaris OS," http://docs.sun.com/app/docs/doc/820-4680.

[SCGEOver] "Sun Cluster Geographic Edition Overview," http://dlc.sun.com/pdf/820-3004/820-3004.pdf, 2008.

[SCInstallGuide] "Solaris Cluster Software Installation Guide for Solaris OS," http://docs.sun.com/app/docs/doc/820-4677, 2009.

[SourceAddr] "IP Source Address Selection, Routing and Outbound Interface Selection, IP Load Spreading, Interface Groups and IPMP," http://sunsolve.sun.com/search/document.do?assetkey=1-61-204569-1, SunSpectrum Document #204569 (available only to SunSpectrum customers).

[SSTAdminGuide] "Solaris Security Toolkit 4.2 Administration Guide," http://docs.sun.com/app/docs/coll/sstoolkit4.2.

[ThorstenBlog] Früauf, Thorsten. "'Secure by Default' and Sun Cluster 3.2," http://blogs.sun.com/TF/entry/secure_by_default_and_sun, 2007.

[Transport] tcp_transport.h, source code, http://src.opensolaris.org/source/xref/ohac/ohac/usr/src/common/cl/transports/tcp/.

[URCCIGuide] "Hitachi Command Control Interface (CCI) User and Reference Guide," MK-90RD011-27, Hitachi Data Systems.

[UsingVLANs] Weiberle, Steffen. "Using IP Instances with VLANs or How to Make a Few NICs Look Like Many," http://blogs.sun.com/stw/entry/using_ip_instances_with_vlans.

[VlanTag] "IEEE_802.1Q," http://en.wikipedia.org/wiki/.

[ZFS] Rich, Amy. "ZFS, Sun's Cutting-Edge File System (Part 1: Storage Integrity, Security, and Scalability)," http://www.sun.com/bigadmin/features/articles/zfs_part1.scalable.jsp, 2006.

[ZFSMirror] Bonwick, Jeff. "Smokin' Mirrors," http://blogs.sun.com/bonwick/entry/smokin_mirrors, May 2006.

[ZonePatch] "How to Apply Patches in Single-User Mode with Failover Zones," http://docs.sun.com/app/docs/doc/820-2558/geubs?a=view.

## Additional Resources

Chen, Leland. "Sun Cluster 3.2 SNMP Interface," http://blogs.sun.com/SC/entry/sun_cluster_3_2_snmp, 2007.

CMM Automaton implementation, http://src.opensolaris.org/source/xref/ohac/ohac/usr/src/common/cl/cmm/automaton_impl.cc.

"Generic Affinity for Sun ClusterScalable Services," https://wikis.sun.com/display/SunCluster/, 2009.

Rattner, Martin. "How Does Sun Cluster Decide on Which Node a Service Runs?" http://blogs.sun.com/SC/entry/how_does_sun_cluster_decide, November 2006.

Read, Tim. "Architecting Availability and Disaster Recovery Solutions," http://mapping.sun.com/profile/offer.jsp?id=65, April 2007.

———. "Using Solaris Cluster and Sun Cluster Geographic Edition with Virtualization Technologies," http://mapping.sun.com/profile/offer.jsp?id=29, April 2008.

Read, Tim, Gia-Khanh Nguyen, and Robert Bart. "Solaris™ Cluster 3.2 Software: Making Oracle Database 10*g* R2 and 11*g* RAC Even More Unbreakable," http://www.sun.com/software/whitepapers/solaris10/solaris_cluster.pdf.

"Round-Robin Load-Balancing Scheme for Sun Cluster Scalable Services," https://wikis.sun.com/display/SunCluster/, 2009.

Roush, Ellard. "Zone Cluster: How to Deploy Virtual Clusters and Why Blueprint," https://www.sun.com/offers/details/820-7351.xml, 2009.

"SCTP Support in Sun Cluster Scalable Services," http://wikis.sun.com/display/SunCluster/SCTP+Support+in+Sun+Cluster+Scalable+Services, 2009.

Streppel, Hartmut. "Why a Logical IP Is Marked as DEPRECATED," http://blogs.sun.com/SC/entry/why_a_logical_ip_is, 2009.

Vidwansa, Atul. "Sun Cluster Service Level Management," http://blogs.sun.com/SC/entry/sun_cluster_service_level_management, 2006.

# Index

# FREE Online Edition

Your purchase of **Oracle® Solaris Cluster Essentials** includes access to a free online edition for 45 days through the Safari Books Online subscription service. Nearly every Prentice Hall book is available online through Safari Books Online, along with more than 5,000 other technical books and videos from publishers such as Addison-Wesley Professional, Cisco Press, Exam Cram, IBM Press, O'Reilly, Que, and Sams.

**SAFARI BOOKS ONLINE** allows you to search for a specific answer, cut and paste code, download chapters, and stay current with emerging technologies.

## Activate your FREE Online Edition at www.informit.com/safarifree

> **STEP 1:** Enter the coupon code: VYGFQGA.

> **STEP 2:** New Safari users, complete the brief registration form.
> Safari subscribers, just log in.

If you have difficulty registering on Safari or accessing the online edition, please e-mail customer-service@safaribooksonline.com